D0864129

Africa
Overland

Plus a return route through Asia
4x4 • Motorbike • Bicycle • Truck

the Bradt Travel Guide

Siân Pritchard-Jones
Bob Gibbons

edition
6

www.bradtguides.com

Bradt Travel Guides Ltd, UK
The Globe Pequot Press Inc, USA

Morocco: Atlas Mountains and Sahara fringes

The Sahara: Algeria, Libya, Niger and Chad

Mali: the mud cities of Timbuktu and Djenne, Dogon people and the Bandiagara Escarpment

West Africa: a melting pot of

Egypt/Sudan: River Nile culture and pyramids

Ethiopia: mountain highlands and rock churches

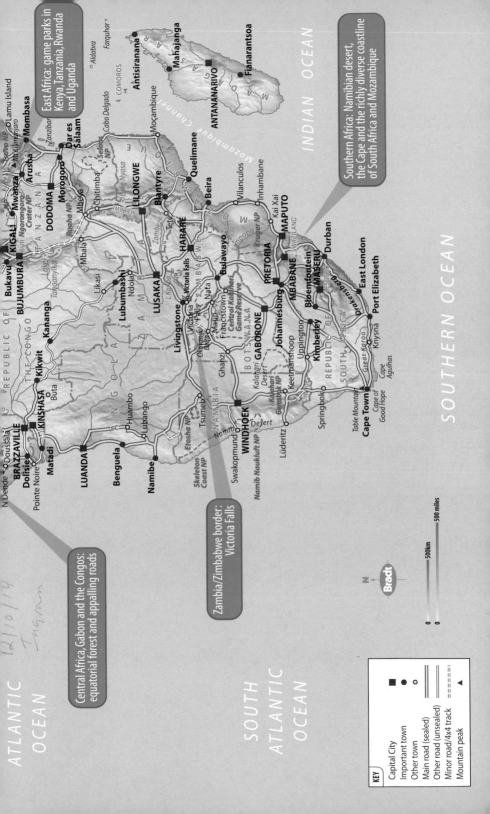

Africa
Don't
miss...

**West Africa, a melting
pot of people and
culture**
Intore dancer, Rwanda
(AVZ) page 289

**Tropical rainforests
and exciting driving,
central Africa**
Overlanding in western Tanzania
(SPJ & BG) page 310

Southern Africa – a variety of adventures in more comfort
Camping on the Liuwa Plain, Zambia
(TH) page 325

The fabulous desert vistas of the Sahara
Camel train in the Guelta d'Archei, Chad
(SPJ & BG) page 223

Game viewing, east Africa
Lions in front of the Ruwenzori Mountains, Queen Elizabeth National Park, Uganda
(AVZ) page 318

Africa in colour

above The sweeping dunes of Kaokoland, northern Namibia, are home to the Himba people (AVZ) page 280

right Tuareg merchants at a camel market, Nouakchott, Mauritania (MM/F) page 270

below School's out in São Domingo, Guinea Bissau (SPJ & BG) page 250

TRAVEL PIONEERS
FOR OVER 40 YEARS
40

We're 40...
how did that happen?

How did it all happen? George (my then husband) and I wrote the first Bradt guide – about hiking in Peru and Bolivia – on an Amazon river barge, and typed it up on a borrowed typewriter.

We had no money for the next two books so George went to work for a printer and was paid in books rather than money.

Forty years on, Bradt publishes over 200 titles that sell all over the world. I still suffer from Imposter Syndrome – how did it all happen? I hadn't even worked in an office before! Well, I've been extraordinarily lucky with the people around me. George provided the belief to get us started (and the mother to run our US office). Then, in 1977, I recruited a helper, Janet Mears, who is still working for us. She and the many dedicated staff who followed have been the foundations on which the company is built. But the bricks and mortar have been our authors and readers. Without them there would be no Bradt Travel Guides. Thank you all for making it happen.

Hilary Bradt

AUTHORS

Both born in Britain, Siân and Bob met in Kashmir in 1983. Bob's overland adventures began in an ancient (1949) Land Rover, which he drove from England to Kathmandu in 1974. Working as an overland driver, he travelled around Asia, Africa and South America, driving trucks as well as decrepit old buses in India and Nepal. Siân worked in computer programming and systems analysis for far too long, until overland travel and the Himalayas captivated her on a trip to Nepal in 1982.

Since then, they have led/organised treks in the Alps, Nepal and the Sahara, driven their overland bus with ageing clients to Nepal, and crossed Africa six times in their own 1983-vintage Land Rover. Their most recent journeys were across Africa (from the UK) and Asia (to the UK from Mumbai).

In 2013 they produced three Himalayan guidebooks: *Annapurna* for Cicerone (UK), and two trekking guides, one to Manaslu and the Tsum Valley and the other to Dolpo, for Himalayan Map House in Kathmandu. Other books written for Pilgrims (Kathmandu) include a cultural guide to the Kathmandu Valley, the monasteries of Ladakh and Mount Kailash. They have also written a trekking guide to the Mount Kailash/Guge region in Tibet and updated a Grand Canyon guide for Cicerone.

AUTHORS' STORY

The story of African overland travel has always been one of risk, adventure, challenge and intrigue. Africa, more than any other continent, still presents hard choices and rugged travel.

As a client on a truck in 1975, Bob was stuck in central Africa for weeks after the drivers and half the other passengers caught hepatitis and left. There were preposterous visa delays, border closures and civil wars. The truck also became very sick. Bob instigated some drastic, if optimistic, repairs and somehow drove it on to Nairobi. The same could still happen to anyone crossing Africa today, but with the combined experience and knowledge found within this Bradt guide, such debilitating dramas can be more easily avoided.

We have explored much of the Sahara together, and our most recent longer journeys in Africa have been in our now 30-year-old Land Rover. In 2003 we drove from England to Gabon, a trip that took us to the mysterious central African rainforests. In 2004 our route went across north Africa to Cairo then south to Cape Town, a trip that was the basis of the fourth edition of the Bradt *Africa Overland* guide. In 2008 our plan was to drive down the entire west coast through Congo and Angola, but in the event visa problems restricted the trip to previously unexplored corners of west Africa, such as Sierra Leone, Guinea and Liberia. Another trans-Africa trip followed, with the return journey being made by shipping from Durban to Mumbai, then driving from India to Europe via Nepal, Tibet, China, Kazakhstan, Russia and Ukraine. This journey, despite its problems, became the basis of this new, even more comprehensive, edition.

And of course, there is always much more for us to discover and share with our readers in the seventh edition!

916
Bra
2014

PUBLISHER'S FOREWORD — *Hilary Bradt*

When I was a child a colleague of my father visited us once a year, having driven his Land Rover from Ghana across the Sahara. I was amazed that it was possible to drive from Africa to England, and enthralled by his stories. This remains the ultimate adventure, yet Bob Gibbons has done it around ten times and Siân Pritchard-Jones six. The combined expertise of these Africa travellers, along with contributions from cyclists and bikers, has produced the book that may literally save the life of a trans-Africa traveller and will certainly enhance the enjoyment of this once-in-a-lifetime trip.

When George and I travelled from Cape Town to Cairo in 1976 there were no guidebooks, so each border was approached with trepidation. We had no idea what to expect, nor even what there was to see in each country. We were using public transport, but occasionally hitched a lift with adventurous souls driving their own vehicles, and envied their freedom to go where they chose and stop when they wanted. But freedom is wasted without knowledge. And knowledge is what this book is about.

Sixth edition published May 2014   First published 1991

Bradt Travel Guides Ltd, IDC House, The Vale, Chalfont St Peter, Bucks SL9 9RZ, England; www.bradtguides.com

Print edition published in the USA by The Globe Pequot Press Inc, PO Box 480, Guilford, Connecticut 06437-0480

Text copyright © 2014 Bradt Travel Guides Ltd
Maps copyright © 2014 Bradt Travel Guides Ltd
Photographs and illustrations copyright © 2014 Individual photographers and artists (see below)
Project manager: Maisie Fitzpatrick
Cover image research: Pepi Bluck, Perfect Picture

12/10/14

ISBN: 978 1 84162 494 5 (print)
e-ISBN: 978 1 84162 791 5 (e-pub)
e-ISBN: 978 1 84162 692 5 (mobi)

British Library Cataloguing in Publication Data
A catalogue record for this book is available from the British Library

Photographs AWL Images: John Warburton-Lee (JWL/AWL); Flickr: Magnus Manske (MM/F); James Gifford (JG); Tricia Hayne (TH); Marco Muscarà, www.marcomuscara.com (MM); Siân Pritchard-Jones & Bob Gibbons (SPJ & BG); Shutterstock: Francesco Carniani (FC/S), CJPhoto (CJP/S), Dereje (D/S), Javarman (J/S), Jbor (JB/S), Pavel068 (P/S), John Wollwerth (JW/S); Ariadne Van Zandbergen (AVZ); Wikimedia Commons: Paulo Cesár Santos (PCS/WC)
Front cover Camping at a tea plantation in Thyolo, Malawi (JWL/AWL)
Back cover Mosque in Kani-Kombole, Mali (SPJ & BG); 4x4 amid Saharan dunes (SPJ & BG)
Title page Rock paintings at Ennedi, Chad (SPJ & BG); reticulated giraffe (*Giraffa camelopardalis reticulata*), Meru National Park, Kenya (AVZ); sand dunes in Libya (SPJ & BG)
In-text photo (page 179) SPJ & BG

Illustrations Illya Bracht and Bob Gibbons
Maps David McCutcheon FBCart.S

Typeset from the authors' disc by Wakewing, High Wycombe
Production managed by Jellyfish Print Solutions; printed in India
Digital conversion by the Firsty Group

Acknowledgements

Thanks to all at Bradt Travel Guides for giving us this opportunity to share some of our experiences with other would-be travellers across the great Dark Continent. Special thanks to David Mozer, Ariadne Van Zandbergen, David Lambeth and Alex Marr.

To the previous authors of *Africa by Road*, first and second editions, Bob Swain and Paula Snyder, and third edition, Charlie Shackell and Illya Bracht, thank you for the original material. Special thanks to Martha, Charles, Angella and Titus in Nairobi, for rescuing us from the roadside! To Arnout and Saskia. To Dr Liz Molyneux in Blantyre, Malawi, for tea and reminiscences in Doogles. To professors Kathryn and Larry, and Annette in Durban, for their exceptional hospitality at the end of one long journey.

Particular thanks for added route information to Debs and Thiemo of Africa Expedition Support in Nairobi, Kenya, and to David of Overlanding West Africa. For the Cabinda Angola route, thanks to Kristy (Princess) and Nev at Oasis Overland, as well as to Andi, Grant and Jeff. Thanks also to Mike Stead for information about Angola. To Kate, Simon and Max, for their updates on west Africa. To Jerry (and Shirley) Kent and Lisa Holyhead after their long overland trips and sojourn in Malawi. Further thanks to Nick Bradshaw and Vicki Muijlaert for all their details. Thanks to Henry John Wright for a great synopsis of the Namibia to Nigeria route via Franceville in Gabon (*www.hjwa.co.za*). For additional material, thanks to Aline Catzeflis (Ivory Coast), Caitlin Reed (women travellers) and Bonita Backhouse (travelling with children) and Mike Robertson.

Thanks to the Dar Daif Hotel, Ouarzazate and Fort Bou Jerif, Guelmime in Morocco; Zebra Bar in St Louis, Senegal; L'Auberge in Segou and Hotel Via Via in Sevare, Mali; Pastor Joseph T Kolleyan at Oasis Lodge, Salala, Liberia; Madame Raby at Hotel Tata, Labé, Guinea; Fiekpani Akim in Kande, Togo; Patrice Pasquier at Mistral Voyages in Libreville and Paul Telfer of WCS; Peggy at SRP Shipping in Durban. In the UK, thanks to Paul Gowen, Eleanor Duvivier and Jennifer Anglin at the RAC, Michelle at P&O Ferries, Sue at Shewee, Valerie and Sam at Haynes Manuals, Phil Haines of Chichester 4x4 and Dr Martin Ridley in Chichester. Thanks also to Amanda of Travcour, for her help with ever-changing visa prices. In France, thanks to Dr Nicolas Poccard-Chapuis of Chamonix.

In Nepal, thanks to Karna, Rajan, Sunil, Susan, Sohan, Uttam, Nabin, Kumar and all the staff at the Kathmandu Guest House, and to Ravi Chandra Hamal for the great parking and workshop spot in Kathmandu. In India, thanks to Ali and Mustafa Merchant in Mumbai for the extraction of the Land Rover (and not too many tips) at Nava Durga port. Thanks to Eugene Pram in Jaipur, Mrs Bhandari's Guest House in Amritsar, Christopher Burchett and Rama Tiwari in Varanasi. In China, thanks to Penny and Tracy of NAVO and the road gang welding crew outside Louliang, Xinjiang, who saved the engine mounting! Also to all the helpful people in Kazakhstan, Russia and Ukraine, whose names we can't spell in Cyrillic. Thanks to Down Under Insurance for rescuing us in Krakow.

In 2014, thanks to Ron Tameris at Wim's in Addis; Naod Haile of K G (G K) Ahadu Tours in Mekele; Luigi Cantamessa and his wife Françoise at Korkor Lodge in Megab; and the Oriental Hotel in Hargeisa, Somaliland. Many thanks also to Karen at Toguna Adventure Tours in Bamako, Mali. To any others whose stories are in here without their knowing it, thanks; and if you are in here, let us know if you'd like a copy.

And, finally, thanks to the peoples of Africa for making our trips memorable, fascinating and so addictive that we can't wait to go back there again.

FEEDBACK REQUEST AND UPDATES WEBSITE

At Bradt Travel Guides we're aware that guidebooks start to go out of date on the day they're published – and that you, our readers, are out there in the field doing research of your own. You'll find out before us when a fine new family-run hotel opens or a favourite restaurant changes hands and goes downhill. So why not write and tell us about your experiences? Contact us on ✆ 01753 893444 or e info@bradtguides.com. We will forward emails to the author who may post updates on the Bradt website at www.bradtupdates. com/africaoverland. Alternatively you can add a review of the book to www. bradtguides.com or Amazon.

Contents

LIST OF MAPS

Introduction

Crossing the vast African continent may seem like a far-fetched idea in the modern world. But if that's your dream, don't hesitate – go for it while you still can.

Africa is vibrant, exciting, fascinating, beautiful and inspiring, yet it can also seem at times depressing, arduous, hot and gruelling. Some days you will be floating

MARSABIT TO NAIROBI

At dawn a grey fog envelops the town, a place of verdant forest in a sea of desert. The heavy dew cloaks everything with a damp veneer. A monkey scurries away, disturbed outside the lodge by the guests' early morning preparations for the day's journey. Breakfast is a tasty affair; greasy fried eggs cooked in days-old butter/ghee, with blackened toast and Lipton's tea. It could have been breakfast anywhere in India, but this was northern Kenya, a land of wild-eyed, colourful tribesmen and spectacular desert scrub dotted with stunning isolated boulders the size of mountains.

As the first cracks appeared in the heavy fog, we began the long descent from the island of hills that make Marsabit such a rich oasis. Mohammed from the Kenyan security forces, a gregarious family man with a gun stuffed in his pocket, accompanied us. At the time taking an armed guard between Marsabit and Isiolo was recommended due to insecurity issues. Whether having Mohammed along would make the day safer was not something we cared to dwell on. At least Mohammed could enjoy a comfortable trip to his family home near Isiolo, and we could learn more about life in these torrid zones of northern Kenya.

On leaving the cool hills, the sun broke through and a crystal-clear sky accompanied us across the dry plains. Dramatic rocks reared skyward; acacia scrub and low bushes provided suitable cover for wild animals (and bandits). We passed groups of Rendille heading to the market. These semi-nomadic tribal clansmen and women carried long spears, wearing brilliant red sashes decorated with silvery-coloured braids, ornaments and bangles. Tall and slender, they presented a picture-perfect image of a proud, self-assured independent people.

The road deteriorated from a sandy strip into a dreadful, rough and rocky gash through the boulder-strewn countryside. Even at 15mph the Land Rover lurched in disgust, suspension banging and wearing itself away, the doors rattling constantly. Slowly we progressed to the northern slopes of Mount Kenya, its jagged, snow-dusted peak peering out above a wispy band of clouds in the distance.

From Isiolo, where we parted company with Mohammed, the desert gave way to the rolling farmlands of the white highlands, graced with quaint colonial farmhouses. Such contrasts – gone were the tense, testing hours in hostile country, with joy at those little things that make it such a worthwhile venture – the children's welcoming smiles, the happy villagers, the tall, incredibly shaped trees, the fabulous desert landscapes, the shady beaches, driving on a fun dirt road, that cold bucket 'shower'… The next day – struggling with the heat, the dust, the flies, the corrupt border officials, the endless bush with nowhere to camp, the mayhem of a capital city with no signposts and, of course, the absurd visa problems – you might want to be somewhere else.

If you're contemplating a journey across Africa overland and beyond – then read on; hopefully you will be inspired to put your dreams into action, or at the very least we will have whetted your appetite. We have included some anecdotes taken from our various trips. These may or may not persuade you to get out of that armchair and do it for yourself!

There are pitfalls and risks, for sure, but nothing in life is completely risk-free and there is so much to be gained by overland travel. Whatever you have read from other early or more recent explorers may only awaken your imagination to the endless possibilities. You will never have enough time to do everything; life is not long

replaced with scenes reminiscent of Wiltshire. We passed a smoke-belching old Bedford truck, not a local model but a British Army training vehicle; it was none too healthy. We sailed on by, all the cares of the world blown away by the cool air and a super tarmac highway with fuel stations, shops and animated markets. The Kenyan capital with its modern towers, coffee houses and vivid happy memories beckoned. We would make it before sunset at this rate. Nairobi at last!

Just 12 miles from the city, in the bright lights of the northern suburbs, at the crest of a rise and just before some poor shanty areas, the clutch gave out with a shocking suddenness. With little prior warning, we were engulfed by impatient traffic, horns blasting and drivers fuming. Desperately we struggled to push the stricken vehicle to the side of the road. 'Nairobi is a city with substantial areas best avoided at night, with rampant crime,' quotes a line in a guidebook. Our thoughts were racing, with a sudden sense of dread. What if this had happened earlier in the day – why were we doing this? And then that detached sense of resignation, of being in the hands of a higher power… and then the need for a practical solution.

Within five minutes we were approached by a local couple on their way home from work – Charles and Martha. What an amazing breath of humanity within the sea of hurried, detached masses of evening commuters. Within an hour the Land Rover had been pushed and cajoled into the armed-guard security of the local supermarket, and the night staff happily rewarded for their kindness. Charles and Martha had invited us to stay with them, their enquiring young son Titus and Martha's younger sister Angella. The flat was in a secure compound on a third floor. They offered us a sumptuous dinner, a comfortable bed and a hot shower, heated by a giant electric ring set in a bucket. Such kindness was embarrassing; would this generosity have been offered to complete strangers in our own country?

On this single day we had enjoyed a homely breakfast, endured a harsh, hot and dusty desert crossing, passed sombre nomadic tribal clans, avoided bandits, experienced exhilaration in the highlands, broken down 12 miles from Nairobi and been welcomed as honoured guests into a private house.

Although written some time ago, this story still encapsulates the essence of *Africa Overland*. We remain close friends with Martha, Charles and their family.

enough for that. So decide your main objectives and be prepared to change your plans as you go. Don't think it will be a once-in-a-lifetime trip; when you return life will never ever be quite the same again. Africa may grab you wholeheartedly; you may find it hard not to return time after time.

Because of changing events, your route may have to be modified once you're on the road, so you should always build as much flexibility into your planning as possible. You'll meet other travellers who may tell you of something they have just discovered and which you really shouldn't miss. Political events may block or open up routes. However, do have a good outline plan before you start out and don't rush off without thinking it all over carefully. Try to avoid disasters before they happen.

It is likely that no-one else will understand or be interested in your travels beyond a quick 'Where did you go? What did you see? What was the weather like?' But your memories will live on forever and you will find inspiration and understanding that no book alone can ever hope to impart. Others will think you are crazy, but surely the call of the open road lurks deep within the human spirit – the need to break free of constraints. Perhaps if more people had a true spirit of adventure, and tolerance for other ways of life, the world might be a safer place.

This book – the first three editions were entitled *Africa by Road* – describes the various ways to travel overland through Africa and beyond. If you don't think driving your own vehicle is for you, then you may want to join an organised trip. The tour companies will do most of the planning for you, leaving you just to find the money and set off to enjoy yourself – although you should still be prepared to do your share of hard work while on the road.

This new edition also outlines a journey 'out of Africa' from Mumbai to Europe through India, Nepal, Tibet/China, Kazakhstan, Russia and Ukraine as an alternative to shipping the vehicle back or if borders shut routes. It also gives hints to those who want to travel overland across Africa on public transport – an option that is far less stressful when unexpected political crises or worse incidents occur, barring the planned route forward. This book is tailored towards planning, preparation and route possibilities, detailing highlights and other factors specific to travel in Africa as well as adjacent areas. It does not aim to replace country guides and we strongly recommend that you take other relevant books. Bradt of course! How long will you wait before embarking on your own trip of exploration?

Part One

BEFORE YOU LEAVE

1

The Basics

Starry desert nights, wild animals roaming through acacia trees, tropical azure skies and silver sands, exotic jungle vistas, camping in the bush listening to the distant beat of drums – this is the Africa we picture, this is the dream awaiting discovery. We hope this book is the beginning of that alluring journey. Exploring Africa will be worth every moment and every pound, euro or dollar (or yuan!). Planning a big trip to Africa begins with dreams, but eventually the practical necessities have to be considered.

Flexibility, time and extra cash are the keys to overland travel these days, when politics, bureaucracy and startling world-changing events seem more frequent than ever. Disruptions must be expected. On our last trip we actually left the UK planning to cross Asia from the Middle East to Kathmandu in Nepal, but that plan was dependent on getting a Saudi visa in Amman and shipping from Dubai to India. Just 20 minutes in the Saudi consulate in Jordan determined the course of the year to come. No transit visas were possible for Saudi Arabia, so it was back to Plan B, southwards via Egypt to Africa. In anticipation of this blockage, we had already obtained our Ethiopian visas as an insurance against the failure of Plan A.

The overall cost will vary widely according to your abilities and facilities, your luck in finding the right type of vehicle, and the length of time you have available. Different routes are described in some detail; though the possibilities ought to be endless, some routes may be impossible for a time because of political considerations. Planning and preparation, both before and during your trip, are important; you don't want to have to fly back to your home country just to get a visa, miss some vital spare part or even forget that favourite food for emergencies!

Any number of things can change your route once you're on the road, so you should always build as much flexibility into your planning as possible. Other travellers are sure to tell you of some priceless discovery that you can't afford to miss. Keep an open mind, but don't just rush off – you need an outline plan before you start out to make the most of your journey. Think it all over carefully in order to avoid disasters before they happen.

Like it or not, your budget will inevitably determine some of your plans. For how long and in how much comfort do you wish to travel? The initial plan will have to consider which countries are currently accessible, and which routes avoid troublesome hotspots. How will the local weather patterns influence the timing of the trip? You will need to take a long look at some maps in order to work out an outline itinerary. Calculating the time to get from place to place will depend on the state of the roads, the nature of the terrain and the type of transport you have, as well as the inevitable bureaucratic delays *en route*. Some countries are expensive, imposing high visa fees or border charges; others are much cheaper. Already you can see the difficulties in estimating a budget. You need to keep in mind any number of unexpected costs that will inevitably arise along the way. Sometimes, of course, it works in your favour, but don't plan on it.

Taking your own vehicle offers you unrivalled freedom, but you will undoubtedly find that the cost is surprisingly high. Most of it will probably be before you even set off. All the peripheral things add up – spare parts, visa fees, insurance, carnet, and so on. Basic day-to-day expenses can be very low; fuel is often dirt cheap, and food, where available, is also often very inexpensive. But if you decide to visit a game park, or your vehicle breaks down, the costs can go sky high.

Taking a motorcycle or bicycle is much cheaper, but you will need to sacrifice comfort, choice of some destinations and personal space to do it. These days there is a lot to be said for taking a motorcycle – it's easier to avoid hotspots and visa problems, because shipping or flying over a problem is an option. It is also, of course, possible to cross most of Africa on very public local transport. This will not always be easy and is often extremely uncomfortable. The other option is to join an overland truck group. This is a good option for a first-time trip if you are happy to mix in with other like-minded travellers and can forgo the independence you have when travelling on your own.

It's possible to calculate many fixed costs in advance, such as visas, ferries, estimated fuel costs, and planned shipping expenses. You can determine the cost of spare parts, equipment and tools. You can decide which vehicle to take, but remember that the vehicle carnet bond cost will relate to the vehicle chosen and its age. This can be the most significant consideration when choosing your vehicle. The level of comfort affects costs – camping or hotels or a mix. You can map out a route and check costs for each country from relevant guidebooks.

What you can't budget for are 'African factors'. These might be border closures or the necessity of some unexpected shipping that could add considerably to the cost. There might be other delays, whether due to bureaucracy, road damage, breakdowns or just bad luck. Try to make a realistic assessment of all known costs and then add a couple of thousand dollars or more, just in case. Make sure you can get extra funds on a debit or credit card if necessary. If you have a major breakdown, you may need more than you could possibly foresee or carry; be prepared for any eventuality.

THE BUDGET

EXPENDITURE Trying to predict expenses and work out a budget is very difficult for an overland expedition. Each person has different needs and expectations. Some can survive on only US$15, while others cannot survive on less than US$80 or more per day. You probably need to find a balance between the two. We have indicated below some of the costs involved before you go. Some are more or less fixed; others are very variable, such as the vehicle chosen.

Costs *en route* will vary according to personal needs. We would estimate an average of US$80 per day, allowing US$40 for fuel and other costs for the 4x4 vehicle, and US$40 for personal expenses such as accommodation and living expenses for two people. Our latest expedition was a three-month trip from London to Durban driving almost 20,000km with a total on-road expenditure of US$6,500. The Nile route down through east Africa is much cheaper for fuel and accommodation than any expedition to west Africa. If you camp in the bush where possible, avoiding air-conditioned rooms, the costs can be reduced. But it would be better to assume a daily expenditure of nearer US$80–100 for two people, with fuel prices likely to rise continually in future.

In some countries, like Sudan and South Sudan, your expenses will be minimal, as fuel is almost free and there isn't much else on which to spend your money. But countries like Kenya, Tanzania and Botswana can be much more expensive because of the activities on offer, like climbing Kilimanjaro or visiting the various national parks. Some days we would spend as much as US$70 and the next only US$12 (sometimes nothing at all in the desert). West Africa is expensive, with fuel prices almost as much as Europe. Food is economical in local markets, but add an air-conditioned room and your daily expenses could rise to well over US$100 in some west African capitals.

Realistically, if you are buying a vehicle specifically for this trip, you will need to budget for around US$15,000–20,000 in total before you leave, plus US$300–400 or more per person per week in your own 4x4 vehicle. Even with a bicycle, the total initial investment will be over US$2,000. Planning a trip by motorbike will fall somewhere between the two. Taking public transport is the cheapest option of all and has an attractive degree of simplicity in these days of over-organisation. However, even on these trips, visas can become a headache.

ESTIMATED COSTS

The costs listed below are based on taking your own vehicle. Information on taking your own motorbike or bicycle is discussed later in this chapter and *Chapter 3*. The figures below will vary enormously according to the amount of work you can do yourself, and where you get the vehicle, parts and tools. A toolbox bought in a car boot sale will cost much less than one from a good stockist, but be careful. You don't want your cheap spanner to crack up in a dodgy place.

BEFORE YOU LEAVE
Vehicle
Based on a secondhand Toyota Land Cruiser or Land Rover 110/Defender

Fully equipped, ie: overland ready	US$9,000–17,000
Vehicle only	US$7,000–13,000

Vehicle preparation If you were lucky enough to find a fully equipped vehicle, you may only need to check that everything works and fine-tune the vehicle for your trip. If you are starting from scratch, it may cost around the full amount. US$4,000–7,000

Equipment	US$2,500–3,500
Spares and tools	US$3,000–5,000

Medical insurance
Based on each person for one year full cover — US$500–1,000

Medical kit
The lower amount if buying in Africa — US$300–700

On the road
Per person, per day, based on two people in one vehicle — US$80–120

The preparation costs quickly add up: the purchase of a vehicle; equipping it appropriately; getting a carnet, full medical insurance cover and a medical kit; and many costs that you might not have considered. Doing it more cheaply may be fine but as a general rule the less you invest, the harder your trip is likely to be. At the other extreme you could buy a fully converted six-wheel drive and spend something like US$100,000 before you even start. We would not recommend this, as the more complicated the vehicle, the harder it will be to fix if it does go wrong. Even an expensive vehicle is not immune to breakdowns. Also remember that the cost of the customs carnet is proportionately related to the cost of the vehicle.

But don't be put off! If you have the abilities and facilities to do most of the preparation yourself, you can reduce your expenses considerably. The following are some of the major costs you will have to meet, but the figures quoted are only a rough guide. Ideally, you should look at your own requirements under each of the headings listed in *Chapter 3* and check out the costs.

SPONSORSHIP Don't think that sponsorship will fall into your lap as soon as you announce to the world that you are off to explore Africa; obtaining sponsorship is a tough nut to crack. Most obvious companies have been approached in the past. Local firms are more likely to be sympathetic than national names, but are unlikely to have as much to offer. Is the massive investment of time attempting to find any sort of sponsorship worthwhile?

In aid of charity With forward planning, some travellers have managed to raise cash for charities by approaching sponsors and private donors. Some benefits can be derived from this approach, but a lot of effort will be required. Some of the larger charities such as CARE have given help to overland travellers who have raised money for them. This could be one way of raising awareness and giving something back to Africa. (See *Travelling positively*, page 196.)

ROUTE PLANNING

It has been lamented by some famous travellers that the planning and the expectations of the journey are sometimes greater fun than the execution of the subsequent travel itself. Planning the trip within the comforts and confines of your own home is certainly a lot of fun.

MAPS Africa is big and distances are on a massive scale. Travel times in Africa can be several times longer for a given distance than they are in more developed countries.

Although the Michelin maps we highly recommend are excellent for planning, they have a few surprisingly significant errors. We mention some of these later in the route sections. You will need at the very least the following map numbers: 741 (*Africa North and West*), 745 (*Africa North East and Arabia*) and 746 (*Africa Central and South*). These maps have a wealth of mostly accurate information on them, showing all the salient points, distance, type of road surface, wells and quality of water, dunes, possible fuel and rest stops, altitudes, scenic routes, etc. Other Michelin maps that may be of some use are 742 (Morocco), 743 (Algeria and Tunisia) and 747 (Ivory Coast).

Some roads shown as a tarmac highway really do exist, but others will be pot-holed, have broken sections, have rough uneven surfaces and, at worst, are just plain diabolical with little tarmac left. Other roads shown as gravel might be new super-highways. Some gravel roads are excellent, such as those in Namibia; others, like those in Ethiopia, are exceedingly rough, stony, rocky and tyre-eating. In the central African rainforest zone, roads can be extremely muddy, with large puddles often the size of ponds. Bridges here may be broken, have planks missing or be constructed of parallel cylindrical logs. During the wet seasons, some roads are impassable and others might be closed off to vehicles by *barrières de pluie* (rain barriers) across the road until the muddy surfaces have dried sufficiently.

CLIMATE On the Michelin maps you will see charts indicating the approximate average temperatures, high and low, as well as the rainfall for various cities and towns in Africa. When you are planning the best time of year for your trip, these give a very good basic insight into the climatic conditions of each area.

Attempting to cross the Sahara in summer between late April and early October or heading into a rainforest in the rainy season is pretty crazy. If you plan to invest a lot of money in driving across Africa, why go when the dangers are high and the journey

BLAME THE MAP

Maps are a wonderful thing until you realise that a road on a map in North Sudan is in reality the sand beside the railway line, and on which side of the line does it go? This road is a complete figment of Michelin's imagination. We followed the railway line but, even before leaving Wadi Halfa, we were in quite deep sand. More by luck and guesswork than map-reading, we found the way for over 200 miles by following the line of telegraph poles alongside the railway tracks; occasionally the sand was very deep. We met just one vehicle all day and that was only ten miles out of town. Despite the railway lines, this route is surprisingly remote and devoid of life.

At Station Four we encountered some workmen sweeping sand off the tracks for the expected train. They were not pleased with us as we pulled into the station astride the lines, carefully avoiding the points and steel cables. 'Which way to Khartoum, please?' They were not amused and directed us out into the deepest sand 100m from the station. Horribly bogged now, we discovered that the low-ratio gears on the Land Rover would not engage. Fortunately some digging and then diff lock got us out. Away from the station, we again headed as close to the railway tracks as possible, sneaking on to the embankment at the next deep sand. The track was surprisingly smooth as the rails were buried by hard sand and the only problem was avoiding touching the lines themselves. It was lucky for us that the train comes only once a week in each direction, as we were stuck on this embankment for many miles with no way off. Today there were no trains, because of a mass wedding party in Wadi Halfa, to which all were invited and no-one could leave.

That evening it was great to camp wild in the desert, below some low rocky hills with a tremendous view. Having just parked and made a cup of tea, Bob said to me, 'Look, what's that over there? It looks almost like a train!'

'It is a train,' I replied.

Thank goodness we were no longer on the lines. It was a large freight train, which was obviously too late for the wedding party!

In 2010 a brand new tarmac road was opened along the banks of the river, providing a much easier alternative to the railway line... with no danger of getting lost!

exceedingly uncomfortable? Remember too that altitude can significantly affect the temperature and climate. In Ethiopia or on the slopes of Mount Kenya, for example, the highlands bring welcome relief from the sometimes-oppressive heat of the plains.

Further south, planning a trip through any areas subject to seasonal rains really can wreak havoc on daily schedules, particularly where roads are not paved. It is surprising what a short, sharp rainstorm can do to some roads. In the Sahel, on the southern fringes of the Sahara, this can mean seriously sticky conditions, where sand and soil are mixed. In the humid rainforests it can manifest in hours of digging away thick heavy mud while up to your waist in brown water. There is a certain amount of masochistic fun to be had in these predicaments, but not for three weeks at a stretch.

No departure date is likely to suit all the optimum weather patterns. If you plan a long journey across Africa, it becomes even more difficult. Somewhere *en route* is going to be awkward; you will just have to work around these things at the time. But time is what you might have most of.

OTHER FACTORS AND LIMITATIONS Below are some of the parameters that you need to determine: total number of days available, daily travel distance, local climate, geography, road conditions, level of accommodation, flexibility with food, availability of fuel and water, delays obtaining visas *en route*, unexpected festivals and even what wildlife you want to see.

With so many fascinating destinations in Africa, your inclination might be to try to fit too much into too little time. Seven game parks in seven days in a 4x4 can be as gruelling as a European bus tour of seven countries in seven days. Some travellers suggest that quality is better than quantity, but if you don't want to miss anything, it's amazing what you can pack in with some determination. Don't be

IT NEVER RAINS BUT IT POURS...

Dawn. It was a bitterly cold morning outside El Golea; the army personnel were drinking black tea and smoking French cigarettes. Breakfast for them was bread and oranges. We waited and waited. And waited. Until 16.00. Finally they told us the bad news: 'Today no convoy.'

Dawn again the next day. A soldier gave us a bottle of Orangina in exchange for a fresh orange. The convoy set off, but within minutes we were alone in the desert, being hopelessly unable to keep up. There were no police or army in the so-called convoy. Soon it was pouring with rain, so much so that we had the windscreen wipers on all day long. Could this really be the Sahara? A day later large pink flowers blossomed in wild profusion, taking full advantage of this unexpected manna from heaven.

At In Salah, the first fuel station was unreachable because of the truck-swallowing mud. The second was slightly better, but with a long line of vehicles attempting to fill up. In the old streets children played happily in the swimming pools made by the unusual precipitation; perhaps some of them had never seen such an event before in their short lives. We camped outside the poshest hotel in town. Inside, the lobby was almost a swimming pool too. The ceiling dripped, and the beautiful carpets had to be moved to a drier part of the building. We watched BBC World and Al Jazeera briefly, before retreating to the inside of our cosy metal box, listening to the 'tap tap tap' on the roof with a comforting sense of security.

surprised if your planning chart begins to look a complete mess, with rows of 'if, then, maybe' conditions for each separate possible itinerary. It's a good idea to use an Excel spreadsheet so that you can shift the options and dates around easily and view them side-by-side.

ROUTE OUTLINES With regard to actual routes, things change constantly. In the heyday of African overlanding in the late 1970s and the 1980s, almost all the continent's big routes were open, except for those via Angola, Mozambique and, at various times, southern Sudan. In the early 1990s the trans-Saharan routes across Algeria closed, due to Islamic insurgents in the north and the Tuareg rebellion in the south. But then the route into Mauritania opened via Western Sahara, so the great trans-Africa route remained possible. When the turmoil of Zaire erupted, combined with instability in the Central African Republic, the routes across the great rainforests of the Congo Basin became history.

Yet routes did remain tenuously possible, as is often the way of African travel. Chad and Sudan allowed a trickle of adventurous travellers to cross from Cameroon to Ethiopia, but then hostilities in Darfur closed that route in 2004. The Nile route through Egypt to Khartoum, so long a big no-go area, opened. More recently, it has been possible to drive south from Cameroon into Gabon, across the two Congos and into Angola, although getting a visa for Angola is a bit of a lottery. Failure means a big detour and recently Angola was requesting that visitors obtain visas in their own country. This meant overlanders required two passports, one of which could be flown by DHL to their home country – a very big hassle and expense indeed!

With the 2003 kidnappings in Algeria, vast tracts of the **Sahara** became effectively off-limits to independent overlanders. The continual threats of al-Qaeda in the Maghreb have effectively closed virtually the entire Saharan region of Algeria, Niger, eastern Mauritania and northern Mali. One would hope that most of Mali will soon become accessible after the recent troubles. Organised tours do periodically operate in parts of Algeria with security guards. Mauritania is proving do-able but there is also a risk. Running the gauntlet between the borders of Western Sahara and Senegal will be nerve-racking, but sometimes risk-taking proves to be a worthwhile gamble – after the event.

Following the uprising in Egypt, it is still possible to follow the **Nile route**, but expect volatility to persist for some time. Apparently the road around Lake Nasser is now complete, though political considerations mean it may not be possible for overlanders to use it. However, at least one overland group has already done so. Of course getting to Egypt itself is now the problem, with the tragic events in Syria and some lawlessness in Libya. Shipping from Turkey is another option. The Nile region of Sudan is currently trouble-free and it remains to be seen what the effects of the Libyan revolution will be. Surprisingly, Chad seems to be getting more accessible of late, although not for independent overlanders in the north. Point Afrique, a French company, started operating direct charter flights to Faya in 2013. New oil-financed roads in the southwest of Chad may improve options there and on into Sudan if the Darfur crisis continues to improve.

West Africa has some great routes that are now mostly safe, exciting and practical. Relatively good routes from Mauritania lead to Mali and Burkina Faso, fascinating Sahel countries with spectacular mud-walled towns, picturesque mosques and varied scenery, but do check the latest security situation in Mali before travel. Along the coast, only Ivory Coast needs to be watched, remaining uncertain. Liberia is at last creeping out from the disasters of the war years. Senegal, Gambia, Guinea

Bissau, Guinea and Sierra Leone are currently as safe as Africa gets. Ghana, Nigeria, Cameroon and Gabon complete the coastal route and are also to be contemplated when planning your route. The chance of encountering crime in all the big coastal cities (Lomé, Cotonou, Lagos, Douala and around Port Harcourt) should be borne in mind, though.

East Africa has become a delight for overlanders, safari enthusiasts and just about anyone looking to experience Africa at its best. Now that the lingering conflict between opposing groups in Burundi is said to have been resolved, most of east Africa – Kenya, Tanzania, Uganda, Burundi and Rwanda – can be visited with keen anticipation. Heading south, the routes to the Cape in South Africa and Namibia are all stable, with even Zimbabwe presenting few serious dilemmas. All this is not to say that muggings in big cities and opportunistic crime cannot be ruled out, but that can happen in any part of the world now.

If Syria returns to some kind of normality, don't dismiss the route across the **Middle East** from Europe to Istanbul and then south to Egypt. Jordan (and Syria before) were exceedingly hospitable countries. We must all just hope for peace in Syria now. Don't go through Israel, though; you will not be able to get into Sudan later. On the downside, the Egyptian authorities have increased the carnet duty percentage from 500% to 800%, making it very expensive to obtain the paperwork necessary for travelling there. Unfortunately the maximum cash deposit that the RAC will accept is now £10,000, so for vehicles with a value of more than £1,250, the carnet bond is no longer an option for Egypt. Check the insurance option, which will unfortunately add more cost.

By linking up the different options, a variety of routes can be contemplated. Over the past 30 years, various routes have always been possible, enough to keep the flickering candle of African travel passion alive. Check out various websites, including our own, www.expeditionworld.com, for travellers' stories as well – many people now carry laptops with them and update their blogs as they go. Keep abreast of the latest political situations and do check the visa regulations for the countries ahead.

You should definitely consult the various government foreign travel advice websites, such as the British one at www.gov.uk/foreign-travel-advice. Of course, if you took complete notice of the information given out in these websites, you might never get beyond Dover. They are by their nature somewhat cautious, over-protective and sometimes out of date. The nanny state is all around; one is not supposed to be this adventurous! We found that the difficulties in assessing the risk were illustrated by the previous warnings about Chad north of the capital N'djamena, which categorically advised travellers not to venture anywhere in the whole area. While the Tibesti region was certainly dangerous, the Ennedi area was not, except for the known existence of mines. If we had heeded the FCO warnings when we visited the Ennedi in 2002, we might have missed an incredible experience. But maybe we were just lucky that time! This is not to say that we recommend that everyone should go to all parts of Chad – just don't write it off immediately.

Things need to be put into context and, above all, good and reliable local advice must be sought for such areas. Some places in Africa are frankly best avoided by people like us in our own cars, and are better visited with experienced local operators, as we did both in Chad and in parts of Niger.

More detail on the routes that exist across Africa, including the Middle East and even Asia, are included below. Whether you are contemplating a short foray into north Africa, a longer trip through west Africa or the complete trans-Africa, the process of planning will reignite the dreams that you had when you first decided that this journey was for you.

Useful planning websites

www.africa-overland.net
www.tracks4africa.co.za
www.expeditionworld.com

www.horizonsunlimited.com/hubb (known as the Hubb)

Note on place names Confusion arises between the Democratic Republic of the Congo (DRC) – formerly Zaire – and the Republic of the Congo. In this edition we have used Democratic Republic of the Congo or DRC for the former and Congo for the latter.

GETTING TO AFRICA BY FERRY All routes to Africa involve ferry crossings. See *Getting to Africa*, page 21, for more overland route information.

Spain to Morocco One popular route is from Algeciras, Málaga or Gibraltar to Ceuta or Tangier. Those with a vehicle or motorbike will probably opt to go via Ceuta, because the city forms part of Spanish Morocco; its tax-free status means that fuel is cheaper than Spain but more expensive than Morocco. It's always a good idea to fill up your jerrycans going north.

It is not necessary to book in advance for the Algeciras-to-Ceuta ferry. Shop around when you arrive. Most ferries between Spain and Morocco run regular services every 30 minutes or every hour both ways. A standard ferry crossing from Algeciras to Ceuta usually takes up to 45 minutes. Prices vary according to the shipping line and the type of seat or the size of car/trailer but may be as low as US$120 or as much as US$300.

Other routes are from **France** (Marseille) **to Morocco or Tunisia**. Ferries to Algeria are not currently advisable. Ferries that ply routes from France and Spain to the north coast of Africa include **SNCM Ferryterranée** (⟨ *0891 701 801, +33 4 91 56 32 00; www.sncm.fr*) and **Compañia Trasmediterránea** (*information & booking:* ⟨ *+34 90 245 4645;* e *correom@trasmediterranea.es; www.trasmediterranea.es*). See also www.maroc-ferry.com for ferries between Morocco and Spain.

Italy to Tunisia Italian ferries go primarily from Genoa, Naples and Trapani (in Sicily) to Tunis. Ferries also connect the Italian ports of Genoa, Livorno and

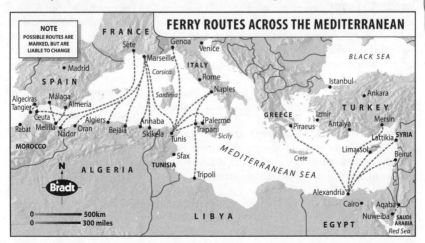

FERRY ROUTES ACROSS THE MEDITERRANEAN

NOTE
POSSIBLE ROUTES ARE MARKED, BUT ARE LIABLE TO CHANGE

FRANCE — Sète, Marseille, Genoa, Venice — BLACK SEA — Istanbul — Ankara — TURKEY — Izmir — Antalya — Mersin — Lattikia SYRIA — Beirut — Limassol — Alexandria — Cairo — Aqaba — Nuweiba SAUDI ARABIA — Red Sea

Madrid — SPAIN — Algeciras — Tangier — Ceuta — Melilla — Rabat — Nador — Málaga — Almería — Oran — Algiers — Bejaia — Skikela — Anhaba — MOROCCO — ALGERIA — Corsica — ITALY — Rome — Sardinia — Naples — Palermo — Trapani Sicily — Tunis — TUNISIA — Sfax — Tripoli — GREECE — Piraeus — Crete — MEDITERRANEAN SEA — LIBYA — EGYPT

N — Bradt

0 — 500km
0 — 300 miles

Naples with Palermo – you can visit Sicily without driving all the way down through Italy. Ferries to Tunisia are cheaper from Italy than France, and the drive to Genoa is almost as fast (allow three days from London). For the best prices these routes should be booked well in advance. They are very heavily booked in summer, but most overlanders will not be going then anyway. Return fares are good value, although none are that cheap. The ferries take about 24 hours. Approximate prices are US$1,400–1,600 return. From Trapani (Sicily) to Tunis the ferry takes seven or eight hours. This is best booked in advance, as it only runs once a week! It is much cheaper, as a cabin is not required: it costs US$180 single for a car plus two passengers.

We have used the following agencies: Viamare Ltd (⚲ *020 8206 3420;* e *ferries@ viamare.com; www.viamare.com*) is an agent for Grandi Navi Veloci and Grimaldi; Southern Ferries (⚲*0844 815 7785;* e *mail@southernferries.com; www.southernferries. com*) deals with SNCM (French), CTN (Tunisian) and Trasmediterránea (Spanish). Check with them for changes to ferry schedules and routes.

Italy to Greece Ferries run daily from Brindisi and Bari in southern Italy to Igoumenitsa near Corfu in Greece. These are good for those heading to Africa via Turkey and the Middle East who want to avoid the cold in eastern Europe.

Greece to Egypt Ferries operate periodically from Greece to Egypt. Depending on the political situation in Libya, it may be better to ship your vehicle into Tunis, a very well-organised port, and take the excellent road from Tunis to Libya and on to Cairo when it's safe. For Greek ferries, look at the website www.greekislands.gr.

Turkey to Egypt Since the Syrian civil war erupted, vehicle ferries have been introduced from Mersin in Turkey to Port Said in Egypt.

Mersin to Port Said Alcor Shipping (⚲ *+90 324 233 5030;* e *ilker.sagay@ alcorshipping.com*) sails Fridays or Tuesdays from Mersin. The trip takes 34 hours and costs from US$175 each way for a cabin only, plus vehicle.

Iskenderun to Port Said It would be worth checking whether or not Sisa Shipping or any other company has been able to restart services on this route.

Jordan to Egypt It is quite easy, although not cheap, to ship a vehicle from Aqaba in Jordan to Nuweiba in the Egyptian Sinai. However, with the troubles in Syria, this option is not of much use for the moment. That said, it's much better and cheaper to drive through the Middle East under normal circumstances. The Turkey to Egypt ferry makes it redundant for the time being.

NB: At the time of writing, Egypt had a temporary import ban on 4x4 vehicles in the Sinai, and ports were liable to be closed at short notice.

Aqaba to Nuweiba The ferry takes one to three hours and costs from around US$450 for a car and two people. It can be booked in Aqaba a day or two in advance. Egyptian visas are available in Aqaba – sometimes the same day. See www. abmaritime.com.jo for inconvenient schedules and expensive prices.

Sudan to Jordan We understand that there is now a shipping service between Port Sudan and Aqaba in Jordan (allowing northbound overlanders a route via Israel and shipping out to Greece etc).

Sudan to Saudi Arabia One final ferry route that might be of some use to those travelling north from Sudan to the Middle East is the one from Port Sudan to Jeddah in Saudi Arabia. It's shown as route ME2 on the map of trans-Sahara routes on page 24. This cannot be done southbound because of difficulties in obtaining the Saudi transit visa, which is only valid for three days and is not given to unmarried couples. This visa was issued in Khartoum for direct travel from Jeddah to Jordan only – again for only three days. Security issues may affect this option. Do not attempt it during Hajj, the annual Muslim pilgrimage to Mecca.

For more information on the routes, see *Chapter 2*, page 21.

NB: When asking about ferry prices note that harbour tax, embarkation fees and GST (VAT) are not always included in the quote. Some of the ferry companies offer concessions, depending on the season.

SHIPPING YOUR VEHICLE

4X4 VEHICLES Shipping your vehicle either out to Africa or back from there can be a major expense. The lowest prices from Mombasa, Dar es Salaam, Accra, Walvis Bay, Durban or Cape Town to Europe are around US$2,000 for a container. Small containers for a single vehicle are available. Beware of all the hidden port extras; these can add more than the cost of the basic container. Shipping a vehicle from Europe to South Africa is reasonably easy, if a little more expensive. At least the overall costs are quoted in advance. However, once the vehicle arrives in African ports, hidden costs are an issue, as problems can occur where red tape is complex and certainly some bribes may be necessary.

In Africa you will probably need to use a shipping agent. Although this may add to the cost, it should give you peace of mind and save a lot of time. For shipping from Mombasa, dealing with the bureaucracy and corruption needs patience, and the costs can never be ascertained in advance. In west Africa, Accra seems to be the least difficult place to sort out shipping. Other ports are Lomé and Douala, while both Libreville and Pointe Noire offer irregular services, but of course they have 'French-speaking' paperwork!

Coming back from or going out to South Africa, there are sometimes cheaper roll-on roll-off services between Durban and Rotterdam/Southampton in the UK. In 2004 we shipped our vehicle back from Durban through P&O and a local agent. This service was offered approximately once a month and the vehicle was put on to a ship bringing hundreds of new cars into Europe. Vehicles sent by 'roll-on roll-off' ferries are not in containers. It took three weeks. This can be arranged through P&O Ferrymasters in the UK or SRP Shipping in Durban, South Africa (see page 14).

After the last Africa trip we shipped our vehicle to India (Mumbai Nava Durga port). The overall cost, including all taxes, fees, port charges, loading and a small one-car container was US$2,000. This was again done at SRP Shipping in Durban. Don't expect the ship to leave and arrive on time. In fact ours was three weeks later than expected, so allow lots of slack in your planning and have loads of time to spend doing it. (You could always go via Madagascar or the Indian Ocean islands between South Africa and India while the vehicle is in limbo *en route* (or in the dock still!)

In India we paid a grand total of US$1,300 for the week-long unloading, taxes and port fees. Of course a lot of the cost covered oiled officialdom. We used SECO Shipping in Mumbai (see page 14). It took about a week for the paperwork to be done, which is a bit irritating when coming into India by road takes less than a day at Attari Road/Amritsar. Getting insurance in India is another merry-go-round, but then you do have lots of spare time in Mumbai in between paperwork delays. We managed to get a year's cover including Nepal through New India Assurance Ltd (*ask for Rajesh Merchant; www.newindia.co.in*), for US$80. Usually Oriental Fire and General will do it in Amritsar, but not in Mumbai.

MOTORBIKES Of course, shipping a motorbike is much cheaper. It is even possible to hitch a lift by putting a bike inside a vehicle already being shipped. Airfreight for motorbikes is also pretty reasonable and much quicker.

BICYCLES It is generally possible to take a bicycle as luggage on most airlines.

INTERNATIONAL SHIPPING COMPANIES The following are good website addresses for shipping lines, agents and costs.

In the UK
Complete online freight services (international) www.freightquote.com
P&O Ferrymasters www.poferrymasters.com or www.routesinternational.com
Grimaldi www.grimaldi.co.uk or www.grimaldi-freightcruises.com. Services to west Africa into Accra, Abidjan, Lomé, Douala & Luanda have been recommended.

In Durban
SRP Shipping 65 NMR Av, Durban ☎+27 011 304 5791/6; e srpship@mweb.co.za; www.srpship.co.za

In Mumbai
Sadikally Esoofally & Co 32 Dock View Bldg, 1 WH Marg, Ballard Estate, Mumbai – 400001; m +91 22 22621107/22621643/22690281 or +91 98921 17786; e info@secoshipping.com or secoshipping@hotmail.com; www.secoshipping.com

STARTING A TRIP FROM SOUTH AFRICA

Updated from original notes by Arnout Hemel and Saskia de Jongh, and Mark Sharp

FINDING THE RIGHT CAR Toyota Hilux and Land Cruisers, and Land Rover Defenders are common. South Africans like the outdoors and 4x4s, so there is plenty of outdoor equipment. Recommended places to look are guesthouses, garages/dealers, special overland equippers and private sellers; there tend to be more overlanders wanting to sell their cars in Cape Town than in Johannesburg. Try www.autotrader.co.za and www.ananzi.co.za. For peace of mind when buying, you can do a Test & Drive check at one of the AA test stations (*www.aa.co.za*).

COST Cars cost about the same or a little less in South Africa as in Europe. Equipment is much cheaper (rooftop tents, fridges, etc). Labour costs are lower in South Africa, so it's cheaper to add an extra fuel tank, get things fixed or get your rooftop tent installed.

BEFORE YOU LEAVE HOME Check whether your local Automobile Association issues a *carnet de passage* for a foreign vehicle (normally they do not, but for example the Dutch ANWB might do). If they do, it gives you the flexibility to sell the car in your home country as well as in South Africa. Also the process for depositing the money is easier and more reliable.

MONEY AND PAPERWORK Getting money transferred to a South African bank account can be quite a hassle. It is possible to withdraw money with a debit/credit card and pay with cash. This is the easiest but not the safest option. Check at your local bank to find the best system to transfer money to South Africa.

According to Mark Sharp, a British overland traveller in 2010, it has now become more difficult for foreigners to buy a car in South Africa. For two British citizens who did this, the registration process took over two (solid) weeks, and involved not only dealing with the Licensing Department, but also Home Affairs, to acquire the correct visa (upon arrival, tourists are granted a Temporary Resident's permit – which is not accepted by the Licensing Department). There are clearly other ways around this issue, such as the tourist asking a South African citizen/resident to register the vehicle in their name, and then provide a separate authorisation letter for the tourist to use for transit through international borders, etc. There is also an issue with non-South Africans obtaining the carnet de passage (at a reasonable cost for the bond!), which the reader should also be aware of. The process includes:

1 The seller needs to get the car through a roadworthiness test.
2 The buyer and seller need to fill in two copies of the selling papers, which the seller sends off to get the car de-registered from his name. The buyer needs to go to a local municipality office with one copy to buy a licence disc, and to register the car in his/her name. Total costs are less than US$150, but you need an address in South Africa to be registered as a South African road user. Ask the guesthouse where you are staying if they will support you.
3 You need a carnet de passage. This is not necessary if you stay in southern Africa (Mozambique, Namibia, Botswana, Zimbabwe, Zambia, Malawi). If you plan to go to other countries, it's mandatory. Make sure Egypt, Jordan and Syria are on the carnet, as you might need to cross these countries if the situation there improves, and many AAs tend to exclude those countries.

TIME The state of the vehicle will determine the time needed for preparation. It can be done in two to three weeks, but expect longer. In South Africa you need a safe place to prepare your vehicle to avoid theft. The best option is to find a guesthouse with a parking lot, a spacious campsite or friends with a big home. In the Gauteng area, you can visit Leimer's Land Rovers.

GUIDEBOOKS AND MAPS Check out MapStudio's *Southern & East Africa Atlas* (*www.mapstudio.co.za*). Maps are not easy to find in South Africa. However, detailed 4x4 maps with GPS co-ordinates for southern Africa are available in Johannesburg and Cape Town. Check out Getaway Magazine (*www.getaway.co.za*), a good source of information.

INSURANCE If you want comprehensive insurance, try Cross Country Consultants (*www.allterrain.co.za*). They have a modestly priced comprehensive insurance for southern Africa, Kenya, Tanzania and Uganda. See *Chapter 5*, page 117 for more details on insurance matters.

EQUIPMENT South Africa has a great selection of spares, tools, accessories, outdoor and camping equipment and skilled mechanics; prices are considerably lower than Europe. You can find portable fridges (National Luna, Engel), and many rooftop tents originate from South Africa (Eezi Awn, Echo, Howling Moon, Hannibal). When buying equipment, make sure you haggle over the prices (you will get at least 10% discount for paying cash). Rooftop tents can sometimes be bought directly at the factory for great prices. When you leave South Africa, if you don't intend to return, you can get the VAT refunded on all goods not permanently attached to the car and not consumed (eg: your rooftop tent). All you have to do is keep the original receipt and fill out the forms at the border when you leave South Africa. You must do this within three months of purchasing the goods.

When it comes to buying accessories, everything – hi-lift jack, winch, tyres, fuel jerrycans, long-range fuel tank – is available and often the seller will install it free of charge.

Some useful outdoor stores
Camp World www.campworld.co.za
Makro www.makro.co.za
Outdoor Warehouse www.outdoorwarehouse.
co.za

MECHANICS South African mechanics are skilled and the labour is cheap compared with Europe. A recommended Toyota mechanic and safari outfitter is Baillies Off-Road (*www.baillies.co.za*). For another excellent mechanic, thoroughly recommended by Mark Sharp, contact William Beets in Jo'burg on his mobile (**m** *0833 207244*) or by email (**e** *william_beets@yahoo.com*).

SHIPPING/SELLING Selling a South African car in South Africa is easy, but a foreign-registered vehicle is much more of a problem because of new restrictions.

PLANNING A MOTORBIKE TRIP

See also *Motorbike preparation*, page 89.

Much of the planning for a motorbike trip can be based on the above details. The major differences will be in costs, which will be significantly lower. The other main difference concerns route planning. The chosen itinerary will to some extent depend on the quantity of fuel and water you can carry and how far off the beaten track you feel confident to go. That said, motorbikes are much easier to handle in many situations. They can be carried across rivers on canoes, put on trucks, buses and even planes. They offer a greater degree of freedom in many respects and generally are less worry if they go wrong. They also do not look extravagant and desirable.

PLANNING A BICYCLE TRIP
David Mozer of Bicycle Africa Tours (www.ibike.org/bikeafrica)

See also *Bicycle selection and preparation*, page 93.

Those driving across Africa might be surprised to learn that an adventuresome bunch is planning the trip on a bicycle. With time and an enjoyment of physical effort, cycling when done intelligently can be a very rewarding way to see the continent. It certainly brings you into closer contact with both the people and the environment. But you must take into account the geography, weather patterns, political reality, culture and availability of food and water.

As with any travel, there is something different, even inspirational, about arriving almost anywhere in Africa by bicycle. In the cities, bicycles are efficient – African streets are congested and parking spaces few, which is not a problem with a bicycle. Cycling through the countryside is liberating, reducing your dependency on mechanically questionable, overcrowded and unpredictable public transport. As you cycle, you are certain to meet people whom you would not meet any other way. The physical activity benefits your health, and the unrestricted access to the environment puts you in the middle of an exciting world that begs exploration.

Even if you aren't the rugged type, you can experience certain areas of the continent that give the benefits of a long bike tour in Africa without needing to rough it. Because of the flexibility of a bike and the ease with which it can be transported on planes, trains, buses and boats, itineraries can be tailored and you can start and stop your road adventure almost anywhere. You should be in good health – cycling across the sands of the Sahara or through muddy forest trails can be extremely hard work. If your interests are more modest, then for a cycling tour on the sealed roads in Africa your preparation is similar to that for Europe or North America. You still need a basic level of physical activity in your life, and proper equipment. Of course there are no written rules, and how you approach the challenge is a personal matter.

Bicycle Africa Tours regularly have complete bicycle and Africa touring novices on their programmes, who do very well because they have so much enthusiasm. In most ways, the fundamentals of long-distance cycling in Africa differ very little from those of long-distance summer cycling anywhere: the hills go up and down; the weather can be wet and dry; the temperature is hot and cold; the humidity varies widely and it seems that, no matter which direction you are going, there is a headwind! But there are also differences in Africa to keep in mind:

- Repair facilities are fewer and farther between, so that the initial quality and ongoing upkeep of your bike and your general self-sufficiency are more of a concern. See the sections on selecting and preparing a bike for remote areas and the bike tools section of the packing list (see pages 93 and 104).
- Although there are thousands of kilometres of paved roads in Africa, the prevalence of deteriorating paved roads and of unpaved roads is much higher than in most developed countries. The recurring joke for countries that have fallen on hard times is, 'What do you call a driver going in a straight line?' Answer: 'Drunk.' However, new stretches of roads are being improved each year and the dust is gradually disappearing.
- Cycling in Africa can easily be made more rigorous if you are motivated to get off the highways and off the beaten track into the villages. On any long-distance tour in Africa you will find a mix of riding conditions and you will enjoy it a lot more if you prepare appropriately.
- Don't expect generic highway McFood. If you keep your expectations modest and learn to like African food, you will find plenty to eat in most areas. Cuisine in Africa is not homogeneous; some is more elaborate than others. The chances are that you will find some excellent hole-in-the-wall restaurants and great local cooks and dishes. Unless you have heard that a specific area is suffering from famine, it probably has adequate, if not abundant, food supplies.
- Quiet and personal privacy may become a luxury. Personal space, private property and 'the individual' have very different implications and associations in African culture. Even where the general population density is sparse, where people are living can be crowded, active and communal. Many Westerners find the gregariousness of African culture a challenge.
- Things that we take for granted, like finding water, need to be carefully planned. Bottled water, carbonated drinks and beer are not always available in stores, restaurants or bars. When they are, they probably won't be as cold as you would like and the choice will be limited. Even coffee, in countries that export tonnes

of it each year, may not be brewed and sold outside the major cities. If you are drinking water from non-bottled sources, it may need to be treated so that it is a blessing and not a curse.

- Toilet facilities may not meet the standards of cleanliness and freshness of a five-star hotel, or may be absent altogether. Smells engulf markets, towns, people and all aspects of life.
- Lastly, unless your initial cycling is in Burkina Faso, or the few other spots where cycling is a popular activity, you will quickly note that cycling does not command the status in Africa that it does in much of Asia, or the west. This is not a point of concern per se, but may explain some bewildering looks and questions of disbelief. Hold your ground. Cyclists may be in the minority, but Africans are used to minorities and they are willing to bestow respect on deserving innovators.

The watchwords are 'plan well, be flexible and be tolerant.'

Bicycle touring is one of the most economical means of travel. The main costs you incur are your bike, visas, food and accommodation. If you eat the local cuisine and camp or stay in rock-bottom guesthouses, you can keep expenses to the absolute minimum.

If the idea appeals to you, a good first stop would be to contact the Internet Guide to Travel in Africa by Bicycle (*www.ibike.org/africaguide*), or the Cyclists' Touring Club (CTC) in the UK (\ *01483 417217;* e *cycling@ctc.org.uk*).

Once you join the CTC, you get a wide range of services – insurance, technical advice and touring itineraries. Information sheets are published by the CTC on various aspects of travelling with a bicycle, and on specific countries and areas in Africa – including west Africa, South Africa, Seychelles, Malawi, Gambia, Zambia, Zimbabwe, Algeria and Tunisia, Egypt and Sudan, Morocco and the Sahara. Information is also available for trans-African journeys and those planning round-the-world trips.

CONSTRUCTING YOUR ITINERARY Planning an itinerary for a bike tour is a multi-faceted project; the places to visit, the limitations of daily range, the need for food and lodging and the complications of weather and topography can make it seem like solving a Rubik's cube.

Mileage Experienced international bicycle travellers find that for a variety of reasons their daily mileage in foreign countries is less than they would typically ride at home. For starters there is a lot to see, and because everything is so different you will want extra time just to look around. Secondly, everyday chores (ie: banking, internet and buying supplies, transportation and unfamiliar procedures in a foreign culture) generally take longer than at home, sometimes double or quadruple the time. As a practical tip, it is more comfortable and better for your health to plan your itinerary with conservative estimates of daily distance, so that most of the bicycling can be done in the morning or late afternoon. Since this is perhaps a once-in-a-lifetime opportunity, you want to enjoy the places, not merely pass through. Don't overestimate the daily distance you will cover.

Planning for daylight Because Africa straddles the Equator, in most of the continent the sun rises at about 06.00 and sets around 18.00 (natural time), plus or minus half an hour, all year round. An excellent, practical and recommended routine on cycling days is to live by the sun. Pack the night before, get up at 06.00, eat breakfast around 06.30 and try to be on the road by 07.00. For the next few hours bicycle, sightsee and stop as necessary to eat and drink. If you don't reach your destination before the midday heat hits, stop from 12.30 to 15.30, eat a good meal, take a siesta, read, write and/or watch the local life. When it starts cooling down, saddle up and finish the day's ride. If you are staying in villages where there is no electricity, there is all the more reason to get washed, fed and set up for the night early; it is easy to be in bed by 20.00. You will then get a good ten hours' sleep before you get back on the road again.

Route One approach is to push pins for the places you want to see into a map and then cogitate on how to connect the dots. As modernisation continues, new stretches are paved every year. Even unpaved, the laterite (clay) and black cotton soil roads, common in Africa, can be nearly as smooth to ride on as paved roads – when dry. When wet, laterite and black cotton soil roads are viscous and virtually impossible to ride on. Depending on the situation, they may take from a few hours to several weeks to dry out after the last rains. Washboard, rocky and rutted dirt roads create their own discomfort and fall somewhere between dry and wet laterite roads in difficulty. It is on the unpaved roads that you tend to find a much more traditional and interesting side of Africa. To best enjoy these areas you need to schedule your visit during the dry season – though nature always reserves the right to be spontaneous. Even where the roads have good, all-weather surfaces, you should take note of the prevailing winds for the time of year you plan to travel. The wind can determine the direction of travel. If the route is a loop – *c'est la vie*. If your itinerary involves large changes in elevation, the geography may also be a major influence on your choice of starting and finishing points and your direction of travel.

Climate The weather often determines the ease and enjoyment of bicycling, especially in less-developed areas. Try to schedule your travels for the cool part of the dry season. This varies from month to month and place to place and is further complicated by the fact that the lowest temperatures and lowest humidity do not always occur at the same time. In general, the best time for cycling is usually near the beginning of the dry season, just after the end of the rains. This period has the added advantage that the dirt roads are packed and the dust is relatively low, though the high-altitude harmattan dust affects west Africa a couple of months into the dry season. Try to keep that wind on your back!

2

Overland Routes

We had hoped that the following section would have been expanded since the last edition, but sadly even more routes have fallen victim to the rise of terrorist activities in northern Africa. It's also fair to say that despite high-tech mobile communications, some new roads and more sources of travel information, things are not getting any easier for overlanders regarding visa bureaucracy, paperwork and regulations.

With the complete trans-Africa trip a bit tenuous, some may wish to plan a shorter overland journey in west Africa, east Africa or southern Africa. Since the last edition, getting so many visas for very long trips is more problematic. Countries like Nigeria, Cameroon, Angola and Sudan are a bit sticky for visas, although in the end there's usually a way through the bureaucracy, like any mud hole *en route*. Angola seems to be the one country that regularly refuses visas.

For those planning the big overland all the way, the best route is down the Nile. If the security issues in Mauritania don't get any worse, the route along the Atlantic coast from Senegal to Cape Town is still an unpredictable possibility. It's certainly a possibility for public transport travellers, as they can just fly over any hotspots or barred country – usually Angola.

With so many problematic routes in Africa, and to maximise the return adventure, you could plan to ship your vehicle from Africa to India in Asia. After so much investment and preparation, it is well worth consideration. We recently drove our Land Rover back from India and Nepal through Tibet.

GETTING TO AFRICA

For information on ferries see *Getting to Africa by ferry* in *Chapter 1*, page 11.

Many roads cross France and Spain to Algeciras for Morocco, but remember French winters are cold. Camping is difficult in winter in France, so try the F1 chain for the cheapest lodgings. One or two campsites are open in central Spain in winter. Look for St Elena near La Carolina on A4/E5 and at La Cabrera, north of Madrid on the A1/E5.

EUROPE TO EGYPT DIRECT
Route NA: Europe, Tunisia, Libya to Egypt
The quickest route to Egypt from Europe was from Genoa to Tunis and along the Libyan coast to Cairo. The roads are excellent. Until the civil war, the formalities at the Libyan border were handled by a local agent. You then had to travel with a Libyan guide, in your own vehicle or accompanying you in his own car. Things may have been turned upside down since the conflagration. Learning some basic Arabic will help with reading road signs! Along the way, the old part of Tripoli, the Roman ruins at Sabratha and Leptis

Magna are the main attractions, while a sobering visit to the solemn war graves at Tobruk should not be missed.

Entering Egypt and dealing with the bureaucracy has thus far been a minefield, but everyone has been at pains to welcome you, and take a little reward for services rendered. The road to El Alamein, Alexandria and on to Cairo is excellent, if a little busy nearer the capital. It should still be possible to drive around the oasis route via Siwa, Farafra, Dakhla Oasis and El Kharga. Heading to the Gilf Kabir Plateau is probably only an option in the company of an Egyptian guide/vehicle.

VIA THE MIDDLE EAST
Route ME1: Europe, Turkey, Syria and Jordan to Egypt

WARNING! At the time of writing, transiting Syria is said to be possible still, and it need only take a day, but this may continue to be a big risk. The following is included in case of miracles in Syria or Iraq.

Heading via the Middle East this way, it will take a little longer to reach Egypt than going via Tunisia and Libya directly, but when possible it offers a whole new world of historical attractions, varied scenery and hospitable people. Coming from Europe, you previously needed a visa for Syria in advance, but Turkey and Jordan issue them at the borders. Going northbound, Syrian visas can be a problem, so check the options and hope it's not a question of flying somewhere to obtain them. Visas were once easy to get in Amman. Other considerations are the vehicle taxes charged on the borders of both Syria and Jordan, which can be a significant amount. Fuel, though, is cheap, as a counter to these charges. Campsites do exist, and some hotels will allow parking/camping in their grounds. Look at the map and you can see that roads go from eastern Turkey into Iraq and on to Jordan. Keep an eye on this option; it might happen one day.

From Istanbul any number of excellent roads head to Syria and, with time, a fascinating trip can be made along the southwest Turkish coast. Here are many ancient Greek and Roman attractions, as well as fine beaches and rugged mountains. In central Turkey, not far off the direct route from Ankara to Aleppo in Syria, are the amazing underground churches, settlements and volcanic chimneys of the Cappadocia area near Göreme. In Syria, the city of Aleppo, with its bazaars and ancient citadel, used to be one of the highlights. Crusader castles dot the country, the best preserved being Krak des Chevaliers. The aromatic bazaars of Damascus are atmospheric and, a little off the route to the east, are the ruins of Palmyra in the desert. Jordan has some great attractions too; at the top of the list are the wonderful desert canyons at Wadi Rum, the world-famous Nabataen Petra and the Roman ruins at Jerash. A ferry links Aqaba in Jordan to the Sinai Peninsula in Egypt. All the roads on the way are good throughout. We are still waiting to take a convoluted historic route through Iraq to Jordan!

Route ME2: Saudi Arabia to Jordan A ferry operates between Port Sudan (Sudan) and Jeddah in Saudi Arabia, across the Red Sea. If you are lucky enough to get a three-day transit visa for Saudi Arabia, this could enable you to bypass a lot of the famed Egyptian border/customs/Lake Nasser bureaucracy! Roads in Saudi Arabia are superb and heading north to Aqaba in Jordan is quick and generally safe. The main road goes via Medina, the second holy city of Islam, which foreigners must bypass, and then to Tabuk. The scenery from here to the Aqaba border of Jordan is superb, reminiscent of southern Jordan's Wadi Rum,

with red craggy canyons. A new road along the coast is another option, but we have not managed to visit Saudi since 1974! In any case, three days is easily enough time for this sector.

We have not heard of anyone being able to do this route in the opposite direction, because it is difficult to get a Saudi transit visa to go south.

AFRICAN ROUTES

NORTH AFRICA AND THE SAHARA This section includes the following countries: Morocco, Western Sahara, Tunisia, Algeria, Libya, Mali, Niger, Mauritania, Chad, Egypt and Sudan. Plan to cross the Sahara between October and March, when temperatures are generally pleasant. Routes S1 and S6 are possible with some risks. Most of the other routes are not possible at present, so only abbreviated detail is given in case the world ever becomes sane again.

Route S1: Morocco to Mauritania

WARNING! There is still a viable risk in Mauritania, due to threats of kidnapping by terrorists. Check the latest advice and enquire about any armed escorted convoys operating between Fort Guergarat to Senegal, which might reduce the risks. If you decide to run the gauntlet of Mauritania (the only security risk on the north–south Atlantic route), be sure to transit directly between the borders of Western Sahara and Senegal.

This route, apart from the Nile option below, is the only viable trans-Saharan route at the moment. The road all the way through Morocco, Western Sahara and on to Nouakchott is tarmac. Within Morocco, main roads are excellent, with Fes, Marrakech, Todra Gorge and the Road of the Kasbahs being some of the highlights. Going south, you enter Western Sahara, which is currently administered by Morocco and awaiting a referendum on its status. Laayoune is the nominal capital of Western Sahara and it is possible to camp along the coast. Be sure to carry enough fuel, as there are long stretches of uninhabited desert. For a limited overland trip, the north and some eastern areas of Western Sahara provide a great introduction to the Sahara Desert that is now so sorely missed by most modern-day 'explorers'.

The Moroccan/Mauritanian border immigration and customs are at Fort Guergarat. There is a 5km rough sandy/stony track between the two border posts. The Mauritanian and Moroccan governments have normalised all overland travel northbound into Morocco now. The border area was heavily mined in the past, so you should keep to any marked tracks until the road is completed. A word of warning, though – in early 2008 the Mauritanian government imposed new visa rules stopping the issue of visas at the borders, after the cancelling of the Paris–Dakar rally. It would be very wise to get the visa in Rabat (or Bamako for those heading north).

A new super-highway between Nouadhibou and Nouakchott avoids the beach road of the past. (The beach route is no safer at present, due to kidnapping threats.) Until the 2008 Paris–Dakar rally cancellation, the desert areas of Mauritania offered great pistes. A desert track ran from Nouadhibou to Choum and Atar beside the railway (a two- to three-day trip). Close to Atar, the routes between Chinguetti, Ouadane and Guelb Richat were fun enough for any desert addict. For serious desert motoring and a big challenge, the route between Chinguetti and Tidjikja

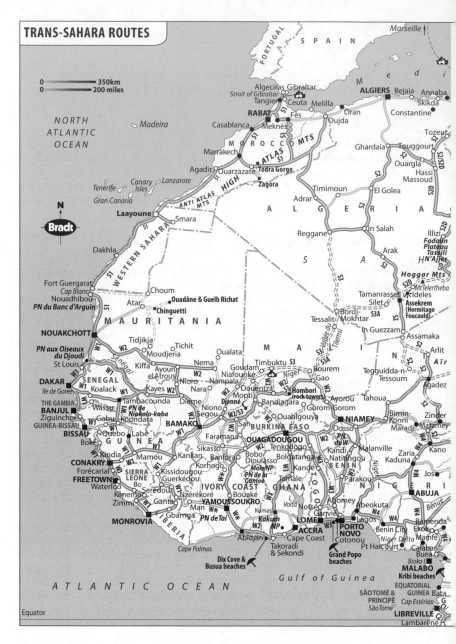

TRANS-SAHARA ROUTES

to the south was a serious affair, needing guides. The ancient camel caravan routes from Tidjikja to Tichit and on to Oualate were also exciting desert options for experienced Saharan drivers with a guide.

The road heading east of Nouakchott towards Nema and Mali was deteriorating in places in 2008, adding a day or so to the driving time. A new sealed road now heads into Mali via Nioro to Bamako and the stretch to Tidjikja via Moudjeria is also sealed. Sadly this route is **not safe** at present.

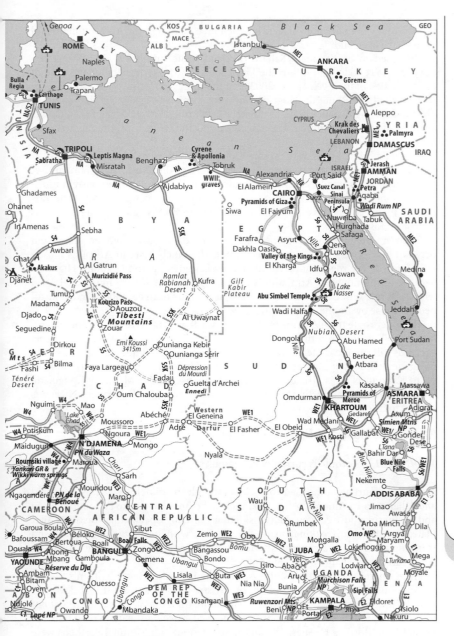

Route S2: Tunisia to Nigeria

WARNING! This route is currently dangerous.

For those willing to take some risks, parts of Algeria can be visited with a local guide. How much security this adds to the trip is debatable. At the time of publication Niger is improving but experiencing insurrections, banditry and kidnapping threats. Many nomads and villagers have left their homes in the Aïr Mountains and mines have been laid.

This used to be the main Sahara overland route until 1993. By 1999 a few travellers were following it, but the kidnapping of 32 Westerners (at the time of our last visit!) in their vehicles in 2003 shut the route again. The main trans-Sahara route (called the Route du Hoggar) ran from Tunis to Agadez via Tamanrasset. The total driving distance is approximately 3,800km (2,370 miles) and used to take about 12 days. The stunning desert scenery and the Hoggar Mountains were the most memorable highlights.

The road from Tunis via Tozeur, Ouargla and Ghardaia to Tamanrasset is paved, but some sections south of In Salah were poor. South from Tamanrasset to In Guezzam is finally sealed. With only one fuel dump and famously no fuel, getting supplies in In Guezzam was notoriously hard, especially since the fuel station manager had many wives in different locations and finding him was almost impossible.

From In Guezzam, the last town in Algeria, there was a section of no-man's-land between border posts, with some deep sand. The lonely piste to Arlit was mostly well defined. The road from Arlit to Agadez is known as the Uranium Highway, because of the mines at Arlit, and is paved. Agadez is a superb mud Sahel town with great markets, camels, a famous mosque, riotous festivals and lively, colourful people. Close by are the Aïr Mountains.

The other route from Assamaka to Agadez via Tegguida-n-Tessoum is not paved, hard to follow now, and there is no fuel available. There are salt mines, and camel caravans still run the route. In the rainy season it became a muddy quagmire. South of Agadez, the road to Zinder should be all paved by now. A tarmac road continues on to Kano in Nigeria. The best border to cross used to be Matamey/Kongolam. (Not the one shown directly south on the Michelin map.) Sadly northern Nigeria is subject to its own terror activities now.

Route S2D: Algeria to Niger via Djanet

WARNING! This route is currently dangerous.

From Touggourt a good sealed road runs through the oilfields via Hassi Messoud and Ohanet to In Amenas. After Illizi the road climbs on to the Fadnoun Plateau and to Iherir, a lost canyon, before skirting the truly spectacular Tassili N'Ajjer Plateau to Djanet. Trekking on to the plateau, with its fabulous rock art and stunning outcrops, is a superb experience. It has remained a possibility for those flying directly to Djanet in recent winters.

From Djanet the route was almost all piste to Tamanrasset, with no fuel *en route*. Remember to carry extra fuel for the stretches of soft sand that devour it rapidly. It was recommended to travel with more than one vehicle and GPS, if not with a local guide. The route was often ill-defined, once off the main road north of Djanet from Bordj el Haoues. The fort at Serouenout and Mount Telertheba were prominent waymarks. The piste was more clearly defined to Ideles and Hirafok, but climbing to the hermitage of Assekrem in the Hoggar involved a dangerously steep track.

Most opted for the longer, but easier route, west to the main road and south to Tamanrasset. The better track of the two from Tamanrasset to the Hermitage du Père de Foucauld and the viewpoint at Assekrem was the eastern one. From Tamanrasset the route to Niger was the same as route S2.

Route S3: Algeria to Mali

WARNING! At the time of publication, this route is impossible because of the recent war in northern Mali.

Known as the Tanezrouft, this route was less popular than S2 because the distances between water and fuel stops were much greater – Adrar to Gao is approximately 1,500km (930 miles). Fuel was generally available in Reggane, but should not be counted on. The driving time from Adrar to Gao was approximately six to seven days.

This route was often preferred by those travellers using VW Combis, Citroën 2CVs and motorcycles, as its surface tended to be harder. The road is paved from Adrar to Reggane. South of Reggane, there is new tar and then the piste was mostly hard-packed sand and quite fast, with only a few softer spots. The terrain is flat and less interesting than the Hoggar route, but nonetheless had a certain remote feel. The Algerian border post is at Bordj Mokhtar and the Malian customs is at Tessalit. The last section from Tessalit to Gao along the Vallée du Tilemsi is the hardest section, with areas of soft sand; it was often impassable during the wet season. This area is the hideout of the baddies at present.

Once in Gao, a paved road runs to Bamako. This route offers some fascinating destinations, such as the Hombori rock towers, the Dogon villages, and the mud mosques at Mopti and Djenné. Heading southeast from Gao, the route to Niamey along the river Niger is scenic. A very sandy track headed west from Bourem, crossing dunes in places, to Timbuktu. Sadly, access to northern Mali and Timbuktu is not currently safe.

Route S4: Libya to Niger

WARNING! This route is not advised at present due to the disturbances in Libya and Niger.

Travelling in convoy with at least one other vehicle was essential, and taking a guide from Gatrun to the border advisable. In Libya, roads south from Tripoli are excellent. Diversions to the Akakus Mountains near Ghat and the dune lakes near Awbari were well worthwhile. The dune lakes must be visited with at least one other vehicle and are only for the experienced; the dunes are seriously big here and potentially extremely dangerous. At the campsite it is possible to hire a 4x4 with driver for the day trip to the lakes if you don't want to risk it yourself! From Ghat a wild and sandy route goes to Djanet in Algeria. From Sebha, paved roads lead to Gatrun and then it is piste to the border at Tumu.

When possible, the most common route in Niger is from Tumu to Madama, Seguedine, Dirkou and through the Ténéré Desert direct to Agadez. The route via Bilma and Fashi is serious dune driving and dangerous for the inexperienced. It is therefore not recommended except with a local operator. The total distance is about 1,500km (930 miles), with fuel previously available at Sebha, Dirkou and Agadez. Fuel for approximately 1,200km (745 miles) is needed. The roads west in Niger from Agadez/Zinder to Tahoua, Maradi and Niamey are pretty good, with the odd pot-hole; beware!

Route S5: Libya to Chad

WARNING! This route is currently unsafe due to political problems in Libya, but much of Chad has improved. The Tibetsi route is still generally an unknown risk.

For when things improve, details are included. The Libya to Chad routes are not for the inexperienced. The rough, rocky and severely punishing tracks of the Tibesti area in northern Chad are very remote and renowned for landmines and bandits. It is reputedly one of the most spectacular areas of the Sahara, with volcanoes, crater lakes, hot springs and mountains up to 3,200m (10,500ft) high. Sadly it may remain off-limits. Routes were: Gatrun – Murizidié Pass – Kourizo Pass – Zouar to Faya; or, longer but more scenic, Gatrun – Murizidié Pass – Aozou – Zouar to Faya Largeau.

From Faya to N'djamena, the piste is reasonable but quite sandy. Fuel is generally available in Faya. Some small settlements such as Moussoro might have diesel drum supplies, but this cannot be guaranteed. Some road building is supposed to be underway north and east of N'djamena. The crossing is about 1,250km (775 miles) via Zouar and an extra 300km (185 miles) if you go via Aozou. Fuel is extremely cheap in Libya, so fill up regularly and particularly in Gatrun.

You must be very well equipped, research all the latest information and travel with at least two vehicles. Take a local guide, despite the costs. In fact you will be forced to take a guide anyway to satisfy local etiquette and contribute to the local economy. Even agents in N'djamena do this. Let's hope this route becomes possible to salvage some of the magic of the Sahara for overlanders.

Route S5K: Libya to Chad via Kufra

WARNING! This route is currently unsafe due to political problems in Libya, but not in Chad, surprisingly – so it could become a winner!

Another perhaps more feasible option to cross the Sahara if eastern Libya settles is this exciting route. It is, however, only a possibility for very experienced Saharan travellers. It crosses eastern Libya from Ajdabiya to Kufra (Al Khofra) close to the Egyptian/Sudanese border. A minimum of two vehicles is essential, and you would need a Libyan guide in his own car. This would also be advisable in Chad because of mines. The remote and little-used piste from Kufra heads around the Ramlat Rabianah sand desert. It then crosses into Chad north of the outstandingly beautiful Ounianga Kebir and Ounianga Serir lakes. Mines are said to be a serious issue on this route near the border area, and normal border formalities do not exist.

From Ounianga Serir, an ill-defined piste goes to Fada, passing some smaller lakes. From an isolated settlement at Demi, whose inhabitants do not appreciate visitors, a treacherous piste continues adjacent to the Dépression du Mourdi and through some amazing rock formations in the northern Ennedi. Gigantic rock arches and the famed Guelta d'Archei with its colony of rare dwarf crocodiles are the highlights here. After Fada the route via Oum Chalouba to Abéché is fairly obvious. Taking a local guide is essential, though, to smooth a path through the larger settlements. We have met only one couple who have done this complete route; a remarkable achievement, some years ago and they were not so young either.

Route S6: Egypt to Sudan and Ethiopia This route (assuming access to Egypt is possible and safer since the military crackdown) is currently the best option for a complete trans-Africa trip by road, avoiding most major political hotspots. Sudanese visas are available in Cairo in a few days. Bear in mind that evidence of having been in Israel renders your passport useless for travel in any other Arab countries. Some travellers who have crossed from Israel into Egypt and onwards

have carried two passports, but be careful about this. Apart from troubles in Syria, the expensive carnet bond for Egypt is the main obstacle on this route. The new ferry between Turkey and Egypt keeps this route open.

Before the Arab Spring, the Egyptian authorities sometimes required all tourist vehicles, including tourist coaches and private cars, to run in daily convoys from the Red Sea resorts of Hurghada or Safaga to Luxor and south to Aswan. The antiquities of Kom Ombo and Idfu are well worth a visit *en route*. Tourists can normally drive to Abu Simbel with pre-arranged permits. The whole area south of Aswan is run by the military and is generally off-limits at present. Apparently one overland group managed to drive to Wadi Halfa and recent reports suggest it may indeed be possible soon for a very large fee – but then it would save the time-consuming and expensive ferry. The route shown on the maps along the Red Sea south from Safaga to Port Sudan is currently not an option.

The ferry from Aswan to Wadi Halfa runs once a week each way. Recently this was on Sundays heading south and Tuesdays heading north, but do check! The ferry is quite expensive (extortionate if you are the only vehicle wishing to travel) and can be a great deal of hassle. Last time most of the price was 'fixed', but nothing is forever in Egypt. Patience, tact, restraint and a sense of humour are needed to deal with Egyptian officials, who know that there is no other normal route south at present. Sometimes a separate barge is used if there are a number of vehicles waiting, which hardly ever arrives the same day as the passenger ferry, meaning a couple of grotty nights in a Wadi Halfa hostelry. Heading north, the ferry can also be expensive and difficult to get on to at Wadi Halfa. Mr Takourny Salah in Aswan and Midhat Mahir in Wadi Halfa have both been helpful to overlanders.

In Wadi Halfa, be sure to get an alien's registration stamp added to your visa stamp. This is a time-consuming mystery tour and will cost around US$20 per person (see *Sudan, Red tape*, page 305). A bank nearby changes cash; note that travellers' cheques cannot be used in Sudan. From Wadi Halfa to Khartoum there are two routes, following either the Nile or the railway line. The new Nile route is now sealed and used by all local vehicles to Dongola, where fuel is available. Sealed roads run to Karima and Atbara. From Abu Dom a good highway leads to Omdurman and Khartoum. Allow two to three days.

The desert route beside the railway is surprisingly isolated and the train, if it's running at all now, crawls slowly once a week in each direction. You must follow the railway or watch for the telegraph poles at all times, otherwise getting lost is a serious possibility. Because there is a lot of very soft sand close to the tracks and even nearby, you might be forced in some sections to drive with your wheels astride the railway lines. We don't imagine the Sudanese railway company approves of this, so try not to be seen doing it near a station. Do remember what day a train (goods or otherwise) is scheduled! Driving on the line is hard but not bumpy, as the line is submerged in hard-packed sand. For your safety, though, try to use the line only as a last resort, and be very careful not to hit the rails with the sidewalls of your tyres.

Allow almost two days to reach Abu Hamed, and don't expect much when you get there. Another lonely piste, indicated by tall metal kilometre markers, goes to Berber, where the tarmac road used to begin. Fuel can be obtained here and at Atbara. A new desert highway runs to Khartoum east of the Nile and passes close to the famous Pyramids of Meroë, not to be missed. You can camp nearby in the bush; the local people were very friendly to us and got down off their camels to help us change a wheel. Their camels needed little maintenance! Other antiquities along here are hard to find without some local help.

From Khartoum an excellent new tarmac road runs south through the Gezira cotton fields to Wad Medani and on to Gedaref (and to Port Sudan). From Gedaref the once ghastly weather-dependent track to Gallabat and the Ethiopian border is now an all-weather gravel road. On the Ethiopian side, road improvements have been underway to Gondar and to Addis Ababa, a scenic and spectacular drive. Roads are continually improving in Ethiopia, but previously rough gravel roads led north to Axum and east to Lalibela. Heading west from Khartoum, roads are being improved, but not yet into Darfur or far into South Sudan.

Sudan to South Sudan If the peace holds, an interesting option might be the route to South Sudan from Khartoum via El Obeid and Kadugl. The road is said to be bad after Kadugl through Keilak and on to Abiye. The disputed border is somewhere south of Abiye and then a bad road goes to Wau, Rumbek and Juba. According to locals in Khartoum, truckers are already using the above route.

WEST AFRICAN ROUTES West Africa includes southern Mauritania, Senegal, Gambia, Guinea, Guinea Bissau, Sierra Leone, Liberia, Ivory Coast, Ghana, Mali, Burkina Faso, Niger, Nigeria, Togo and Benin. Since obtaining an Angolan visa is still unpredictable, west Africa is a good destination for an extended Africa trip, assuming the security aspects of Mauritania improve.

With ever-improving roads, west Africa is a great region for some exciting new non-trans-Africa options, especially as Sierra Leone and Liberia are back on the list. Niger is off-limits, but Ivory Coast looks to be improving at present. In Senegal, Gambia, Guinea, Mali, Burkina Faso, Ghana, Benin, Togo, Nigeria and Niger, main roads are generally paved and in good shape, but pot-holes soon appear when away from these. Traditional routes in southern Mali and Burkina remain popular and can be linked into the coastal route for a complete trip around west Africa. Further east is the coastal route between Ivory Coast, Ghana, Nigeria and on into Cameroon, as well as options into Benin and Togo from the Sahel regions of Burkina.

Route W1: Mauritania to Senegal, Guinea, Sierra Leone, Liberia and Mali

WARNING! The situation in Mali will hopefully improve, but keep south of Mopti for the time being and be sure to check out the security aspects if contemplating a trip to Timbuktu.

A fairly good paved road leads due south from Nouakchott to St Louis and Dakar. Crossing the border into Senegal is better (and currently cheaper in 'non-value-added taxes') at Diama and gives a taste of dry dirt-road driving. Senegal has some of the best roads in west Africa, but surprises are always possible. Variations across Senegal could involve the Senegal River route, a poor road, or through the central baobab tree-covered countryside via Touba, a religious centre. Super new empty roads link this pilgrimage town with Keberma on the main St Louis–Dakar highway and with Kafferine on the road east of Koalack. The road from here to Tambacounda has now been resurfaced – thanks for that! Another new route in Senegal involves a visit to the Parc National du Niokolo-Koba, where some of the animals lurking include lions and elephants.

Many people follow the coast from St Louis to Dakar, then into Gambia on good roads. Routes beside the Gambia River are bad, but the coastal roads are good. Find out about security issues in the Casamance region around Ziguinchor before visiting.

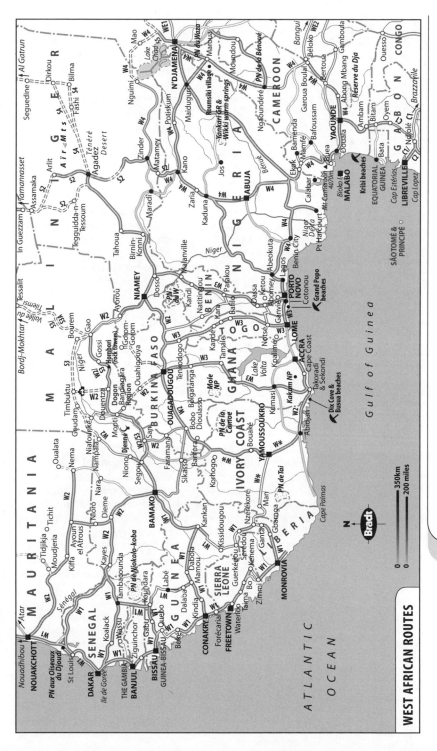

WEST AFRICAN ROUTES

Guinea Bissau If you are continuing from Gambia/Senegal into Guinea Bissau, the roads are steadily improving but have some testing stretches inland. The main route between Guinea Bissau and Guinea is from Bissau to Gabu, then from the border to Koundara in Guinea. Another route into Guinea is from Quebo to Boké. This is a dry-season option only. Check the road conditions, whether local transport is going, and that any ferries *en route* are working before heading this way.

Guinea Heading into Guinea from Tambacounda in Senegal, there are two routes. The dangerous rocky one via the Parc National du Niokolo-Koba and Maliville in the mountainous Massif du Tamgue is not recommended if you want to keep your vehicle in shape. The preferred route into Guinea is via the new road (a mix of tarmac and fairly good piste) through Koundara towards Labé. Koundara has a couple of extremely basic but friendly places to stay, though you will probably want to sleep in your vehicle even if you do pay for a room. From Koundara, the road winds its way over hills, through thick pleasant Sahelian bush and between isolated friendly villages. There are no other places to stay except the bush if you plan to do it in two easy days from Tambacounda to Labé.

Watch for a junction at about 50 miles where you go left (Labé is 158km from here). A ferry interrupts your drive and the operators work by hand to take you across. We paid US$8 with tips, but there was no hassle. The route heads through Bori and Poopodara into Labé.

Once in central Guinea, the main roads close to the capital Conakry are quite good. In the Fouta Djalon region, Labé and Dalaba via Mamou and Kindia are serviced by good but very twisting roads. Watch out for other vehicles on blind bends. Heading inland after Dabola to Kankan, the roads are reasonable, with some occasional pot-holed sections. The Kankan to Bamako road should be complete, a breeze to drive on and not busy. Further south and east of Kankan, the condition of the roads is variable. The road is patchy and pot-holed from Mamou to Faranah, but then new to Kissidougou. From here to Gueckadou is bad, then it's good as far as Lola.

Coming **into Guinea from Liberia**, the first section of the route from the Ganta border to Nzérékoré is another fun road through some sections of exotic dense forest. It's extremely isolated, though, with a few villages but no facilities. Allow three hours for this route via Diéké. From Nzérékoré to near Serédou, a brand-new highway has been completed (it came to a sudden end at 103km), but then the section on through Macenta to Kissidougou was appalling and mainly dirt. Follow the route through Guerkédou, not the 'lane' suggested at a signpost. This is another slow-going, rough section. From Kissidougou the road out of town to Mali was not obvious and was appalling for 96km (60 miles). After that, improvements made it faster to Kankan. Beware, though, of isolated holes and enjoy the last 30km, which are nearly perfect, into Bamako. Hooray!

Sierra Leone and Liberia Coming from Guinea on what is now mostly a good road, take care at Forécarial as the correct route is not obvious; take the right fork at the town roundabout and head initially south. From the border at Pamalap, the main highway to Freetown has now been completed, funded by the EU. There is a choice of roads into Freetown, either on the main road or via the much slower and longer coastal route, where all the unspoilt beaches are found. The road from Freetown to Makeni is also paved and in reasonable condition. Provincial roads and tracks in the Outamba-Kilimi National Park and the Loma Mountains are rutted, washed out and very slow.

The horrors of driving around Freetown are a shock. The streets are crowded, the markets tumble on to the highways; nudging your way out of here takes hours and that's once you've found the road out (Kissy Road) from the clock tower beyond the massive and notoriously unsafe 'Eastenders' market. Going east to Bo and Kenema, the road is good. Just before Kenema town is the junction for Zimmi and the route into Liberia. The direct secondary route on the Michelin map from Bo to Zimmi was not recommended in case of problems at the ferry across the Mole River.

From Kenema, the main 'international highway' is a fair dirt road and it takes an hour to cover the 18 miles to Joru. This road becomes a narrow lane and passes through friendly villages south for 36 miles (two hours) to Zimmi. One could call this a fun road in the dry; nonetheless this is very remote countryside with almost no traffic – it was previously RUF (Revolutionary United Front – former rebels) territory. The road naturally deteriorates more close to the border – another

DIAMONDS ARE FOREVER

The two men sat drinking beside the pool as dusk settled over the country hotel just outside Bo in Sierra Leone. They looked like missionaries; who else would be driving around here apart from us?

'Sit down; have a beer.' It was abruptly clear that the two guests were not missionaries. One had been living in the country for most of the last dozen years. The other had arrived from, among other places, Guinea. 'With the war over, where is all the promised development?' we asked. 'Well, the war is technically over, but come into town (Bo, which was the rebel RUF headquarters during the struggles) and I'll show you where to buy an AK47 for a couple of hundred dollars.'

In the streets of Bo there are many shops advertising diamonds for sale. So how was the road to Liberia, we asked. 'It's not good, but it's fine during the daytime; the villagers will help you and look after you if you have a problem. Just don't break down at night! … And don't stop to help anyone along the road – it might be a set-up,' they said. Very encouraging!

We had already done that in Guinea, when a *taxi-brousse* full of desperate-looking locals had broken down and needed engine oil. For us, not to stop would have seemed harsh. It's a gut reaction thing; react as you see fit for a given situation and be wary.

'So what is your mission in the country?' they asked.

'Just tourists,' we replied. We started to feel rather silly. 'Tourists in Sierra Leone!' one exclaimed. 'I thought that had stopped years ago! Even then it was only along the beachfronts of Aberdeen and Lumley, which the Chinese have bought up recently.'

Our hosts were clearly wise to many things that we could only imagine from media hype of the past and the film, *Blood Diamond*, which portrayed the country in a poor light. So far we'd had a pleasant time in the country – the coastline near Freetown is spectacular, a paradise lost. Even frenetic, sweaty, overcrowded, dilapidated Freetown has a certain disintegrating charm.

PS: The drive was exciting, but only because the route was another fun, off-road, dry muddy lane to the Liberian border. The village people were very friendly and we didn't break down. The first people to greet us at the Liberian border were Pakistani peacekeepers, but that's another story (see the box *Salaam aleikum in Liberia*, page 134).

grinding 30 miles in two hours – and gets worse. The forest is beautiful, though, as the area near the border is the Gola reserve. The Morro River forms the border. There are a lot of 'checkings' of papers, but it's a relaxed place.

Once in Liberia, the road from the Bo Waterside border post to Monrovia is sealed and reasonable all the way. Heading up country through Gbarnga and on to Ganta is also mostly OK, but a few sections slow the pace here and there. The road from Ganta to Ivory Coast is a dirt route and initially fair. We did not explore further, because of political problems in Ivory Coast. The route into Guinea from Ganta is remote and little more than a lane out of Ganta. The Liberian side of this border was relaxed. See above for the route onwards into Guinea.

Expect some improved sections between Monrovia and Harper via Zwedru but ideally go in the dry season.

Route W* Ivory Coast If you are contemplating continuing east to Ghana, the security situation in Ivory Coast needs to be checked as things improve. Roads were formerly in a good state of repair, but they are now full of pot-holes. That said, getting to Man via Sanniquellie and Danane is not apparently such an ordeal. From Man, the road is OK to Yamoussoukro then north to Bobo Dioulasso. Heading east, the route goes via Yamoussoukro to Abidjan and on to Accra in Ghana via Sekondi and Takoradi.

Route W2: Mauritania to Mali, Burkina Faso and Niger

WARNING! Although there are two main routes south into Mali from the Mauritanian highway between Nouakchott and Nema, the routes are currently very unsafe. These are from Ayoun el Atrous and Nema. It was all sealed from Ayoun el Atrous to Nioro and on to Bamako. The road west from Dieme, south of Nioro, was also sealed to Kayes and the Senegalese border. However, for the safest option, head down the coast quickly to Senegal.

From Bamako, the most interesting route and probably the only option at present involves heading through Segou, San and Djenné to Mopti. Travellers contemplating heading to Hombori, Gao or Timbuktu should check security issues following the French intervention. Beware – there are almost as many 'sleeping policemen' built into the roads near villages on this main route as there are sleeping policemen in Mali, and luckily in this heat, there are lots of those!

For Timbuktu, if safe, the best route is from Douentza, although the road is quite badly corrugated on the middle section around Bambara-Maoundé. Route-finding is easy and the first section is a fun road, but with many small creek beds to watch out for. The scenery is stunning for much of the way. Despite rumours of rip-off rogues at the ferry across the river Niger to Kabara/Timbuktu, we had no such problems. Allow plenty of time, though, for the crossing. Leaving Timbuktu in the morning, we had to wait several hours in a queue before we could even get on the ferry.

After taking in the cultural sites of the Dogon region around Bandiagara, good, well-used routes now head to Burkina Faso from Bankass or Bandiagara through Koro and Ouahigouya to Ouagadougou. A fairly good but not all smooth road runs from Segou or Sevare via San to Bobo Dioulasso. It might still be bad between Kimparana and Kouro. After the border at Faramana, it's a super-highway to Bobo.

The main roads in Burkina Faso – Bobo to Ouaga, Ouaga to Niger and Ouaga to Togo – are very well-made new roads. Burkina is very pleasant with welcoming people everywhere; your arms will get plenty of waving exercise here.

Route W3: Burkina Faso, Niger, Ghana, Togo and Benin

WARNING! Much of Niger is currently unsafe, so check before travel.

Two good options link Burkina Faso (and Niger) with the coastal roads of Ghana, Benin and Togo. Heading south from Ouagadougou via Bolgatanga in Ghana, the countryside is the typical Sahel of dry scrub that later transforms into denser forest. Few traces of the rainforest remain in Ghana, but, along the coast, interest lies in the slave ports of Elmina and Cape Coast as well as good beaches. Traffic is hectic in Accra and Kumasi, but the condition of the roads will not need as much patience.

From Ouagadougou into Togo the main highway is mostly fine through Tenkodogo. Once in Togo, some sections are a bit scrappy. The Tamberma villages should not be missed; these can be visited from Kante (Kandé) by a reasonable dirt link road that is controlled by guides just out of town. All visitors to the area are expected to take a guide, mainly to prevent offending local tribal people and contribute to the economy. Potential visa issues aside, it's possible to divert into Benin near Kara through the Tamberma and Somba villages.

The road south to Lomé should not present any surprises, but watch out on a couple of hilly sections for huge numbers of very slow or broken-down trucks. There may be a diversion on this road around a government installation, which is confusing, but just keep asking which way to go. Just near Bafilo is an amazing cutting on the southbound lane! It may be possible to get into Benin from Notsé in Togo to Abomey, but Benin 48-hour transit visas may not be available at the border. Watch for a few poor road sections before Lomé; the traffic here, and lack of any signposting, will test the most patient of drivers.

We believe the road east from Lomé Airport will take you around the worst of the traffic to reach Benin and Grand Popo. The coastal road east of Cotonou is very busy and best avoided for those wanting a quieter introduction to Nigeria, or who want to put off the inevitable. A border exists at Ketou, from where the road heads into Nigeria around the north of Lagos via Abeokuta.

From Niamey in Niger, via Dosso, a good road headed south to Benin. The border is across the Niger River, at Malanville. After Kandi, south and west of the main road, a visit to the Somba people around Natitingou is a must. Parakou and Dassa are the main overnight options heading south. Don't forget to visit Abomey to experience Benin culture at its best. A boat trip on the lagoons at Ganvié just before Cotonou is another unmissable but touristy sight. Cotonou is best avoided, with much-discussed crime statistics.

Route W4: Nigeria to Cameroon and Chad

WARNING! The very north of Nigeria near the Cameroonian border has become extremely dangerous due to the terrorist activities of the Islamist movement, Boko Haram. This includes the northern routes east from Kano via Potiskum to Cameroon and Chad. The long, lonely, sandy and insecure option around Lake Chad via Nguigmi in eastern Niger and Mao to N'djamena is a big 'must NOT do'. Most main roads in Nigeria are good and looked after by police at many checkpoints. In central Nigeria, the new capital Abuja is linked by motorway through Kaduna (civil inter-communal disturbances possible here) to Lagos. Various good roads link Abuja with Ekok, the border town with Cameroon, in the south. Those who have avoided Lagos, or braved its horrendous traffic, crime and general hullabaloo, can relax as they head east through Benin City. Give the insecure Niger Delta around Port Harcourt a wide berth and head further east. Calabar is a pleasant place, and there is a Cameroon consulate here that issues visas. From Calabar the border is northeast at Ekok.

Cameroon has some excellent roads and some dreadful ones. Avoid routes in the north, due to the Islamist kidnapping threats. The road from Ngaoundéré to Yaoundé was patchy with good and bad sections. The Michelin map indicates that a road via Abong Mbang is a better option, and this is now apparently true. South of Bertoua a decent road runs to Yokadouma and the dense rainforest of the pygmies. It continues in a bad state, only passable in dry periods, almost as far as Quesso in Congo. We do not know whether the rivers along the border can be crossed by car-carrying barges. The road from southern Nigeria via the Ekok border into Cameroon had some bad truck-swallowing sections. It is said to be improved by now, as is the road from Mamfé south to Buea (for Mount Cameroon's cool retreats), but things are never certain. Further south along the coast is the beach resort of Limbé, from where the road goes on to Douala then Yaoundé.

Those heading to Bamenda from Mamfé to escape the heat in the cool high country and then travelling on to Yaoundé should check road and security conditions in Mamfé before going on up. Before heading into Chad, do check the latest security situation. Roads in some areas of southwestern Chad have improved, now that oil has been found. These run close to the new oil pipeline from Chad into Cameroon through Moundou.

CENTRAL AFRICA Central Africa comprises southern Chad, Cameroon, Gabon, Central African Republic (CAR), Congo, Democratic Republic of the Congo (DRC) and Angola.

Central Africa has plenty of rain and mud to slow you down; this is where a 4x4 really comes into its own. The easiest time to cross east–west (or vice versa) is in the drier season from about December to February. There is also a 'less wet' season in June/July. The 'rain barriers' set up on roads during the rainy season could cause you considerable delays. Most of these routes have been closed to travellers for years, but hope springs eternal for crazy overlanders.

Central Africa north–south routes

Although the security issues on these routes have improved, the bureaucratic obstacles have increased. Check the security issues between Dolisie and Brazzaville now that peace has broken out. Consider the route via Franceville to reach Brazzaville, but be prepared for bridge-building and delays. Be prepared to keep up-to-date with the latest situation.

Since the last edition, more travellers are trying routes via Kinshasa in the DRC. Oasis Overland, one of the leading overland truck operators, runs trips on this route, although some trips have had Angola visa problems. Private travellers face a lottery over the Angola visa and where it can be obtained. It is still to be hoped that the DRC and Angolan authorities will clarify the situation in order to stop putting black holes on the map and to encourage tourist dollars into areas of outstanding natural beauty.

That said, it is likely you will still encounter some gun-toting soldiers, difficult bureaucracy and bad roads – the worst countries being the two Congos. Cameroon and Gabon are fairly stable at the time of writing and thus reasonably safe. Visas for the region are increasingly expensive, though.

Route C1: Gabon via Congos and Angola to Namibia
Gabon Heading south from Yaoundé, the road is good but hilly tarmac and very pretty, with dense jungle and occasional distant mountain ridges. From Ambam

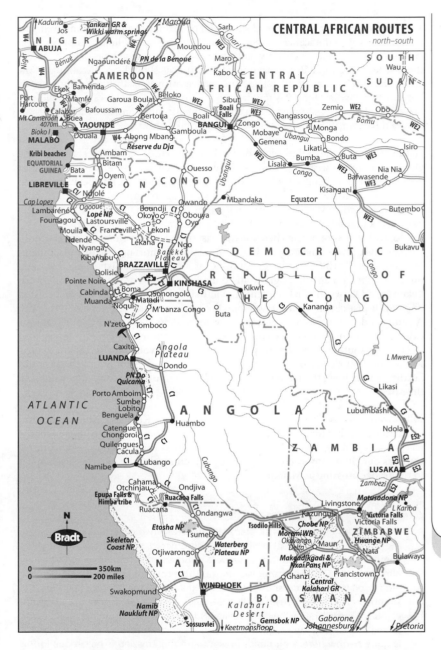

CENTRAL AFRICAN ROUTES
north–south

there are two routes. The main one heads south from town to the Ntem River, where a new bridge must surely be finished by now. Then a wide road heads towards Equatorial Guinea. East of the border post of Meyo, the route was a dirt track to Bitam in Gabon. The other route heads east from Ambam on a very narrow muddy track with ageing log bridges. A friendly ferry crosses the river here to Gabon. Most formalities are carried out at Bitam.

Going south in Gabon, the road should all be tarmac to Libreville and well past Lambaréné. Again the scenery is spectacular. The road from Ndjolé to Lopé National Park is little more than a country lane and very hilly. The road has deteriorated in the last few years, but if you have plenty of time it should be OK, though slow and isolated. Fortunately, after Lopé the road improves, with more hilly sections but a better road surface. It should, under normal circumstances, be possible to drive from Lopé to Lastoursville in a comfortable six-hour day. The route improves between Lastoursville and Franceville and may take only three to four hours.

Congo There seem to be two potential routes from Franceville around the Congolese border area. According to Paul Telfer of WCS (Wildlife Conservation Society) in Franceville, a small sandy track leads from the Batéké Plateau into Congo and on to Lékana, where roads of a sort lead to Ngo on the main Owando to Brazzaville road. We have only sketchy information about this route, so you will have to ask around in Franceville about its viability.

Most others have reported heading due east from Franceville to Lekoni (Leconi), where some canyons make a good if hairy diversion. A short new section of Chinese-built tarmac exists here. The border of Congo is 30km further east (marked as Akou on the Michelin map). Immigration is done in Mbie. It's around 125km between Lekoni and Okoyo, the first settlement of any size in Congo, but you might do it in one day. It just depends on the weather, the rivers and the bridges along the way. A sandy and then rough track leads on for more than 100km to Boundji. New tar exists from Boundji to the town of Obouya on the main road.

Heading south now on a mostly good tarmac road, you come in 160km to Ngo, where the other route from Lékana meets the main road. Another much easier day heading south along the main road leads to Brazzaville, but beware of pot-holes all the same.

DRC From Brazzaville you have to cross the river to Kinshasa. The actual ferry takes little time, but formalities make this an all-day affair. Expect to bargain for the ferry tickets. Do NOT take any photos of the Congo River from anywhere, or get cameras out either, anywhere near it. They will confiscate the lot. This also applies to the bridge crossing at Matadi.

ALTERNATIVE CONGO RIVER CROSSING

According to overlander Nick Bradshaw there are two other ways to cross the Congo River but neither should be considered unless there are very compelling reasons. Both are southwest of Brazzaville. The first is at Luozi, already in the DRC. The other is at Pioka. This route is closer to Brazzaville, with good tar to Boko as shown on the Michelin map. The border papers are stamped at Ntombe Manyanga, but the road is a little dangerous with bad cambers. The village by the river is called Ndendanga and entry to the DRC is done here. The ferry will require some (lots – say 20 litres) of diesel! The river is quite narrow here, with rapids in view, and the crossing is hazardous to say the least, with no proper ramps. The next 20km might take eight hours and the 'road' is dangerous, with massive erosion. The route heads to Gombe Matadi with some bad bridges, mud pools and more erosion. It improves to Mbanza Ngungu and thereafter is tar to the Angolan border turn-off at Songololo. Expect a three-day adventure!

From Kinshasa to Matadi, the road is in a variable state. If you have been lucky enough to get your Angola visa in advance, you will not actually need to go as far as Matadi. Currently the turn-off for Angola is in the small crossroads town of Songololo, 81km east of Matadi. Be sure to get your carnet stamped here. A poor dirt road goes south to Luvo, with the DRC immigration 11km from the turn-off. Another Angolan border at Noqui, close to Matadi, has been used by Oasis Overland. A pretty awful stretch of dirt then leads to Tomboco.

Angola After another 3km from the Luvo check-post you reach the Angolan immigration. The infrastructure in much of Angola is still in a bad way; mines are still a big hazard away from the main routes. Possibly impassable in the wet, the next 75km is a single-track route with a few sealed bits on to M'banza Congo. The small ruined church was the first Catholic place of worship built in central Africa.

In very good weather conditions, you might get as far as the delightful beaches south of N'zeto. The road surface, though, changes a lot, from new tarmac to lousy. The distance is around 300km from the border through Tomboco to N'zeto, of which about 200km is sealed. Don't expect any good road to the capital from N'zeto. The coastal road is still to be completed to Caxito. The road from Caxito on to Luanda is much better, but there could be endless check-posts on the way. Improvements towards Luanda are likely to be done by the time this edition is out, though – but how many times have we said that before! Once in Luanda, beware of theft and street crime. Luanda is also one of the most expensive cities in Africa.

There is now a choice of route to the south. Latest reports from travellers who have made it into Angola suggest that many new Chinese-built roads are now completed. From Luanda to Lubango via Huambo can be done in just two long days on good, surfaced roads. The entire 640km to Huambo can be navigated in one very long day. The first section of good road goes to Dondo. The scenery is more varied from here on and the road newly rebuilt all the way to Huambo. From here the next 400km or so to Lubango is also new tarmac road.

Heading south via the coastal route it will take a couple of hours to the Parque Nacional da Quicama, but at least you've got through the capital. With interesting, varied scenery and a new road, the coastal trip down to Benguela could take a day (or two allowing for a side trip to the Quedas de Água do Binga waterfalls). From Benguela the best road is via Chongoroi and Quilengues, where the road is almost finished. The going is good for the last 90km from Cacula to Lubango.

If you are continuing along the coast, be sure to follow the correct road to Santa Maria and on to Lucira. The route is not yet rebuilt and is said to be slow. Closer to Namibe the road improves, then you head inland to Lubango. The road is mostly OK as it climbs into high country with great views. Lubango is likely to become the tourist destination of southern Angola, as more people discover its long-unexplored delights. Above town and with great views is the Statue of Christ, looking like the Corcovado version above Rio in Brazil. The fantastic Tundavala Gorge is the prime destination, about 17km from Lubango. Carved from the Chela Escarpment, sheer 1,000m cliffs drop into a verdant green canyon; don't miss it!

On the road south via Cahuma and on to Humbe, roadworks should be completed in a year or so. From Humbe it's fine to the border with Namibia. There is also a possible optional road through Otchinjau direct to the Ruacana Falls border with Namibia. Once in Namibia, the roads are a joy and so is Etosha National Park. It's one big holiday from here on, whether down to the Cape or back up to Nairobi.

Route C2: Gabon to Angola via Cabinda While the route above (C1) via Franceville to Matadi via Brazzaville and Kinshasa is proving interesting, it is quite demanding after rains. Another possibility for those with the right Angolan visa, allowing double entry via Cabinda, is to follow this west-coast route. Some of the information in the route notes below has been updated by drivers Kristy (Princess) and Nev of Oasis Overland.

The road is good in from Libreville through Lambaréné to Mouila. A side trip to the abandoned old missions at Sindara village and the rapids on the River Ngouniets is worthwhile; it should be possible to camp in the bush there. The unsealed road is relatively reasonable from Mouila to Ndendé to the border. Gabon exit procedures start at Ndendé and, after a final check *en route*, it's across the bridge and on to a far worse road in Congo.

The **Congolese** border fun starts at Moussogo; further formalities are normally done at Nyanga an hour or so south. (Expect some road barrier checks along the way throughout Congo.) The route emerges from the forest into more open grassy savanna. Watch out for deep ditches on the side of the road and try using old quarries for bush camping. Things are grim as far as Kibangou and then for a further two hours before new tarmac is reached. This brand new tarmac section starts well before Dolisie and runs down to Pointe Noire. The Cabinda Angolan border is about an hour's drive south. With OK roads now, it's not far to Cabinda via Landana. From Cabinda town to the border takes less than an hour, but remember the DRC border could be shut on Sundays and public holidays.

Welcome to the **DRC** – it's only 300km to **Angola** and it's all one big, exciting, grinding wonderland of delay. Still sure you wanted to come to this final African frontier? No? Well, there's no going back now! It's straight on to sand at the border and from here to Boma are some of the worst sections. In the wet it can become almost impassable. Don't expect things to get much better between Boma and Matadi either, with check-posts as well as poor road conditions. From Matadi the road is – surprise, surprise – good for 81km to Sorongolo/Songololo. The route described above, via Franceville, Brazzaville and Kinshasa, joins here. (See *Route C1*, page 40.)

Route C3: DRC to Zambia

WARNING! Travel within the DRC from Kinshasa to Zambia is still a little-travelled option at present and has been for many years. From Kinshasa, roads of an unknown nature head southwest towards Lubumbashi via Kikwit, Kananga and Likasi. Many years ago you had to obtain permits in Kinshasa to cross the mining region. Look out for travellers' blogs on this route, as a couple have appeared recently. It may also be possible to put a vehicle on the train at Kananga. Motorcycle travellers might be able to trailblaze the route more easily – any news welcomed.

Central African west–east routes
Route WE1: Chad to Sudan and Ethiopia

CAUTION! Although this route has been plagued by the conflict in the western Darfur region of Sudan adjacent to the Chadian border, there is some light at the end of the tunnel, so check the latest security situation. Information collected by the previous authors (of the third edition), Charlie and Illya, is included here in case things improve.

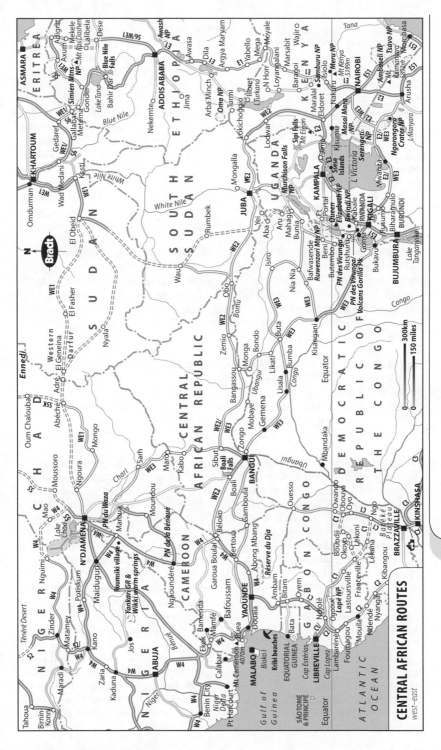

CENTRAL AFRICAN ROUTES
west–east

41

The main route (recently sealed) is from N'djamena to Mongo and Abéché near the Chadian border at Adré. Then it's on to El Geneina (Sudanese border), Nyala, or El Fasher, El Obeid, Kosti and Khartoum. Allow 12 to 14 days during the dry season. Make sure you get your Sudan visa before entering (either in Chad, Ethiopia or Kenya) and check whether you need a travel permit stating your route. (See also *Red tape* under *Sudan* in *Chapter 9*, page 305.)

Once into Sudan, the tracks are generally hard-packed sand. There are usually two tracks, one for the Bedford trucks acting as the local taxi service and another for cars. The deep ruts left behind by the trucks are trying at times for smaller vehicles to navigate through. If you get this far, be sure to check out the options for exploring the amazing volcanic Jebel Marra region. It is hard to lose your way later on, but if in doubt, just follow the railway line or drive on it (oh no, not again!). A few police checks are evident along the way, but if your paperwork is in order, it's an absolute breeze. Charlie Shackell and Ilya Bracht wrote: 'More often than not we politely had to decline the invitation to lunch at most police check-posts! The hospitality in Sudan is extraordinary.'

From Khartoum it is possible to get to Ethiopia via the Gedaref/Metema border and Gondar to Addis Ababa. Currently you cannot go via Eritrea, as the border with Ethiopia is closed, and going from Assab south to Djibouti is not advisable without local assistance, if even possible. It might, one day also be possible to head southeast from Darfur into South Sudan via Abiye, Wau and Rumbek to Juba. It all depends on progress between the two Sudans over the peace pacts. Roads are poor, especially after rains. Check the latest travellers' reports and blogs.

Route WE2: Central African Republic to Sudan and Kenya

WARNING! If you take the various government warnings about the situation in the CAR as gospel, **this route is not to be trifled with yet**, with armed insurgents abounding. However, it is in fact quite hard to verify how bad it really is. Any news on this route would be particularly welcome.

With a tentative peace in South Sudan, the old route from Bangui in the Central African Republic (CAR) to Nairobi via Juba might reopen. A none-too-comfortable unsealed road used to run through dense savanna forest over rolling hills from the Cameroonian/CAR border at Garoua Boulai/Béloko to Boali Falls – an amazing spectacle when in full flow. A sealed road then continued to the capital, Bangui. When 'Emperor' Jean Bedel Bokassa ruled the roost here, things were unpredictable, and there is little hard evidence to indicate that things are very different today. The road to Sibut was good before, but it's likely the stretch to Bangassou is badly pot-holed by now.

From Bangassou the route, formerly a rather dreadful narrow track through quite dense, dry forest, runs east through Zemio and on to Obo. A number of ferry crossings also made this route slow going. Things were little better in Sudan between the border and Juba through Maridi. This was also slow going but OK in the dry. A rough track leads north to a place called Wau, an apt name for it! (Wau was a big church and a few huts.) After Juba this was a superb but isolated route through friendly villages with varied mountain scenery. The road surface was not superb, though. Once in Kenya, the route passes through dry acacia scrub, inhabited by the Turkana people. Improved roads lead on to Nairobi via Lokichoggio and Lodwar. Today a good road links Juba with Uganda and Kampala. Travellers are already exploring South Sudan, so check the online travel forums.

Route WE3: Cameroon via CAR, DRC, Uganda and Rwanda to Kenya

WARNING! This was the classic trans-African route, but it is **dangerous at present** due to the antics of the LRA (Lord's Resistance Army – a bunch of well-armed rebels holed up in the CAR) and the rebellion in the eastern DRC. It was renowned for broken bridges and enormous bog holes. It was the only time you needed your winch, snatch blocks and full capacity of fuel, not to mention your reserves of inner strength and patience. Ferry river crossings were a big headache. Operators needed to use your battery to start the ferry, your diesel to run the ferry and your donation in order to begin the process. But remember, this is why you planned to see Africa in the first place, isn't it!

Entry to the Central African Republic is from Cameroon or Chad – south of Sarh at Maro and Kabo – but it's unlikely that anyone has done this for years. Once in the CAR, things deteriorate. Bridges can be down and rain barriers are set up during the wet season to stop vehicles using and damaging the roads. After the spectacular Boali Falls, the road used to improve the closer you got to the capital. At present Bangui may not be very safe for tourists.

There were two routes across Zaire, now the DRC. One crossed the Ubangui River directly from Bangui to Zongo and then slipped on a muddy way via Gemena, Lisala, Bumba and Buta to Kisangani. The other route involved driving east from Bangui via Sibut to Bangassou. Once across the river from Bangassou, a narrow and overgrown road used to head south via Monga, Bondo, Likati and Buta to Kisangani.

After Kisangani the route headed east through Bafwasende and Nia Nia into Pygmy territory around Ipulu. Overland parties used to go into the forest with the pygmies on hunts and also visit the rare okapi reserve. The rainforest continued until Komanda and nearby Mount Hoya. Here the route headed along a ridge with spectacular views, south to Beni, Butembo and on to Goma via the Virunga National Park. Another little-used and currently very unsafe bad road went north through some grassy, rolling hills around Bunia to Aru and Aba. Some dreadful bridges caused heart-stopping moments before the route crossed into southern Sudan near Yei. A better track continued through superb scenic boulder areas to Juba.

Until the political situation improves in the eastern DRC, we can only speculate about this future option. Apparently some of the roads above have seen some work and improvement. It was also possible to cross into Uganda from Beni some years ago before the troubles. Once in Rwanda the roads are better, but slow and hilly. From the Rusumo Falls border the route heads into Tanzania, to Lake Victoria, through the Serengeti, up on to the Ngorongoro Crater and Arusha, before reaching Nairobi.

EAST AFRICA East Africa includes southern Ethiopia, Djibouti, Kenya, Tanzania, Uganda, Rwanda and Burundi. Somalia is off the planet at present, although Somaliland is not.

Hitting the wrong climate in eastern (and southern areas) is more likely to be a nuisance than a disaster, as the roads are mostly good. Most rain in the east falls between March and June and October to December.

Route E1: Ethiopia to Kenya The main route from Ethiopia into Kenya or vice versa is the Moyale to Isiolo road; most would not describe it as a road. From Addis Ababa a good sealed road goes via Awasa as far south as Dila before becoming pot-holed, very hilly and slow. After Argya Maryam it improves and is generally good through Yabello and Mega to the border at Moyale.

Once in northern Kenya the road is soon shocking; it would be wise to check at the border about the latest **security concerns**. A convoy system is in use periodically due to isolated banditry. Before Marsabit the road is dreadful, allowing speeds of no more than 10–15mph. You might consider breaking the trip to Marsabit by staying in the village of Sololo's friendly missions. After Marsabit, a veritable haven of civilisation, the road is patchy. The Chinese are working on the road to some mines, so the last 70 miles to Archers Post should be good. Allow nearly two days to get to Isiolo from Moyale. Do not use the track via Wajir – it's too close to Somalia.

With security issues in northeast Kenya, more travellers are going via the Omo region around Arba Minch *en route* from Addis Ababa to Banya Fort. On the Kenyan side, going via North Horr and Lake Turkana is an increasingly attractive possibility, but check at the border about security.

The road from Addis Ababa to Djibouti is good, and Djibouti is an exciting country. There is also a mostly good road east from Kembolcha to Mille on the highway to Djibouti. The road from Mille via Awash and Nazret is also very good and busy with truckers. It's probably unwise to take your own vehicle into Somaliland (eg: to Hargeisa from Harar).

Route E2: Kenya, Tanzania, Uganda, Rwanda and Burundi For a shorter trip around the classic east African region, this loop is a superb choice, taking in some of the most famous game parks, Lake Victoria, gorilla-tracking in Rwanda, the Mountains of the Moon and the highlights of Kenya, such as Lake Nakuru. Burundi is now back on the travellers' map.

Those with their own vehicles can enjoy the comforts of travel here and those looking for an organised trip by truck or safari vehicles can look forward to a great immersion in Africa's famous charms. Try not to time your visit here during the rainy season, as some black murram park roads become boggy or very slippery. Before setting off from Nairobi, don't miss the famous Carnivore restaurant.

Heading northwest, the famous flamingos of Lake Nakuru are close to the Kenyan capital. Further north on a bigger loop to Eldoret are the lakes of Baringo and Bogoria, with flamingos and hot springs. After crossing into Uganda, most stop in Jinja for a view of the Nile and perhaps some rafting. When Idi Amin held sway, no-one dared to stop here, even at a broken-down traffic light – we speak from personal memory of this. No such fears today as you pass through Kampala, Masaka and Mbarara to Kabale on good roads. Gorilla-tracking is possible in Bwindi, while nearby are the cloud-hugging peaks of Ruwenzori. Check the latest security concerns when visiting Bwindi, as it's close to the DRC border.

Rwanda also offers gorilla tracking near Ruhengeri, adjacent to the Virunga National Park. Rwanda is a beautiful country of big rolling hills. Lake Kivu is tranquil and the roads are mostly also tranquil and sealed. To continue on the loop to Nairobi, you can head to Rusumo (or add Burundi first) and then enter Tanzania. Roads have generally improved a lot through the savanna around Lake Victoria. That said, heading into the Serengeti after Mwanza has pitfalls in the rainy season, as some black dirt roads turn into a boggy mess. The open plains of the Serengeti and the drama-filled Ngorongoro Crater are magical. Then as you descend through Karatu to Lake Manyara the road is fine in the dry but awful in the wet. From Arusha a good road runs to Nairobi, with the beautiful Amboseli National Park stretched out below Kilimanjaro.

Route WT: western Tanzania On our latest trip we headed from Kenya to Uganda, then south through Rwanda into Burundi. The route south from Burundi

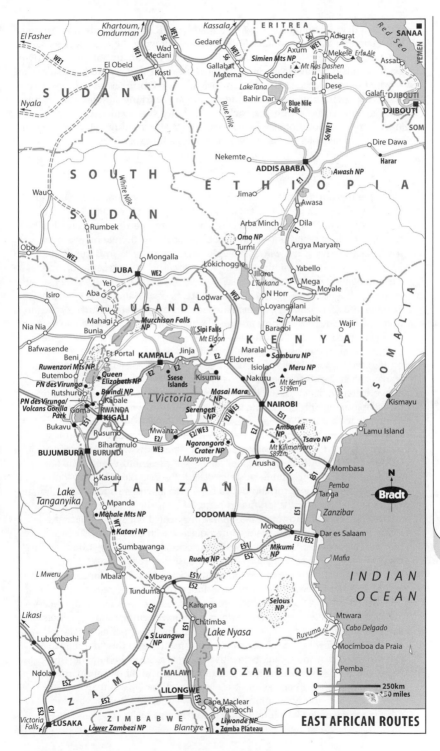

EAST AFRICAN ROUTES

0   250km
0   150 miles

Bradt

N

is generally a dry season option only. The road from Kigali to Bujumbura is good, and spectacular as it drops to Lake Tanganyika. Following the lakeshore south to Nyanza-Lac, it then twists and climbs steeply to the Tanzanian border. From here the road south is dirt but OK; at 5km turn left on to a smaller road to Kasulu, the first town (the main road continues on to Kigoma). From Kasulu it's about two hours' drive to Uvinza; the Mpanda road is right at the triangle before town. Cross a big bridge and go uphill on the rocky road. Later this road is OK with some long, fast 30mph sections; otherwise it's slow. It gets very muddy in the wet season, bordering on impassable. Uvinza to Mpanda takes about six hours.

MUD, GLORIOUS MUD

Since the days of mud paradise in Zaire (DRC), it's been a rare experience to relive those 'exciting' times. Looking back, the memories are a lot more romantic than the real thing, when we camped knee-deep in thick goo, tried to cook on green wood bombarded by bugs and were then kept awake by the cicadas. Leaving the windy shores of Lake Tanganyika in Burundi, the surprisingly good road climbs the Rift Valley Escarpment in a series of long zigzags. Can this great road really last?

Of course not, this is Africa! The short no-man's-land between the Burundian and Tanzanian borders is a shocker, but so rare is such a road that it's a fun drive. The people are friendly, the villages picturesque and the weather's holding up – it is the rainy season. At the Tanzanian border we search in vain for any sign of immigration or customs. The 'road' is a great gash, sliced through layers of exotically coloured mud. A tall bamboo ladder leans against the vertical edge of the chasm. 'Jambo Jambo,' shouts a man above, tottering dangerously close to the edge. 'Come on up!' It was the most pleasant immigration post of the whole trip and there was no extra charge. 'Welcome to Tanzania! What are you doing here? Are you lost?'

Evidently few foreign vehicles or travellers come through this outpost. Customs was an equally pleasant treat; this time there was no precarious ladder to climb, with steps two feet apart. The drive into Kasulu was fine and we found an enchanting hostelry called the God Bless Hotel. What a revelation this area was turning out to be – such a surprise and so friendly. We had high hopes for the journey to Zambia.

Next day the road was quite reasonable, not sealed but smooth dirt. After Uvinza, however, conditions deteriorated quickly, with endless mud holes in the semi-wet season. The holes often have rocks and wood buried in them, requiring slow, careful driving. Tiny Mpanda boasts the quirky Super City Hotel. Here a strange-looking wood-burning heater dominates the interior courtyard and actually does give off heat – it's surprisingly cold here after rain.

In Katavi National Park, beware the ferocious tsetse flies – it's the only place in Africa where we have ever been in open combat with calculating aggressors like this. In our haste to escape them, the handbrake was accidentally left partially on. A few minutes later, smoke seeping through the floor into the cab indicated that something below us was on fire. Luckily no damage was done, but it does show how hard it is to keep cool at all times. Along the 40 miles through the park, keep your windows closed! In Sumbawanga we stayed at the relatively luxurious Moravian Mission, and it was with some relief when we pulled into Tunduma, once again on a real road.

The road south through Katavi National Park is passable, with the odd muddy hole. After the park, variable road surfaces are encountered. After rain some sections are very poor; sticky wet mud holes are common and some are clogged with hidden logs – beware. There are some OK bits with short, good 30–35mph sections. The last 30 miles to Sumbawanga is a dreadful section. The road to Tunduma is worse than the two previous days, with rough sections, bumps, pot-holes but less mud. Of the 135-mile trip, only about 15 miles are well graded.

Be warned that taking this route involves some challenging and hilly driving with real mud driving 'at its best' after rain. Don't underestimate the remoteness of the region and be well prepared with fuel, food and spares.

EAST AFRICA TO SOUTHERN AFRICA ES routes are covered on the East African Routes map (see page 45) and the Southern African Routes map (see page 49).

Route ES1: Kenya to Tanzania, Malawi and Mozambique From Nairobi,

any number of good roads and routes lead south into Tanzania, the most popular being directly south to Arusha. Heading to Mombasa and south to Tanga, or going via the game parks circuit, including Masai Mara, Serengeti and Ngorongoro Crater, are also possible routes.

The road from Arusha, below the southern flanks of Kilimanjaro, and on to Dar es Salaam, makes for easy motoring. Through southern Tanzania, another good road goes all the way from Dar es Salaam through Morogoro and the Mikumi National Park to Mbeya, then on into either Zambia or Malawi.

After Mbeya, a good road heads south into northern Malawi and then passes the 'beach resorts' along the shores of Lake Nyasa. From Malawi it is perfectly feasible to head south into Mozambique from Blantyre across the Zambezi River to Tete, then south to Chimoio, in a scenic area near the Parque Nacional da Gorongosa. The roads are mostly good, but some sections are breaking up and pot-holes are an issue. The route has very little traffic or fuel and other supplies are sparse, particularly north of Vilanculos. Be prepared for an isolated journey much of the way. Hassle from traffic police has lessened.

From Maputo into Swaziland and on into South Africa, the roads are generally excellent. Be vigilant on the South African side of the Swazi border, though, where car hijackings are said to be a hazard. Signs around here recommend no stopping!

Other Tanzanian routes The road from Arusha south to Mbeya via Dodoma is said to be very rough and quite remote. Nearly all the roads in the western part of the country leave a lot to be desired. For something different, the route south from Dar es Salaam to the old Muslim ruins at Kilwa Kisiwani is sure to attract attention. We don't have any firm reports about road conditions, but expect the worst and plan for a dry season run. A bridge between Mwambo (Mozambique) and Mtwara (Tanzania) has reportedly been planned for ages. There might be a ferry at least, which runs at high tide only. However, new reports suggest that a new Chinese-built bridge, the Unity Bridge, exists at the Mtambaswala border. Head west from Mtwara through Newala and Masasi, preferably in the dry season. We have no other information, though, so before trying to take this coastal route, check the status of the border, road and bridge.

Route ES2: Tanzania to Zambia and Botswana Further south of Tanzania, the

main route goes directly from Mbeya to Victoria Falls, then either through Botswana to South Africa, or into Namibia and down to the Cape. Roads are mainly fine.

The main route from Dar es Salaam to Lusaka is the same to Mbeya as ES1, see page 47. Once in Zambia, the road passes through quite hilly areas and is slow going at times. From Lusaka, the road heads to Livingstone and Victoria Falls. To reach Botswana you'll need to go to Kazungula until work on the new bridge is finished. Currently, visiting Zimbabwe doesn't normally present any significant issue. However, local politics are not predictable.

SOUTHERN AFRICA The countries of southern Africa are Namibia, Botswana, Zambia, Zimbabwe, Mozambique, Swaziland, Lesotho and South Africa.

With so many varied routes through southern Africa, it is impossible to list them all. The standard of roads is excellent compared with the rest of Africa, and indeed most roads in southern Africa are as good as those in Europe. Roads in Lesotho are the exception, especially in the mountain areas away from Maseru. Gravel roads in Namibia are generally very well maintained and offer some spectacular drives. The trans-Kalahari route across Botswana from Lobatse to Windhoek via Ghanzi is now paved throughout, as is the Caprivi Strip in the north. Security concerns in South Africa are, perhaps, sadly, more of a problem than any road, route or geographical obstacle. Don't camp away from secure sites or backpackers' hostels.

There are a few routes through southern Africa that are 4x4 only and will get you into the unknown. For further information, read *Southern Africa 4X4 Trails* by Andrew St Pierre White and Gwyn White, or *The Complete Guide to a Four Wheel Drive in Southern Africa* by Andrew St Pierre White.

SUGGESTED ITINERARIES

The following itineraries are listed as suggestions only.

LESS THAN SIX MONTHS Below are some suggestions, but the timescales are limitless. And after so much investment, you will want to enjoy the fruits of your labours.

NORTH AFRICA Perhaps as a warm-up or with limited time: Morocco and Western Sahara; or Italy–Tunisia.

NORTH AND WEST AFRICA With visa difficulties further south, many overlanders are planning trips around west Africa, accessed from Morocco and Western Sahara. Apart from the kidnapping threat in Mauritania, the downside at present is repeating the Atlantic coast, although the interior of Western Sahara around Smara is an alternative new area.

Guinea–Sierra Leone–Liberia–Guinea or Ivory Coast when safe–Mali–Burkina Faso–Ghana–Togo–Benin–Nigeria and then eventually back via the Western Sahara route. With a radical improvement in security and more time: Nigeria–Cameroon–Chad–Sudan–Egypt (or Saudi Arabia–Jordan).

CENTRAL AFRICA Cameroon–Gabon–Congo–DRC–Angola. This route will surely become easier within the lifetime of this guide. Good luck!

EAST AFRICA Ethiopia–Kenya–Tanzania–Malawi or Zambia–Mozambique or Botswana–South Africa.

Plus, in addition the varied and exciting options, Kenya–Uganda–Rwanda–Burundi–Tanzania.

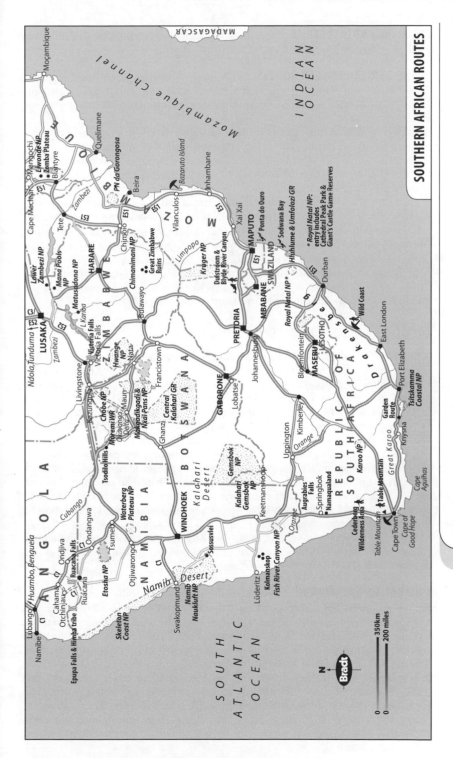

SOUTHERN AFRICAN ROUTES

SOUTHERN AND EAST AFRICA Cape Town–Namibia–Botswana–Zambia–Zimbabwe –Malawi–Mozambique–Swaziland–Cape Town.

TRANS-AFRICAN LONGER ROUTES The routes we have suggested are completely dependent on the political situation at the time. A full overland trip from London to Cape Town or vice versa can be done in as little as four months, but taking at least six to eight months would be more relaxing.

At the time of writing, the following routes are feasible: ferry Turkey–Egypt (or maybe soon Tunisia–Libya–Egypt); then Sudan–South Sudan–Ethiopia+ (Djibouti)–Kenya–(or Uganda–Rwanda–Burundi)–Tanzania–Zambia–Namibia– South Africa; or Tanzania–Malawi–Mozambique–Swaziland–South Africa– Lesotho plus Botswana and Namibia.

Currently the following has risks in Mauritania and is not a guaranteed option. Success will depend on the visa situation in DRC and Angola: Morocco–Western Sahara–Mauritania–Senegal–Gambia–Senegal–Guinea–Sierra Leone–Liberia– Guinea–Mali–Burkina Faso–Ghana–Togo–Benin–Nigeria–Cameroon–Gabon– Congo–DRC–Angola–Namibia–South Africa.

In future, when Darfur is safe perhaps, as above, then Nigeria–Cameroon– Chad–Sudan–Ethiopia (or South Sudan)–Kenya–Uganda–Tanzania–Malawi– Zambia–Botswana–Zimbabwe–Mozambique–South Africa.

OUT OF AFRICA – THE ASIAN OPTION

With so much turmoil across the Middle East, and with much of the Sahara off-limits, we have turned our thoughts beyond Africa for return routes. We have included a brief outline of the possibilities for a return journey, not back across Africa but through Asia. Shipping a vehicle from South Africa to Europe is likely to cost more than sending it on to Asia. It can make sense if you are on a long, extended trip.

We had been hoping to do another *Asia Overland* since 2000, but adverse political and security issues have scared us away from Pakistan. This has been unfortunate, for Pakistan has so many truly welcoming people. On our last trip, with some trepidation, we shipped our Land Rover from Durban to Mumbai in India. In fact it did not prove that daunting to send it in a small container. Most of the costs are in the loading and unloading procedures. We were also able to park up in Kathmandu for a few months to get back to our summer work. For details of shipping, see *Chapter 1*, page 13.

Summaries of each of the countries covered on this route can be found in *Chapter 10*, page 331. For more detailed country and routes notes for Asia, please contact us or take a look at www.expeditionworld.com.

MUMBAI TO KATHMANDU Mumbai is the gateway to India and from there myriad routes exist on mostly good main roads. Country roads tend to be narrow, often rougher and less maintained, although some are a delight, being quiet and actually in good repair. With so many spectacular historic sites, varied scenery and the kaleidoscope that is 'incredible India', you will never be short of exciting times in India. Driving in India is also incredible; you either hate it or you love it, sometimes both at once. Might is right here, with no quarter given by the trucks, buses or elephants. Rickshaws, scooters, bicycles and bullock carts may occasionally deign to move aside. Be prepared for diabolic drivers, unexplained delays and a generally frenetic time. Savour the crazy atmosphere and even occasionally the quiet places that can be unearthed. Accommodation can be found to suit all budgets. The monsoon (June to September) is not the best time to visit, but winters are fabulous.

The sights, sounds, smells and vibrancy here are definitely full-on. There are stunning palaces, forts, fabulous mosques and the whimsical concoctions of the Maharajas' exotic palaces, along with scruffy camels and amazingly colourful, industrious, friendly people. Rajastan and Gujarat are exceptionally varied. In the north is the cool of the Himalaya; in the south, the heat of the tropical beaches. The holy Ganges at Varanasi and the hill station of Darjeeling, renowned for its tea, are to the east, while in central India are some heady religious historic monuments and sites.

For tranquillity and peaceful spectacular scenery, head to Nepal and luxuriate in its enchanting valleys and historic cities. The Himalaya are the natural draw, of course, and driving around the foothills will certainly give you a feel for the sheer size of these stupendous peaks. Nepal was made for adventure travellers, with welcoming people and magical, magnificent historic cities like Kathmandu. These days, though, Kathmandu, like all major capitals, has become the domain of the motor car instead of the street dogs of old, when hippies chilled out and the lemon meringue pies had a kick. Across the country there are stunningly deep river gorges, impressive terraced rice fields where farms cling to precipitous hillsides, and thick bamboo cloudforests. Along the plains below the foothills, take an early morning safari through the dewy jungles. Nepal is magical for trekkers, travellers, tourists and overland drivers alike. A home from home in Kathmandu is the famous Kathmandu Guest House (*www.ktmgh.com*).

KATHMANDU TO LHASA Our latest Asian overland route took us into Tibet from Kathmandu across the Himalayas. Driving your own vehicle there is a relatively recent possibility and it is still an on/off erratic option. We tried for four years to get permission to enter from Pakistan, but we could not have dreamt we would enter Tibet from Nepal – the stuff of fantasy. Tibet has been forbidden for most of its history and reaching the forbidden city of Lhasa almost impossible. Even now, Tibet is frequently closed to visitors.

We crossed into China at Zhangmu and climbed rapidly on to the Tibetan Plateau, between the 7,000m (25,000ft) peaks of Jugal Himal and Gauri Shankar, through the deeply indented gorge of the Bhote Kosi River. Chilly Nyalam (an hour from Zhangmu) is the first Tibetan settlement, where it's necessary to stop to aid acclimatisation to the altitude. If you need a day here, there are some walks up the valley west towards Shishapangma Base Camp.

Leaving Nyalam (3,750m), the road climbs relentlessly, passing the cave of Tibetan poet-philosopher Milarepa, to the Lalung La Pass (sometimes called the Tong La). At 5,200m (17,050ft), it has a breathtaking panorama of the glittering Himalaya, now to the south. The massive giants of Gauri Shankar, Menlungtse and Shishapangma are an astonishing sight. On this side of the Himalaya the mountains seem close and inviting. From Tingri village there are superb views of Mount Everest and Cho Oyu. The appearance of our Land Rover in their midst provided the local village people with immense fun as they gathered around to examine it in minute detail – the foreign invader from Solihull!

We stayed in grotty lodgings near the old citadel monastery of Xegar Dzong (4,350m/14,270ft) for the night (four hours from Nyalam). The 'hotel' had no running water, outside corridor loos, draughty windows and strange visitors in the night. Tibetan landscapes are truly 'other-worldly', with vast vistas and never-ending mountain peaks floating on the horizon. From Xegar to Xigatse (3,900m)

2

the road climbs to a pass, with a great view of Everest before the summit. Lhatse is a further two hours. More small passes and undulating barren countryside leads on to Xigatse. Here is the enormous Tashi Lhunpo monastery, but before sightseeing, to our surprise, we spent most of the time doing paperwork. We needed to have a Chinese MOT-style check on the vehicle before being given our road travel permits, a new number plate and Chinese driving licences in order to continue to Lhasa.

Our route from Xigatse to Lhasa was via Gyangtse (3,950m) – an enchanting Tibetan town with a great monastery and towering citadel fortress (two hours' drive). After Gyangtse, the road climbs into a defile and continues steeply up, passing a glacier on its way to the 5,010m Karo La Pass. This is where Sir Francis Younghusband's British military expedition fought the poorly armed Tibetans during their march to Lhasa in 1903–04. It is a 20km descent to the lakeshore and the small town of Ngartze is a few kilometres north around the lake (four to five hours' drive from Xigatse).

Next day, the views around the turquoise blue Yamdrok Lake and from the formidable Kamba La Pass (4,900m) are truly sensational. From the pass there are more fabulous vistas – westwards over the shimmering lake to the gleaming white Himalaya, while to the north lies a landscape of dark, jagged peaks. Far below and ahead is the silvery ribbon of the Tsangpo River, the gateway to Lhasa.

It's a very steep descent from the Kamba La to the Tsangpo River Valley that eventually heads into the Kyichu Valley. Lhasa begins at the Yangbajain turn-off,

A DAY IN KATHMANDU

As a misty dawn stirs over the valley's stupas and temples, the dog patrols fall silent. A chaotic cacophony erupts; pedestrians lose the battle with bicycles, cycle rickshaws, motorbikes, taxis and minibuses in the vibrant, colourful streets and alleys. Yet in quiet corners, little has changed; a few holy cows linger beside a grotesque, gargantuan gargoyle or a serene, stony-faced idol. Hidden in the intricate maze of the old cities, potters spin their wheels by hand; antique sewing machines spin their cotton threads. Reverent Buddhist pilgrims spin their prayer wheels. The rumour mill is in full swing down in Durbar Square; Bob Dylan or Cat Stevens are in the low-roofed, dingy café around the corner. People offer devotions to the golden Ganesh idol near the old 'pie and pig' alley of the 1970s, behind the Kasthamandap Temple. Trekkers scurry about trying to find the current location of the immigration department. Others seek out the cheapest sewing shop, getting a T-shirt embroidered with their latest trekking route, or 'Yak Yak Yak'! And the dog patrols lie dormant, gaining strength for another night of barking …

BEWARE OF YAKS – DRIVING NEAR THE DEATH ZONE

'Beware of Yaks!' says the sign. When yaks ahead bar your road, you know you've reached an overlander's Shangri-la.

Most of Tibet lies above 4,000m, with formidable obstacles to entry placed in the way by nature. Seen from Kathmandu, the Himalaya often appear dreamy, floating above the fluffy clouds, draped in dazzling glaciers and snowfields. Only one road currently crosses the Himalaya into China and it's just 60km east of the Nepalese capital. Kathmandu lies in a lush, semitropical verdant valley, once a paradise for hippies, then trekkers and now for countryfolk seeking a better life in the big city. Beyond the mountains the plateau is barren, harsh, wild and unforgiving – a truly exotic contrast from the soft light of the Nepalese foothills. How would our faithful old Landy cope with this amazing physical and geographical step up?

We initially expected some problems concerning the effects of the high passes, not just on ourselves, but also on the ageing Land Rover. Would it cope with the 5,000m (16,400ft) passes running on possibly badly refined diesel? We even kept some Indian diesel from the high country around Nainital for this purpose, thinking it would be better than Nepalese fuel. We worried about the bitter cold – would it prove too much for our vehicle? Could we drive at very high altitude, at times only 3,000m below the '8,000m Death Zone'?

The ever-industrious Chinese have recently sealed the road. Much to our surprise, the vehicle coped admirably with the high altitude; hardly any loss of power was noticed. In fact, as the air cooled down, the vehicle seemed to gain in strength. The draughty old doors of our ancient steed, however, kept us awake with an icy blast.

where there are now two main roads into town. Despite massive construction, the city is incredible, and nothing, absolutely nothing, can diminish the impact of the towering Potala.

LHASA TO GOLMUD North of Lhasa is the vast high plateau country of backcountry Tibet. There are three main passes *en route* to Golmud, where the altitude is high! Snow, white outs, blizzards and high winds can occur at any time, so you need to be well wrapped up with warm clothing and equipment. Basic food and lodgings can be found a day's drive apart. The road is not particularly busy, although quite a few big trucks do use it. It's about 90km to Yangbajain, passing the Tsurphu monastery turn-off (40km from Lhasa) on the left. The road heads northeast below the Nyenchentangla Peaks to Damzung, with cosy truckstop cafés for oodles of noodles for lunch. It takes seven hours to Naqchu.

From Naqchu to Tuo Tuo there are some strange speed restrictions to adhere to – only 70km per hour – so you might have to wait on the roadside together with the truckers to comply, as it's calculated from your time between check-posts. Amdo is a grubby place at about 140km. There is a steady climb to the Tanggula La Pass (5,180m). Snow is common here and it's bitterly cold for much of the year. A truckstop town, Yangsping, is reached 60km after the pass. The road continues across the bleak country to Tuo Tuo River town (eight hours' drive).

From Tuo Tuo to Golmud it is 85km to the Feng Liang Pass (5,010m) and on to the snowy Wu Daliang Pass (5,010m), at 170km, often the worst pass, with frequent whiteouts. The route continues across open red plains on a good road for another 100km to the Kunlun Mountains. After the Kunlun Pass (4,767m/15,570ft), it's only 160km more down to Golmud (nine hours' drive). It's a dramatic descent through the dry canyons, surrounded by eroded cliffs and gaunt peaks.

GOLMUD TO ÜRÜMQI From Golmud a new highway leads to Ta Tsaidam, with the countryside more desert-like. There are three passes of between 3,335m and 4,000m to cross before reaching Aksai down at 1,800m. The Silk Route city of Dunhuang is only two hours ahead through some interesting dunes. Don't miss the fabulous 7th-century Buddhist art of the Magao cave complex here and the high dunes of the Crescent Moon lake area. The caves are 11km east and 14km south of town.

A rough but sealed road leads north for two hours from Dunhuang to Louliang. Be sure to turn off for the Hami 'motorway' 5km before town. The road to the Hami oasis should be finished by now (eight to nine hours' drive). Hami, famed for its melons, is 10km south of the motorway. Hami to Turfan is along an OK motorway but the drive below sea level can get hot, dusty and windy (seven hours' drive). Turfan has an impressive mosque and a few remnants of the old Uighur town. The next day, a good motorway runs through the Tien Shan Mountains, with views of Mount Bogda on the right after three hours, to Ürümqi. This town has become a sea of high-rise blocks with flashy restaurants, supermarkets, malls and modernity at every corner.

ÜRÜMQI TO KHORGOS The route crosses the brown soils of the Dzungar plains with the distant Altay ranges to the north and the peaks of the Tien Shan to the south. It's a good dual carriageway road to Shihezi for three hours. The good motorway (G30) continues to Jing He (three to four hours). After Jing He is Samui Lake, about 100km and over two hours west. The area is beautiful, with mountains, lakes and nomadic herder's yurts. Before the border at Khorgos there is a dramatic drop down from the barren Tien Shan. It is about two hours to Khorgos, another modern Chinese town. There is an indigenous, Turkic-speaking Uighur historic area to the south of town.

KHORGOS TO ALMATY A very bumpy road leads to Zharkent for 30km (an hour max). From Zharkent to Almaty is 330km, via Shankyn and the Lower Charyn Gorge. It's a nice, quiet desert route with gorges and mountains. To visit the Charyn Gorge, leave the main road at a marked junction and go south for some 19km. The gorge is a further 9km from another junction. From this main junction above it is approximately 172km to Almaty, which takes in all five to six hours, driving at

LHASA

The spirit of old Lhasa remains; the simply stunning grandeur of the former residence of the Dalai Lama, the Potala Palace, dominates the town. Equally atmospheric is the magical Jokhang temple, where hordes of Tibetan pilgrims gather at the holiest shrine of Tibet. The noises, smells and animations of the Tibetan traders in the Barkhor markets are memorable. The great monastic cities of Ganden, Sera and Drepung are unforgettable; these vast monk temple cities still resonate with monks and stirring prayers. Modernity has of course reached these once remote and alluring places, but look around and you can still find the mystical, spiritual qualities of old Lhasa and Tibet.

The lodge in Tuo Tuo was so new that the TV sets were still in their boxes. We awoke to a freezing room and fresh snow. At least we were up-to-date with the news from China CCTV: a new high-rise in Shanghai was opened yesterday. As usual the gearbox needed oil, so the cardboard from the TV packaging prevented that icy snow from attacking Bob's back, even if the snowflakes still swirled around. The spanner was a terror to touch, sticking to skin exposed through the holes in the tatty Nepalese woolly gloves. After self-help muesli, tea (not Tibetan), filtered coffee and a few minutes in the icy outside 'bathroom', it was off to Golmud.

The Feng Liang Pass and Wu Daliang Pass are not the best places to be in April. Visibility is only 3m; the horizon is lost, the side of the road has disappeared and heavily laden, smoky trucks are almost sliding off the edges. Who said Tibet is the last Shangri-la? On this day Shangri-la could have been lost forever beyond the horizon!

Somehow we negotiated the skating rinks of the road in the lowest gear. Even the gearbox oil refused to leak out in this bitter arctic swirl. It was fortunate that we had smuggled a new heater radiator into the subcontinent in anticipation of this 'new experience'. In all the truck-slipping kerfuffle, Siân's phone slipped out into the mist, lost forever on the Tibetan Plateau for the Buddhist demons to check out the ancient texts. Descending now, we left the snows of Shangri-la as quickly as we'd engaged them. Bliss – the fast run across the Kunlun plains and on to Golmud for take-away noodles and Earl Grey tea. That British kettle was priceless in Tibet, despite the funny plugs.

around 40mph from Zharkent. Almaty is a Russian- and European-styled city, with some classic museums and stylish buildings. The impressive Cathedral of the Holy Ascension is a colourful highlight here, especially since it is mostly constructed of wood.

ALMATY TO TURKESTAN After leaving the traffic chaos of Almaty, the road west is good for a while. To avoid the Kyrgzystan border, a bad and bumpy detour loops around the forbidden 20km or so, taking hours extra via Shu (Chu) to Merke. Once back to the westerly main road, the surfaces range from awful to fair as far as Taras, (over ten hours' drive). Taras is a typical Soviet-style town with attitudes to match in some quarters. A very bumpy road continues to Shymkent, a historic town dating back to the heyday of the Silk Route. A rather confusing ring road leads around the town; follow the signs for Tashkent. It seems a long way. When you finally reach a major roundabout – near a large mosque – turn right to head north. The road to Turkestan is mostly good and takes about six hours. Turkestan is a great place and one of the few in the country to display the rich tapestry of Islamic building. The Khodja Ahmed Yassaui Mausoleum Complex, a UNESCO World Heritage Site, is a stunning vision in blue tiling and brown brickwork that matches any in Iran. Be sure to look for the massive metal cauldron that dates from 1399 and the time of Timur (Tamerlane). Yassaui was born in nearby Sayram and studied in Bukhara, the great centre of learning in central Asia.

TURKESTAN TO ARAL After leaving Turkestan, be sure to stop at Sauran *en route* (about 50km north on the left) – there is a dirt track under the railway to where

You could of course spend months driving around Kyrgyzstan, Tajikistan and Uzbekistan, with their high mountains and superb Silk Road mosques and madrasas. Kyrgyzstan is a mysterious land of great mountains. The Tien Shan ranges are home to herders and horsemen who still live in the time-honoured fashion, in yurts and summer camps. In Uzbekistan are the fabled cities of Khiva, Bukhara and Samarkand, with Islamic architecture the equal of any in Persia. Tajikistan is a little-known country hosting the lofty plateau of the Pamirs and a curious blend of Soviet and Muslim culture. Turkmenistan does not throw its doors wide open for travellers, but those who are willing can be escorted around the bizarre monuments of Ashgabad. Out in the black desert of the Karakum is the lost Silk Road city of Merv.

The paperwork is much the same as for Kazakhstan, but don't put a foot wrong with any documentation in Uzbekistan or they will 'nab' you for some infringements – they will probably ask for some generous gifts in any case. Be very wary of the currency declaration forms in Uzbekistan or your money could be confiscated. You currently need to be escorted in Turkmenistan by a local tour operator. None of the hassles should be enough to deter the overland traveller, though, and in fact visa difficulties are continuing to ease across the region.

you see the historic mud remains. It's vaguely marked by a turquoise signpost about 4km after a small village. At one time Sauran was the largest settlement in the region of Kazakhstan, being the capital of the 'White Horde' Mongolian ruler, Sasibuqua. Bad, bumpy roads continue to the ghostly industrial city of Kyzlorda (five to six hours). This forlorn place is confusing, and it's hard to find the road out. To be honest, it is easier to follow the bypass, but if you do venture into town, the exit road is roughly on the NE factory zone side, with barred roads and detours. Follow signs to Aktope to avoid this muddled town. Otherwise follow signs to Zhalagash for 75km, then go left under the railway lines, over the Syra Darya River and join the 'main road' to Khosaly (320km in nine hours).

The previously bad road, with lots of ridiculously short 2km and 10km new sections, could well be completed to Aralsk by now. The road bypasses the Baikonur Cosmodrome, with only a slight hint of its location given by a few radar dishes very far away on the right. Before the town of Aral (Aralsk), you may catch some fleeting glimpses of the Aral Sea. The old harbour at Aral is a sight no-one can miss; dried-up, bleak and decaying. Even the old Soviet-era and once-grand hotel seems to be high and dry, with cracked concrete, crumbling staircases and rusty toilets.

ARAL TO THE RUSSIAN BORDER From Aral to Aktope the new road via Karabuk should be done, cutting the driving time in half from our 11 to 12 hours. Camping should be fine along the road, although getting off is not always easy. Aktope is a modern town with high-rises, busy streets and chaotic traffic. The road from Aktope to Oral (Uralsk) was surprisingly bad for 80km but then good into the town. When you finally manage to locate the central area of old Uralsk, you will be surprised at the grandiose public buildings, churches and theatres. Reminiscent of a bygone era, the buildings are all restored and speak of a Soviet past of pomp and culture. From Oral (Uralsk) to Saratov, a terrible road ensues as far as the border;

it's bumpy, pot-holed and feels very remote. The border is a surprisingly friendly spot, if a bit desolate. Change cash if possible here.

THE RUSSIAN BORDER TO SARATOV Once in Russia, the flavour is much more European, but Saratov is well worth a stop. An alternative route if you have time would be to go via Aktau and enter Russia at Astrakhan, with a typical citadel (Kremlin) to visit. The endless steppes of Russia are hardly inspiring, nor are the roads.

SARATOV TO BELGOROD The 230km to Saratov from the border is on mostly shocking bumpy roads with pot-holed sections. The last 50km are OK and improving up to the huge ring road, an apparently massive detour before reaching the town from the north. (You could try the direct town route through Engels – it might be better.) Follow the motorway over the river Volga on the long route, then turn left for the old town centre. Saratov has some striking mansions and old streets, as well as impressive onion-domed churches. Getting out of and then around Saratov takes hours. Roads continue the same to Voronezh and even the dual carriageway 'motorway' sections are poor and bumpy. It will take seven to eight hours to reach Borisoglebsk, from where the road improves to Voronezh. This town is interesting, but finding a way through is an epic only slightly less confusing than Saratov. Head directly through town, going left and right in the central area to the signposted A144 road. As you leave Voronezh, there is a cosy roadside restaurant/café on the right in which to unwind after surviving the town's traffic. The route continues 50km west to the turn-off to Stary Oskol, an awful-looking town really. Belgorod is reached on a good road. Take the ring road around Belgorod to avoid snarl-ups and then head 40km to the Ukrainian border and countries that don't need time-restricted visas. Phew!

THE UKRAINIAN BORDER AND EUROPE Ukraine has some superb places to visit, with super food. From the border to Poltava a fair road goes via Kharkiv, with a ring road to avoid the big city. Poltava has an interesting heart, with a grand circle of impressive buildings and churches. The road is reasonable to Kiev, with some dual carriageway sections (five to six hours' drive). Kiev is bursting with superb churches, monasteries and fine gardens. The Lavra complex is one of those must-not-miss sights. From Kiev to Medivizhy, we followed the E40 to Zhyntomyn and then headed south to Kamyanets. The massive castle here is very impressive. To the south is the equally picturesque Kotyn castle. From Chernivtsi to Lviv, some surfaces are very poor to Yeremche and from Ivano to Lviv the route is on the H9. Ivano has dreadful signposting. Lviv is a historic city with many attractions well worth a day's stopover. The road to the Polish border is not great as yet. Once across the Polish border, all roads are well surfaced, although the section to Krakow is slow with many towns *en route*. Be sure to spend a couple of days relaxing in fascinating Krakow and Wroclaw. Berlin is worth the detour; from here good motorways lead all across Europe.

Whether overland travel to either Africa or Asia in future will get any easier is anyone's guess. All we can do is keep abreast of events and keep on dreaming!

Vehicle Selection and Preparation

Once the budget and route choices have been assessed, you can think about your biggest expense of all: the vehicle. An eye for detail now will help you to avoid some potential pitfalls later on. Planning and preparation is half the fun.

If you are taking your own vehicle, we would recommend a planning period of about a year. You should have your vehicle for at least six months or more before you leave, especially if you are preparing it yourself in your spare time. It may sound like a long time, but you will be amazed at how much preparation is necessary and how many things there are to consider.

The chapter is divided into vehicle, motorbike and bicycle sections, detailing every requirement before and during your trip.

At the end of the book (*Appendix 3*, page 347) we have included a checklist to help you with your planning decisions.

SELECTING YOUR VEHICLE

Travelling in your own vehicle might distance you from the environment you are visiting, cocooning you in a self-contained world. However, this is true only if you allow it to be. The major advantage is that you are free to go more or less anywhere, stopping for tea or a snooze anytime. With relative comfort and the capacity to carry a fair amount of supplies, this is the best option. The biggest decision is which type of vehicle to choose, since all have their advantages and disadvantages.

4X4 This is the best option if you can afford it. The range of 4x4s is quite varied now, but most are being used on the school run. Of the more suitable models, there is a choice of permanent or part-time 4x4 and, more usefully, low and high (normal) ratios for all gears. Some have diff lock and others have varying degrees of automation. Diff lock is when all four wheels are able to rotate without the loss of traction that normally occurs if one wheel is spinning. Diff lock should never be used for normal driving any longer than necessary, as the gears will 'wind up' and create excessive stress on gear components. The other significant factor when choosing a 4x4 is the type of suspension it has. Some have leaf springs, others have coil springs and some have a mix. Coil springs rarely give trouble, but can induce a rolling effect. Leaf springs are more stable, but prone to breaking. There is never a perfect answer!

Petrol or diesel? It's hard to see any advantages in taking petrol, so we recommend you to stick with diesel. Diesel engines usually offer superior fuel consumption. Diesel is safer to carry, unlike petrol, which is lethal once it has been shaken about in hot jerrycans. Diesel engines are also simpler in that they have no points, coils, condensers or distributors, though they do have more complex fuel systems. Make sure your injector pump and injectors have been professionally serviced before you leave. Diesel engines produce high torque at low revs, whereas petrol engines tend to produce maximum torque at high revs, which can be a disadvantage in difficult conditions where wheelspin is a problem.

Most of the 4x4 manufacturers have now moved on to diesel engines that are turbo-charged. To gain more power, some have inter-coolers. These two systems basically make use of exhaust gases and colder air to boost power levels. Being more complicated, they have some disadvantages. Buying such models secondhand can have risks. Ideally you should ask for the servicing record of the vehicle. Wear rates can be higher with the faster motion and greater heat generated by these models. Of course the power gains are significant and undoubtedly an advantage in deep sand.

Fuel availability (either diesel or petrol) varies from country to country. As a general rule, however, diesel is cheaper throughout Africa and more readily available than petrol. Vehicles that use unleaded petrol have a definite problem, since such petrol is not available in many countries.

Short or long wheelbase?
A long wheelbase has the obvious advantage of space. Remember that you are likely to be planning to live in and on your vehicle for long periods. It will be a close companion, and so will the person you share it with, so you might as well start out with the idea of making it comfortable. Having more space means more flexibility; more equipment can be stored inside and out of sight. Pick-up versions of long-wheelbase vehicles with added rear box units are extremely good for storage capacity. Rear box shells are available; some are rather low. Otherwise, if you are lucky enough to have access to welding and fabricating equipment, you can make your own metal- and aluminium-clad box. Some people put custom-made caravan-style boxes on to pick-ups. Some are quite good; others look unstable and are not ideal in sand dunes.

A short-wheelbase vehicle does not really have the capacity or the convenience. Attaching a trailer to a short wheelbase for extra storage space is a possibility, but we don't recommend it. Towing a trailer can be a severe hindrance in some terrain, particularly sand or mud and over loose, uneven or sloping surfaces. There is potentially some danger when manoeuvring trailers at difficult angles or on sloping muddy roads. A badly loaded trailer can cause instability when cornering and braking. Trailers do spread the load better, but overall are best not considered.

Further information on storage and driving techniques regarding a short-wheelbase vehicle with trailer can be obtained from major 4x4 or trailer outlets. Companies offering 4x4 courses will also be able to assist.

Age and value
Buying the latest model or the most expensive vehicle might be desirable ordinarily, but there is one important factor to consider. Remember that the level and cost of your customs document for the vehicle, the carnet de passage, is related to the value of your vehicle. The bond or insurance-cover fee you must arrange before leaving your home country depends on the value of the vehicle you choose, its age and, in some circumstances, its initial cost when new. When a country like Egypt charges an 800% mark-up on the assessed value of your vehicle, new or old, it can be a seriously daunting amount to put up as collateral. If you are planning a limited trip and to travel in countries that do not require a carnet, the problem is not an issue.

See *Red tape* in *Chapter 5*, page 115, **before** deciding on the vehicle. Unless you have a lot of money, this effectively means buying an older model, preferably in good condition, and spending some considerable time fixing it up. How old it is depends on your mechanical ability, the time and enthusiasm you have, and the depth of your pocket.

Vehicle makes By far the most common 4x4s in Africa are the Toyota Land Cruiser, Land Rover, Toyota Hilux (4x4) and the Nissan Patrol in southern Africa. You are more likely to find spares and experienced mechanics for these vehicles than any other.

The older models are more common, such as the Land Rover 110 and Defender, and the 60, 70 and some 80 series of the Land Cruiser and mid 1980s Hilux. There aren't many spares for much older models now. You will also find Land Rover and Toyota dealers in most capital and larger cities, although the stock of spares varies greatly from dealer to dealer. They will sometimes only stock spares for the newer models.

Unless you are a very experienced mechanic, have a very reliable vehicle or can afford to have spares sent out to you, avoid the seriously overcomplicated computerised newer models for which bush mechanics will not have the tools or know-how. Go for an older Land Rover, Land Cruiser or Hilux.

The following is a brief rundown of the vehicles available and a few of their advantages and disadvantages.

Land Rover (*www.landrover.com*) It is often lamented that 'a Land Rover is always sick but never dead!' That said, there are still more overlanders using Land Rovers than Toyotas, thus defying logic, but then so is crossing Africa these days!

The ageing Land Rover Series IIIs are no longer advised, as most will have rusted away. Favourites now include the 110 and Defender Land Rover series, which are the most suitable for African roads. Their fairly simple and robust design makes them ideal for the wide variety of difficult conditions. They are available in long or short wheelbase, with six-cylinder petrol or four-cylinder diesel engines. The smaller 2,286cc engine is too underpowered. The 2.5 engines normally have turbocharging and injection - the Tdi series. The later models are more powerful but more complicated. The early 2.5 turbo is best avoided, but the following 200 Tdi-engine models are quite popular. The later 300 Tdi originally had some timing-belt problems, but is now considered to be the best engine. The very latest Td5 is more sophisticated; some servicing is probably best done by main dealers in African capitals.

The 110 and Defenders have permanent 4x4. With coil springs, they are a joy to drive on rough terrain. This is not to say that even Land Rovers are sufficiently robust to ignore bad conditions. They actually need constant attention and nurturing throughout the journey. Land Rover fans are an enthusiastic lot, spending happy hours underneath, admiring their steeds and keeping an eye out for oil leaks and loose bolts.

Range Rover (*www.landrover.com/RangeRover*) The Range Rover offers greater comfort than the Land Rover but for a trans-African journey it is of fairly limited use. It does not have much in the way of storage capacity and the compensating advantages of its powerful engine and comfortable interior can now be found in the newer Land Rovers.

Land Rover Discovery (*www.landrover.com*) Although the Land Rover Discovery has virtually the same engine, gearbox and axle specifications as the Land Rover Defender, it has fewer practical advantages. It does have greater comfort, though. It is not common outside southern and eastern Africa. This vehicle has either the 200 or 300 Tdi engine, which are now fairly reliable. The gearboxes are still liable to early wear and the shape of the vehicle is not ideal for tinkering with or living in for long periods.

Toyota Land Cruiser (*www.toyota.com/landcruiser*) The Land Cruiser's design is rugged and very reliable, and spare parts are readily available throughout Africa. Toyota is rapidly taking over Africa! Toyota have a rather confusing numbering system for their various Land Cruiser models. They started with the 40 series and worked up to the 80 series in the early 1990s. The FJ prefix denotes a petrol engine and the HJ series diesel engines. Just to confuse you further, BJ refers to the short wheelbase. The engines tend to be large but very reliable and, in particular, the H2 engine (fitted in the HJ 60 series) will go on forever if looked after. The suspension is solid axle and leaf springs, and the older models are all part-time 4x4 with a two-ratio transfer gearbox. Watch out for chassis rust when buying older secondhand models.

The HJZ75 and HJZ78 are still probably the best models for the Sahara and Africa as a whole. The 78 had coil springs fitted to the front and retained leaf springs on the rear, which can mean broken springs if you drive too fast. Toyota's four-cylinder 3.5 and six-cylinder 4.2 engines are still reliable workhorse power units. The 80 series came along in 1990 with all coil springs, and the VX models have permanent 4x4. It may be better perhaps to look out for the GX models, which do not have permanent 4x4. Local mechanics tend to be more familiar with these earlier vehicles. The later Toyota 100 series are a step backwards for overlanding – far too complex and an impractical shape. Toyotas are now made in South Africa, but specifications can vary.

Toyota Hilux (*www.toyota.com*) The Hilux is available as a double or single cab with either a 2.2-litre petrol or 2.4/2.8-litre diesel engine. The engines are fine unless you expect to be dune-bashing for most of your trip. It also has part-time 4x4 with a two-ratio transfer gearbox. They are quite popular vehicles in Africa and nearly rate up there with Land Cruiser and Land Rover. They are a little easier to roll over on to their roofs if you are not careful, so take particular care when crossing slopes and cornering at speed. If you are considering buying a Hilux pick-up, be sure to keep the height as low as possible when designing the rear living/storage area.

Following on from the Hilux are the 4Runners. These have part-time 4x4 and a three-litre turbo diesel engine. The Hilux is still more common at the moment in Africa.

Nissan Patrol (*www.nissanuk.com* and *www.nissanusa.com*) These vehicles have a good reputation in Australia and South Africa and are reported to be very reliable. They are increasingly seen in southern Africa, where spares seem to be available in larger towns. They have coil-spring suspension and part-time 4x4. The later Patrol GR had a six-cylinder 2.8 turbo diesel engine. The TD42 models have a larger engine. These two versions kept the part-time 4x4. We do not have any direct experience of these vehicles, but their shape and size certainly have no apparent disadvantages.

Jeep (*www.jeep.com*) The Jeep Wrangler is probably a bit small for all the equipment and the Cherokee range tend to be gas-guzzlers. We met one Dutch couple with a Jeep and, although new, it suffered from suspension problems. Again it is virtually impossible to find even basic spares and is not recommended.

Mercedes Unimog (*www.unimog.net*) The Unimog is popular with some German travellers and it is indeed a wonderful vehicle. It is a powerful 4x4 truck with very high ground clearance; it also offers a lot of storage space. The living quarters are separate from the driving cab. Although you can buy Unimogs quite cheaply at auction in Germany, costs can really start to mount on the road. The fuel consumption can be very high indeed, and some are petrol. You should test-drive the Unimog in various conditions, as it can easily tip over in soft sand.

Bedford and other trucks Bedford 4x4 trucks, especially ex-British army models, were much favoured by British-based trans-Africa overland tour companies years ago but are far too old to be considered now. Very old J6 Bedfords are still seen along the desert tracks of Sudan as transport for the locals (and hardy travellers) who have to sit on top of the loads. Some Europeans like small trucks converted into quite spacious mobile homes. Both Mercedes and MAN have 4x4 versions, but preparation costs are high. MAN has the smaller models. Trucks are a pain when stuck in sand, though.

Isuzu Trooper (*www.isuzu.com*) This is undoubtedly a comfortable vehicle. It is reported to suffer from a very sensitive accelerator that may cause difficulty and excessive wheelspin in sandy and muddy conditions. Some are seen in east and southern Africa.

Mitsubishi Pajero (*www.mitsubishi.com*) The Pajero is reportedly one of the better vehicles when it comes to off-road ability, but its front suspension is said to let it down.

Mitsubishi Colt (*www.mitsubishi.com*) The Colt is another vehicle in the same vein as the Hilux. It has part-time 4x4 with automatic free-wheel hubs.

Top of the range These models are best avoided. That said, for a go-anywhere vehicle there is the Austrian Pinzgauer – a phenomenal vehicle at a phenomenal price. Others are more likely to be found in supermarket car parks or outside schools in the smart suburbs of London or Sydney than crossing Africa. More seriously, you will struggle to find a mechanic who can fix them, or any spares outside Europe or South Africa.

TWO-WHEEL DRIVE Although not really suitable for more adventurous, full-blooded trans-Africa trips, 2WD vehicles can be used quite happily if you plan your route with care or will be travelling in areas with better roads. A 2WD vehicle is feasible between Kenya and southern Africa keeping to main roads. Twenty-five years ago it was possible to drive across the Sahara, and even right across Africa, in a vehicle like a VW Combi, but most are only now found in car graveyards. Some smaller 2WD cars, like the ancient Citroën 2CV and Renault 4, were surprisingly

---

TIMING CHAINS AND BELTS

Your vehicle timing chain or belt, where there is no reliable service record, should be replaced before departure. Even if it is not causing you any problems before you set off, you could get into big trouble if it were to break while you were on the road.

good in all but the muddier sections of central Africa. They were economical on fuel and capable of desert crossings on main tracks with some pushing and cursing. The only problem was the lack of ground clearance.

CAR HIRE With much of north Africa off-limits, it's perfectly possible to hire cars/4x4s in major centres or through specialist companies at home. Much of southern Africa and parts of the east and west are perfectly accessible by 2WD vehicles that can be hired locally. If you want to get off the beaten track once you arrive, you should be able to find more substantial vehicles for hire in some of the major tourist centres. In cities like Windhoek and Nairobi, for example, it is possible to hire 4x4 vehicles such as Suzuki, Isuzu Troopers and Land Rovers, already kitted out with camping gear, cooking equipment, water containers, etc. Some useful websites are www.bushlore.com (self-drive safaris, based in South Africa), www.safaridrive.com (self-drive safaris) and www.africatravel.co.uk (Africa Travel Centre).

VEHICLE PREPARATION

The range of possibilities for vehicle preparation is obviously enormous – from paying someone else to do the job for you, to having the fun of tackling most of it yourself.

Some companies can provide a vehicle completely customised to your own requirements, while others will give advice and help so that you can prepare your own vehicle. It is crucial to know your vehicle well. This is extremely important if you have not had a hand in the preparation. Keeping the vehicle close to the standard is best; try not to overload it.

What follows is a guide to some of the more important issues to bear in mind. You will all have your own ideas about what is essential and what optional extras are necessary.

The first and most important part of vehicle preparation is to ensure that the basic vehicle is in sound mechanical order before you add on any extras. If you are not a mechanic, you will soon become one! In the meantime, it would be advisable to take it to a garage for a major check/overhaul. This should include the engine, cooling system, fuel system, suspension, gearbox, transfer box, clutch, differentials, brakes, electrics and chassis condition.

Initially take the vehicle on some test-drives. It is really preferable to take it on an extended drive before going to Africa. This applies whether or not you have some mechanical knowledge. If you are already in southern Africa, you will be well ahead of the game. Teething troubles are most likely to occur earlier on and many can be ironed out over these initial forays. Try to identify any problems and get them fixed while you still have access to good mechanics. With thorough and conscientious preparation beforehand, the number of problems, and hence headaches, will most probably be limited later to the effects of African conditions.

Make sure as many nuts and threads as possible have been greased before you go; there is nothing worse than rusty nuts on the side of the road.

Once you have the basic vehicle in good working order, you can start to fit it out for overland travel. From a security angle, it is desirable to limit the amount of equipment placed on or around the vehicle. With gear all over, it can look a bit pretentious; it certainly shows a level of wealth undreamed of by most Africans. This in turn might attract petty thieves. The more you keep hidden, the more you blend into the local ambience.

FACTORS TO CONSIDER Some personal preferences will come into play.

Sleeping options
You have the following choices: a rooftop tent, sleeping space inside the vehicle, a tent or hotel accommodation. The ultimate choice is obviously dependent on where and for how long you intend to travel.

The option of hotels every night is only a consideration if you are travelling in places like Morocco, Tunisia, Egypt and southern Africa, where towns are frequent and roads good. Although you will find hotels in some places in all countries, you should always be prepared to camp out, as you never know where you might end up.

Tents Pitching a tent with a sewn-in mosquito net and groundsheet is the cheapest option, but invariably inconvenient. When sleeping on the ground in Africa you will never be alone, as all manner of bugs will find your presence attractive; a camp bed helps, but takes time to set up. Getting tent pegs in can be a bind; sand is too soft, mud too sticky and the Sahel too hard. Aren't holidays a hassle! Pitching a tent daily can be a nuisance when driving for long stretches over a long period. Finding suitable rough camps is not so easy in a continent with a rapidly increasing population. Dome tents (requiring fewer pegs) are better in any event, except in tropical downpours, but they do dry quickly.

Rooftop tents Most overland vehicles that you see throughout Africa have convenient rooftop tents of various designs. They do not require much space, are quick and easy to put up, and keep you away from people as well as from large and small wildlife. Being well above ground, they afford good ventilation. There are various designs that can be fitted to most vehicles. Normally they come with a double mattress, which stays in the tent as it is folded up. With a little ingenuity, it is possible to pitch any normal robust tent on the roof rack, assuming your rack has a plywood base. This is a cheaper option if you already have a good tent.

Sleeping inside the vehicle Even if you have a roof tent, it is a good idea to plan some way of sleeping inside the vehicle. This can be handy in certain situations, foul wet weather, sandstorms, borders and some rather public places. If you intend to sleep inside the vehicle a lot, try to devise a system that minimises the number of things you need to move when you go to bed. Sleeping inside can sometimes be

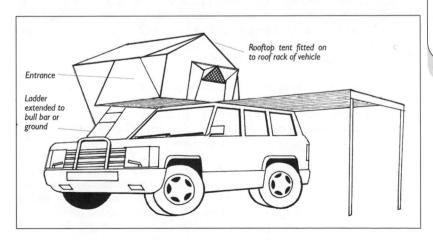

Rooftop tent fitted on to roof rack of vehicle

Entrance

Ladder extended to bull bar or ground

too hot and ventilation needs to be considered. It is useful to have a multi-purpose platform that can slide in and out, and which lies above the equipment. Part of the platform can double up as a table by attaching legs to it. Sleeping in the vehicle is clearly the most secure option for both you and your belongings. See the *Suggestions for vehicle layout* diagrams on pages 70–1 for options.

Roof rack Roof racks are available in all shapes and sizes. They can be used as a low-cost alternative to a rooftop tent by simply adding a sheet of plywood so you can sleep under the stars. You might consider extending the plywood over the windscreen for added shade. It will be seriously appreciated under the burning hot African sun. Do not overload a roof rack. Most 4x4 vehicles are not built for heavy loads on the roof. Structural parts, like windscreens, also have a habit of cracking under the strain if overloaded. Roof racks should only be used to store light equipment like sand ladders and empty jerrycans. Try to keep as much equipment as possible inside and out of sight. Overloading the roof increases the risk of tipping over on uneven or sandy roads. Anything removable on your roof rack should be secured with padlocks.

Security It is surprisingly hard to find good places to camp wild in Africa. That idyllic spot you found may prove to be a much-used track between the local village and its distant well. Total security is impossible to achieve, of course. The most important security system will ultimately be your own vigilance. It is worth mentioning here that security concerns and how you plan to camp are linked.

More about this later under *Accommodation* in *Chapter 5,* page 138.

Padlocks and hasps Padlocks should be put on any items mounted outside the vehicle, and may be put on some doors. Avoid combination locks, which will very quickly become clogged by the thick dust that will cover your vehicle once it hits the African roads. Ideally buy a set of padlocks with a common key, or it will take forever to find the right one. If you can't do this, paint them different colours. Hasps can be forced, so you should consider some form of internal mechanism to back them up, such as additional locks or bolts.

Windows Windows are another problem area, so they should be kept to a minimum. Rubber surrounds can easily be cut away. Metal grilles on windows will help, but they also have the adverse effect of making you look as if you have something worth stealing. If you intend to sleep in the vehicle, metal grilles covering the windows mean you can sleep with the windows open. Sand ladders can be mounted and locked over windows.

Curtains It is worth putting up curtains, whether or not you intend to sleep inside all the time. They provide instant shade and dissuade prying eyes. Simple strips of fabric on curtain stretchers can be fitted inside most vehicles, or you can fit curtain rails with proper hooks. Bungee cords are useful for many things: curtains, drying washing and holding equipment in place for starters.

Safety box for valuables This is tricky. You don't want to be with your vehicle all the time, and carrying vital documents, passport, carnet and cash on your person all the time is not ideal. But leaving them in the vehicle is not ideal either. Bolting in a safe box is one possibility, but don't keep everything in it, just in case the worst happens. It's best to have a few hiding places around the vehicle for spare emergency cash; carry the rest with you in a money belt along with your passport. Be extra careful about losing the carnet. It's very bulky, so if you don't want to carry it, do find a secure hiding place, but, you guessed it – be sure to remember where it is!

Hide copies of all documents in some other area of the vehicle. If staying overnight in a hotel, whether cheap or expensive, take the carnet and main valuables with you before retiring. Another good idea is to scan all valuable documents – passports, driving licences, carnet and other vehicle papers, yellow fever certificates, travellers' cheque receipts, insurance policies, credit card numbers and other important documents, madrasas etc – and store them in a folder in your email account. That way, even if you lose everything, you can print off a copy in the next internet café.

Alarm systems This may help, as it should deter a thief from continuing with a break-in, but do not depend on it. A wide selection is available from all accessory shops.

Bull bars These help to protect the lights and radiator from anything you may hit. Bull bars are optional. However, bearing in mind the amount of general debris on the roads, it is recommended. Cows, goats and camels, in particular, will often stroll out nonchalantly into the middle of the road just as you are passing. The bars can also be used to install mesh to prevent stones breaking your headlights. Additional lights are best placed higher.

Baffle/bash plate A baffle plate is a steel plate fitted beneath the vehicle, helping to protect its vulnerable underside from rocks. They can make routine maintenance more awkward. You should consider covering the tie rods on your vehicle, as these are vulnerable. An old tie rod can be bolted on in front of them with a little thought and can even be designed to act as a tow bar. Putting baffle plates under the sump and gearbox is only really worthwhile for extended sand driving, where rocks are hidden. It is better to drive with caution where potential obstacles exist; get out and check first if in doubt.

Suspension The biggest enemy for vehicles and their suspensions in Africa is the state of the roads. Ideally fit new springs and shock absorbers all round before setting off. Strengthening the chassis is only a good idea if you are likely to be carrying very heavy loads.

Opinion is divided as to which springs are the best. Fitting heavy-duty springs for the additional strains of African roads might sound fine, but African mechanics will often tell you that lighter springs are suppler and less likely to break under the strain. The chassis will also vibrate less.

If you can afford it, Old Man Emu shock absorbers and springs have a good reputation. Take plenty of spare rubber bushes, as they will disintegrate with great rapidity on some road surfaces. Some people take poly bushes, but, being less supple than rubber, they can induce more vibration. By driving carefully, you can reduce the worst effects of rough roads. Old car tyres are cut up and made into bushes in Africa. They usually last much longer than ones purchased from the manufacturer, though they probably won't pass any vehicle roadworthiness test such as the British MOT!

Spare battery and split-charge system Carrying two batteries is only necessary if you are intending to be out in the wild for long periods. It is necessary in the depths of the Sahara. Batteries can fail without warning. The cheapest option is to change the batteries periodically to keep them charged. It is a bit of a bind, however, and, in storing the second battery, you must ensure it cannot tip over. If you are intending to run other electrical items, like a refrigerator, off your battery, we would suggest a dual battery and split-charge system. This enables the second battery to run other electrical items while the vehicle's main battery stays unaffected.

Many campervans have a deep-cycle-type second battery. This is designed to cope with charge and recharge. These batteries are not ideal for starting, though. You might consider having a dry cell, sealed battery as the second battery. A split-charging system ensures both batteries remain charged. Since these need to be in good order, we strongly suggest you seek appropriate advice. As with all things, the more complicated, the more risk of problems. Maybe it's easier to change the batteries manually after all. Don't forget to take some good-quality jump leads anyway.

Oil cooler Recommended by many, ignored by many others. Probably a good idea if you are likely to take full advantage of fast roads in the hottest conditions. Less useful if you are in an older vehicle.

Raised air intake This is standard on many African 4x4 vehicles, reducing the intake of large quantities of dust and acting as a safeguard if you intend to drive through deep water. It will certainly do no harm to fit one and might help to save your engine from damage. The Australian Safari Snorkel is suggested and is available at most off-road outlets.

Axle breathers These are small air valves, mounted on the top of the axles and gearbox, which allow air to be drawn in or out as the parts heat up and cool down. The problem is that, when you go into deep water, the axles cool quickly and suck in water through the breathers. The easiest way to deal with this is to fix a length of plastic tube over the breather and thread it up into the vehicle.

Wheel rims Riveted steel rims should be selected for tougher terrain, as they are more reliable. Magnesium alloy rims are not very convenient because the bead, the part of the rim most often damaged in tougher terrain, cannot be hammered back into place like a steel rim. If you have a puncture repaired by an African, he will usually use a very heavy hammer, often skilfully, to break the bead; that is, to separate the tyre from the rim. Sometimes it's best not to watch!

Some older cars are fitted with split rims, which are very convenient when you are repairing your own tyre. Ensure that the tyre is properly deflated before splitting the rim, as air pressure remaining in the tyre could cause an explosion and serious injury. Some people fit a ring of shaped rubber around the inner wheel rim to stop the tube wearing and ripping.

Tyres Set off with a completely new set of tyres, including two spares, if you are planning a long trip. Aim to fit the best you can afford. You will be facing a wide variety of terrain – sand, mud, laterite, rocks and tarmac roads. Good-quality, all-terrain tyres are the best bet. Many people opt for Michelin or the Continental Super All Grips. BF Goodrich tyres are significantly cheaper than Michelin. Tyres need to be suitable for mixed terrain on a general African trip.

There is little need for specialist sand tyres, with fewer chances nowadays to drive in the desert. Multi-purpose tyres are good for sand as well as tarmac and mud. In any case, you can do a great deal to cope with sandy conditions by reducing tyre pressures until you get back on firmer roads.

The main spare wheel is sometimes fitted on the rear doors; if so, the hinges and clamps should be periodically checked and tightened. Those fitted under the rear fuel tank reduce ground clearance. Those fitted to the bonnet can be a real nuisance, making the bonnet very heavy to lift and restricting the view. The second spare may well have to be fitted on the roof. We fitted our two spares inside; much better if you have the space.

Tubed or tubeless tyres? Tubed tyres are generally easier to remove from the rim, as the bead does not need to be so tight, but it is possible to fix a puncture in a tubeless tyre without removing it from the rim. We switched to tubeless after so many badly repaired punctures on the last trip. Tubeless tyres can be repaired from the outside using the 'gluey plug', but, since this method is outlawed in Europe now, getting the kits could be a problem. Surprisingly perhaps, tubeless tyres can be run with low air pressures in sand without many snags. In the end it comes down to personal preference.

Inner tubes If you take tubes, be sure to pack a few spares, as they cannot always be found in the correct size or make. It is best to inflate, deflate and re-inflate the tyre once the new tube has been fitted to remove twists in the tube. This takes a lot of effort in some circumstances, so try to be careful, inflating slowly if you do it once only.

Valves It is better to fit your tyre with a short-stemmed valve rather than the longer one often found in African parts shops and garages. In some places it's possible to find tubeless valve stems to cut out tube usage. Longer valve stems are more susceptible to breakage, particularly in tough terrain. Always carry some extra valve cores with you. Valves have a habit of flying off into the sunset when being removed to let air out, so beware!

Extra fuel and water tanks
Fuel In most parts of Africa fuel is actually more readily available than you might think. There are not many places where you will need to go more than 640km (400 miles) without supplies. But you can't always guarantee that you'll find fuel when you expect to, and you may want to take full advantage of cheaper supplies when you have the chance. The final judgement on how much you should carry is always likely to be something of a balancing act. For the most extreme trip (Sahara – only when possible) we would recommend 1,000km (620 miles) capacity. Work out your fuel consumption to determine your desired capacity.

Keep things as simple as possible. The cheapest and simplest option is to take metal jerrycans. The more complex the system, the more things can go wrong. African roads will constantly cause things to shake loose, leak and wear away. Fuel pipes are notorious for shaving and becoming holed, and it's very difficult to find such leaks. Unless you are going into remote desert, four will probably suffice, unless your vehicle has a high fuel consumption.

If you really want to avoid filling the vehicle with jerrycans, then you may consider fitting extra tanks, particularly for models with higher fuel consumption. Land Rovers can be modified to add an extra tank, but you will need to have either an electric pump to transfer the fuel from the extra tank to the main one, or have a two-way fuel valve. Both options add to the list of things that can go wrong.

Customised tanks with larger capacities for both fuel and water are also available and can be fitted to most vehicles. Plan to carry as much fuel as possible, but always bear in mind weight restrictions. Fuel and water, two essential items, are incredibly heavy. There is little point in being well prepared if you destroy your suspension or even break your chassis in the process.

Water Make sure you carry enough. The cheapest option is to take good-quality plastic jerrycans that also enable you to see how much water is left. You should aim to carry at least 40–50 litres, preferably in two or three containers in case one of them leaks. Keep one untreated water can for boiling and cooking, one for treated cleaner water and keep some extra plastic bottled water for drinking as well. Ensure all jerrycans stored inside are held securely in place. These containers can be worked into your general interior plan – of course there is always something in the way inside; that's life.

A built-in water tank can be more convenient than a vehicle full of jerrycans. However, filling the tank can sometimes be quite awkward. You will need a hose where taps are inconveniently located. Tanks need to be drained periodically, as sludge can build up and, with it, contamination. Keep it simple. Jerrycans can be stored between inside lockers below a sleeping platform, keeping them secured. Don't put them on the roof rack when full or you will overload it. See *Suggestions for vehicle layout* diagrams, opposite and on page 72.

Jerrycans You *must* use metal ones for fuel. **Never** have petrol in jerrycans on the roof; it spells double trouble, as the sun will soon make it hot and explosively dangerous. Avoid storing water in jerrycans that were previously used for fuel – the taste never disappears. The number you take will depend on fuel consumption, tank capacity, route, load and how much you plan to take advantage of cheaper fuel supplies when you find them. For water, your route is the most important factor. Long stretches in the open desert will mean you need to carry substantially more.

Oils You are likely to get through more oil than in normal conditions. Engine oil is generally available, but some specialised gear oils, brake and clutch fluid are more difficult to locate. You will find everything you need in the bigger cities like Accra or Nairobi, but don't count on it elsewhere. We carried 25 litres of engine oil, in different containers, which gave us two oil changes, ie: one emergency change (broken sump) and one regular change. Try to buy internationally recognised brands of oil, as some local supplies may be substandard.

Storage Careful planning of your storage facilities can make all the difference between ease of access, general comfort or a permanent nightmare. Try to achieve a closely packed but accessible arrangement. Avoid having anything loose that can be thrown about in the back. Fitted cupboards and storage space can be built by customising companies or you can do the job yourself. Remember the whole thing can easily get shaken to bits unless it has been well made.

You need to be able to pull things out quickly, find what you are looking for and repack into the same space you started with. This process is generally a lot harder than it sounds. Ideally split your storage space into compartments and, within this, into a series of rigid sections or boxes.

Over the years we have found that a locker system works quite well. You can build in sections for spare parts, food supplies, oils, grease, etc, spare battery, and even valuables. Try to keep your toolbox safe but accessible – you'll need it daily for maintenance checks. To make simple lockers you need only a drill, saw and energy, or get the plywood cut by your friendly wood merchant. Before you start, though,

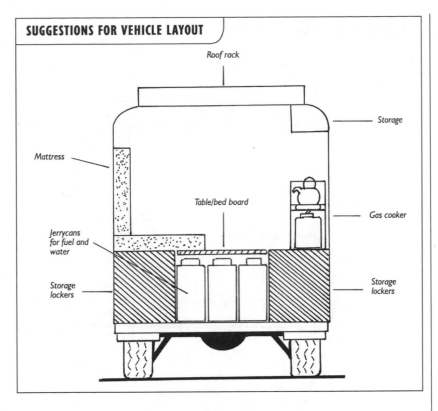

SUGGESTIONS FOR VEHICLE LAYOUT

Roof rack

Storage

Mattress

Table/bed board

Gas cooker

Jerrycans
for fuel and
water

Storage
lockers

Storage
lockers

consider the width and size of any jerrycans. You will need to work out a basic design first and calculate the sizes. It should be possible to keep the jerrycans in place between the lockers. Further wooden sheets can be cut to fit between the two lockers to separate fuel and water cans if necessary. It can be fun devising such units.

Using 11mm plywood cut and bolted together with metal angle pieces from a hardware store, you can make a series of compartmentalised lockers. These can have hinged lids attached. Use spring washers on all bolts or they will quickly shake loose. Make two long lockers and fit them in each side of the rear part of the vehicle. The jerrycans need to have good seals, as they may need to be stored lying down. Two or three central plywood sheets can then be put horizontally between the two lockers and above the cans. One might be a table and all together can provide a platform on which to sleep.

If you don't have the time or inclination to do the above, then use rigid plastic storage boxes, or even light metal cases. Elastic bungee cords and canvas or webbing belts are useful for lashing things down. Anything removable on your roof rack should be secured with padlocks. Whatever system you adopt, something that you need will always be at the bottom or in 'the bloody locker'!

Cooking Always ensure that the cooker and gas cylinder are well secured, and turned off when leaving the vehicle for long periods of time or while driving. Refrigerators should also be secured tightly with straps. You should have a **fire extinguisher** with you. It is not only compulsory in many countries, but might be needed at some point. Make sure that it works properly.

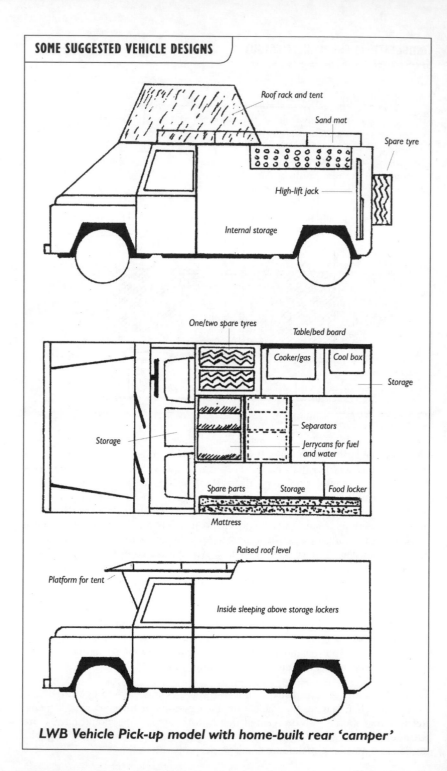

SOME SUGGESTED VEHICLE DESIGNS

Roof rack and tent

Sand mat

Spare tyre

High-lift jack

Internal storage

One/two spare tyres

Table/bed board

Cooker/gas

Cool box

Storage

Storage

Separators

Jerrycans for fuel and water

Spare parts

Storage

Food locker

Mattress

Raised roof level

Platform for tent

Inside sleeping above storage lockers

LWB Vehicle Pick-up model with home-built rear 'camper'

Comfort

Seat covers The choice of seat covers depends on the vehicle. Plastic will be very uncomfortable in the hot sun. Towelling is ideal. With removable covers you have the added advantage of their being washable. Even if you have fabric-covered seats already, you will appreciate washable covers – you will pick up more dust and grime than you could believe possible! A set of beaded seat covers might ease your back over long drives and help prevent soreness in extreme heat.

Steering-wheel cover Standard black plastic steering wheels can become extremely hot in direct sunlight and your hands can easily slip. It is advisable to fit some type of non-slip cover before you leave.

Canopy An optional canopy may keep you dry during the wet season, offer shade and a certain amount of privacy. Make up your own canopy with strong canvas or vinyl-based material, or have one fitted to your vehicle.

Music/radio You may not be able to hear anything over the engine and road noise, but at least when you stop you can relax to your favourite tunes. It's a good idea to keep the unit out of sight and also away from the direct heat. We also recommend a short wave radio, to tune in to the BBC or similar and keep up-to-date with what is going on around you or further down the line.

VEHICLE EQUIPMENT

Deciding what to take and what to leave behind can be difficult. Ask yourself if you really need it. When your springs sag or break, you'll regret every kilo of unnecessary weight. With four wheels you will be nothing like as restricted as with a motorbike or bicycle in terms of what you can carry.

RECOVERY GEAR You will need equipment to extract the vehicle from mud and sand or rescue another vehicle.

Hydraulic jack You will need a hydraulic jack for punctures, changing springs or lifting the engine to change engine mountings, for example. Make sure you have an assortment of flat and chunky wooden blocks for jacking. Old-style hydraulic jacks are hard to find now, because trolley jacks are the latest preference. These are too bulky and not very good on sand and mud. Hydraulic jacks, made in the Far East, can be bought in many places in Africa, but you might need one before you get there.

High-lift jack The versatile high-lift jack could be one of the most useful tools that you will carry with you to remoter areas. The classic high-lift jack is the red American-made one, which is simple and reliable. Other makes in the market are now just as good. Remember to use wooden blocks or some sort of base when jacking the vehicle up. Also ensure that your vehicle is in gear and that the handbrake is on. Older vehicles often have heavy-duty bumpers that make good jacking points, but you will find that a jacking point

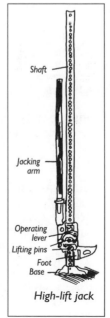

Shaft

Jacking arm

Operating lever

Lifting pins

Foot

Base

High-lift jack

may need to be fitted to your vehicle if you have a newer model. If you store the jack outside, ensure regular cleaning, as dust can get trapped in the oil. Cover the jack with canvas for further protection. See also *High-lift jack* in *Chapter 6*, page 147.

Sand ladders (sand mats) With luck and careful driving, you may not need sand ladders at all, but it would be crazy to leave home without them. As well as getting you out of soft sand, they can have other uses, for example on broken bridges and, with extra support, for bridging some holes. Various types are available, including some made from lightweight alloys that are expensive but easier to use. Perforated steel sand ladders are just as good, although heavier.

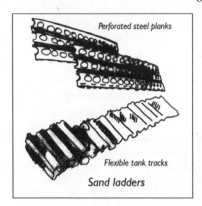

Perforated steel planks

Flexible tank tracks

Sand ladders

The flexible variety that look like tank tracking do not have to be laid flat like sand mats, so you can save yourself some digging. DIY fans with welding equipment can make ladders from square or round metal tubing. These can be just as effective and are much cheaper. See also *Sand ladders* in *Chapter 6*, page 147.

Electronic or manual winches Winches are of limited use and possibly not worth the expense or extra weight. In practically every situation it is easier to be towed out of trouble. A winch may give you the confidence to explore further off the beaten track but if you plan to be that adventurous, it would be wiser to team up with at least one other vehicle anyway. As a compromise, consider getting a good hand winch; Tirfor has been suggested. Another simple winching technique makes use of a high-lift jack. If this is chained to the vehicle at one end and to a winching point, such as a tree trunk, at the other, you can slowly pull the vehicle out of trouble. Unfortunately you can only winch the length of the jack (1m/3ft) at a time. If you are using a tree as an anchor, use canvas, or the purpose-made anchor straps to protect the tree. In general, a winch is not your highest priority. See also *Winching* in *Chapter 6*, page 148.

Towing points Ensure you have adequate, easily accessible towing points on your vehicle, usually mounted below the vehicle at the back and front.

Towing straps/short cable Kinetic straps are slightly elastic, flat towing straps, known as snatch straps. A popular brand is Tuggum. These are specifically designed for pulling other vehicles out of a difficult situation. Snatch straps have a limited life of about 20 tugs as the line becomes static. A short cable of sufficient strength can also be used with care. Carry at least two towing straps of either type, and have sufficient **shackles** to connect them.

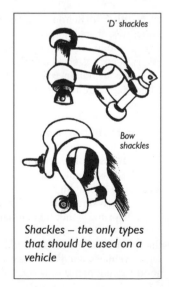

'D' shackles

Bow shackles

Shackles – the only types that should be used on a vehicle

Shovels A small shovel may be useful as a companion to the sand ladders. Failing to scoop out sand or dig out mud from around your tyres will result in more strain. Sand can be cleared by hand, whereas clearing mud manually may be fun for five minutes but not for hours.

For sand, a shovel with a concave blade is better. In mud, a flatter angle is better. Compromise, but take only one. A shovel can be used for rubbish; always burn or bury anything you are planning to leave behind. Be careful not to bury jagged cans or broken glass in game parks where animals may dig up your rubbish and injure themselves. Also be aware that locals can use empty cans for water storage if they are cleanly cut with a tin opener. A garden trowel is useful for toilet trips.

SLEEPING GEAR You will need a mattress, pillows, duvet or sleeping bag and sheets. A covered duvet or quilt is much more comfortable than a sleeping bag, which over long periods can feel restricted, and proper pillows will make you feel much more at home. If you have limited space, use a roll-up mattress, fold-up pillow and a sleeping bag. A washable, three-season bag should be adequate, but some parts of Africa can be very cold. For the cover of your mattress and pillows, use some thick cotton material. You can watch the grime accumulate over the weeks! See also *Hammock*, page 81.

Mosquito nets A mosquito net is not an optional item; it could be a lifesaver. Whatever type of sleeping arrangement you have, it is very important that you equip your tent, rooftop tent or sleeping space inside the vehicle with a net. Even if you opt for local accommodation, it is advisable to carry your own mosquito net. Some places in Africa do provide them, but they are not always in the best condition. Nets can be bought in specialist shops. It is not always easy to find them abroad and/or the choice is limited.

Lighting Fluorescent strip lighting is bright, convenient and doesn't put too much strain on the battery. Festoon bulb lights also use little power, but are less bright. Bring some electrical wire in case you need to adapt things, or have a mobile lighting strip as well as normal internal lights. Gaz lights are not a good idea, as the canisters are almost impossible to find. Whatever you do, remember to bring a torch with spare bulbs and batteries.

Map light Standard map lights that can be attached to the cigarette lighter are available for reading maps at night. A torch would do as well, or a mobile phone with a light. Avoid night driving unless absolutely essential. Never plan to do so!

WASHING GEAR
Portable shower Not really essential, although a pleasant luxury. Various devices are available: a plastic bottle, pump-action shower which holds enough water for a seven-minute shower using heated water from the stove is one. Another is a solar-heated shower, which heats four litres in about an hour; or a simple plastic tub with holes and filled with hot water from the kettle or a plastic bucket. Of course, unless you are showering fully clothed, you risk providing amusement for the locals or causing some offence; be discreet.

Portable washing machine (ie: a bucket!) Use a bucket with a lid as a portable washing machine. Before driving off, fill the bucket with washing detergent, water and dirty clothes and strap it firmly in the vehicle. Remember to put the lid on

Vehicle Selection and Preparation   **VEHICLE EQUIPMENT**

3

and make sure it fits securely. The motion of the vehicle will act as a washing machine, leaving you only to rinse and hang up the clothes once you've reached your destination. Take a washing line and clothes pegs. A plastic bucket will also have many other uses (like draining the oil or radiator too, but don't tell your better half!).

OTHER GEAR

Table and chairs These might seem like a luxury, but on a long trip having folding chairs and a table is a very good idea. Canvas-covered chairs have a fairly long life and can be washed regularly.

Compass and/or Global Positioning System (GPS)
Many travellers today use GPS as a navigational aid. GPS is essential and fun if you are going into really isolated areas like the Sahara, and you can set your co-ordinates accordingly. Most guidebooks specifically relevant to the Sahara and southern Africa have recorded GPS co-ordinates for the area.

It is best to hide your GPS when crossing borders. It could be misconstrued as a transmitter and get you into trouble with the security forces. Remember that the electrics will throw off a normal compass, so if you have a hand-held type, stop and walk a few paces away for an accurate reading. Also remember that, without a good map, a GPS or compass is often useless.

Mobile phone With ever more sophisticated mobile phone systems, most travellers will have a normal mobile phone, smart phone or even a satellite phone. See www.thuraya.com and all the mobile phone operators' websites for details of coverage.

OTHER ESSENTIAL EQUIPMENT

Axe or machete Very useful for chopping wood and hacking through vegetation.

Warning triangles/jackets In many African countries it is compulsory to carry two warning triangles. Some European countries now require a fluorescent jacket for each passenger in the vehicle.

Foot or electric tyre pump This is an essential item when repairing tyres on the side of the road, or pumping up an airbed. Try using a foot pump in the heat of the African day and you will wish you had purchased a cheap electric pump. They have crocodile clips to attach to your battery. Extra wire may be required with some models.

Tyre repair kit Getting normal tube patches is increasingly difficult in Europe, but once in Africa patches or something usable can be found. Chris Scott suggests in his excellent book *Sahara Overland* (see *Appendix 5*, page 364) taking a bicycle tube to assist when pumping up tubeless tyres in the desert after a puncture. It is used to fill the gap between the tyre and rim before a seal is made under pressure. It should be the same size as the tyre rim.

Pressure gauge A good pressure gauge is essential and particularly useful in the desert, where you will be deflating and re-inflating tyres continually.

Assorted wooden blocks As mentioned above, these are essential to place under a jack in soft sand or mud.

FOOD AND COOKING
Water and water purification methods As discussed under *Storage* in this chapter, page 70, your best bet for carrying water is in 20-litre jerrycans. One of these should be accessible at all times to be easily filled with water. Some plastic containers have a tap, but this may leak. Any major outdoor equipment retailer can supply them. Traditional nomads carry water in goatskin sacks called *guerbas*. These keep the water remarkably cool, as the skin allows for slow evaporation.

In the wilder regions, you may have to obtain water from local wells. You should be careful not to contaminate them. Wells in places like Niger are often the only source of water and it can be very pure. Getting such water up is an art form in itself. It may sound easy, but have you ever tried throwing an empty bucket 50ft down a well so that it lands upside down? You will certainly create some amusement for the nomads, who will most probably give you a lesson in the art of extracting well water. Wells in the Sahel are a pivotal point for the community and are places of social interaction for all: local villagers, nomads, long-horned cows, goats and occasional tourists. Some wells are astonishingly deep. The water is raised in containers attached to exceedingly long ropes and often hauled by recalcitrant camels.

Unless you are certain the water is safe, you will need to purify it. The simplest, cheapest and safest option is to boil it. Another popular option is Chloromyn-T. You need only an amount equal to the tip of a matchstick to purify 25 litres. Allow it to work for one or two hours, until the Chloromyn-T has settled. Micropur, Puritabs and iodine are other purification methods. Iodine is an effective purifier but shouldn't be used on a long-term basis, as your body absorbs it (see *Health* in *Chapter 5*). Some people use 'filter socks', but no method completely guarantees the killing of all evils that may lurk in the water.

Ideally, you should take a water filter with you, particularly if you are going to be travelling in more remote areas. Cyclists should definitely have one. There are many filters on the market. Top of the range are the Katadyne filters used by the Red Cross throughout Africa; though excellent, they are expensive. Mountain Safety Research (MSR) also make a range of filters. The UK-based company First Ascent (*www. firstascent.co.uk*) supply filters, as does Outward Ventures (*www.outward.co.za*) in South Africa.

Refrigeration Refrigerators for vehicles run on either gas or electricity, 12V DC or 240V AC; some refrigerators are built to run on all three. If you have the space, a small fridge might be one of the first luxuries to take. Whether the added cost and space it takes are justified for the cold drinks it provides is a matter of debate. It is surprising how cold some things can keep when buried in the depths of a good locker after a cool night.

Ordinary camping shops can be a good source. The Engel fridge has been recommended as an efficient but expensive option. The simpler option is to have an insulation box. We have managed like this every time; cold drinks can be found in many places along the way. Keeping margarine and yoghurt is a little more difficult. The traditional bush method of wet towels draped over boxes and even bottles is very effective at keeping things cool.

Cooking equipment When it comes to cooking, your choice of fuel and equipment depends on how long you intend to be on the road.

Gas stoves Gas stoves are the easiest, cleanest and most reliable option. We have always used Camping Gaz, but it is not a complete answer. The bottles are quite small, so we have had to carry at least four. A Camping Gaz (size 907) bottle can be made to last about three to four weeks with very careful usage and easy-to-cook food supplies. We have always used a standard Camping Gaz cooker mounted inside a riveted, aluminium box structure that offers windbreaks around three sides. Bringing vegetables, etc to the boil and then leaving them to cook in the hot water will save your valuable fuel, whichever you choose.

Many local families cook with gas (particularly in the Sahara) and most gas stoves have a choice of regulators to cover a range of gas fuels. The larger gas bottles can be filled in some of the larger towns. Perhaps taking two Camping Gaz bottles and later buying a larger refillable butane bottle in Africa might be better. On a very long trip, using a purely gas system might have its limitations, but its simplicity is a prime factor. It invariably comes down to personal choice and the route chosen in the end.

Petrol stoves The wide variety of camping stoves available means you can exercise a fair degree of choice, though bikers and cyclists tend to opt for small, lightweight petrol stoves or burners. These can be fussy to light but are fairly reliable, though even expensive models can let you down. Several people have recommended Coleman petrol stoves (one, two or three burners) as very reliable, though they are rather bulky and so not suitable for bikers or cyclists.

Disadvantages of petrol stoves are the blackening of pots (though the soot does rub off much more easily if you smear the outside of your pans liberally with soap or washing-up liquid before you cook) and smoking when you first light them.

Kerosene stoves The Chinese-made kerosene wick stoves can be found almost everywhere in Africa. There is virtually nothing that can go wrong with them, and the small amount of fuel they burn means you can easily carry enough to last until the next source of kerosene. They can be a bit messy to operate.

Open fires Although open fires are harder to control for cooking, they are an instant focus when camping, particularly when it gets cold at night. Take a small fire grille, preferably self-supporting. Otherwise you can do it 'nomad-style' with a few strategically placed rocks. Nomads use very little wood by using the burnt ends of small branches or the charcoal remnants. It's a bit slow, though. And remember that rocks aren't available everywhere!

Potatoes and other vegetables, wrapped in foil with a few herbs or spices for extra flavour, can be roasted in no time on an open fire. If you do build a fire, be sensible in dry areas where sparks may set grass or scrub alight. And never cut green wood for a fire, particularly in the desert and Sahel areas or game parks. Africa has enough deforestation problems of its own without your adding to them. If your transport allows you to carry firewood as you go, you can dry it out by lashing it to the roof rack of your vehicle.

Remember from a security point of view that an open fire may be visible for miles.

Matches/lighter Matches are available almost everywhere, but it is a good idea to carry a spare box. A couple of lighters are advisable too.

Cooking utensils Like everything else, keep these to a minimum and adapt what you have for a whole range of purposes; cooking on the road is all about using your imagination. We use two small stainless-steel cooking pots, which fit inside each other and have flat lids, plus a small non-stick frying pan and kettle.

Other favourites are pressure cookers and woks. It's a matter of space, personal expectations and dietary requirements. If you are in a reasonably large group, bring cast-iron pots, which can be left sitting on an open fire to stew away for hours.

A small Thermos flask is a good idea for easy hot drinks on the way or at borders. Other items needed are a decent sharp knife, a wooden spoon, something to strain boiled pasta or vegetables (unless you have a saucepan and lid that are suitable), a tin opener, a bottle opener, Swiss army knife or Leatherman's knife, vegetable peeler, bread knife and a small chopping board.

Go for plastic plates and bowls, with plastic or melamine mugs for tea and coffee, as enamel gets frustratingly hot. Plates are best with raised edges; bowls are easier to eat from without a table and safer for runny dishes. Take a plastic box for the cutlery; teaspoons love inaccessible corners in a vehicle. And don't lose the lighter! Always keep a spare somewhere else.

Food to take It is surprising how your taste buds change in Africa. That salad cream or ketchup you never finish at home might suddenly be the missing ingredient you are craving. It's a good idea to assemble a store of basics and emergency supplies before you go. As a rough guide, the following food items are mostly available on the road: bottled water, bread, bananas, tomatoes, carrots, garlic, tinned fish, potatoes, eggs, rice, pasta, couscous, cooking oil, spices and dodgy meat as well as good fresh meat. Items like margarine, yoghurt, other fruits and vegetables can be found, depending on location and climatic zone. Across north Africa, some towns have reasonable supermarkets with a limited choice. In west Africa you will find French supermarkets in all the capitals; these have a good but expensive selection. Nairobi has large supermarkets, while further south things are mostly just as good in the capitals and larger cities. You won't find tinned curries, assorted tinned meats, puddings and dehydrated meals for emergency rations.

Good basic supplies to take with you include plenty of salt for the extra fluid loss; sugar (even if you do not normally use it – sweet tea is great if you are ill and cannot face food); herbs and spices to liven up vegetables; tea and coffee. Take some cereals and muesli for an easy breakfast when bread is not available. Some boil-in-the-bag rice, instant mash and pasta are easy and quick to cook. Tomato purée in tubes, stock cubes, oil in plastic screw-top bottles, cornflour for thickening and dried milk are always useful. Parmesan cheese is a wonderful addition to basic pastas.

Always have a week's supply of emergency rations, as you never know if you are going to be unavoidably delayed along the way and not find any food to buy. Good standby meals are instant potato, dried vegetables/fruit, tinned tuna, tins of meat, peas or beans, long-life cakes, peanut butter, Marmite (said to keep the mosquitoes

COOKING WITH ONE BURNER?

Even if you only have one burner, you don't need to restrict yourself to one-pot meals. Bring your rice or pasta to the boil for a few minutes, then leave to continue cooking in its own heat. You can then make up a basic vegetable sauce, or heat a tin of chicken curry. If you are cooking with meat, cook that first and leave it to stew for however long is necessary. Always bring your food back to the boil and check it is thoroughly cooked before eating. If you find yourself travelling in convoy, meeting up with other travellers in campsites or free camping, you can pool resources and end up with some really adventurous meals.

at bay), Vegemite (said to keep the Brits at bay), jam and/or marmalade, instant desserts, etc. The list goes on: mustard, dried mushrooms or onions to liven up pasta or rice dishes, lemon juice in plastic bottles, custard, biscuits or crackers. Boiled sweets are good for when you need a burst of energy, and Kendal Mint Cake when you are flagging (a high-glucose bar that goes into the supplies of every major expedition). An indispensable item on all our expeditions has been a homemade Christmas cake, always delicious at any time of year!

Occasionally you will be unable to cook anything hot because of the weather or some other circumstances. Then you will feel a lot better for having some provisions that can be turned into a cold meal. For example, a refreshing salad can be made from a tin of tuna in oil, with beans in lemon juice and a freshly chopped onion or tomato.

With a vehicle you can afford to carry quite a number of tins, some as standby. Sadly, your chocolate won't go far. Take the odd luxury item, such as a bottle of wine, boiled sweets, Christmas pudding and other goodies, specifically for those arduous days when you need to spoil yourself. You can always survive on bread and, generally, bananas. And don't forget some small plastic bottles of mayonnaise, ketchup and Branston pickle. (Be aware that they will go off if kept open but unrefrigerated for a long time in the heat.)

Storing food We kept our food reserves in a locker, but any vermin and bug-proof containers would do. Food storage boxes need to be kept reasonably clean. Choose storage containers with care. Square ones pack better. Rough conditions will shake things around so much that jars will literally unscrew themselves, lids will pop off, and tubes of tomato purée will puncture. You can minimise these nuisances by having the right containers in the first place. Pack loose spaces with towels and toilet rolls so that things do not jump around.

Plastic jars and bottles with deep screw tops are best used for storing things like sugar, tea and coffee. Tupperware-style boxes should have very tight seals. Be sure to keep cooking oil in a container with a screw top! You are only likely to forget this once! An open cardboard box is a good idea for fresh vegetables, or tie them up in a cloth local-style to keep them as dry as you can.

Washing up A plastic bowl is fine. Washing-up liquid, a cloth and a scourer are essential. Some travellers wash their dishes in Milton (a gentle disinfectant). Giving all your dishes, cutlery and pots a good clean when hot water becomes available should be sufficient to keep the germs at bay. If you are struggling to clean that burned-on mess at the bottom of the pan, use sand or gritty mud – the best scourers you could ever find.

A few tea towels are useful, but they do need frequent washing. Some travellers either leave their dishes to dry in the sun or flap them vigorously to dry them off. You will see a lot of overland tours doing this, to the amusement of onlookers.

PERSONAL ITEMS

Clothes Take as few clothes as possible; you will not need much once you are on the road. You'll need warm clothing for nights in the desert and in the highlands; something to keep the rain off is also useful. Otherwise, lightweight cotton is the general rule, along with certain modern technical fabrics that dry quickly and don't make you sweat.

You should also be aware of local dress customs. In Islamic countries women in particular should take care; even the tops of your arms can be regarded as offensive. Men also should wear long trousers and long-sleeved shirts. Look at what local people are wearing. Their reactions will soon let you know if you have crossed acceptable levels of modesty.

Taking one 'smart' item of clothing helps when having to deal with a recalcitrant embassy or border crossing. Besides, you never know whom you might meet on the way! If you meet us, we will not be dressed in black tie and evening dress.

Shortwave radio A shortwave radio with plenty of bands is great for picking up news from home and information about conditions in the countries you may be visiting. We once sat alone in the silent vastness of the Sudanese desert listening to news about the conflict in Darfur.

Camera Take spare batteries in case you are far away from electricity and recharging facilities.

Fun and games A pack of cards or backgammon is useful for those lonely nights in the middle of nowhere. The most popular game throughout Africa, played on street corners, is a kind of backgammon, most commonly known as *woaley*. It changes its name and rules slightly from country to country. It's called *awalé* in Ivory Coast, *ayo* in Nigeria, *aju* in Togo and Benin, *ouri* in Senegal and *aware* in Ghana.

Pocket calculator Useful for working out fuel consumption and exchange rates. These days you're sure to have one on your phone too.

Hammock This is a non-essential item, but one that people on long trips recommend. After a hard day's driving, if you are intending to stay a few days, there's nothing like stringing up the hammock and relaxing under the African sun.

Gifts It is quite amazing just how important a small supply of inexpensive gifts can be, particularly for children who are desperate to help you fill your jerrycans at wells, guard your vehicle or give directions. On the other hand, you should never hand out gifts just for the sake of it. Constant handouts can mean that the local economy comes to depend on them, and later travellers will suffer because the same will be expected of them.

There will, however, be occasions when people have greatly helped you. Generosity can be thanked with a simple gift. Pens and postcards of your home country are always welcomed. Empty containers of any kind that can be used to carry water are highly sought after in many areas. You don't need to bring everything with you from home – you can top up your supplies at local markets, thereby helping the local economy, too.

Also see *Travelling positively* in *Chapter 8*, page 196.

Shewee What more can wee say? A unique product specially designed for women only, for use in awkward places. See www.shewee.com for more information.

SPARES AND TOOLS

Working on your vehicle before you leave will give you some idea of what you are likely to need. Check through your workshop manual or talk to an off-road enthusiast to find out if you are missing any essential spares or tools. In many cases you will be able to limp along to the next big town where spares are available. In general, labour is cheap but parts are expensive. It pays to be as well equipped as possible.

Some places in Africa are better than others for picking up spares. The high cost of imported parts means old spares may be the only viable option. Even official dealers for your vehicle may not have what you need, although they will generally direct you to the best secondhand source. The hammering all vehicles take on African roads means that in most sizeable towns something can be found to fix the job.

Working for various overland companies over many years with often 'knackered' trucks has shown us just how many things can go wrong. Perhaps our list of spare parts reflects this expectation and is more comprehensive than most. You make your own choices.

SPARE PARTS Deciding what spares to take is a bit of a guessing game. It's Murphy's Law: it's always the part you didn't include that fails. Too many heavy parts are likely to damage your suspension, but not taking sensible items isn't very wise either. Take more lightweight spares than you think you will need, like gaskets, oil seals or bearings. Some can then be sold or exchanged for heavier parts if necessary.

What you include depends on the make, model and age of your vehicle, as well as the amount of space available. The actual list will also depend on the amount of preparation you have undertaken on the basic vehicle. Did you have a reconditioned injector pump or a new starter? What spares may be available locally?

You should get advice from a good mechanic, who may know of typical problems regarding the make and model of your vehicle. Always remember to take all your workshop manuals with you. We have assumed you have a diesel engine. Ideally have the engine, gearboxes and clutch all reconditioned; that is, unless you are on a very tight budget and not too concerned about what happens to your vehicle afterwards. The front and rear axle differential units should be in good order.

It's best to have the following parts new or reconditioned: radiator, brake and clutch master cylinders, clutch slave cylinders, brake wheel cylinders, starter, alternator, water pump and brake hoses. Also suspension rubbers, engine mountings, brake pads and fuel lift pump. The injectors and injector pump must be reconditioned. Injector pumps rarely go wrong if in good condition, but if they do it's a rather serious matter. Taking a spare would be a good idea if you can find an old version that works, but it is expensive. In any case all used parts should be kept as spares.

Take items that you will have to replace as part of a service: oil filters, fuel filters and air filters, unless your vehicle has an oil bath air system. Old-fashioned oil baths are very good in dust and sand and there is no need to carry bulky filters, but most newer models don't have these. Take as many of these various filters as you can fit in: one for every 3,000–4,000 miles, as some local units may not be up to standard. You will have to change these more often than recommended by the manufacturers. How often you change them partly depends on the terrain, dust, sand and temperature, as well as the quality of your oil. As a bare minimum, carry three of each. Air filters can be cleaned out and re-used at a pinch.

Don't forget all the little extras that save the day like radiator sealer, Araldite glue, plastic metal glue, bits of metal, string, duct tape, fuses and countless other items.

The following is a list of suggested spares, which should be tailored to your requirements. An asterisk denotes a part for a petrol engine.

Consumable spares
- 3 oil filters
- 4 fuel filters
- 2 or 3 air filters
- oil (enough for two changes)

- 5 litres of gearbox/differential oil (check whether the same oil is used in each)
- grease
- 1 or 2 litres of brake and clutch fluid oil
- 1 litre of radiator coolant (you can use water)

General spares
- heater plugs/spark plugs*
- 1 diesel injector
- set of engine gaskets
- set of all oil seals (wheels, gearbox, engine, differential)
- set of wheel bearings
- set of engine mountings
- set of radiator hoses plus other hoses
- accelerator cable
- 2 fan belts
- set of brake pads
- brake master cylinder rubbers/kit
- clutch master and slave cylinder rubbers/kit
- wheel cylinder rubbers/kit (or kit for disc brakes)
- water pump
- lift pump
- suspension rubbers and bushes
- condenser*
- distributor cap*
- contact breaker points*
- spare fuel cap
- spare radiator cap
- U bolts/centre bolts for leaf springs
- main leaf springs (coil springs rarely break with careful driving)
- track rod ends
- clutch plate
- wheel nuts
- water temperature sensor unit
- sump/gearbox drain plugs (the silly things can fall into the sand – not guilty!)
- propshaft UJ
- flexible brake hose
- alternator (better a complete unit or at least the brushes)
- fuses
- light bulbs
- plastic fuel line and connectors

Other optional parts
- starter (for remoter areas, Sahara and Congo)
- fan (for seriously remote areas or when constantly fording rivers)
- injector pipes
- injector pump (remoter areas, Sahara and Congo)
- injector pump solenoid if applicable (remoter areas, Sahara and Congo)

Useful bits and pieces
- funnel (make sure it fits the filler of your fuel tank and has a gauze filter)
- electrical tape

- electrical wires
- masking/duct tape
- assortment of wire
- assortment of nuts, bolts and washers
- 2m of fuel hose (long enough to be used as a siphon)
- flexible 'bathroom' sealant for leaky bodywork
- instant gasket paste
- plastic padding/instant fibreglass
- exhaust repair putty
- gasket paper
- WD40 or Q20
- radiator sealant
- towing eye/cable
- assorted small sheet metal, short drainpiping, square tubing, etc
- assorted bits of rubber, inner tube
- old rags – lots and lots
- self-tapping screws
- cable ties in various sizes
- contact adhesive/Evo-stik
- Araldite and/or plastic metal epoxy glue
- superglue
- old bicycle/car inner tube
- wire or bicycle spokes
- thin gardening wire
- long piece of chain or steel cable
- small length of lighter chain
- plastic from oil tubs or similar containers
- pieces of sheet metal/aluminium sheet
- small pieces of plywood
- metal strips/old pipe/square tubing
- lots of assorted Jubilee clips/clamps
- various lengths of electrical wire
- assorted small springs (throttle, clutch, etc)
- various lengths of nylon rope/string/small rope
- ladies' nylon tights (not for evening attire!), for temporary filters or fan belt (you should be carrying a couple of spare fan belts anyway)
- assorted driver relaxants, tea, chair, hammock, etc, etc!

TOOLS Take a comprehensive set of tools. Requirements vary from vehicle to vehicle and many jobs need 'special service tools'. However, there are general tools that will cover most jobs and, with a bit of lateral thinking, can be used in place of special service tools.

- a good set of spanners (imperial or metric as required by your vehicle)
- a good set of sockets with a power bar and ratchet
- extra large sockets (check sizes needed)
- assortment of screwdrivers
- adjustable spanner
- mole wrench (large and small)
- pipe wrench (Stillson and adjustable-size versions)
- grease gun

- metal and rubber hammers
- torque wrench (essential for all engines)
- pliers (various)
- circlip removers
- multi-size puller
- jump leads for battery
- set of feeler gauges
- hacksaw and spare blades
- multi-meter electrical tester
- flat metal file
- coarse flat file
- small round file
- hand drill and bits (9V cordless drills can be connected directly to your battery)
- tyre levers
- tyre valve tool/valve extractor
- set of Allen keys
- centre punch/assorted punches and metal drifts
- wet and dry sandpaper
- length of pipe (to extend your power bar for stubborn nuts)
- arc welding rods – a few
- G clamp/small vice to attach to bumper
- magnetic retrieving tool – for when you drop a nut that gets trapped
- hydraulic jack

These lists are not exhaustive; again space, weight and money determine which extras to take.

SUPPLIERS AND USEFUL CONTACTS

VEHICLE MANUALS A very good source of information specific to your chosen vehicle is the series of manuals/technical books produced by Haynes (*www.haynes.co.uk*). They cover most vehicles for all the technical data that the manufacturers will not divulge these days.

VEHICLE SELECTION Various motor magazines can be found at major newsagents, with information on used and new vehicles to sell or buy. Also look in local newspapers. Check the various Land Rover/Toyota magazines for a full list of dealers and suppliers.

VEHICLE PREPARATION
UK
Ashcroft Transmissions e info@ashcroft-transmissions.co.uk. For reconditioned gearboxes in the UK.
Black Diamond Warrington Transmission Centre Ltd www.blackdiamond-ltd.co.uk. One of the largest independent re-manufacturers of gearboxes, differentials & axles.
Brownchurch Ltd www.brownchurch.co.uk. The largest supplier of rooftop tents in the UK.
Chichester 4x4 www.chichester4x4.co.uk

Essential Overland Preparation www.allisport.com
Footloose 4X4 www.footloose4X4.com
Formula 4X4 Ltd e info@formula4x4.com; www.formula4x4.com
Harwoods www.harwoods.uk.com
LAS Garage (North Wales) www.lasgarage.co.uk
Mantec Services www.mantec.co.uk. Their latest product is 'Tufflift' for spare wheels.
Superwinch www.superwinch.com

Westfield 4x4 www.west-4x4.demon.co.uk.
Unimog agent.

South Africa
Avnic Trading www.avnic.co.za or www.garmin.
co.za. Suppliers of Garmin products.

OFF-ROAD DRIVING COURSE
UK
Ian Wright Off-Road Driving Centre West
Malling, Kent; www.thewrightevent.co.uk

OTHER SOURCES
Africa Travel Centre London; ☏020 7387
1211/0845 450 1528; www.africatravel.co.uk

Outdoor Warehouse www.outdoorwarehouse.
co.za. Specialists in outdoor equipment in
Johannesburg, Pretoria, Durban & Cape Town
Safari Centre www.safaricentre.co.za. The
longest established 4x4 outfitter in South Africa.
Also has driving courses.

Expedition Advisory Centre Royal
Geographical Society, London; ☏020 7591 3000;
www.rgs.org
Nomad London; www.nomadtravel.co.uk

MOTORBIKE SELECTION

*David Lambeth (Rally & Overland ☏ 01205 871945; e bigbluecoach@hotmail.com; www.
davidlambeth.co.uk; see also advert on page 142) and Alex Marr*

For those prepared to sacrifice comfort and space, travelling by motorbike offers
a very exciting alternative. Although frequently physically demanding, most bikes
also give the traveller unparalleled freedom to explore wild Africa. A bike can cope
in a number of situations that a 4x4 cannot. Whether crossing rivers by canoe,
negotiating narrow, rocky climbs or simply weaving a line along a badly pot-holed
road, two wheels beats four nearly every time.

Another factor, often overlooked, is that bikes are not perceived by locals as
great symbols of wealth (unlike cars) and they tend to be friendlier as a result. It
helps at checkpoints and border crossings too – there is something about turning
up at a remote road control tired and dirty that generates a sort of sympathetic
admiration in all but the most heartless of officials. Someone getting out of a shiny
new Land Cruiser is far more likely to be invited to participate in some underhand
redistribution of wealth.

Of course, travelling by bike has its downsides. It's hard to convince yourself it's a
good way to travel if you get a puncture in a thunderstorm the day after you've had
your tool kit stolen. Also note that bikes are not allowed into any national parks in
Africa and must be left behind while you make alternative arrangements.

MAKES AND MODELS In virtually all of Africa a bike with some degree of off-
road capability is essential. These days there are myriad four-stroke bikes which are
given an 'off-road' label by the manufacturers. The degree of 'off-roadability' varies
enormously, ranging from superlight enduro bikes (designed for racing), which
can tackle virtually any terrain, to large twin-cylinder bikes which are given sharp
off-road styling but are really designed more for comfortable tarmac touring. The
large middle ground is made up by versatile 'trailbikes' offering a good compromise
between comfort, features, weight and off-roadability.

Just to confuse the issue, note that trailbikes are often called 'enduros' in Germany
and are also sometimes referred to as 'dualsport bikes' in America. What the British
call enduro bikes – for competition use – tend to be called 'hard enduros' in Germany.

Listed below is a non-exhaustive selection of models that a fairly adventurous traveller who is not content with sticking to the main roads could consider. As with 4x4 vehicles, buying the latest models is not a good idea.

Yamaha (*www.yamaha-motor.co.uk*) The legendary reliability and unsophisticated engines of the XT500, and subsequently the XT600, meant Yamaha were the most popular overland bikes from the 1970s to the 1990s. The XT600 Ténéré models, with their 23–28-litre tanks and bulletproof simplicity, were for a long time *the* bikes to use in Africa. Discontinued in 1991, they are rarer, but there are still those who would never use anything else. Unfortunately, finding decent secondhand models can be a problem. One big advantage of their popularity is that a number of XTs are still found in Africa, having been sold by overlanders at the end of their trips, and scavenging spares is a reasonable possibility. If you do choose a 600 Ténéré, the best by far is the 1988–91 twin-headlamp electric-start-only 3AJ model. The earlier kick-only and kick-and-electric models suffer from some serious engine and gearbox problems.

The more recent electric-start XT600E is another good option, which was available new until early 2005 and can easily be 'Ténérised' with the addition of a large tank, a good screen and an 18-inch rear wheel. Go for the 1997-onwards 4PT/DJ02 version with a rev counter and right-hand-side clutch actuator. The XTZ660 Ténéré, a water-cooled, five-valve single, is a little over-complicated for overlanding, but worth a look if a good 600 can't be found. The XTZ750 Super Ténéré is Yamaha's twin-cylinder offering. It is a bit of a monster, but reliable and a good option for two-up travel.

The TT600s are truer off-roaders than the XT, but are more limited in availability. The best overlanders are the TT600R (kick start) and RE (elec start) models. Both use the reliable XT600E motor in a high-spec chassis and have proper high-output generators.

As travel kit, tools and spares get lighter, you might consider Yamaha's mighty little XT225 Serow or TTR250. Superlight, agile bikes like these are becoming very popular, the only downside being ultimate top speed. If 60 or 70 mph is fine, don't dismiss them.

More recently the XT660Z Ténéré has arrived on the scene and it's sure to feature among the top overlanders' choices of the future once people become familiar with it. Don't be frightened of fuel injection – cars have had it for 30 years and it's reliable.

Honda (*www.honda.co.uk*) The XR600, and since 1996 the XR400, are extremely robust off-roaders and utterly dependable. Offering the usual Honda high quality, they are an excellent choice, with no frills – air-cooled and no electric start (electric start kits can be fitted), not even an ignition key. Comfortable they may not be, but they are built to last. Partly as a result of their use in desert rallies, a good range of accessories, such as large tanks, is available.

The XR650L is a 20kg/44lb heavier, more street-legal version of the XR600 with the Dominator electric-start motor and a high-output generator with a high seat that suits tall riders. The NX650 Dominator is slightly more road-orientated, but also a good candidate if fitted with an 18-inch rear wheel. Many high-mileage or overheated examples suffer from exhaust valve seats falling out – be careful! A good XL/XR/Dominator engine should make no rattling noises at all, hot or cold.

The Honda XR650R replaced the XR600 in 2000. With an aluminium frame and compact kick-start engine, this is an incredibly light bike for the power it produces, weighing in at under 130kg/285lb. It makes a good overlander with a whole host of overland kit available including electric-start conversions.

The Transalp, Africa Twin and Varadero are comfortable, larger, twin-cylinder bikes, but because of their weight, most people travelling on their own would consider them too cumbersome for a trans-Africa trip. Note that they also have expensive fairings, which would almost certainly not withstand the rigours of African travel.

Suzuki (*www.suzuki-gb.co.uk*) The long-established DR350 and DR600/650, simple air- and oil-cooled machines, have their fair share of fans, the smaller version having a reasonably low seat and being particularly popular with female riders. Unfortunately, the 650 has a 17-inch rear wheel. The DRZ400 (also badged as a Kawasaki KLX400R) was introduced in 2000, with a water-cooled motor which comes in both kick- and electric-start versions. It makes a great, lightweight, economical overlander. All the overland gear is available for the DRZ at affordable prices.

Kawasaki (*www.kawasaki.co.uk*) Not so frequently seen in Africa, the water-cooled KLX range (250, 300, 450 and 650cc) are very capable off-roaders, although, as with the Suzuki DR, the larger model takes a 17-inch rear. The KLR650 is heavier and more road-orientated. These models are popular in the US, so check out the internet for more information. We consider the KLR/KLX range a little over-complicated for overlanding, with its twin cams, water-cooling and twin-balance shafts.

KTM (*www.ktm.co.uk*) The 640 and more recent 690 'Adventure' is the closest you can get these days to a dedicated lightweight overlander's bike. With large tanks, twin tripmeters and options like side panniers, these bikes are almost ready to go straight from the crate. However, they are expensive and there are question marks over engine vibrations and long-term reliability. One to consider for the more affluent overlander could be a retired 660 Rallye. Hugely expensive new (£20k), but built to endure the Dakar rally and more, it has a 60-litre fuel capacity, top-spec suspension, wheels and chassis, and comes with a full navigation equipment set-up. The 660 LC4 motor also seems now to have become reliable, while remaining simple to maintain and repair. You have four separate fuel tanks, so you could use one for water storage (if it is brand new and has never been used for fuel). Post-2001 models have better fuel consumption and a generally smoother response.

If you really think you need and can handle a 200+kg bike off-road, then the 950/990 Adventure is the one to go for. It's a proper trail/enduro bike, with fine suspension and serious performance.

BMW (*www.bmw-motorrad.co.uk*) The F650GS/Dakar/G650X is BMW's single-cylinder trailbike, but at over 190kg (420lb) it is more at home on the road. Go for the Dakar or G650X, as they have 21-inch front wheels.

The F650/700/800GS is the new parallel twin-cylinder trail/adventure bike and looks to have all the makings of a seriously refined overlander if a single cylinder just won't do.

The GS 800–1,200cc series of large boxer twin-cylinder bikes have been available throughout Africa for decades. These smooth, shaft-driven machines are a pleasure to ride on the road, but for most people their sheer weight makes them a handful on tough terrain. Even so, the latest R1200GS and HP2 are certainly marketed as real off-road machines and the GSs will probably never lose their faithful band of supporters. Needless to say they are not cheap, and a massive range of equally expensive accessories is available from a number of German manufacturers.

WHICH TO CHOOSE? Your choice of bike depends upon a number of factors:

- Your mechanical knowledge. Don't choose a bike you can't fix, because you *will* have to fix it. You must at least be able to carry out basic servicing. Go and do a short mechanics' course and take your own bike to work on.
- Your intended route. Generally speaking, the harder the terrain the more suitable a lighter bike will be. For example, someone crossing central Africa in the rainy season would have a gruelling time on an Africa Twin. At the other extreme, if you are going to be cruising around southern Africa, most of the time on tarmac roads, you may find a Honda XR400 slow and uncomfortable.
- Your size. Those with short legs will not enjoy the comparatively high seat of an XR650L. Also very important for those travelling alone in remote areas, you need to be able to pick the bike up on your own – and you have to be pretty strong to right a fully loaded XTZ750 lying on its side in the mud. Try it before you go – if you can't manage it, choose a smaller bike.
- The availability of extra equipment, such as large tanks and luggage carriers. Yamaha XTs, Honda XRs, KTMs and BMWs are the most popular overland bikes and so offer the best choice.
- How much the standard bike has to be modified – especially important for those people short on time or not mechanically inclined.
- Your budget.

MOTORBIKE PREPARATION

Thorough pre-trip preparation is the key to a successful time in Africa. Cutting corners at this stage will result in problems *en route* and you can almost guarantee that they will occur in the most remote and inconvenient places. As well as having a mechanically sound engine and chassis, considerable thought should be given to any peripheral items, such as mounting racks for luggage, fuel, water, tools and spares. These are the things that are going to break or cause problems.

Whichever bike you use, it should be given a thorough mechanical overhaul before you leave. At the very least, you should start with new oil, filters (air, oil and fuel), spark plugs, chain, sprockets, clutch, tyres, inner tubes, brake pads and cables. Items which you know are going to get considerable wear, such as the non-engine bearings (wheel, swingarm, steering), should be thoroughly checked if not replaced with new. Whether or not you go for a complete engine strip-down depends on the age of the bike, how long you have owned it yourself and its general condition.

TOOLS It is a good idea at this stage to think about what tools you intend to take with you. With a view to keeping things as light as possible, select the smallest number of the best-quality tools you think you will need on the trip and prepare the bike confining yourself to using only these tools. It will soon become obvious what you do and don't need. Try to keep your tools in a dedicated, solidly mounted, waterproof, lockable toolbox.

BIKE MODIFICATIONS/ADDITIONS How you go about modifying the bike really depends on the length and intended route of your trip. When planning a trans-continental trip, for example, the following essential points need to be considered:

Fuel and water tanks Generally speaking, the ideal size for a fuel tank is around 25–30 litres. This is a good compromise between not being overly heavy or bulky and giving a decent range, around 500–600km (300–380 miles) for most

MOTORCYCLE TOOLS AND SPARES LIST

- spare rear tyre
- heavy-duty inner tubes
- wheel and cush drive bearings and seals
- good-quality puncture repair kit with lots of feather-edge patches
- small mountain-bike pump or compact electric pump
- a few spare spokes of each type – there can be two types per wheel
- connecting links for chain – clip and rivet (better) links
- short section of chain for repairs
- sprockets and lock washers
- clutch, brake and gear levers
- brake pads/shoes
- clutch cable
- throttle cable(s) – usually only pull cable
- air filters – fewer if cleanable type
- oil filters
- fuel filter
- spark plugs and HT cap and lead
- fuel hose and hose clips
- bulbs and fuses
- electrical wire and connectors
- regulator/rectifier
- stator/pickup/ignition pack/HT coil – if a very long trip
- assorted nuts, bolts, washers and Loctite
- gasket set
- clutch friction and plain plates
- duct and electrical tape
- assorted cable/zip ties
- spare bungee rope/straps
- instant gasket
- multimeter electrical test meter
- epoxy glue
- liquid steel/JB weld two-part epoxy
- nitrile rubber gloves
- small tub of grease – 35mm film pot?
- 1 litre of engine oil
- air filter oil, if using foam air filter
- small, high-quality toolkit (combination spanners, 3/8-inch drive ratchet and relevant sockets, screwdrivers, ball-end Allen keys, small mole grips, spoke spanner)
- Leatherman-type multi tool
- chain-splitting/riveting tool
- feeler gauges
- tyre pressure gauge (if not on pump)
- file
- spark-plug spanner
- tyre levers
- repair manual

bikes. This will be sufficient in all but a few circumstances. Realistically you are more likely to be constrained by what large tanks are available for your particular bike. Companies like Acerbis, IMS and Aqualine make large plastic tanks for a wide range of off-road bikes, though most of them tend to be slightly small, in the 18–24-litre range. The extra capacity can be achieved using side- or rear-mounted small auxiliary fuel tanks or cheap ten-litre jerrycans. Always fit transparent fuel filters to all your fuel lines. You can then see when you have contamination early enough to do something about it.

It's worth pointing out that in areas where you actually need more fuel than this, such as certain parts of the Sahara, for safety reasons you are more than likely going to be travelling with at least one other vehicle (a 4x4 or truck) which will be able to carry extra fuel in jerrycans or plastic containers for you.

For a long trip in the desert you will also need a considerable amount of water, say 20+ litres, which just adds to the difficulty of carrying fuel on your bike. If there is no extra vehicle and if you don't have jerrycans to carry extra fuel, you can usually find cheap plastic containers, which can be disposed of after transferring the fuel into your main tank. Another way is to use water 'bags', such as those made by Ortlieb, or flat foldable emergency fuel bags. They are very resilient and are fine for carrying fuel for short periods – and of course they take up very little space when not in use.

Hard luggage There are essentially two ways of carrying your gear, and the hard or soft debate among experienced overlanders will continue forever. Hard luggage usually involves mounting hard aluminium side-boxes at the rear of the bike on to some sort of steel rack attached to the mainframe and subframe. This method is very popular in Germany and a number of companies manufacture the equipment.

Aluminium boxes offer a greater degree of security from theft than soft panniers. However, they are also heavy, unwieldy and annoyingly hard to mend if they break in a crash. Over time, friction on the aluminium creates a dark-grey dust, which means clothes and other sensitive items have to be kept covered. Tough fabric inner bags will prevent this problem and ease removal of contents. Tools and spares can be kept low in the boxes under a false bottom for protection.

Soft luggage Soft waterproof side-panniers are also fitted at the rear sides. Unless the contents are very light, they cannot just be thrown over; some sort of frame is needed to support the weight and resist constant abrasive movement and fatigue. Much cheaper and lighter, soft luggage is becoming a popular choice these days as quality and design improves.

Actually, good-quality soft panniers are surprisingly hard-wearing and, provided they are well supported, should easily last a long trip. If damaged, they can easily be repaired with patches or stitching. Soft is the right option for those who travel light and have learned what *not* to take.

Custom-made racks are best for soft panniers – keep everything as close to the bike as possible and protect the panniers from exhaust heat.

A combination of soft panniers, a small lockable waterproof 'Peli' type topbox, a small rucksack, various things hidden away under panels and fuel tank should get most of your clobber carried. An Ortlieb roll-up drybag, containing your tent and bedroll, on the back of the seat makes something comfortable to lean against on long days.

Within the luggage, it is important to protect all your belongings from the constant vibrations they will receive. Most things can be neatly stored in small Tupperware boxes and clothes within plastic bags. Apart from the main luggage, lightweight, regularly needed items can be kept on a fork-mounted front rack.

3

Tyres One important point to note is that trailbikes that take anything other than a 21-inch front and an 18-inch rear tyre will have a restricted choice.

On a long trip, tyre choice requires careful thought, mainly because sourcing decent tyres in Africa (apart from some places in southern Africa) is a perennial headache. Tyres are always available in big cities, but they tend to be rather narrow and of light construction for small-capacity bikes. With a bit of persistence you can usually find something, but in west and central Africa, generally speaking, it is very difficult.

Ultra-knobbly motocross tyres offer the best grip in rough terrain, but they are not really practical because of their very limited life, particularly when ridden on tarmac, which is more often than you think. A better choice in tough conditions is a tyre like Michelin Desert, Pirelli MT21 or Metzeler Karoo. They have much harder-wearing knobbles, which are spaced closer together and consequently have a much longer life, although they still wear fast on the road.

More versatile 'trail tyres' – such as Metzeler Sahara, Avon Gripster and Dunlop Trailmax – with a broader, shallower tread pattern, are generally a good compromise, offering a longer life and an acceptable amount of grip in sandy or stony conditions; they are not so good in mud, however.

For those entering north Africa and crossing the Sahara, it is best to leave southern Europe with a pair of new Michelin Desert tyres and to carry a spare at the rear, space permitting.

For ultimate puncture and pinch resistance you can do no better than use Bridgestone, Conti or Michelin Ultra Heavy Duty inner tubes, lubricated with Michelin mousse gel and treated with a puncture-resisting 'slime'-type product.

Make sure your rims are true, that your spokes are tight and the nipples are free to be adjusted. Choose a good-quality rim tape to protect your tubes from spoke ends.

Miscellaneous Other essential modifications are:

* A bash plate, to protect the crankcase from flying stones.
* An X-ring chain. The rubber seals keep the lubricant inside the chain cavities and keep the dust out, increasing longevity. Try to stick with DID, as you will find it easier to find spare links. Always use a rivet link rather than a clip, as clips can come free with time. Use steel, not alloy, sprockets. They last a lot longer and are stronger.
* Good-quality, alloy-reinforced handguards, which protect your levers in a fall.

Desirable modifications include:

* For those who intend to use a GPS (Global Positioning System), a power lead and some sort of vibration-isolating mounting bracket on the handlebars are necessary.
* Bland looks. The less new and shiny a bike looks, the better. Removing stickers from new bikes helps.

SPARE PARTS For those who have never travelled in Africa, one of the problems is not knowing in advance what spares you are likely to be able to pick up on the way. Generally speaking, very little is available for large bikes north of South Africa. In some large capitals you may find basic items, like oil filters for popular models, but not much more; there simply isn't the demand. In the more westernised capitals, like Harare, Windhoek, Nairobi and most of South Africa, you will find more choice, especially non-model-specific items such as tyres and chains.

What spares you take with you is a compromise between trying to cover all eventualities (the wrong approach) and taking as little as you can get away with (the right one). Only take what there is a good chance you will probably need. This may sound naively optimistic, but it is really a case of logical risk evaluation. If you have a fundamentally good bike, well prepared and properly looked after, it is pretty unlikely that anything serious will go wrong mechanically. If the worst does happen in the middle of nowhere, you will be able to get help and eventually get your bike to the nearest town, where you can try to repair it. You may need the right spares to be air-freighted out from your home country and you might be able to convince customs that, as you'll be exporting the spares again as part of your bike, you should not have to pay any duty. Carriers like UPS or DHL can get most parcels, fairly cheaply, to most places in a matter of days.

Lots of bodge-it items such as wire, glue, chemical-metal, duct tape and plenty of cable ties are invaluable for temporary repairs.

OTHER ITEMS

Clothing Choice of riding gear is yet another compromise: protection versus practicality. While some degree of protection against a crash is essential, don't underestimate the amount of time you'll be off the bike, walking around villages or cities. A strong, well-ventilated enduro jacket with built-in back, shoulder and elbow pads is a good choice.

Most riders use full-length motocross-style boots – an excellent safety measure – although some people find them too cumbersome when not actually riding and prefer the flexibility of normal strong walking boots which cover the ankle. This is something of a risk, given how vulnerable feet and legs are in the event of a crash, but again it boils down to personal preference.

As with the bike, the blander you look the better.

Helmet An Arai Tour-X or XD4 type helmet offering the use of a visor or goggles is best for overlanders.

Camping equipment A lightweight tent, sleeping bag, Thermarest and mosquito net are essential. A high-quality petrol stove (such as MSR) is the most practical way to cook.

Water A Camelbak-style water system is essential. Store extra water in their plastic bottles in your panniers.

If you are going somewhere very remote, get a compact water purification filter.

Personal items Clothes, hygiene, books, electronics, etc are of course subjective things, but it is really a question of common sense based on available space. Most people take far too much, so consider every item carefully.

See also *Appendix 5*, page 362, for relevant books, magazines and websites.

BICYCLE SELECTION AND PREPARATION   *David Mozer of Bicycle Africa Tours*

The bias of this section is 'Africa-friendliness', not what might impress a gear-head friend, so it tends towards keeping it simple. Things are interconnected, so that some decisions on equipment will dictate the tools required and the weight of your load, for example.

TYPES OF BICYCLE Most people cycling across Africa use mountain bikes. For some regional trips, touring and hybrid (or cross-bikes) are also practical.

My default recommendation is mountain bikes (MTBs) over touring bikes for most excursions in Africa. The MTB is versatile, durable and stable, and its shortcomings are few. I have found that once a bike is loaded with gear, an extra kilo in the frame is immaterial. The tyres and wheels are probably more of a factor, because that is where there is extra rotational weight. For most excursions in Africa you won't want to give up the durability and choice of MTB tyres.

Because the bike is going to be loaded with panniers, it is more important that it be able to accept sturdy racks than have a suspension system. The added weight of your belongings will help your bike to hug the road. Having a suspension system adds weight and it could have mechanical problems. In my opinion, the hybrids, or cross-bikes, are crossed the wrong way. Instead of narrow tyres and straight bars, I would select fatter tyres and drop bars. Fat tyres increase stability. Drop bars facilitate a lower riding position, which reduces wind resistance, lowers the centre of gravity to increase control and increases the number of hand positions. This is especially useful if you know you will be doing considerable mileage on paved roads, along with some challenging terrain on dirt roads. If you are looking for less rolling resistance and straight bars, put narrower tyres on a MTB.

As the airlines reduce their baggage allowances and increase their excess-baggage charges, folding-suitcase bikes become a serious consideration. I have ridden a Bike Friday 'World Tourist' in the sands of Mali, the rutted roads of Ethiopia and the mud of Cameroon without failure. But the small wheel can drop further into holes and alter the inertia of the bike, while the shorter wheelbase puts the centre of gravity much more over the front wheel. This is likely to catch up with you most going downhill on a rutted gravel road. Unless you are skilled at this, you will be better off with a full-size bike. If you already have a MTB and want to increase your choice of grip positions, options include getting some bar extenders or replacing the whole handlebar assembly with the set-up you prefer. I have put drop-bars on a MTB with good results.

There are many good mountain bikes on the market and the choice comes down to personal preference. Though their names are different, many are made in the same factory, with the same inputs. Basically you get what you pay for. A rule of thumb is to pay enough to get what you feel you need.

SELECTING YOUR BICYCLE

Frames In addition to the geometry and size of the frame, there are other important factors: the size (diameter and thickness) of tubing; the quality of workmanship; the kind of metal; and the size of wheel that the frame uses. Many of these factors play more of a role in how comfortable the bicycle is to ride than how durable it is under normal use. Under normal conditions there is little or no performance difference between frames with high-top tubes (men's bikes) and slanted-top tubes (women's bikes).

Generally, new models have more efficient frame geometry than older bikes. Once you have the right style, you probably won't have to worry too much about the specifics of the frame angles. In considering the kind, size and quality of the tubing, it is not necessary to get lured too far upmarket. Low-end bicycles, above the lower mass-market levels, simply don't fall apart very often.

Our advice is to not overlook the cost effectiveness and advantages of the solid US$500 bike with a frame of a weldable metal (chrome-moly steel). In the unlikely event that it should break, you usually don't have to go far to find someone who can fix it in some fashion. I have seen steel frames brazed over a blacksmith's bed of coals! On the other hand, be wary of expensive frames made of materials or assembled with adhesive that might be weakened by vibration. I have seen expensive bikes shake apart even on 'paved' roads. Aluminium frames face the same problem of being difficult to repair if they break in a remote area.

An important variable dictated by the frame is wheel and tyre size. Not all frames use the same size of wheel, and not all wheels have the same selection of tyres. For remote areas, consider a frame with a wheel that takes a sturdy tyre. Collectively, in terms of geometry, tubing, tyre availability and workmanship, this suggests a modest 26-inch wheel MTB as a starting point.

Size A bicycle that is too big or too small for the user can be a safety hazard and tiring to ride. Bicycles are sized, in inches or centimetres, by the measurement along the seat tube from the top tube to the bottom bracket (theoretically – it varies by brand). The final determination of a safe size comes when the bicyclist straddles the top tube, stands with both feet flat on the ground, and checks the clearance between the top tube and his/her crotch. The recommended clearance depends on the type of riding you will be doing: 3–5cm (1–2 inches) for road riding and double that for off-road riding. Your crotch and 7.5cm (3 inches) below it is obviously a fixed distance above the ground, but because the bottom bracket isn't the same distance above the ground on all bicycles and 'sizing' varies by brand, the 'right size' may be different from bicycle to bicycle. Typically, people use MTBs 5–10cm (2–3 inches) smaller than they use touring bicycles.

PREPARING AND MAINTAINING YOUR BICYCLE

Speeds Once upon a time there were only single-speed bikes, then three speeds, then that expanded to 5, 10, 12, 15, 18, 21, 24, 27 and 30 speeds. Is there a difference? Is it important? Sometimes. Between 1, 3, 5, 10 and 15 speeds there are functional differences that can be important. In a flat area, with short trip distances and no loads, a one-speed might be sufficient and cost effective. In hilly terrain, on rough roads, over long distances and/or when hauling a load, 15 speeds are advantageous. Each additional chainring (front gear) you combine with a basic five-gear freewheel cluster (the rear gears) creates a substantial increase in the range of gear ratios. It's the range that is important!

This is not true for changing from a 5, 6, 7, 8, 9 or 10-gear cluster. The incremental difference between speeds is smaller, but the range is usually unchanged. At the efficiency level that most people ride, the benefit from reducing increments between gears is not measurable. In fact, the fancy freewheels can add problems.

Gear clusters, hubs and axles There are two systems for attaching the gears to the rear hub: traditional threaded freewheel units, which screw on to the hub, and rear hubs with built-in freehub mechanisms that use cog cassettes. These are not interchangeable. To change from one system to the other, you must change the hub, which requires rebuilding the entire wheel. In terms of remote-area maintenance, the main significance of this is on the rear axle. Mountain-bike rear hubs with screw-on freewheels generally use an axle similar to those on Chinese bicycles (and local knock-offs) found around the world. If you break this axle, you can get a replacement axle almost anywhere.

3

Traditional hubs are available with solid nutted axles or hollow quick-release axles. Unless you need to take a wheel off frequently, solid axles are an economical and practical choice. Hollow axles can be replaced with solid axles and vice versa. Hub bearings can be loose or sealed. Loose bearings may require adjusting (use standard-size bearings) and can be serviced and rebuilt easily with a set of cone wrenches. Sealed bearing hubs are difficult to service and require special parts and tools.

Protecting freewheels and hubs (from dust, grit and rain). Usually the manufacturer's instructions tell you to lubricate most of the ball bearings on a bicycle (the headset, bottom bracket and hubs) with grease, but to lubricate the freewheel with light machine oil. If you are using a freewheel, in some extreme wet or dusty climates and cycling conditions, it also may be practical to protect the bearings in your freewheel by packing them with grease.

On hubs where the dust cap doesn't rotate with the axle (usually older), you can keep foreign material out of your bearings by wrapping the exposed part of the cone with a pipe cleaner and then twisting the two ends back on each other so that it fits snugly. This technique can also be used on the bottom bracket.

Chains It used to be that all chains more or less fitted all bicycles. No longer! The new seven-plus speed cassettes require narrower chains, and some of these chains require their own special tools, replacement rivets and service techniques for maintenance and repair. The high-tech chains are hard to repair if they fail on the road. Unless you have a certified mechanic working on your bike, you may want to stay away from some of the advanced technology. You have more options if you stay with five- or six-cog gear clusters and the standard chains that fit these assemblies.

An ongoing concern for chains is lubrication. Africa is often dusty or wet. If you over-oil, your chain will get caked up, and if you under-oil, your chain will wear prematurely. The goal is to have the chain clean and dry on the outside and lubricated inside between the moving parts.

Derailleurs Derailleurs are now built to close tolerances so that a specific movement of the shift lever moves the derailleur to a specific gear (indexing). To use this system the derailleur and shifter have to be matched. The differences between the derailleurs within one manufacturer are indexing, weight, price and quality. As the weight goes down, the price goes up.

A higher price doesn't necessarily mean better quality. Grams can be shaved by using more plastic or alloy metals, but this can also compromise strength. Generally, at the level of performance at which MTBs are ridden, a few grams of weight is not as important as durability. Unless you are certain of their durability, derailleurs with plastic parts should be avoided. For remote locations, high-quality, all-metal derailleurs are preferable. To continue to use an index system, any replacement components need to match the other components. Whatever you use, if you go far enough on bad roads, it will take a beating.

Gear shifters For years gear shifters were disks with a lever sticking out rotating through a continuous range of settings. To shift gears, the user moved the lever to the desired setting and the disk stayed in place by friction. Any shifter would work with any derailleur. Engineers have now calculated the distance the disk needs to rotate for a specific derailleur to shift gears and have put stops (indexing) at these locations on the shifters. Shifters with both 'index' and 'friction' modes are few and far between now. If you have one of these, even if the system came out of calibration from cable stretch or some other reason, you could switch to friction mode and things would work. Even if you needed to replace the derailleur with an incompatible model, you could move a lever, release the indexing, return to the friction system and continue on your way.

Parts are no longer as interchangeable. The latest 'advance' is grip shifters, which twist, and two-lever ratchet systems (just push one lever to ratchet up a gear, push another lever to release down a gear). Neither system offers a friction option. If the derailleur breaks and you can't get a compatible replacement, the shifter is useless. Furthermore, the shifters are virtually impossible to repair. The best thing about a broken ratchet shifter is the opportunity to replace it with a dual-mode shifter. Grip shifters don't protrude out from the handlebars as far and have fewer moving parts to jam and break, so they are less prone to malfunction. But they are still single mode. If you are selecting a new bike, shifting systems with a friction-mode alternative are highly recommended. Short of this, grip shifters are the choice.

Bottom brackets The bottom bracket is the mechanism inside the frame, between the two crank arms that hold the pedals. There are bottom brackets with sealed bearings and bottom brackets with free-bearings. The former are more expensive and harder to service. In contrast, the latter can be serviced worldwide and the bearings are available in many remote areas, assuming there are bicycles in the area.

Brakes It is said that a bicycle will always stop – brakes just let you determine where. If you want that choice, choose your brakes carefully. The heavier the loads and the more downhill travel, the stronger the brakes need to be. Among the strongest type of brakes are cantilever, v-brakes and disc brakes.

Disc brakes are more expensive and heavier, but they are the best. Rim brakes have tended to be more problematic and clog with mud very fast under African conditions. The simplest, most cost-effective brakes on the market today are cantilever brakes. The more unique part of cantilever brakes is the way the two sides are connected. The simplest use a straddle-cable between the brakes, with a fixed anchor at one end and an adjustable cable-pinching plate on the other. These can be repaired with a short piece of standard brake cable. Each style of brake has its own design of brake pads. Carry replacement pads that fit your brakes.

Wheels and spokes There are alloy rims and steel rims. Alloy rims are more effective with rim brakes when wet, easier to keep true and easier to tap dents out of, but they do dent more easily. Steel rims are strong, but they are dangerous with rim brakes in wet weather, and when they start having problems they can be tough to re-true. Spokes are available in different gauges and lengths. The standard spoke is 15g, but 14g spokes are stronger. Double-butted 14/15/14 spokes are strong and light. The preferred material for spokes is stainless steel. The length of the spoke is a function of the hub flange, wheel size, weave pattern and dish. Rear wheels may use two different lengths of spokes. Carry spare spokes selected for your wheels.

Tyres One of the major features of 26in-wheel MTBs is their durable wheels and tyres. The wheel is a small diameter and the rim is wider, so they are stronger, more trouble-free and more stable than comparable touring bike wheels. The beefy 2½in tyres on MTBs are also relatively trouble-free and, if properly inflated, they are very effective at protecting the rims from dents. The wider the tyre, the higher the rolling resistance, so if you will be doing a lot of riding on smooth roads this is a drawback; a 1½in tyre may be more appropriate. If you will be cycling on both

3

paved and unpaved surfaces, consider combination side tread with a solid raised centre bead. The centre bead makes easier rolling on paved roads and the tread will help you in the dirt.

Though the supply line for good tyres may be long, the longer life, less downtime and additional versatility of MTB tyres usually make them a good choice. MTB tyres are becoming more widely available in Africa's large cities. With a little planning ahead, it's not hard to keep a sufficient number of spares on hand. The price often bears very little relation to suitability. Cheaper, gum-walled tyres can be better than skin walls at taking the weight on bad roads. On desert tracks, deflate your tyres slightly, increasing the surface area in contact with the ground. Skin walls invariably split under this kind of treatment. Tyres with little tread have proven to be the best at sitting on top of the sand.

Inner tubes These can be made out of a variety of materials and there are at least three types of valves. Airless tubes are also available. The material of a pneumatic tube may affect its puncture resistance; it will also determine what type of glue and patches you need to repair a puncture. The most common inner-tube material is butyl rubber, which can be repaired with the glue and patches found in patch kits around the world.

'Thornproof' tubes are probably better labelled 'puncture-resistant'. They are usually two to six times as expensive as regular tubes. Puncture-resistant tubes can be made of extra-thick butyl rubber, or of totally different materials, such as polyurethane plastic. When the latter punctures, it requires its own special patch kit (twice as expensive as kits for butyl tubes). Combination latex/butyl tubes are an expensive hybrid (eight times the price of regular butyl) that can be patched with a standard patch kit. Puncture-resistant tubes may be of the greatest advantage where there is a lot of glass or short, sharp objects on the road. If there are no sharp objects on the route, all tubes are about equal. If you have long thorns to contend with, the best thing to do is avoid them!

Automobile tyres and tubes and most recreational US bicycles use a 'Schraeder valve'. European cyclists often use a 'Presta valve'. Parts of Europe, much of Asia and some developing countries use a third type called a Dunlop valve. One solution to the valve issue is to make sure that every bicycle has a pump that fits the valve for its tubes. Many modern pumps can be switched from Schraeder to Presta, and used on a Dunlop with an adapter.

Airless tubes solve some problems, but they offer a harsher ride, slam spokes, are six to ten times as expensive as regular tubes, at least twice as heavy, have twice the rolling resistance and don't carry heavy loads well. It is still probably most practical to use butyl compound tubes that are repairable.

Tube protectors Some people praise tube protector strips. I know of several cases where the edge of the strips wore a line of holes in the tube, causing irreparable punctures. The most plausible explanation is that the hot weather softens the tubes more than the plastic strip, making the tube vulnerable to abrasion from the edge. For off-road riding, there is no final decision on the effectiveness of protective strips. I have never used them in Africa and have only rarely had problems with a flat that I think a tube protector would have prevented. They would be most strongly advised for sections in severe thorn veld.

Pedals and toe-clips If you are likely to be dismounting in dirt (anything from dust to mud), it is best to stay away from any pedals that require special matching pairs of shoes with hardware underneath. This pretty much eliminates cleats and older clipless pedals, though some of the new designs of clip-in systems are not as susceptible to clogging. Conventional pedals give you the flexibility to use multi-purpose shoes, which cut down on the number of pairs of shoes you will have to pack. You can gain some efficiency as you pedal by using traditional toe-clips. If you are trying them for the first time, or don't have a high level of confidence, don't tighten the straps initially nor when you are in urban traffic, sand, mud, rocks and other technical situations.

Saddles You are going to have an intimate relationship with your saddle; get one that is comfortable. Those that are too narrow or too wide may not support your pelvic bones properly or comfortably. Spring saddles will have you bouncing about all day. Gushy soft or rock-hard can also leave you constantly searching for a comfortable way to sit. If you are not used to riding a bike, almost any saddle will leave you sore to begin with. Experiment with different saddles before you start your tour.

The angle of the seat and what you wear also play a role in posterior comfort. Thick seams and bunched clothing between you and your saddle quickly take their toll. Probably the most useful piece of specialist bicycle clothing is padded cycling shorts, which are designed to be worn without underwear. If you are having a problem with chafing, a comprehensive application of non-petroleum skin lubricant (eg: bag balm, KY Jelly or something similar) over the affected surfaces of your body will help!

Accessories The best advice on accessories is to be sure they are strong enough to take the beating they will get, and attach them securely. If accessories fail while in use, it may not be fatal, but it can be very frustrating. Buy equipment that is properly designed and sufficiently durable for its intended use. One way to minimise lost screws is to apply Loctite (medium strength) or tyre patch cement to the threads before bolting on racks and cages.

Racks and packs There are two schools of thought on carrying anything on your back in a rucksack or backpack. Some people find that their back will ache very quickly and will overheat sooner. Even water packs can be a problem for some people, while others swear by them. If you plan to carry things on your back, test your system on a long ride in hot weather before your big journey. Waistpacks (bumbags) are more manageable, but can still be annoying. I like the versatility of a waistpack, but I rig it in front of the handlebars while I'm riding.

To carry large loads you need a sturdy rack and saddlebags (panniers). Racks and packs can wear fast and screws loosen quickly when they vibrate for several hours on a daily basis. Choose racks and packs that are sturdy and stable enough to handle the conditions they will be subjected to. The weak points on racks tend to be the welds and eyelets. The weak points on panniers tend to be where the hooks screw into the backing.

Bicycles travel best if the weight of any load is distributed evenly and kept low. Four slim packs, two front and two rear, are better than two giant bulging ones. If you are travelling with only a moderate amount of baggage (say 10kg/22lb), you can get by with just a rear rack and medium-size panniers on each side. If the weight is too heavy at the rear, the front wheel becomes hard to handle and you will expend extra energy trying to keep the bike under control. For heavy loads, split the weight between front and rear.

Assuming you are looking at panniers made with strong materials and good workmanship, the trade-off tends to be between waterproofness and pockets to help you keep things organised. Regardless of which feature you favour, packing your items in plastic bags will help them stay more organised in a one-compartment waterproof pannier, and will help them stay more waterproof in a multi-compartment pannier. Strong lighter-weight racks divide into two groups: those made with aluminium rods or with steel alloy tubing. I have seen a lot of aluminium racks break and they tend to be hard to fix in the field. I have never seen a steel alloy tubing rack break. If it did, it would be easier to get it repaired.

The best mount is to screw the rack directly on to the frame. Look for a frame with rack braze-ons on the seat-stays and threaded eyelets on the axle drop-outs. If you expect to be riding on roads, trails or streambeds with high rocks or roots, do not use low-rider racks. Low-riders will give your packs more of a beating than racks that hold them higher. And if one of those rocks or roots gets hold of your pannier, you may take a beating as well!

If you will be travelling on rough roads, it is preferable that the attaching system for the packs consists of strong hooks and non-stretch webbing straps with buckles or Velcro fasteners. Packs with suspension systems that rely solely on elastic cords and springs can bounce off when you hit bumps and pot-holes. Similar advice applies for attaching articles to the top of the rack: you will have more flexibility and fewer problems if you use non-elastic nylon webbing straps with buckles instead of elastic straps, shock cords or bungee cords. Webbing is also lighter.

Handlebar bags or waistpacks are not essential, but they are very convenient for cameras, snacks, sun lotion, notepads, etc. As they sit so high, you don't want to carry too much weight in a handlebar bag. The advice on water-bottle cages is the same as for racks; they should be sturdy enough to handle the conditions they will be subjected to. It's best if they mount into braze-ons on the frame.

Mudguards/fenders and kickstands There are pros and cons when it comes to mudguards/fenders and kickstands: on trains, planes, buses and during the course of a normal day, mudguards/fenders get knocked out of alignment. They are inconvenient to detach, reattach and keep adjusted. In dry weather they keep a little sand off the chain. In rain they will keep you happy and stop the chain from being washed, but if you ride off paved roads, they can quickly clog with mud and become a major aggravation. If you have a rear rack, a less fragile (although less thorough) protection is available from snap-on commercial products which can be fitted to the top of the rack. Alternatively, you can improvise by cutting up a 1.5-litre plastic bottle and taping it on to the racks to provide a splash guard which keeps body, drive train and baggage drier.

The disadvantage of kickstands is that they are often not designed to support the weight of a loaded touring bike. If your bike is going to be fully loaded most of the time most kickstands are not worth the bother. You will have more success finding walls and other things to lean it against.

Mirrors Rear-view mirrors are not a substitute for good cycling technique, but they are useful. They tend to lead a rough life on tour. Whether they are attached to the handlebar, helmets or glasses, they tend to get a good bashing and have a short lifespan. I still find them valuable and love them.

Lights It is generally a good rule of thumb to make every effort to stay off the roads at night. A disproportionate number of accidents happen at night, and they are often fatal. If you have to be on the road after dark, lights and reflectors are essential. Plan ahead. If you don't expect to be riding very much at night, you won't need a particularly elaborate system. There are four kinds of power source. In ascending order of initial cost, they are: battery, generator, rechargeable battery and combo generator/rechargeable battery. Prices can range from US$5 to US$300. Your budget, location and pattern of use will dictate which is best for you.

A versatile solution is to use a headlamp strapped around your helmet or head, providing hands-free light on or off the bike. If you decide on battery power, choose a model that uses batteries that are easily replaced (AA are common worldwide). I prefer rechargeable batteries, but they need a charger and electrical current or a solar cell to recharge.

Locks It seems that the further you are from big cities, the less sophisticated the bike thieves, the rarer the bolt cutters and the less need for heavy locks and chains. While on tour, my bike is usually loaded and conspicuous, securely stored at the hotel, or left for only a few minutes while I run an errand. In the latter cases I lock it. I use a rather ordinary lock and long, thin cable. The long cable is attached to a fixed object to prevent snatch-and-ride. If you expect to be parking your bike unattended in cities, you will need a more sophisticated locking system.

Tools and spare parts To fully enjoy the self-sufficiency and independence that a bicycle can provide, you need to carry a few tools and spare parts – and know how to use them. They do not add much weight and could prevent you from having to push your bike on a long walk or having a long wait for a taxi. Select the tools and spare parts you need to do basic adjustments and maintenance on your bicycle, and any special tools if your bicycle has esoteric components. Check with your local bike club to find out about classes on bike maintenance, if you need to bone up on this.

For a long solo trip, or any kind of group trip when supply lines could be long, bring enough tools and spare parts to be able to completely overhaul your bike and repair everything, short of a broken frame or rim. Essentially turn yourself into a mini-portable bike shop. Usually only one complete set of tools is needed for a trip. Ideally, though, everyone should have their own tools for a tube patch and basic adjustments. The group leader should be organising the group tools.

If you should need a spare part or tool sent to you in an emergency, DHL, USP, FedEx and other worldwide package services are now available in most African capitals and many other major cities. You will need a contact back home or an account at a bike shop that can buy the part and send it out via courier. Unfortunately, the shipping is not cheap.

WATER Dehydration can hit very quickly. Feeling thirsty is not a good indication; by then you could well be in serious trouble. Drinking frequently will improve your performance and enjoyment. Basically there is no substitute for drinking plenty of water in a timely manner.

Water bottles It is essential to take a water bottle on every trip. In hot weather you will be drinking a litre of water or more every 15km (10 miles). For long trips you need a large water supply, such as water bags. Be sure you have sufficient water capacity for the kind of travel you plan. Safe water is getting increasingly available in Africa, but it is still problematic in many places. It is also possible that some areas may have no water during the dry seasons. Even when there is water, you may find the pump that you expect to use is broken. Use white-coloured water bottles, as the water inside doesn't heat up quite as much as in coloured or clear bottles.

Water purification Bottled water is almost always available in towns, but it is not a preferred solution (see *www.travelersagainstplastic.org*). If you want to avoid the expense, litter and high carbon footprint of bottled water, bring re-usable water bottles and water filter or purifier; they will be put to good use. Iodine and chlorine tablets are useful only in emergencies – if you have half an hour to wait, and once a week at the most! Don't rely on iodised water, because you will poison yourself. The three better choices are a filtering pump (search: hiking water filter), an ultraviolet light purifier (search: SteriPen) or an oxidant purifier (search: MSR MIOX). Filtering pumps tend to be the most versatile, labour intensive and require the most maintenance. The latter two hi-tech methods require cleaner water and use batteries, which can be rechargeable. The MIOX also needs salt and adds a little taste to the water, which is mostly only an issue if you start with a high mineral water that already has a taste. The UV pen is generally the fastest.

FOOD AND COOKING Even if you start the day with a good breakfast and full of energy, as the day goes on you will burn it up. If you do not eat again, the calories will be consumed and you will reach a state of hypoglycaemia, or low blood sugar. It can hit you very quickly and leave you dead in your tracks. On any trip, have extra food with you at all times. It needs to provide not just quick, but also sustainable, energy. Breads, local pastries, biscuits and bananas are widely available and are good choices. You should carry emergency packets of dried food for times of need. The dehydrated meals available from camping and outdoor shops are expensive and none too generous in size, so unless you are very wealthy with a small appetite, you will have to look at alternatives. Good buys, particularly if weight is a problem, are packet soups, packets of instant Chinese noodles and other dried 'instant' food.

There's a wide range of lightweight billycan sets, though if you go for collapsible pots and pans, pay particular attention to handles and how they clip or hook on. If some plastic slot-on handles chip, you will never get them to stay put again.

PERSONAL EQUIPMENT
Helmets and gloves Many sports present a risk of head injury. Bicycling definitely has this hazard also, and it warrants precaution. Scrapes and broken bones heal, but scrambled brains may not. A helmet also serves to protect your head from direct sun, which significantly reduces fatigue. Helmets are not a substitute for good skills and judgement, and they won't prevent an accident, but they can reduce the severity of the consequences. Compared with the lifetime cost of a head injury or even death, the cost of wearing a helmet is small. I know of several crashes in remote locations in Africa where the cyclist's helmet took a hard hit and the cyclist rode on. None of these cases involved an automobile.

The value of gloves is similar to a helmet. Gloves don't prevent accidents but they can reduce injuries, such as the amount of gravel embedded in your palms. They are also invaluable in reducing road vibration.

Clothing On extended tours in remote areas, all clothing (and bodies) gets really filthy. Although it is mostly possible to wash your body and the day's clothing at night, there can sometimes be a long time between washing opportunities. Perhaps the hardest aspect of travelling by bike is going for two weeks at a time without a decent wash, sweating every day in the same smelly clothes. At the very least take measures to control bacteria around your crotch! As the trip progresses, it is easy to get increasingly sloppy about things, for example cycling in flip-flops after shoes become too smelly and start falling apart. Leather gloves get forgotten for the same reasons. Don't lose sight of why these items were chosen in the first place; have a plan for replacing them.

In choosing your clothes, consider comfort, visibility and social standards. You can never make yourself too visible as a cyclist. Brightly coloured cotton T-shirts work well. Special cycling shorts have padding in the crotch, relatively long legs and no heavy inseams. Leather in cycling shorts is less durable than good synthetic material.

If you are going to be cycling at dawn, dusk or at night, an oversize, long-sleeved white shirt is an excellent item. It can be slipped on over anything and does not take up much space. A long-sleeved shirt also doubles during the day as protection from the sun. By covering your arms, you will reduce the amount of moisture you lose (for more information see *Health* in *Chapter 5*, page 122). Worn separately or together, a medium-weight sweater (or pile jacket) and nylon wind jacket will prepare you for a variety of changes in temperature and weather conditions. A pair of loose trousers or a wraparound skirt that can be slipped on over your cycling shorts will make you more presentable away from the bike in modest cultures.

You can get shoes specially designed for cycling, but they tend to be uncomfortable to walk in. If you have a pair of shoes that you can cycle in without getting cramp in your feet and also walk in, then they are probably fine for general bicycle touring. As a rule, cheaper athletic shoes have stiffer soles, so are better for cycling. If your feet get cramp using multi-purpose shoes to cycle in, then you will need to have two pairs of shoes.

Dust and exhaust are another problem. The irritation from exhaust can be the worst. When pollutants reach a choking level, a bandana over the mouth and nose and sucking on a lozenge helps considerably.

Sunglasses If you are used to sunglasses, you will want to wear them most days. They will not only protect your eyes from the sun, but also keep dust out of your eyes and reduce eye fatigue from the drying wind. Do not wear sunglasses with opaque side blinders. They restrict peripheral vision, which is very important if you have to manoeuvre in traffic or swerve to avoid a hazard. In the afternoon, just when you are ready to take off your sunglasses, new irritants appear: gnats and small bugs. If you are going to be riding at dusk, it is worth buying a pair of glasses with clear lenses.

First-aid kit Travel to unfamiliar surroundings can mean more injuries than usual. A lot of these are cuts and scrapes. Carry a first-aid kit and be able to give minor first aid. Prompt attention to even the smallest scratch is very important.

For an extended tour you should also prepare a medicine kit with prescription medicines and remedies for headaches, colds, upset stomachs, allergies and other common ailments. If possible get pills in 'blister packs' or individually packaged forms. Bulk-packed pills tend to vibrate into dust on long cycle tours. If you take a prescription drug, carry a duplicate prescription that gives the generic name.

Camping equipment You only need camping gear if you plan to camp. If you are taking a tent and/or stove, make sure you have all the pieces before you leave.

One of the problems with camping on a cycling tour is the security of your belongings – you're pretty much tied to your camp. Note – when it rains in Africa, it generally pours, so no tent is going to be as nice as the simplest hotel room. Outside the rainy season, what you really need, included in many hotel rooms, is a free-standing mosquito net. In the US the most practical is made by Long Road Travel Supplies (*www.longroad.com*).

If planning to rough camp or village camp, you'll either need to take a tent or plan to sleep under the stars inside your mosquito net. It is useful (if not essential) to have a dedicated groundsheet/cloth, ie: a piece of plastic, a woven mat, an old sheet or sleep sack, etc.

To self-cater, you need not only a cooker, but also the pots, pans and utensils (bowl, cup, spoon, knife) to use with it. You will also need space to carry some staples that you will need frequently but won't want to buy for every meal, like cooking oil, salt, pepper, sugar and spices.

SUGGESTED CYCLE KIT LIST

EQUIPMENT
- bicycle
- helmet
- cycling gloves
- luggage rack(s)
- water-bottle cage
- panniers, eg: Ortlieb, www.ortlieb.com
- toe-clips
- mudguards
- rear-view mirrors
- lights
- cable and lock
- tool bag

SPARES AND TOOLS
- spare tyres (number depends on length of tour)
- inner tubes (number depends on length of tour)
- puncture repair kit
- pump
- tyre levers
- gear and brake cables
- brake pads
- lubricants: grease and oil
- bearings
- wires and straps
- pliers
- set of Allen keys
- cable cutter
- spoke tensioner
- set of spanners
- freewheel or cassette remover tool
- screwdrivers, blade and Phillips
- set of cone wrenches
- spokes
- box of nuts and bolts, etc
- chain link extractor
- gear brush or old toothbrush

The most versatile stoves are multi-fuel designs. Mountain Safety Research (MSR) and Coleman make ones that are highly regarded. You will need a safe container for carrying fuel. Make sure you have enough fuel storage capacity to last between fuelling points.

Other items for bicycle touring Depending on your plans, there are a number of other special items worth taking:

* If staying in local houses or small guesthouses that don't necessarily provide linen, take sheets and a towel.

MEDICAL EQUIPMENT
* rehydration mix and spoon
* gauzes, bandages and creams
* suture kit
* anti-malaria tablets
* antibiotics
* antacids
* antihistamine cream and/or tablets
* prescription medicine
* eye ointment
* non-petroleum skin lubricant
* Paracetamol or acetaminophen
* tooth repair kit
* mosquito net

WATER
* water treatment tool
* water bottles or bags sufficient for your tour

COOKING
* Colemans multi-fuel cooker
* eating utensils
* cooking pots

CAMPING EQUIPMENT
* tent
* sleeping bag
* mattress

MISCELLANEOUS
* toiletries
* torch
* maps
* whistles (as a warning and signal)
* binoculars
* compass
* camera

- If travelling in the cold season or at altitude, you might want to take a sleeping bag or blanket as well as the above.
- Rubber thongs or flip-flops are good for those slimy loos.
- Business cards are useful for impressing officials and honouring requests for your address.
- Extra passport photos are essential in case bureaucracy invents an unexpected new form or you need to apply for an additional visa.
- Binoculars are good in game parks, but otherwise they are just extra weight.
- Camera, memory cards and batteries, because some may be hard or expensive to obtain *en route*.

MORE TIPS

Accommodation and food If you plan to stay overnight outside major cities and tourist destinations, which is the norm for cyclists, it is usually difficult to plan your accommodation too specifically without the help of a travel consultant who has been there. In small towns and villages, you rarely have a choice. You will get to stay in the best – and probably the only – hotel in town. Where there is a choice, your budget will determine the selection.

Many budget African hotels have only a few rooms and beds, so if you are travelling with a large group your choices may already be narrowed and the group may exceed the capacity of a village hotel. While camping is an option, we tend not to camp for a combination of reasons: you have to carry more gear (both shelter and cooking) or include a support vehicle (which negates much of any environmental or financial savings); setting up and taking down a camp uses time that is better spent seeing Africa; camping tends to be on the outskirts of towns and separated from the community.

I prefer to be more immersed in the villages. The modest cost of most accommodation and meals does more to help the village economy and may be no more expensive than camping. Furthermore, many parts of Africa don't lend themselves to camping and there can be security problems. Meal planning is similarly influenced by budget and the availability of markets, cooking facilities and restaurants. In rural areas, selection may be so limited as to constitute no choice. But if you are in an area where any Africans are travelling, cooked food is usually available.

Seeing wildlife One of the best experiences is seeing free-range animals from the freedom of a bicycle seat. If you know where to look, it is possible to see a wide variety of wildlife and birdlife, but with the continuing encroachment on wildlife habitats by man, this is getting further and further away from inhabited areas.

If you choose to search for wildlife, be selective about your objectives. These are wild animals and, when threatened, they can be very dangerous. They have their own ideas on how to handle intrusions into their personal space. I have seen baboons and elephants from a bicycle in Burkina Faso, Togo and Zimbabwe, watched giraffes, zebras and gazelles in Kenya and Cameroon, and enjoyed monkeys jumping overhead in Ghana and Liberia. I once heard the growl of a lion while on a bicycle and an elephant has chased me – not a relaxing experience.

Without an experienced guide, do not go in search of Cape buffalo, lions, elephants or rhinos by bicycle or on foot. Most countries help you with this by not allowing bicycles or foot travel in the major game parks. To see the big game, you will have to store your bike and take an excursion for a day or two. Unless you pre-arrange it, you will not find transport for game drives waiting at the park entrance. Usually game-watching safaris begin from major cities, so you need to plan accordingly.

4

Organised Tours and Public Transport

The concept of organised overland tours was pioneered in the mid 1960s by Encounter Overland. A number of 'fly by the seat of the pants' companies soon began venturing across Asia and Africa, with little backup but a hammer and screwdriver. By the 1970s overland was booming and with its success came an equally rapid expansion in adventure travel. So successful were the destinations that the big travel companies finally followed suit, making 'adventure' a fashionable holiday. Sadly, overland and, to a degree, those off-beat original trips are now dwindling in popularity. Political events and ever-burgeoning bureaucracy stifle the much-cherished and fortunate freedoms of those able to travel. It is to the credit of the few remaining overland and adventure companies that such travel is still an option.

An organised overland trip may be the best choice for you if you are willing to sacrifice a degree of independence and prepared to live and travel with a large group. However, there are quite a few compensations for this cheaper option.

There will be none of the planning, preparation and expense involved in getting your own vehicle ready. No carnets, no spare parts to worry about, no engines to overhaul and definitely no greasy hands to clean. Dealing with border officials is made easy; you can just lie back while some other mug – usually the co-driver deals with any cantankerous officials. You can enjoy the camaraderie of like-minded travellers, while the countries roll by. You might even fall in love! Some of you may already be wondering why you would even think of taking your own vehicle.

The company will brief you about things like visas, vaccinations, insurance and what to pack for the trip. All you need to do is be on time for departure. There are trips to suit all budgets. The company will be familiar with the routes, security, daily planning, good and bad places to camp and where to get water, fuel and food. The driver will have done most, if not all, of the trip at least once before.

Those who do choose an organised tour will probably never realise quite the extent to which they have been protected from African bureaucracy. Most truck trips operate some kind of rota system, giving those not on cooking duty time to explore at the end of the day. Tasks can be more efficiently divided and shared out. Travelling independently, you have to deal with all the daily tasks of guarding the vehicle, motor maintenance, shopping, pitching camp, making a fire, purifying water, cooking, cleaning and so on. Also, on a group overland trip, costs such as fuel, equipment, spares, carnets and insurance are spread across a much larger group.

The biggest headache for independent travellers is the need for constant vigilance over their vehicle and its contents. This can make it difficult to get away from the vehicle, perhaps reducing the possibilities for hiking and visiting more inaccessible spots. With an organised tour, there are more people to ensure a permanent security rota, allowing members to leave their gear behind and take off by foot, canoe, train or bus. Individuals can generally leave the tour at any time and travel independently (at their own expense) to a pre-arranged rendezvous point.

So what are the disadvantages of organised trips? You will have to put up with long hours in the back, covered in dust, sitting next to the most obnoxious member of the group. Despite some pretence of democracy, the driver generally dictates that safety, security and the well-being of the group take precedence. You will have to muck in with the daily chores, buying group food, cooking and, dare we say it, washing up 20 people's plates and mugs, as well as the black pots and pans. You will definitely have to push the truck out of sand and probably have to dig it out of thick, sticky mud. You might fall out with your better half or significant other. Does this sound like fun?

There is also the lack of independence, which is why most of us consider doing a trip to Africa in the first place. The routes will be pre-designated and changing them can risk disagreement within the group. The leader will generally permit a measure of democracy, perhaps allowing the trip to deviate a little from the published route, but this isn't the same thing as finding a particularly nice beach and deciding to hang around for a week or so, deciding to miss some countries out altogether or to take a completely different route from the one originally planned. Only independent travel gives you absolute freedom.

Despite the common interest of crossing Africa, there is no guarantee that the members of the group will get along. On a six-month trip the group dynamics could be a university degree subject in its own right. Groups with a good cross-section of participants often work surprisingly well, but then again you could be on the trip to hell! However, you are very unlikely to be landed with an entire group that you can't stand. It mostly requires some team effort, but you don't need to be caged in with the group all the time.

Mixing with the local people is all part of the routine, but perhaps making genuine friendships is more difficult. When a truck comes into town, the people will react very differently from the way they might react to a solitary Land Rover. Then again, coming into town in a solitary Land Rover might not be so relaxing either. So many decisions…

The boxed story on page 167 may perhaps be a good reason to join an organised tour if you are a little nervous!

THE ROUTES

There's a vast selection of trips, from two-week tours in Morocco or a month around South Africa to trans-African expeditions lasting several months. Many of the routes are the same as those outlined earlier. For years the favourite routes were across the Sahara, central Africa and what was formerly Zaire (DRC) to Nairobi before continuing south to Johannesburg.

Most companies who still operate trans-Africa will take the route from Morocco via Mauritania and through much of west Africa then down the west coast through the two Congos and Angola. Some groups fly to Nairobi, usually from Accra in Ghana, Douala in Cameroon or Libreville in Gabon. Another truck will then be waiting in Nairobi, where the trip will continue around east Africa before heading south. With the Nile route opened up, a few companies are now running trips each way between Cairo and southern Africa via Ethiopia. It was possible to link these with extensions into the Middle East and Asia. A limited number of shorter trips now operate in west Africa, but costs are higher.

INTO THE CAULDRON OF FIRE

Despite a scary brush with armed militia while having a tea stop en route to Djibouti in 2004, we were still keen to return to the Danakil. Taking a 4-day tour from Mekele, our group of nine independent travellers descended into the Rift Valley via Berehile and some impressive canyons to Hamedella. Located close to the vast salt lake of Assale, this scruffy Afar settlement provided little but hot wind, tatty wooden beds and a mobile phone mast, but no toilets or running water. Its best attributes were the colourful camel caravans and a stunning starry sky.

Dallol, 25km to the northeast, is a multicoloured, earth-shattering wonder of nature -- a series of weirdly shaped fluorescent formations, exotically shaped outcrops and smoking chimneys. Green and blue bubbling pools bordered with dazzling white salt crystals are studded with colours in all imaginable hues. Close by is a forest of grey volcanic towers and a large blue pool with bubbling yellow sulphur fountains.

It's a six-hour desert drive from Hamedella followed by a three-hour hike in the dark from El Dom to reach camp on the crater rim of the Erta Ale volcano. No words can describe the sense of awe that is felt on arrival at the top in the darkness of the night. Glowing a fiery red, the lava lake is approached after a short descent from the crater rim into the hopefully dormant cauldron of this hell fire. We walked across contorted lava flows, frozen into brittle serpentine coils and vast tubes, the petrified crust crunching at every step. Standing at the lake rim, only 10m below us the turbulent molten lava, boiling and cracking loudly, exploded periodically into sensational fiery crescendos of white, yellow and red.

Super-heated red jagged lines zigzagged across the treacle-like flows in the eerie darkness of the midnight hour. Mesmerised by the primordial display, two hours passed in a flash (or two!). Before dawn the show began again, as we watched the exploding lava eruptions before the orange glow of dawn. Noxious gases drifted and swirled across, making the picture one of sheer amazement.

Erta Ale is intoxicating and hard to leave.

Currently there is a boom in overland truck travel between Nairobi and Cape Town, by routes either through Malawi and Mozambique, or west through Zambia to Victoria Falls and Namibia. These shorter tours allow you to fly into a region for a few weeks and get a taste of it in a concentrated burst. Shorter expeditions also mean you can add them into your schedule once you arrive in a particular area, so giving you even greater freedom of movement. An organised tour could easily fit in with other parts of your journey if you combine it with a hired car. Often, as one region closes off, others open up; that's the beauty and intrigue of Africa.

Throughout east and southern Africa, there are a number of good local operators. Smaller companies in South Africa and Zimbabwe now offer a variety of expeditions, including South Africa, Mozambique, Namibia and Botswana. Local tours can respond to changing conditions much faster than the UK-based operators, perhaps providing a more interesting trip. The downside is that you have no way of assessing the quality of their operation until you arrive, and you probably have no 'comeback' options if you have a major complaint.

WHAT TO EXPECT

How the tours are organised varies from company to company. They will generally explain how the trip will work, the everyday practicalities and precisely what you need to arrange in advance in the way of documents, vaccinations and so on. They will usually also offer or suggest a comprehensive insurance policy, essential for any form of travel. Don't leave home without it.

Most tour operators aim to make the experience feel as close to independent travel as possible. As mentioned, there will be a fairly democratic approach to deciding on day-to-day details. Members of the group will normally set up a rota to cope with all the daily chores, especially cooking and security. Before leaving, most trucks will be partially stocked with food supplies, but fresh items will be bought locally and shopping will generally be the responsibility of those on cooking duty for the day.

Even where a company provides a cook as part of its team, you will be expected to help out with much of the actual work, with the cook acting more as an adviser. Participants will also be expected to volunteer for additional jobs such as stores, fire-lighting, water purification, security, first aid and rubbish collection. These vary from company to company and according to the number of people on the trip. Many drivers will also suggest the option of setting up a bar, which tends to be a popular job!

You will normally pay a deposit on booking. Most companies ask for a kitty at the beginning of the trip to cover food and other communal expenses, but others include this within the overall cost of the trip. Some companies only include transport; others will cover camping, game-park fees and other admission charges. It is important to be clear what is and what is not included in the basic price. A few companies add a 'local payment' in addition to the main charges. This may cover direct costs along the way such as national park entrance fees. Remember to add in the cost of any airfares when you are budgeting for your trip. These will not be included in the tour cost.

You will generally have to supply your own bedding, but tents are normally provided. Sleeping is generally in shared, two-person tents. Check the availability of camp beds and mosquito nets, as most do not supply these.

Most companies use Mercedes trucks, MAN or Scania, customised with their own seating configuration. They have very different layouts, but all of them can accommodate a group of 18 to 24 people. South African companies often use Japanese trucks (Izuzu or Hino).

A few trucks still pack luggage and tents into a separate trailer, making more space in the truck itself. It is worth checking out the seating design of trucks in which you are thinking of travelling. Has it been organised simply to fit in the greatest number of bodies, or does it look relatively comfortable with a decent view? Does it offer forward-facing or inward-facing seats? You will be spending a long time in that truck, so you ought to be quite sure you are happy with the layout.

Your drivers/leaders have an incredibly demanding job. They also have to be a motor mechanic, a diplomat, an actor, a social worker, an expert on everything and a friend to everyone. Most companies have extensive training programmes for their drivers, including both workshop experience and travelling with another leader/driver.

Some companies also provide couriers or cooks. On a short journey a good all-round leader/driver should be adequate. On a longer trip, a second team member is invaluable in order to help with visas, bureaucracy and paperwork, as well as helping out with the driving and mechanics.

CHOOSING A TOUR

You can pay anything from £3,000 to £5,500 for a full trans-African trip, but the variations between them are not just a matter of cost. The range of choices offered can be quite bewildering. Make sure that you find out exactly what is included in the price and how the trip is organised.

As with most things, the general rule is that the more you pay the more you get. The cheaper end of the market can also tend to have less experienced leaders/drivers and use older and less dependable vehicles, but this is not always the case. Leaders/drivers with the larger operators keep in constant touch with full-time staff back at base, who can help out in the event of problems or emergencies.

One-off expeditions and budget trips are less secure when the going gets tough, but may offer a different style of trip. You might have to accept the possibility that

THE DEPRESSING MOURDI – NO WAY

Where are the Depression du Mourdi and the Ennedi? For those seeking the wildest part of the Sahara that is still accessible, these places are on the map – in Chad.

For years we have wanted to get to the Tibesti (we still do!) but the chance to do a trip in Chad was a dream come true. Hooking up with three French adventurers living in N'djamena allowed us to set off to Faya in two ageing but reliable Toyotas. The oasis is beautiful, with swaying palms, mud mosques, mud houses and a lively market. Today the airstrip accepts group charters from France (Pointe Afrique). Our route wound through the Wadi Doum sand fields to Ounianga Kebir. An astonishing, vast turquoise lake spreads out from the barren escarpment as far as the eye can see, especially on a clear day. This massive expanse of water is not alone in northern Chad. Close by is the equally impressive lake of Ounianga Serir. Perhaps the smaller lakes to the east are more picturesque; serenely intimate and surrounded by orange sands backed by purple outcrops and vivid cliffs.

The village of Demi is a wild place where hardy Tubu eke out a living digging for salt – it's not even shown on the map, unlike the Depression du Mourdi. If you like challenging sand dunes, weird-shaped outcrops and pushing a Toyota for fun and necessity, this is the least depressing place on the trip. Adventure can't get much more exciting than this.

Saving some of the most incredible places for last, the trips head to the Ennedi Plateau. It is sensationally sculptured and carved by wind and the powerful forces of nature. Massive outcrops soaring skywards, huge red rock arches and finely trimmed needles dominate the horizon, concealing prehistoric rock art below overhanging cliffs. Guelta d'Archei is a lost canyon, a Shangri-la for those with a passion for the Sahara. Lurking in black, uninviting pools in the stunning canyon headwaters are dwarf crocodiles. Every day, long trains of frisky camels, camel men and goat herders come to water in this forbidding defile, hemmed in by ghostly turrets and whispering walls.

South of the Ennedi is the dry scrub of the Sahel. Further south, around Abeche are the dry woodland savannas, a fitting conclusion to an amazing adventure.

Tour arranged by Tchad Évasion (www.tchadevasion.com)

the truck may break down more frequently, but this is not always the case. Anyone can break down in any place!

OTHER OPTIONS

For some parts of Africa it can be more beneficial to take shorter trips with local operators, some of whom will have representatives in Europe and elsewhere. Travelling with a European operator affords you the benefit of more financial security, of course. These shorter expedition options apply in particular to the Sahara, parts of west Africa and most of southern Africa. Two or three weeks in the Sahara, when safe, to places such as the Ténéré in Niger, Ennedi in Chad, Tassili N'Ajjer/Hoggar in Algeria are best done with specialist operators, who have experienced local guides and who travel with at least two 4x4 vehicles. Morocco, Egypt, Tunisia, Senegal, Gambia, Burkina Faso, Ghana and, to a degree, Gabon, in the west are other countries where local trips organised through European tour operators have a lot to offer. In east Africa there's no shortage of offers in Kenya, Tanzania, Uganda, Rwanda and Ethiopia. There is a plethora of these shorter tours in South Africa, Namibia and Botswana in particular.

OVERLAND OPERATORS

Many of the UK-based companies above also have representatives in Nairobi, Harare and South Africa, as well as in Australia and the US. There are also other expedition companies worldwide. The following list is not exhaustive.

UK

Acacia Adventure Holidays www.acacia-africa. com. Operating since the 1980s, originally as an overland company. Now a more varied programme, including safaris, trekking, diving & short overland.
Africa in Focus www.africa-in-focus.com. Photographic specialist trips, mostly in southern Africa.
African Trails www.africantrails.co.uk. Have been running trips since 1980 with 1 driver & courier. No age limit quoted – most passengers 18–35. Also offers Kenya/Tanzania game-parks tour, & shorter trips in southern Africa. Nairobi to Cape Town.
Bicycle Africa Tours (see also advert on page 164) www.ibike.org/ibike. Unique bicycle tours in all regions of Africa.
Dragoman www.dragoman.com & also Encounter Overland. Have been running trips for over 30 & 40 years. Offers long & shorter tours in most of Africa for all ages. Some trips feature visits to community projects helping local people.
Drive Botswana (see also advert on page i of the second colour insert) www.drivebotswana.com. Self-drive & fly-in safaris.
Exodus www.exodus.co.uk. Company with over 30 years' experience. Age range mainly 17–55 on

trips from 2 to 12 weeks, mostly in east & southern Africa.
Expedition World www.expeditionworld. com. The authors' website for Africa, Asia & the Himalaya.
Explore Worldwide www.explore.co.uk. Small group holidays using a mix of hotels, lodges & camping.
Intrepid www.intrepidtravel.com. Has taken over Guerba (*www.guerba.com*), which had been running overland expeditions & shorter safaris for over 20 years. Off-road & 4x4 tours with comfort-added camping & no camp chores.
Keystone Journeys www.keystonejourneys.com. Offers overland & small group adventure in Africa.
Nomadic Tours www.nomadic-tours.com. Mainly Morocco & Jordan.
Oasis Overland (see also advert on page 114) www.oasisoverland.co.uk. Small company offering tours in Africa (also the Middle East & South America). Uses Scania & Leyland trucks with a driver/mechanic & courier. Passenger ages generally 18–40. Trips from 3 weeks to 7 months.
Odyssey Overland www.odysseyoverland.co.uk
On the Go Tours www.onthegotours.com. Various tours & expeditions in east & southern Africa.

Overlanding West Africa www. overlandingwestafrica.com. Unique exploratory overland adventure trips in west Africa.
Tucan www.tucantravel.com. An extensive programme, including overland tours for fit, younger-thinking 18–65 year olds.
UKToOz www.uktooz.com. Trans-Africa trips & beyond – partnered with Madventures for Asia.
Undiscovered Destinations www. undiscovered-destinations.com. Includes Somaliland and Congo.

FRANCE
Point Afrique www.point-afrique.com. Chad, Mauritania, Ethiopia, Benin, Senegal, Guinea, Morocco & Tanzania.

USA & CANADA
Adventure Center www.adventurecenter.com. Various trips in Africa; offices across Canada & the USA.

SOUTH AFRICA
There are many companies offering specialist overland tours specific to southern Africa, with representation in South Africa only. You will need to shop around & visit a local travel agent for further information.

Affordable Adventures www. affordableadventures.co.za. Corporate adventures & 'team-building'.
African Encounters www.africanencounters. com. Egypt, Tanzania & Kenya.
Africa Tours www.destination.co.za. Tanzania, Egypt & Mozambique.
African Touch Adventures www. africantouchadventures.com
Africa Travel Company www.africatravelco.com
Bushlore www.bushlore.com. Self-drive 4x4 hire.
Drifters Adventours www.drifters.co.za. From overland tours to exclusive lodges.
Felix Unite www.felixunite.com. River trips in southern Africa.

Karibu Safari www.karibubots.blogspot.co.uk. Now based in Botswana.
Umkulu Adventures www.umkulu.co.za. From camping safaris to luxury lodges.
Wildlife Africa www.wildlifeafrica.co.za. Tailor-made safaris.

EAST AFRICA
Africa Expedition Support (see also advert on page 114) Nairobi; www.africaexpeditionsupport. com. Dynamic company run by experienced overlanders & offering fully guided self-drive trips from Nairobi to Cape Town or Cape Town to Nairobi. A 4x4 vehicle leads these trips. Contact Debs or Thiemo.
Chorra Tours e chorra.tours@gmail.com; www. chorra-tours.com. Italian/Swiss run; based at Addis & Korkor Lodge, Megab. For Gheralta treks lasting 4–10 days & longer.
Dalmar Tours Oriental Hotel, Hargeisa; e info@ dalmartours.com; www.dalmartours.com. For tours to Las Geel & Berbera.
Game Trackers www.gametrackersafaris.com. Kenya & Tanzania.
K G Ahadu Tours & Travel Agency Mekele, Axum Hotel building; e info@ethiopia-tour-travel-ahadu.com, naodgk@yahoo.com; www.ethiopia-tour-travel-ahadu.com. Specialising in Danakil & Tigrai tours. Contact Naod.
Swala Safaris www.swalasafaris.com. In Tanzania, wildlife & cultural safaris.

NORTH AFRICA
Tours to the Tibesti/Ennedi are currently offered usually for a minimum group size of 6.

Société des Voyages Sahariens (Spazi d'Aventura), N'djamena; www.svstchad.com
Tchad Évasion N'djamena; 00235)22 52 65 32/22 52 50 24; m 00235 66 29 21 39; e tchad. evasion@yahoo.fr; www.tchadevasion.com

In some African countries it is also apparently possible to hire a car with driver locally; see various online travellers' forums.

5

Practicalities

RED TAPE

PASSPORTS Make sure you have plenty of spare pages in your passport! Most visas will take up a whole page each, and sometimes the whole of the opposite page for entry and exit stamps when you reach the country. Some African countries are extremely 'stamp happy' and use up a lot of space. You may come across checkpoints where all your documents will be scrutinised and your passport stamped, sometimes over and over again. Some countries, like Egypt and Libya, put details of you and your vehicle in your passport as well as in the carnet (see below).

If you have dual nationality, it may be worth taking both passports, as some visas may be cheaper for different nationalities. However, this can sometimes give you more problems at borders; some officials may be suspicious when you produce two passports, one to exit the country you are in and the second containing the visa for the country you are about to enter.

Remember you will not be allowed into certain countries if your passport has an Israeli stamp in it. Be aware too that a border stamp could imply a visit to Israel. This can happen if you entered Egypt at the border south of Eilat, even when no Israeli stamp is shown in the passport.

Passport photos Some embassies demand two, and sometimes three, passport photos to attach to your visa application. We suggest you take around 30 passport photos with you; if you need more, they are relatively easy and inexpensive to obtain in most African cities.

CARNET DE PASSAGE (CARNET)
What is the carnet? The carnet is an essential and expensive document for everyone taking a vehicle (including a motorbike) across Africa. It is effectively the passport for the vehicle. Carnets are issued by national motoring organisations, eg: the RAC in the UK. This document allows you to import a vehicle into a country temporarily without paying customs duty, which in some cases can be many times its actual value.

Regulations differ between countries over the issue of carnets. Unfortunately, however, you cannot just shop around on the international markets, unless you go to the trouble of re-registering your vehicle. The carnet must be issued by an authority in the country where the vehicle is registered.

Although a carnet is likely to come in useful everywhere, it is not absolutely essential in North and west Africa. If you do not have a carnet here, a *laissez-passer* will be issued when you enter the country, for a 'small' fee. You should be able to cover much of western and southern Africa without a carnet, but in central and east African countries, it is essential.

The carnet is the main factor that makes selling a vehicle at the end of your journey far more difficult than you might expect. When you sell, you have to get your carnet discharged by the local customs office. This means the import duty will need to be paid before the deal can go through. Make sure that all the paperwork is correctly processed, or you could face a large bill later on. If you do sell without discharging your carnet, the motoring organisation or insurance company is entitled to recoup the duty from you.

How do I get a carnet and how much does it cost?
To obtain a carnet in the UK, you should contact RAC Carnets (*Great Park Rd, Bradley Stoke, Bristol BS32 4QN;* ✎ *0800 046 8375 (free in the UK) or +44 1603 605154;* e *carnets@rac.co.uk; www.rac.co.uk*). For full details, see www.rac.co.uk/travel/driving-abroad/carnet-de-passage/.

The cost of the carnet is now £195 for 25 pages, which you will need for driving across Africa. Make absolutely sure your carnet has been validated for all the countries you have requested. Customs officers will check carefully to ensure their country is listed. You may as well play safe and request absolutely every country you may possibly wish to visit – the number of countries covered does not affect the cost.

You will need either to lodge a bank guarantee or deposit equivalent to several times the current value of the vehicle, or to take out a special insurance policy to cover this amount. The sum required is from 150% of the value of the vehicle for most countries, but up to 800% of the value for Egypt. For this reason, you should value the vehicle as low as possible. The carnet-issuing authority reserves the right to adjust the declared value. Current valuations can be obtained from motoring magazines – go for the lowest option.

If you lodge a cash bond, you must pay the full amount to the RAC, who will hold the money until you return the carnet correctly processed to them at the end of your trip. The money will be returned to you without interest. Unfortunately the maximum cash bond that the RAC will accept now is £10,000, so if you're driving to Egypt and your vehicle is worth more than £1,250, you'll have to go for the insurance option.

Carnet insurance is available from R L Davison (*Bury Hse, 31 Bury St, London EC3A 5AH*). The cost is 10% of the indemnity amount, plus of course insurance premium tax; 50% of the premium is refundable on return of the cleared carnet to the RAC. In Great Britain, carnets are only available from the RAC, and in general from the national motoring authority in the country where the vehicle is registered.

CARNET WARNING

In 2008 it took us several hours to extricate ourselves from the border customs department in Guinea. The officials there claimed that we should not have been allowed into the country because our carnet did not state on the back that it was valid in Guinea. Luckily, after much talking in several languages, it took only a small gift (around £5) to smooth our way out, but following this up with the RAC in the UK was not entirely satisfactory.

Try to get the RAC or carnet issuer to list every country to which you might be travelling on the back cover of the carnet. Whatever they say in Europe, it is you who will be there in the jungle or bush trying to move on, not them!

How is the carnet used *en route*? The carnet is a large booklet containing a number of pages that are identical (except for the page numbers). Each page has three sections with details of the vehicle such as chassis number. Details about the owner are also shown. When you enter a country the customs officer should stamp, remove and keep the third section. The first section should also be stamped in the entry part as a record. When you leave the country the second section should be stamped, removed and kept by the customs. The official should also stamp the exit part on the first section, still attached to the booklet, which provides a record for you and the motoring association who issued the carnet.

The idea of this is that the main customs departments in the countries you visit will collect the two matching sections. If those two sections are not collected, they will claim customs duty through the issuing authority. (One might ponder how long these scraps of paper take to find their way to the central customs of some countries.) It is therefore vital that you collect a complete set of entry and exit stamps. If you don't get an exit stamp for a country where you got an entry stamp, you could be in big trouble later on. It could also cost you a lot of money, because the carnet may not be cleared.

INTERNATIONAL CERTIFICATE FOR MOTOR VEHICLE Known as a *carte grise* (grey card) wherever French is spoken (even though it is white) it costs around £10. Available from motoring organisations (the AA in the UK, not the RAC!), it provides an official-looking summary of the details and serial numbers of your vehicle. Generally officials request the original registration document for our vehicle, but it is definitely advisable to have both close at hand at every border and police check-post.

INTERNATIONAL DRIVING PERMIT These are available from national motoring organisations (such as the AA or RAC) on production of a current driving licence. You must get your international licence in the country where your domestic licence was issued. In the UK the cost is around £8 and requires a copy of your national driving licence and a passport photo.

INSURANCE

Vehicle insurance If you are departing from Europe, be sure to get the best cover (comprehensive or third party if costs are prohibitive) for most of the countries along the route. Green cards (often not green but paper additions) are issued for all of Europe; that includes Morocco, Western Sahara, Tunisia and Turkey. In addition be sure to get Ukraine and Russia added if possible for those contemplating a trip back through Asia. You can always print off the green card documents on green paper to help in far-flung corners of Europe. You will be lucky to get cover far beyond these countries. You can try to get insurance through Campbell Irvine (*43 Earls Court Rd, London W8 6EJ;* \ *020 7937 6981; www.campbellirvine.co.uk*). They are experienced in meeting the insurance needs of overlanders, though it is almost impossible nowadays to insure a vehicle for anywhere in Africa through a British insurance company. Try also Down Under Insurance (*www.duinsure.com*) for vehicle and personal travel insurance.

Comprehensive and third-party vehicle insurance is not available in advance for most areas in Africa. It is compulsory (policed to varying degrees) to buy third-party insurance locally. However, if something happens, your third-party insurance won't help you much. You will most likely have to pay the costs (typically in cash US$).

Once you reach Senegal, Niger or Mali, it is possible to buy a single policy that will cover you for the whole of west Africa. Similarly, you can get another single policy covering central African countries (Cameroon, Chad, Central African Republic, Equatorial Guinea, Gabon and Congo). In east and southern Africa the COMESA/Yellow Card is one policy covering third-party insurance for Burundi, Djibouti, DRC, Eritrea, Ethiopia, Kenya, Malawi, Rwanda, Tanzania, Uganda, Zambia and Zimbabwe. For other countries you need to buy third-party insurance at the borders. Mozambique, for example, will make you buy its own, even though it may be marked as covered on your existing African policy.

Medical and personal belongings Medical insurance is essential. Shop around for a good deal, as prices and cover can vary substantially. Travel insurance policies generally include some cover for personal belongings, but this is unlikely to include theft from a vehicle.

PERSONAL REFERENCES References could be useful if you are up against big bureaucratic problems. A reference from a bank or other financial representative can be used to prove that you will not be stranded through lack of funds. A character reference may also be helpful if you are in a tight corner; a character reference in French could be useful in Francophone Africa.

VISAS If there is any element of protracted red tape concerning a trip across Africa, it is that of obtaining visas. Getting many of the visas in your own country is sometimes more difficult than in neighbouring countries on the way, and it's getting harder and more expensive. Some countries, however, insist that you obtain the visa in your home country. Bear in mind, though, that for an African to get a visa to visit almost any country outside the continent is very difficult.

A VISA SAGA

Some things never change. It took six weeks to get a Sudan visa in 2004; but what happened on an overland trip to Africa in 1976? Some snippets from the diary…

Bangui 3 January Crossed the Ubangui River, only to be turned back by the Zaïre Immigration. (The great Zaïre expedition falters before it's begun.)

Now trying for the Sudan visa, but the ambassador is a very bored fellow from Khartoum and has other ideas; he wants to wine and dine our girls before a visa is remotely possible. It's a good job the whole truck isn't loaded with females, or we'd never get out of here. Of course our CAR visa will expire before we get the Sudan one.

Managed a day trip down to the Congo border – that's another version of Zaïre run from Brazzaville not Kinshasa. That's if anyone is running Zaïre, with Mobutu Sese Seko Sese Banga Waza partying here in Bangui with Big Daddy Idi Amin and Emperor Bokassa.

9 January Looks like the Sudanese Ambassador is getting bored with our girls; not that anything underhand appears to be going on. Encounter Overland, another party, are here now for visas, so they have become more interesting for the fellow. We might be out of here tomorrow with visas.

It will save you a lot of time *en route* if you can get visas for the first few countries you'll be visiting at the start of your trip, as well as any visas that are difficult to obtain in Africa. Visas for Libya, Nigeria and Angola are notoriously difficult to obtain and it is well worth trying to get them before you leave. Angola may prove impossible beforehand, making planning difficult! Even if they run out before you arrive, at least you have something in your passport and that may just make the difference. For other countries, depending on the route you take and the time you intend to spend in Africa, more often than not your visa will have expired by the time you have arrived in that country. Heading into west Africa, it's easier and cheaper to get them on the borders and within countries such as Burkina Faso, Benin, Togo and even Mali.

It is also not necessarily a good idea to get every visa before you leave, as the political situation in Africa is forever changing and by the time you intend to visit a specific country, it might not be safe or convenient. Clearly, if you are cycling, travelling will take a lot longer than in a vehicle, making visa validity and timing even more important.

On our last three expeditions we were able to get visas for all of the northern African countries in advance. It is now also required for Ethiopia, because they won't issue them *en route* any more. Others are likely to follow this trend. Just be sure to make it clear when you intend to visit and they might post-date the visa. But don't arrive before that date, as we once did! It will cause some consternation at the border. Most visas are issued as you go, from embassies in capital cities or consulates in larger towns. Consulates are often a bit quicker to arrange the visa than embassies, which might mean an enforced lengthy stay in an expensive city if you have several visas to get.

Generally speaking, you should be able to pick up a visa in the capital of a neighbouring country, but do not rely on it if there is tension between them. Major cities – Dakar, Abidjan, Nairobi, Dar es Salaam and Harare – have embassies for most other African states. Addis Ababa has the most representation when it comes to embassies and consulates, because of Ethiopia's early involvement with the OAU (Organisation of African Unity) and UNECA (United Nations Economic Commission of Africa) in 1958; most countries have some type of representation there. The moral is: if all else fails, go to Addis Ababa, so long as you have already obtained an Ethiopian visa in your own country, of course!

Nowadays you can usually get visa information on embassy websites, so you can download visa application forms and make online applications in advance.

Visa agencies It is often easier, and indeed cheaper if you live outside the capital, to get your visas via a specialist visa agency. They will send a courier with your passport to the various embassies, saving you time and effort, and of course money if you are still at work. They may ask you to download the visa application forms from their website, or from the websites of the countries concerned. You then simply complete the forms and send them, together with the fees and the relevant photographs, and of course your passport, to the agency by registered post. Then you can sit back and get on with the vehicle construction and design. Two visa agencies we can personally recommend are:

Travcour London; www.travcour.com
Home Visas Paris, France; www.homevisas.com

Visa requirements Specific visa requirements vary according to nationality. Most requirements for European travellers have now been harmonised, apart from special arrangements for UK travellers in most Commonwealth countries and similar arrangements for French nationals in former French colonies. Other travellers, such as those from Australia, New Zealand and the USA, will have to meet different requirements. If in doubt, contact your own embassy for further information.

There are various factors that need to be considered when applying for a visa. Firstly, costs can vary considerably from one country to the next, depending on your nationality and where you apply for your visa. On reaching a certain border, even though your embassy, and every guidebook, has told you that you are exempt from needing a visa, you may find that you still have to pay to enter. This is true when it comes to most Commonwealth nationals. It is a good idea to ask other

ANGOLA VISA – THE WHAT IF SYNDROME

We should have known better. Setting off into the darkest corners of Africa, one has inevitably to be fairly optimistic. But setting off with barely enough time is not a good strategy for a successful overland. That though was what we did on one venture in 2008 – London to Durban in 15 weeks, including Guinea, Sierra Leone, Liberia, Timbuktu and the two Congos. We tried to ignore the intermittent bad news about Angolan visa procurement.

Atakpame in Togo was the crunch point. We received another email about the Angolan visa problem and more web news of people ahead of us. To go on or not to go, that was the question! Of course, we had always known there was a chance that our African expedition might end prematurely this time; that was why we had explored Guinea, Sierra Leone and Liberia first.

This trip was like climbing Mount Everest – getting to the top would be a bonus but getting safely back down again would be even better. Now we were stuck on the equivalent of the South Col. Retreating from here would mean a long drive back mostly the same way, but going on could be considered foolhardy – like heading up with bad weather on the unstable slopes above. This was the 'Hillary Step' of this trip; the decisive moment when we were almost bound to make the wrong choice.

A group in front of us had been refused Angolan visas in every embassy that they had tried. Apparently some motorcyclists had ridden through a rebel roadblock at high speed in Congo. They managed to obtain their Angola visas in Kinshasa after some weeks, but having then arrived in Angola, found mines floating on the roads after the rainy season floods. Whose idea of fun was this?

With work looming, waiting for weeks in Brazzaville was not a feasible option. Yet going back 'down' the mountain to the UK was 6,000 miles, even more than going on to South Africa. But 'what if' we got to Kinshasa and we really could not get a visa for Angola? A storm on the last summit ridge! Then the Land Rover would have to be shipped out of Pointe Noire, passing through rebel country, or we would have to drive back to Libreville, requiring another expensive Gabon visa and so on. The only sensible decision was to retreat – back to Bamako and Morocco. It was our only real option.

The moral is try to have sufficient time to give yourself the best options to overcome any unforeseen obstacle – that's overland these days. Perhaps if we had 'climbed on up the South Summit Ridge' we might have found the clouds clearing ahead… but then again, perhaps not!

travellers or locals about the latest status on visa applications for the next country you're visiting.

Remember that you may need a valid yellow fever vaccination certificate in order to obtain some visas.

EMBASSIES AND CONSULATES

A good website for further information is www.embassyworld.com, or www. yellowpages.co.za for South African embassies. We recommend that you check various visa websites for up-to-date information.

You can also check the British Foreign Office website (*www.gov.uk/foreign-travel-advice*) travel advice section, which lists the relevant London embassy or consulate for each country. The French equivalent is www.diplomatie.gouv.fr/voyageurs and the German is www.auswaertiges-amt.de. Australians should look at www.smartraveller.gov.au.

MONEY

These days most banks hate travellers' cheques and charge high commissions; others won't even change them. If you take a few for an emergency (if your card won't work, etc), be sure to carry your original purchase receipt, as many banks will not exchange them without it. Keep a list of the cheque numbers separately.

Generally you should take as much hard currency in cash as you feel you can safely carry. At borders you will often want to change a small amount of money before you get to a bank or official moneychanger where you can check the correct current rates. You may also wish to take advantage of changing money on the street (a decision for each individual to make – be extremely careful if you do). In some areas there may be no banks at all and you may have to rely on changing money with local traders. One bank in Cameroon actually sent us to the man 'behind the onion sellers', who they said would give us a much better rate! Some countries will demand payment for certain services in hard currency.

It is worth bringing both small- and large-denomination notes with you. Be aware though that there are a number of fake US$100 bills in circulation; most banks will not accept them because of this. But if you are using a moneychanger, he will usually prefer larger notes such as US$50 or €50. Small notes are useful when you have to pay low charges in hard currency, otherwise you end up getting your change in local money. Bring a mix of currencies to take advantage of swings in exchange rates. You will also find that only certain currencies will be acceptable in some countries. The two most important currencies to carry are euros and US dollars. The US dollar used to be the preferred international currency of exchange, but in some banks in west Africa, particularly in small towns, euros are now the only currency accepted.

Also make sure you have either euros or CFA francs with you when crossing the Sahara into Niger or Mali (you wish!), as they were needed to pay various charges at the border. CFA (Communauté Fiscalière de l'Afrique de l'Ouest) is the common currency of the West African Monetary Unit. There are two CFAs – the West African CFA and the Central African CFA. They have the same value, but they are not interchangeable. The western version is valid in Senegal, Guinea Bissau, Mali, Niger, Burkina, Togo, Benin and Ivory Coast. The latter is used in Cameroon, Central African Republic (CAR), Chad, Congo, Equatorial Guinea and Gabon.

Most big cities have ATMs across Africa, so you do not need to take all the money you are likely to spend. It is sometimes possible to buy hard currency with your credit and debit cards (shop around – different banks in the same town will have different rules).

In a dire emergency (eg: an expensive breakdown) you can have money wired to a bank in Africa, although it can take some time, sometimes up to 12 days. It's much easier if you have someone at home to help to transfer funds if necessary. Western Union or Moneygram are increasingly represented throughout Africa. For peace of mind it's best to arrange for all your regular outgoings to be paid by direct debit while you're away.

Find a relatively safe place in the vehicle to hide some money – a mixture of hard currency and local currency of the country you are travelling in – just in case you are unfortunate enough to be robbed. But do remember where you have hidden it!

HEALTH *with Dr Jane Wilson-Howarth and Dr Felicity Nicholson*

We suggest that you discuss your medical history with your local GP and take any appropriate medication with you. The medical kit list in *Appendix 3*, page 356, includes most that you might need, but this does not mean that every item should be taken with you. Ideally discuss a medication list with your local GP or a travel clinic.

Malaria, bilharzia, various forms of diarrhoea, constipation, skin infections, flu and irritable eyes or ears from the dust are the problems that travellers are most likely to suffer eventually. Women travellers should carry all relevant medication regarding likely infections (vaginal, etc).

Doing a first-aid course before leaving may prove useful. Be prepared with as much medical equipment as you can usefully manage and use. Most travel kits include IV treatment packs, as many medical institutions in Africa do not have them. However, it is best not to undertake intravenous (IV) treatment unless you are a qualified medic, doctor or nurse. Medical staff in Africa welcome good equipment. People new to exotic travel often worry about tropical diseases, but it is accidents that are most likely to carry you off.

Carry a medical self-help book with you such as *Where There Is No Doctor: Village Health Care Handbook for Africa* by David Werner, Carol Thuman, Jane Maxwell and Andrew Pearson – available from amazon.co.uk and the Nomad Pharmacy. There are many other self-help books; ask your local pharmacy for a copy of the BNF (*British National Formulary*). This book documents all the medicines available in Britain and their prescribed doses for the relevant diseases. It is updated every few months, so you should be able to get a recently expired copy.

BEFORE YOU GO

Vaccinations Check your immunisation status. It is wise to be up-to-date on tetanus, polio and diphtheria (now given as an all-in-one vaccine, Revaxis, that lasts for ten years), hepatitis A and typhoid. Immunisations against meningococcus, hepatitis B and rabies may also be recommended. Proof of vaccination against yellow fever is needed for entry into parts of Africa, especially if you are coming from a yellow fever endemic area. The vaccination may also be advised on health grounds to protect you from disease. If you cannot have the vaccine yourself for medical reasons, then obtain an exemption certificate from your GP or a travel clinic. However, you must consider whether it is safe to travel to countries with yellow fever disease without being vaccinated, as the disease is potentially fatal.

Hepatitis A vaccine (Havrix Monodose or Avaxim) comprises two injections given about a year apart. The course costs about £100, but may be available on the

NHS; it protects for 25 years and can be administered close to the time of departure. Hepatitis B vaccination should be considered for those on longer trips (two months or more), working with children or in situations where contact with blood is likely. Three injections are needed for the best protection; for those aged 16 or over, these can be given over a three-week period if time is short. Longer schedules give more sustained protection and are preferred. Hepatitis A vaccine can also be given in combination with Hepatitis B as 'Twinrix', for those aged 18 or over, though two doses are needed at least seven days apart to be effective for the Hepatitis A component, and three doses are needed for the Hepatitis B.

Injectable typhoid vaccines – Typhim Vi – last for three years and are about 70–80% effective. Oral capsules (Vivotif) may also be available and can be used for those aged six and over who can tolerate live vaccines. Three capsules given over five days will provide protection for about three years. They offer a similar degree of protection to the injectable typhoid vaccines provided that they are taken correctly. Typhoid vaccine should be encouraged unless leaving within a few days for a trip of a week or less, when the vaccine would not be effective in time. Meningitis vaccine (containing strains A, C, W and Y) may be recommended for all travellers on longer trips passing through countries considered at risk of disease (see *Meningitis*, page 131). Vaccination against rabies is advised for overland travellers visiting remote areas, more than 24 hours from medical help. They are definitely advised if you will be working with animals (see *Rabies*, page 131).

Oral cholera vaccine (Dukoral) is now available and is recommended for extended trips to Africa or for trips to areas with extremely poor hygiene. Older travellers or those with chronic health problems may be recommended to take the vaccine. A primary course (adults and children over six years old) consists of two doses of vaccine taken between one and six weeks apart, the second dose being taken at least a week before entering the infected area. The vaccine gives good protection for up to two years. A three-dose vaccine course is used in those under six years old.

Experts differ over whether a BCG vaccination against tuberculosis (TB) is useful in adults; discuss this with your travel clinic.

In addition to the various vaccinations recommended above, it is important that travellers should be properly protected against malaria. Ideally you should visit your own doctor or a specialist travel clinic (see page 125) at least eight weeks before you plan to travel.

Malaria prevention There is no vaccine against malaria, but using prophylactic drugs and preventing mosquito bites will considerably reduce the risk. Seek professional advice for the best anti-malarial drugs to take. There are three drugs that are considered effective against malaria in sub-Saharan Africa: mefloquine, doxycycline and malarone. There are pros and cons to each of the medicines and these need to be discussed with whoever is carrying out the pre-travel consultation. Although mefloquine (lariam) is a very effective prophylactic agent it is often not the preferred choice for adults as it has some potentially serious side effects. However, for those people who have used it before with no ill effects then it is a very convenient and reasonably cost-effective way of getting protection. It is also very useful in children who do not tend to get the psychological side effects that adults can experience. If this drug is suggested and you have never used it before, then you should start two to three weeks before departure to check that it suits you. About 25% of people will experience some side effects, but these are nearly always not serious. Stop immediately if it seems to cause depression or anxiety, visual or hearing disturbances, fits, severe headaches or changes in heart rhythm. Anyone who has been treated for depression or psychiatric problems, has diabetes controlled by oral therapy, is epileptic (or has suffered fits in the past) or has a close blood relative who is epileptic, **should not** take mefloquine. Malarone or the generic equivlalent atovaquone/proguanil is an effective alternative to lariam. However, this drug is expensive and therefore better for shorter trips. Malarone need only be started one to two days before arrival in a malarial area. It is taken daily and is continued for seven days after leaving the area. It can be safely used for over a year, though it would be a very expensive way to go. It is also available in paediatric form for children under 40kg. It is prescribed by weight, so it is helpful to know how much your children weigh.

The antibiotic doxycycline (100mg daily) is a very useful alternative, and is often the preferred drug of choice for longer trips, being far less expensive than malarone. Like malarone, it need only be started one to two days before arrival; it is taken daily but needs to be continued for four weeks after leaving the malarial area. It may be used by travellers with epilepsy; however, the anti-epileptic therapy may make it less effective. Allergic skin reactions in sunlight can occur in about 1–3% of people; the drug should be stopped if this happens. It may be unsuitable in pregnancy and should not be used in children under 12 years of age.

All prophylactic agents should be taken with or after the evening meal, washed down with plenty of fluid and continued for the recommended time after leaving Africa. Chloroquine (Nivaquine, Avloclor) and proguanil (Paludrine) are not effective in sub-Saharan Africa and are only ever used now as a last resort.

There is no malaria above 3,000m; at intermediate altitudes (1,800–3,000m) there is a low but finite risk. Much of South Africa is free from the disease, although it is a risk in some parts; elsewhere the risk to travellers is great. It is unwise to travel to malarial areas of Africa when pregnant or with children: the risk of malaria is considerable and such travellers are likely to succumb rapidly to the disease.

Malaria diagnosis and treatment

Even those who take their malaria tablets meticulously and do everything possible to avoid mosquito bites may contract a strain of malaria that is resistant to prophylactic drugs. As well as taking anti-malarial tablets, it is important to protect yourself from mosquito bites, so keep your repellent stick or roll-on handy at all times. Untreated malaria is likely to be fatal, but even strains resistant to prophylaxis respond well to prompt treatment. Because of this, your immediate priority upon displaying possible malaria symptoms – including a rapid rise in temperature (over 38°C), and any combination of a headache, flu-like aches and pains, a general sense of disorientation, and possibly even nausea and diarrhoea – is to establish whether you have malaria, ideally by visiting a clinic.

Self-treatment is not without risks and diagnosing malaria is not necessarily easy, which is why consulting a doctor is sensible. There are other dangerous causes of fever in Africa, which require different treatments. Even if you test negative, it would be wise to stay within reach of a laboratory until the symptoms clear up, and to test again after a day or two if they don't. It's worth noting that if you have a fever and the malaria test is negative, you may have typhoid or paratyphoid, which should also receive immediate treatment. Travellers to remote parts of Africa would be wise to carry a course of treatment to cure malaria, and a rapid test kit.

If you are going somewhere remote in an area where malaria is a high risk, you probably have to assume that any high fever for more than a few hours is due to malaria. With malaria, it is normal enough to go from feeling healthy to having a high fever in the space of a few hours (and it is possible to die from falciparum malaria within 24 hours of the first symptoms). In such circumstances, if you are unable to easily access medical care for testing then you may decide to self-treat until you can get there. Rapid diagnostic tests are available to buy but are notoriously difficult to use unless you have been trained.

Either Malarone or coarthemeter are currently the treatments of choice. However, if you are taking Malarone as a prophylaxis then it cannot be used as a treatment. Always buy your malaria treatment before travel to avoid the pitfall of purchasing counterfeit medication.

Other See page 126 for day-to-day health issues. Be sure to have a dental check-up before you leave home. If you'll be using a coil, get it fitted at least six weeks before departure. Take whatever tampons you may need initially. Finally, see the advice about multivitamins under *Weight loss and gain* (page 126).

TRAVEL CLINICS AND HEALTH INFORMATION A full list of current travel clinic websites worldwide is available on www.istm.org. For other journey preparation information, consult www.nathnac.org/ds/map_world.aspx (UK) or http://wwwnc. cdc.gov/travel/ (US). Information about various medications may be found on www.netdoctor.co.uk/travel. All advice found online should be used in conjunction with expert advice received prior to or during travel.

HEALTH IN AFRICA It can be difficult to strike the right balance between justified concern and outright paranoia. A lot of common problems can be avoided by being sensible about hygiene. Sometimes you are dependent on local standards of hygiene. Some health guides for out-of-the-way travellers will frighten you half to death. Mostly all you need is common sense. Do not hesitate to see a doctor and use your medical insurance cover if you think there is something really wrong with you. Some countries have perfectly adequate hospitals and health clinics; some facilities are so basic they will make you cringe. Trust your judgement, but do not assume that African health care is all bad. After all, the doctors are far more accustomed to tropical diseases than those at home.

Water sterilisation If you drink contaminated water, you will probably get sick, so try to drink from safe sources. Water should have been brought to the boil, passed through a good bacteriological filter or purified with chlorine dioxide tablets. Iodine is no longer recommended for sterilising water. There are also some very effective filters that do not use chemicals and water can be drunk straight away (eg: Aquapure). If you buy mineral water, make sure the bottle is properly sealed. Some mineral water has been proven to be contaminated in many developing countries.

Hygiene One of the main problems is trying to keep clean with only a limited amount of water after a hard day's driving with sweat, dust and sand clinging to every part of your body. Following the advice below will also help prevent dysentery:

- Carry a small, compact flannel with you and use a minimal amount of water, but still wipe the day's activities from your body.
- Disinfectant soap, like Dettol, can be found throughout Africa.
- Always wash your hands after visiting the local market and handling raw meat and vegetables, as well as before eating or drinking.
- When using a cutting board or any other surface to cut meat or vegetables, always use one side for meat and the other for vegetables.

- Wash any vegetables you want to eat raw in potassium permanganate or Milton, and always peel fruit before eating.
- When there is plenty of water available, give all your cutlery a good wash in hot water just to sterilise everything.

Day-to-day health issues

Weight loss and gain Travelling independently can cause weight loss for some, while others gain it. In fact, a lack of activity, sitting and driving all day, means you are more likely to put on the pounds. Constipation is a common problem – bring laxatives with you. Take a multivitamin supplement to ensure your body gets any vitamins missing from your diet. Buy them before you leave home.

Dental care Toothpaste and toothbrushes are available in cities, but err on the side of caution and take everything you are likely to need. When you see some of the African versions of toothbrushes, you'll be glad you did. The wire brush from the tool kit is not even the last resort! Oil of cloves is good for numbing toothache, but of course it will not solve any real problems. Make sure that you clean your teeth in safe water,

Safe sex Travel is a time for all sorts of adventures. Remember the risks of sexually transmitted infection are high, whether you have sexual intercourse with fellow travellers or with locals. About 40% of HIV infections in British heterosexuals are acquired abroad. Use condoms or femidoms. If you notice any genital ulcers or discharge, get treatment promptly.

Condoms are usually extremely difficult to get hold of in Africa; there is reputed to be a black-market stall in Abidjan that sells nothing else, but it's a big detour! And can they be trusted not to burst at that critical moment? Generally you would be advised to bring what you are likely to need – and more.

If you are only travelling with your regular partner, obviously condoms are not your only choice of contraception. If you are taking the pill, you should refer to the guidance set out on the packet for storage (normally in a cool, dry place) and follow it carefully. If you decide on a coil, it must be fitted at least six weeks before you leave, to check you are not at risk from infection or expulsion. Some women experience heavy and painful periods with a coil. You can also use a cap, which can be sterilised easily in a mug with an ordinary water-purifying tablet. But you should think about the number of times you will be using communal toilet facilities or washing in the open air before making a decision to rely only on your cap while you are away.

One other possibility is to have an injectable contraceptive (Depo-Provera), which will last for two or more months. Side effects can include irregular periods, or no periods at all, not necessarily a disadvantage on the road. Fertility can also be delayed for a year after the last injection. Another disadvantage could be the need for another injection when you are miles away from anywhere. If you are thinking of changing your normal method of contraception, talk this over in plenty of time with your doctor.

Tampons and sanitary towels You will be able to buy tampons and sanitary towels in most big towns in Africa. Problem areas are north Africa and other remote areas like Congo and Central African Republic. Take enough supplies to get you through and stock up later on. If you have a definite brand preference and lots of spare space, it's a good idea to bring extra supplies. It might also be worth considering a re-usable menstrual sponge, but make sure you practise before you leave so you know exactly what is involved.

Avoiding insect bites

Mosquitoes It is crucial to avoid mosquito bites between dusk and dawn. As the sun is going down, put on long clothes and apply repellent on any exposed flesh. This will protect you from malaria, elephantiasis and a range of nasty insect-borne viruses. Malaria mosquitoes are voracious and hunt at ankle level, so it is worth applying repellent under socks, too. Sleep under a permethrin-treated net or in an air-conditioned room. During the day it is wise to wear long, loose (preferably 100% cotton) clothes if you are going through scrubby country; this will keep ticks off and also tsetse and day-biting *Aedes* mosquitoes, which may spread dengue and yellow fever. Insect repellents should ideally contain around 50–55% DEET; this can be safely used by children and pregnant women. Lower concentrations need to be applied more often, which is usually inconvenient. Higher strengths offer no additional benefit.

African trypanosomiasis Sleeping sickness (African trypanosomiasis) is a parasitic infection caused by *Trypanosoma brucei*, transmitted by the tsetse fly. There are two sub-species: one predominates in east Africa and usually causes an acute infection, whereas the other predominates in central and west Africa and causes a slower, progressive, chronic infection. In the UK cases that have been reported have usually been associated with travel in Africa.

The parasite is transmitted by the bite of an infected tsetse fly. Tsetse flies are around the size of a honeybee. In east Africa, the main reservoirs for the parasites are domestic and wild animals such as antelope and cattle. The tsetse flies here tend to inhabit savanna and woodland areas. One bite from an infected tsetse fly is enough for a human to become infected. Trypanosomiasis cannot be spread directly from person to person.

For east African trypanosomiasis, first symptoms (skin lesion around the bite with lymph node enlargement) will occur five to 15 days after the bite, with fever occurring after one to three weeks. For west African trypanosomiasis, symptoms may not present for some weeks after the infective bite. East African trypanosomiasis is a much faster progressing disease than the west African form, which can progress over a number of years.

There is no vaccine or drug to prevent sleeping sickness. The only way to prevent it is to avoid tsetse fly bites and be aware of the risk. Tsetse flies are attracted by movement and dark colours, particularly blue. They have been known to follow moving vehicles, so windows should remain closed when driving through endemic areas. Travellers are advised to wear insecticide-treated close weave and loose-fitting clothing and use a good repellent containing DEET on exposed skin. Insect repellents are not as effective against tsetse flies as mosquitoes but are better than nothing. If sunscreen is also being used, repellent must be applied after sunscreen. More information about the disease is available from the Nathnac website (*www.nathnac.org*).

Blackfly Minute pestilential biting blackflies spread river blindness in some parts of Africa between map co-ordinates 19°N and 17°S. The disease is caught close to fast-flowing rivers as flies breed there and the larvae live in rapids. The flies bite during the day but long trousers tucked into socks will help keep them off. Citronella-based natural repellents do not work against them.

Tumbu flies or putsi These flies are a problem in areas of east, west and southern Africa where the climate is hot and humid. The adult fly lays her eggs on the soil or on drying laundry. When the eggs come into contact with human flesh (when you put on clothes or lie on a bed) they hatch and bury themselves under the skin. Here they form a crop of 'boils', each of which hatches a grub after about eight days, when the inflammation will settle down. In putsi areas dry your clothes and sheets within a screened house, or dry them in direct sunshine until they are crisp, or iron them.

Jiggers or sandfleas Jiggers or sandfleas are another kind of flesh-feaster. They latch on if you walk barefoot in contaminated places, and set up home under the skin of the foot, usually at the side of a toenail where they cause a painful, boil-like swelling. These need to be picked out by a local expert; if the distended flea bursts during eviction, the wound should be doused in spirit, alcohol or kerosene, otherwise more jiggers will infest you.

Common medical problems

Travellers' diarrhoea At least half of those travelling to the tropics or the developing world will suffer from a bout of travellers' diarrhoea. The newer you are to exotic travel, the more likely you are to suffer. Taking precautions against travellers' diarrhoea will help you also to avoid typhoid, cholera, hepatitis, dysentery, worms, etc.

Travellers' diarrhoea and other faecal-oral diseases come from getting other people's faeces in your mouth. This most often happens from cooks not washing their hands after a trip to the toilet, but even if the restaurant cook does not understand basic hygiene, you will be safe if your food has been properly cooked and arrives piping hot. The maxim to remind you what you can safely eat is:

PEEL IT, BOIL IT, COOK IT OR FORGET IT.

QUICK TICK REMOVAL

African ticks are not the rampant disease transmitters they are in the Americas, but they may spread tickbite fever and even Lyme disease. Tickbite fever is a flu-like illness that can easily be treated with doxycycline, but as there can be some serious complications it is important to visit a doctor.

Ticks should ideally be removed as soon as possible, because leaving them on the body increases the chance of infection. They should be removed with special tick tweezers that can be bought in good travel shops. Failing that, you can use your fingernails: grasp the tick as close to your body as possible and pull steadily and firmly away at right angles to your skin. The tick will then come away complete, as long as you do not jerk or twist. If possible douse the wound with alcohol (any spirit will do) or iodine. Irritants like Olbas oil or lit cigarettes are to be discouraged since they can cause the ticks to regurgitate and therefore increase the risk of disease. It is best to get a travelling companion to check you for ticks; if you are travelling with small children, remember to check their heads, and particularly behind the ears.

Spreading redness around the bite and/or fever and/or aching joints after a tick bite imply that you have an infection that requires antibiotic treatment, so seek advice.

TREATING TRAVELLERS' DIARRHOEA
Dr Jane Wilson-Howarth

It is dehydration that makes you feel awful during a bout of diarrhoea and the most important part of treatment is drinking lots of clear fluids. Sachets of oral rehydration salts give the perfect biochemical mix to replace all that is pouring out, but unfortunately they don't taste nice. Any dilute mixture of sugar and salt in water will do you good, so if you like Coke or squash, drink that with a three-finger pinch of salt added to each glass. Otherwise make a solution of a four-finger scoop of sugar with a three-finger pinch of salt in a glass of water. Or add eight level teaspoons of sugar (18g) and one level teaspoon of salt (3g) to one litre (five cups) of safe water. A squeeze of lemon or orange juice improves the taste and adds potassium, which is also lost during diarrhoea.

Drink two large glasses after every bowel movement, more if you are thirsty. If you are not eating properly (or at all), you need to drink three litres of water a day plus whatever is departing from you. If you feel like eating, have a bland, high-carbohydrate diet. Heavy, greasy foods will probably give you stomach cramps. If the diarrhoea is bad, or you are passing blood or slime, or if you have a fever, you will probably need antibiotics in addition to fluid replacement. Wherever possible, seek medical advice before starting antibiotics. If this is not possible, then a three-day course of ciprofloxacin (500mg twice a day) or norfloxacin is appropriate.

If the diarrhoea is greasy and bulky and is accompanied by eggy burps, the likely cause is giardia.

Fruit should be washed and peeled. Hot food should be safe, but raw food, cold cooked food, salad and fruit that have been prepared by others, ice cream and ice are all risky. Foods kept lukewarm in hotel buffets are usually time bombs waiting to explode! That said, plenty of travellers and expatriates enjoy fruit and vegetables, so do keep a sense of perspective: food served in a fairly decent hotel in a large town or a place regularly frequented by expatriates is likely to be safer.

Giardia Giardia is a type of diarrhoea or intestinal disorder caused by a parasite present in contaminated water. The symptoms are stomach cramps, nausea, bloated stomach, watery, foul-smelling diarrhoea and 'eggy' burps. Giardia can occur a few weeks after you have been exposed to the parasite and symptoms can disappear for a few days and then return – this can go on for a few weeks. Giardia is basically a form of amoebic dysentery and is best treated with tinidazole (2g in one dose, repeated seven days later if symptoms persist).

Bilharzia or schistosomiasis
With thanks to Dr Vaughan Southgate of the Natural History Museum, London, and Dr Dick Stockley, The Surgery, Kampala

This is a disease that commonly afflicts the rural poor of the tropics. Two types exist in sub-Saharan Africa – *Schistosoma mansoni* and *Schistosoma haematobium*. It is an unpleasant problem that is worth avoiding, but it can be treated if you do get it. It is easier to understand how to diagnose it, treat it and prevent it if you know a little about the life cycle. Contaminated faeces are washed into the lake, the eggs hatch and the larva infects certain species of snail. The snails then produce about 10,000 cercariae a day for the rest of their lives. The parasites can digest their way through your skin when you wade or bathe in infested fresh water.

Winds disperse the snails and cercariae. The snails in particular can drift a long way, especially on windblown weed, so nowhere is really safe. Deep water and running water are safer, while shallow water presents the greatest risk. The cercariae penetrate intact skin, and find their way to the liver. There male and female meet and spend the rest of their lives in permanent copulation. No wonder you feel tired! Most finish up in the wall of the lower bowel, but others can get lost and can cause damage to many different organs. *Schistosoma haematobium* goes mostly to the bladder.

Although the adults do not cause any harm in themselves, after about four to six weeks they start to lay eggs, which cause an intense but usually ineffective immune reaction, including fever, cough, abdominal pain, and a fleeting, itching rash called 'safari itch'. The absence of early symptoms does not necessarily mean there is no infection. Later symptoms can be more localised and more severe, but the general symptoms settle down fairly quickly and eventually you are just tired. 'Tired all the time' is one of the most common symptoms among expats in Africa, and bilharzia, giardia, amoeba and intestinal yeast are the most common culprits.

Although bilharzia is difficult to diagnose, it can be tested at specialist travel clinics. Ideally tests need to be done at least six weeks after likely exposure and will determine whether you need treatment. Fortunately it is easy to treat at present.

Avoiding bilharzia

- If you are bathing, swimming, paddling or wading in fresh water that you think may carry a bilharzia risk, try to get out of the water within ten minutes.
- Avoid bathing or paddling on shores within 200m of villages or places where people use the water a great deal, especially reedy shores or where there is lots of water weed.
- Dry off thoroughly with a towel; rub vigorously.
- If your bathing water comes from a risky source, try to ensure that the water is taken from the lake in the early morning and stored snail-free, otherwise it should be filtered or Dettol or Cresol added.
- Bathing early in the morning is safer than bathing in the latter half of the day.
- Cover yourself with DEET insect repellent before swimming: it may offer some protection.

Skin infections Any mosquito bite or small nick in the skin gives an opportunity for bacteria to foil the body's usually excellent defences; it will surprise many travellers how quickly skin infections start in warm humid climates and it is essential to clean and cover even the slightest wound. Creams are not as effective as a good drying antiseptic such as dilute iodine, potassium permanganate (a few crystals in half a cup of water) or crystal (or gentian) violet. At least one of these should be available in most towns.

If the wound starts to throb or becomes red and the redness starts to spread, or the wound oozes, and especially if you develop a fever, antibiotics will probably be needed: flucloxacillin (250mg four times a day) or cloxacillin (500mg four times a day). For those allergic to penicillin, erythromycin (500mg twice a day) for five days should help. See a doctor if the symptoms do not start to improve in 48 hours.

Fungal infections also get a hold easily in hot, moist climates, so wear 100% cotton socks and underwear and try to shower frequently. An itchy rash in the groin or flaking between the toes is likely to be a fungal infection. This needs treatment with an anti-fungal cream such as Canesten (clotrimazole); if this is not available try Whitfield's ointment (compound benzoic acid ointment) or crystal violet (although this will turn you purple).

Prickly heat A fine pimply rash on the trunk is likely to be heat rash; cool showers, dabbing (not rubbing) dry, and talc will help. If it's bad you may need to check into an air-conditioned hotel room for a while. Slowing down to a relaxed schedule, wearing only loose, baggy cotton clothes and sleeping naked under a fan will reduce the problem.

Damage from the sun The incidence of skin cancer is rocketing as Caucasians are spending more time exposed to the sun. Keep out of the sun during the middle of the day and, if you must expose yourself, build up gradually from 20 minutes per day. Be especially careful of sun reflecting off water, and wear a T-shirt and lots of waterproof SPF 15 or higher suncream when swimming; snorkelling often leads to scorched backs of the thighs. Wear a hat whenever you can.

Foot damage If you wear old plimsolls or flip-flops on the beach you will avoid getting coral, urchin spines or venomous fish spines in your feet. If you do tread on a venomous fish, soak the foot in hot (but not scalding) water until sometime after the pain subsides; this may mean 20–30 minutes' immersion in all. Take the foot out of the water when you top it up, to prevent scalding. If the pain returns, re-immerse the foot. Once the venom has been heat-inactivated, get a doctor to check and remove any bits of fish spines in the wound.

Eye problems Bacterial conjunctivitis (pink eye) is a common infection in Africa; people who wear contact lenses are most open to this irritating problem. The eyes feel sore and gritty and they will often be stuck together in the mornings. They will need treatment with antibiotic drops or ointment. Lesser eye irritation should settle with bathing in salt water and keeping the eyes shaded. If an insect flies into your eye, extract it with great care, ensuring you do not crush or damage it otherwise you may get a nastily inflamed eye from toxins secreted by the creature. Small elongated red and black blister beetles carry warning colouration to tell you not to crush them anywhere against your skin.

Meningitis This is a particularly nasty disease, as it can kill within hours of the first symptoms appearing. Usually it starts as a thumping headache and high fever; there may be a blotchy rash, too. The tetravalent vaccine (eg: Mengivax ACWY) protects against meningococcal A C W135 and Y strains of bacteria, which cause the serious forms of meningitis. The original polysaccharide vaccine (eg: ACWYvax) has been surpassed by the newer conjugate vaccines (eg: Menveo and Nimenrix), which offer better protection against the various strains. In addition they prevent carriage of the bacteria in the nose and mouth and therefore reduce the risk of transmitting the disease to family and friends on return. It is recommended for many countries in sub-Saharan Africa, but specific advice should be sought. Other forms of meningitis exist (usually viral), but there are no vaccines available for these. Local papers normally report localised outbreaks. If you have a severe headache and fever, go to a doctor immediately.

Rabies Any warm-blooded mammal may carry rabies, but be particularly wary of village dogs and monkeys. It is passed on to humans through a bite, a scratch or a lick of an open wound. You must always assume that any animal is rabid and medical help should be sought as soon as is possible. In the interim, scrub the wound thoroughly with soap and bottled/boiled water for five minutes, then pour on a strong iodine or alcohol solution. This can help to prevent the rabies virus from entering the body and will guard against wound infections, including tetanus. The decision whether or not to have the highly effective rabies vaccine will depend on the nature of your trip. It is definitely advised if you intend to handle animals, or you are likely to be more than 24 hours away from medical help.

Ideally, three pre-exposure doses should be taken over a minimum 21-day period.

If any animal bites you, treatment should be given as soon as possible. At least two post-bite rabies injections are needed, even for immunised people. Those who have not been immunised will need a full course of injections together with rabies immunoglobulin (RIG), but this product is expensive (around US$800) and is very hard to come by in many African countries. This is another reason why pre-exposure vaccination should be encouraged in travellers who are planning to visit remote areas. Treatment should be given as soon as possible, but it is never too late to seek help as the incubation period for rabies can be very long. Bites closer to the brain are always more serious. Remember if you contract rabies, mortality is 100% and death from rabies is ghastly.

Treating local people You may be asked to provide medical help. Many local villagers believe that every white person is a doctor, perhaps because most travellers carry a significant amount of medicine with them.

SNAKES

Snakes rarely attack unless provoked, and bites are unusual among travellers. You are less likely to get bitten if you wear strong shoes and long trousers when in the bush. Most snakes are harmless, and even venomous species will only dispense venom in about half of their bites. If bitten, therefore, you are unlikely to have received venom; keeping this fact in mind may help you to stay calm.

Many so-called 'first-aid' techniques do more harm than good. Cutting into the wound is harmful; tourniquets are dangerous; suction and electrical inactivation devices do not work. The only treatment is anti-venom.

If you think you have been bitten by a venomous snake follow this advice:

- Try to keep calm – it is likely that no venom has been dispensed.
- Prevent movement of the bitten limb by applying a splint.
- Keep the bitten limb BELOW heart height to slow the spread of any venom.
- If you have a crêpe bandage, wrap it around the whole limb (eg: all the way from the toes to the thigh), as tight as you would for a sprained ankle or a muscle pull.
- Evacuate to a hospital that has anti-venom.

Here's what NOT to do:

- NEVER give aspirin; paracetamol is safe.
- NEVER cut or suck the wound.
- DO NOT apply ice packs.
- DO NOT apply potassium permanganate.

If the offending snake can be captured without risk of someone else being bitten, take it to show the doctor – but beware – a decapitated head is able to dispense venom in a reflex bite.

Aspirin is particularly useful, as it is unlikely to harm anyone and is often seen as a cure for everything. Vitamin pills also enjoy a legendary status. NEVER hand out antibiotics carelessly, as you risk making someone seriously ill if you give them an inadequate dose or they fail to complete a course. Take care, too, when administering eye drops or bandaging sores, as infection is very easily passed on. If there is a local doctor nearby, it is better to send a person with these sorts of ailments to them. He or she will be there to continue treatment long after you have gone. If you do have some medical background, bear in mind that the local health post may be poorly equipped and may appreciate some of your surplus supplies.

SECURITY

Of course things can go wrong anywhere. More often than not, security issues are a matter of being as well informed as possible and making a sensible judgement. Avoid all current rebel areas and heed local advice. Remember that there are hundreds of thousands of visitors to Africa every year and only a small percentage may have a bad experience.

PERSONAL Africa is generally a safe place to travel and, more often than not, you will be surprised by the kindness and hospitality of the African people. When walking around towns or cities, always look as though you know where you are going and stick to busy roads rather than isolated alleys. As always, dress respectfully and do not flash money, cameras and jewellery around. Money belts next to your body are the best way to carry cash and other valuables when away from your vehicle. If in any way you do feel threatened by a situation, drive away or find the nearest shop, local police station or security guard. In big cities where many people have so little, looking rich will make you more of a target.

VEHICLE Lock everything up at night and always put everything away before leaving your vehicle. Locking yourself in your vehicle at night is generally not necessary, but judge each situation for yourself. We did not carry our passports or other important documents on us all the time, generally only when we left the vehicle unattended in a public place. If you are on a motorbike or cycling, many campsites and backpackers' hostels have secure areas for you to keep your valuables.

WILD ANIMALS Wild animals present a small danger, but the chance of encountering hostile animals is low. Most animal attacks occur when they are surprised, protecting their young or where the animal perceives a danger.

Avoiding these situations is nearly always a simple matter of exercising care and attention. Drivers already have protection in their vehicles, but frightening elephants and other large animals in game parks should be avoided. Be careful around waterholes, particularly at dusk when more animals come to drink. Most accidents occur where hippos are bathing near waterholes; watch out also for buffaloes. Crocodiles are another possible risk in some areas. Attacks on humans by the big cats are very rare. Hyenas may scurry about close to a camping area, but present no threat in the daytime. Even if not a physical danger, monkeys can be pests (especially when playing with your windscreen wipers). Be wary of inquisitive warthogs. Since all visitors to the big parks with private vehicles have to camp in designated areas, the risks are minimised. That said, it is unwise to leave the confines of a tent or vehicle after dark. Plan ahead for that night-time loo stop.

Obviously those hiking or watching game on foot are more at risk. There are some minimal risks on the lower slopes of the big mountains, Mount Kenya, Kilimanjaro, the Ruwenzoris and other remote hilly regions. Never run from a wild beast; in the event of any danger try to get into the protection of trees. Hikers should be aware that there are dangerous snakes, so be careful in thick undergrowth and tall grass. Fortunately most snakes, and indeed most animals, will be long gone before the approach of a human.

Also see vehicle *Security* in *Chapter 3*, page 66, and bicycle *Camping equipment* and *Accommodation and food*, *Chapter 3*, pages 104 and 106.

WOMEN DRIVERS AND TRAVELLERS

We didn't often come across men or women travelling on their own. A lot of single women were either backpacking in loose groups or joining organised tours. There may be hundreds of travellers who have done Africa on their own, but many who start out on their own hitch up with other travellers on a variety of transport. The previous authors met a mother and daughter driving across Africa without any hitches. It did help that the daughter was a professional car mechanic!

Most factors discussed are the same for men and women. At the risk of being sexist, we could hint that perhaps one important difference for women travellers

'SALAAM ALEIKUM' IN LIBERIA

Being greeted by a large white tank and soldiers with blue helmets was both welcoming and intimidating at the Liberian border post of Bo Waterside. 'Salaam Aleikum.' The Pakistani soldiers seemed eager to talk. 'What is your country, madam memsahib? Pakistani cricket team, it is good, yes sahib?' This was the Pakistani Battalion, nicknamed PakBatt, motto 'Brave and Brisk'.

The main cart track 'road' from Sierra Leone had been a shock to the system, and escaping unscathed from the diamond smugglers of Bo was a relief, but getting this far was very exciting. We really hadn't thought it would be this easy to visit the country, nor had we guessed how safe it would feel. How many AK47-wielding rebels would we see? You really can't judge from any government travel website just how sensible it is to make these journeys. Yet on the whole trip we never once felt intimidated by anyone, even on this diversion to the recently war-torn former American colony. Optimistic, happy-looking people greeted us everywhere. We never saw any gun-toting soldiers of any persuasion, except the UN.

So what is Liberia like now? The capital Monrovia shows only a few signs of the wanton destruction of the war. The markets are stuffed with imported goods; huge generators hum all day. The restaurants are expensive, catering to the armies of UN advisers, and the hotel prices match their salaries. Businesspeople are making the most of the new investment opportunities. However, the rainforest in the countryside that we saw is mostly devastated. The main roads are fair tarmac, but electricity is not widespread. The rubber trees are still dripping and the Firestone Tyre Company is working again. Leaving Liberia upcountry for the backroads of southern Guinea, we were in the land of the UN BanBatt, the Bangladeshi Battalion.

Liberia is a great place. It has the first woman president of any African nation; perhaps that is reason enough for hope!

is the weight of some items – parts, jerrycans (ten not 20 litres, etc). Tyres could be kept inside the vehicle, rather than on top of the vehicle, so they are easier to access. Everyone, male or female, will soon learn the ins and outs of their vehicle, motorbike or bicycle. Even with a team of man and woman, it is best to learn and get involved as much as you can. Your male counterpart might fall ill and be completely dependent on your skills. A helping hand is generally not far away in Africa. However, only in very isolated areas or in the deepest Sahara could you run into problems, and there it is best to travel in a convoy of at least two vehicles.

ATTITUDES TO WOMEN If you are a woman travelling on your own, your only other concern is going to be the mentality of the African people. Women are seen as having a specific role within the community, and in our eyes this may seem inferior. Remember that this has been part of their culture for centuries. Although not strictly true for every country you visit in Africa, many border posts, banks and embassies are usually run and staffed entirely by men. Obviously, if you are a woman travelling on your own, you have no choice but to communicate with whomever might be there. Be polite and respectful and you should have no problems.

When travelling through more isolated areas of Africa you will often see men lounging under the acacia trees, enjoying the shade, while the women are doing all the work – collecting water, reaping the fields, cooking, caring for the children and generally running around making sure home and family are looked after. Even if they have the opportunity to start school, most African women never complete any formal education. Girls in particular have to start helping around the house at a very young age. As they are obliged to help the community at such a young age, women are usually very isolated and will speak only the local tongue, even when their male counterparts speak either French or English. You may find that most of your communication is with men.

If you have been invited to somebody's home, the women will often provide the meal and then disappear, eating with the family in the kitchen. This is particularly so in Muslim countries. In that case women are perhaps privileged, because a male guest is only allowed into the guestroom. If he were to venture into the rest of the house he might see the women of the house without their head coverings, and that would never do! As a woman, I was allowed everywhere in the house – the kitchen, living room, the television room, etc. Where we had a common language, I could communicate with the women and the men equally.

Women are also often shy in communicating with an outsider and are not used to being asked for an opinion; their lives revolve around their day-to-day responsibilities and survival. Their attitude may come across as, 'A European woman, what does she know? She is barren, no children, driving this car, no home...' This attitude is quite common and you should certainly not take offence. If time permits and you have the opportunity, it can make entertaining conversation between yourself and the local women. We can learn a lot from one another.

Some of the greatest fun can be had at markets. In some Arab countries it is the men who trade, but elsewhere it is often a woman's world. Sometimes, having walked for miles with their wares on their backs and heads, they transform a dust bowl into a riot of colour, smells and sounds. Children trace your every footstep, shouts offer you the local brew, food, cloth or even a sheep for sale... you'll need plenty of patience and time to barter for whatever you want to buy.

You may never really learn much about African women, their joys and fears, laughter and tears. Just relax and enjoy the unspoken shared moments together. You'll have a lot in common.

5

HOW TO DRESS It is very important to dress in accordance with the social norms in the countries you visit to avoid giving offence, and indeed to feel more comfortable in the heat yourself. There are reasons for local people's choice of clothing beyond religious ones. In north Africa, it is best to cover up with loose tops that hang below your bottom, with loose trousers below. Long sleeves are advisable, again, not only for religious reasons, but because you will also be protected from the sun.

I have always worn a long Pakistani tunic-style dress when in north Africa, over light trousers, giving the advantage of lots of zipped pockets with the added security that no-one else can see them. Dressing down, as you might call it, also goes a long way to avoiding sexual harassment by African men, particularly in Muslim countries. Again, this is dependent on the area you are travelling in and can take many forms. You may be followed, laughed at, constantly touched, hissed or whistled at, usually innocently, but it can become uncomfortable and annoying.

When you're driving, you will probably be most comfortable in trousers, as a skirt can too easily get torn or caught on some protruding part of the vehicle; there's always something sticking out! I usually wore a loose long-sleeved shirt with the sleeves partly rolled up, and a scarf over my hair, tied Tuareg-style in a turban, to stop it blowing constantly in my eyes in the unavoidable wind. It also helps to keep some of the sand out of your hair, a special problem if it's long. I would sometimes wear a T-shirt when driving, but would always cover my arms when in towns or villages in Muslim countries. Some European women in Africa prefer to wear a wraparound skirt, T-shirt and headband. Just be discreet.

Sometimes young women come off organised tours in their shorts and tight sleeveless or strapless tops, and you can see the reaction of the women – often tittering behind closed palms – and men, usually gawping in astonishment. This does not mean that you can never wear shorts, tank tops, bikinis or swimming costumes – just be aware of your environment and what the other women are wearing.

Much of southern Africa is pretty relaxed when it comes to clothing, but it depends on the area you are visiting. Most of the rest of Africa, however, is conservative and should be respected accordingly.

If you are a woman travelling on your own and you find a particular town a little overbearing regarding the attention of the opposite sex, you should find a temporary companion. Having a guide from a recognised agency is another option. If things are too uncomfortable, it's best to move on. Egypt and Morocco can be particularly intense regarding sexual harassment, not as a direct threat but more as an irritant.

AVOIDING HARASSMENT Sexual harassment is not confined to single women. Even if you're travelling with a male companion, some intrusions seem out of place. It is unfortunate that some Arab men tend to think that Western women are promiscuous at the drop of a hat, but it is best just to try to ignore such a situation. There are certain things you can do to minimise sexual harassment:

- Dress conservatively. Your own experiences in Africa will be so much more fulfilling as a result, with both men and women.
- A wedding ring helps in Africa. If you are being hassled, refer to your husband as often as you can, even if you don't have one.
- Avoid eye contact and ignore all rude comments. If you are feeling threatened in any way, walk to the nearest public café and ask the owner for his or her help in getting a taxi home.
- Always know where you are and stick to busy roads rather than isolated alleyways.

TRAVELLING WITH CHILDREN   by Bonita Backhouse

There is travelling, and then there is travelling with children. The latter brings a whole new dimension to the meaning of 'adventure travel'.

The best advice is to do what works for you! However, for those of you paralysed with doubt about travelling with a child, here are some suggestions to help you overcome any fears (we took a four-year-old boy overland across Africa for 13 months).

Be honest with yourself first. If you are not up for the adventure of travelling to the destination, then there is absolutely no point in going with a child. It will be misery for everyone. If you have previously done a lot of adventure travel and know a destination well, then that place may be a good first place to visit. Our first travels with a baby were within Europe, but by 18 months we were travelling with our son around China because it was a destination we had been to before and felt able to cope with.

An obvious point maybe, but travelling with children is slower than normal. Children are less able to spend long hours in the car. On the long driving days we tried to break them where possible and made sure we had plenty of 'down' time. Smaller children will need time for play and naps; older children will need time for home schooling. Trying to stick to a punishing timetable is unrealistic and stressful.

On the subject of stress, remember children take their cue from you. If you are stressed the entire time, then they will be too. Instead, try to relax and explain that travelling is an adventure and that means that things do not always go according to plan. It is how you deal with a setback that matters. Having car trouble in remote northern Kenya was difficult, but we never let on to our son how worried we were – now he remembers it as the greatest adventure.

For younger children, it is worth trying to stick to some familiar routines. All through Africa we managed to give our son some milk, morning and evening (it might have been from a camel, goat or formula – although hot, a plastic bag of camel's milk in Sudan was interesting!). We always read him a story, or made

A SOLO WOMAN MOTORCYCLIST IN AFRICA   Caitlin Reed

Advice: everyone is full of it, especially for women travellers! When people found out my trip was overland and solo, they became instant experts on the disasters, horrors and difficulties I could face. Encouragement was nowhere to be found, with the prevailing sentiment being that women did not, should not and even could not travel independently in Africa.

Six months and 12,000km later when I parked my motorcycle (DAFE), I felt like shouting from the rooftops. Not only was my trip a success but I met other women doing extraordinary solo trips. We all agreed that most advice regarding Africa is overblown and unduly negative. Besides the usual hassles that come with women travelling solo anywhere, Africa proved no more fraught with danger than other continents. The normal rules of good sense sprinkled with precaution apply of course, and since accommodation can be sparse, it's good to set modest daily goals with backup plans in place.

If you want to wander the open (and not so open) African roads alone, DO IT! It is entirely possible, easier than most would have you expect and of course promises the usual great rewards which can only come with taking on adventure solo.

one up, and he always had his favourite bear and blanket. So, whether we were sheltering from a horrendous storm in our roof tent in Rwanda or in a flea-ridden hostel in northern Ethiopia, he felt secure. A few familiar events in the day make all the difference – at any time – be flexible when you are travelling.

And of course, children need toys! Travelling itself is stimulating; that is why you choose to travel with children in the first place. From an early age my son could only bring the toys he could pack in his small trunk, and if it didn't fit, it didn't come! Reading books and drawing materials were excluded from that rule. Friends with older children had them researching the countries they were travelling through, writing journals and learning a few phrases in the local language. Toy batteries may not always be available, and beware of toys that make noises – we drove through most of northern Kenya to the sound of Fireman Sam's theme tune as the button on his fire engine got stuck due to the vibrations!

Another good tip is to give children little age-appropriate jobs or responsibilities. This makes them involved in the adventure and part of the family unit. Simple things like chopping vegetables or looking at maps are fine – even if they get it wrong, it's good practice, and from experience, you are no more likely to get it right – ever tried navigating in Cairo?. Show them pictures in the guidebooks of places they are going to and tell them a bit of history and background. Our son was four or five but remembers huge amounts about the places we visited. He wants to be a naturalist now because the animals so fired his imagination. Your enthusiasm will wear off!

When considering health issues and travelling with children, take comprehensive advice for the Africa trip with regards to malaria medication and vaccinations. Wednesday became 'jam day' when we all took our malaria tablets on a spoonful of jam and pulled a face! Day-to-day simple and basic health rules are needed. We stuck to three: our son always had to wash his hands before eating, he could only drink water that we had said was safe, and lastly, he should not touch animals (eg: local dogs, cats, etc which carry disease including rabies). In 13 months in Africa, none of us were sick – except from overeating or over-drinking (us only!). We also cooked for ourselves on our camping stove as often as possible, allowing us to control food hygiene.

Travelling with children can be tremendous fun. Having a child with you can be a passport to meeting people and being invited into places one would not usually encounter. In Uganda our son played for an entire day with a group of children from the village we camped near while I was invited into the women's houses and became engrossed in their daily lives. In Syria, we walked through the souks and found that our son came out laden with gifts. We were invited into people's houses for tea. Others have trodden the path of travelling with children before you, so take courage from that and follow on.

ACCOMMODATION

In Africa you will always find somewhere to stay, whether it be with the local community, a hotel, bed and breakfast, pension, mission, youth hostel, backpackers' hostel, campsite, or just sleeping in the bush or desert.

One of the more enticing reasons for driving, cycling or biking through Africa is the fascination of meeting other cultures and tribes in the context of the continent's open spaces, beautiful scenery and often complete isolation from the outside world. Opportunities will arise for you to sleep out in the bush, something that you may come to love, giving you freedom to move as you please. The accepted rule that applies is *leave nothing behind but your footprints*.

If bush sleeping is not your cup of tea, or you cannot find a place where you feel comfortable and undisturbed, conventional accommodation is available throughout the continent. In some parts of Africa, such as the east, there are plenty of lodgings. In central Africa you will need to search to find a place for the night. Along the west coast, some countries accommodate campers, while others offer nothing but hotels.

Outside major cities in countries like Congo and Central African Republic, you are unlikely to find any type of accommodation unless you are lucky enough to come across a mission. Throughout southern Africa you will find a plethora of choices, except perhaps that idyllic wild bush camping spot for which you have been longing.

For more specific information about hotels, guesthouses, etc, see *Where to stay* in *Chapter 7,* page 170, and *Chapter 9, A–Z Africa Country Guide.*

POST AND TELECOMMUNICATIONS

Most reasonable-sized settlements will have a post office and a telephone. The question is whether the phone is working. Some systems are so old you wonder how they manage to get a line. And often they don't, or you may get cut off midstream. New mobile phone networks are developing fast and have fairly good coverage in Africa, though certainly not in the jungles or parts of the Sahara. Internet access is available in the most unlikely places, as well as the larger towns and cities. Of course sometimes they are very slow and sometimes they are expensive.

POST In every capital city and larger town there is a post office with post, telephone, poste restante and courier services. If you are sending letters home, ask the cashier to frank all the stamps in front of you; this will avoid stamps being removed from letters that will then never reach their destination.

EST-CE QUE C'EST LA LOIRE?

We cross the river from Cameroon to Gabon. Gabon too has its good bits of road and some strange aboriginal villages. The pygmies are not far from here, but we don't see any. The road becomes a rutted dirt highway through the magnificent trees of the equatorial forest. Later, finding a place to camp is a problem, with very few possible spots. Finally we stop to cook, but a local appears from nowhere and suggests that camping here is not a good idea; there are too many monkeys or elephants, but maybe it's too many inquisitive villagers. We don't really know; it's a bit forbidding.

We drive on and on into the dark night; the road brushes through thick bamboo forest. After hours some lights appear; it is 21.00, we are in Ndjolé, a town on the banks of the wide Ogooué River. We can't believe our eyes as we pull up outside the Auberge St Hubert. The building could be anywhere along the banks of the Loire in France, except it's hot, muggy and the cicadas are deafening. Inside we are greeted by 'Madame la Propriétaire' and some expatriate French guests. We have a beer and find ourselves discussing the state of the country with the expats. One is *en route* to Franceville on business; the other is out from the capital Libreville. Our room temporarily transports us to France, to a small hotel, a little tatty, a bit smoky and with rather tacky curtains. It could be in Amboise or Blois.

Poste restante This is a postal service in the main post office of almost every capital city. Hardly anyone uses this service now; however, letters and parcels are kept for up to four weeks. Some form of identification will be needed for collection. You may also have to pay to collect it. Make sure that your name is marked clearly in bold, black capital letters: for example, Joe Bloggs, c/o Poste Restante, Central Post Office, plus the location. Note that for all French-speaking countries you need to write 'PTT' instead of 'Poste Restante.' Remember that it can take at least two to three weeks for a letter to get to its final destination. If you are collecting a parcel, it usually needs to go through a customs check, and if it's valuable you may have to pay duty.

Alternative mail services If you need to collect valuable items, spares or papers, you can use a courier service like DHL; although fees are high, the hassles are less.

Telecommunications Telephone and email facilities are widely available now, often even in the smallest towns. All capital cities and most larger towns will have public telephone, Skype and internet facilities, so there is no excuse not to keep in touch!

All these facilities obviously rely on the individual country's telecommunications network, the quality of which varies greatly. An overseas call is often clearer and easier to make than one to a neighbouring town. Telephone calls to Europe vary widely in cost. It is much cheaper to use Skype or similar if the network speed is adequate, or some other system of internet phone calls.

See individual country sections in *Chapter 9* for more details.

A LAND ROVER LOVE AFFAIR

Everybody loves their Land Rover. We have yet to meet anyone who is in any way emotionally attached to any other form of vehicle!

Let us know why you love yours and we'll publish it on our websites *www.expeditionworld.com* and *http://africaoverlandguidebook.webs.com*.

Part Two

ON THE ROAD

142

6

Your Vehicle

This chapter provides you with information about driving in Africa, recovery techniques and an overview of daily maintenance, breakdown and repairs.

DRIVING TECHNIQUES

Driving in Africa can be hot, harsh and exhausting – days can be unavoidably long. It is preferable to share the driving and the experiences as much as possible. Do not drive at night unless it is completely unavoidable. With cattle and people straying on to the roads during the hours of darkness, there is constant danger. Many African vehicles have either pathetically poor or blindingly brilliant lights stuck on full beam. Some loads are wider than the vehicles and can be invisible at night.

Be very careful when you first reach the continent; watch out for the local drivers. Some drivers go phenomenally fast, including those share-taxis that have 11 people crammed inside and screech around corners with bald tyres! Buses are not always much slower, but are equally overloaded. The African travelling public has to put up with a lot!

You need to anticipate the driver's actions; many do not do the obvious. In fact expecting the unexpected should become second nature. Many vehicles don't have mirrors. Even when fitted, mirrors may not be used. You will soon learn how Africans drive!

Remember that a lot of African roads are quiet most of the time, and therefore people will not be alert for passing vehicles. This means you must drive **very slowly** through villages and towns; children may run out unexpectedly, and women with heavy water pots balanced on their heads will be oblivious to any passing traffic. If you should be so unfortunate as to knock someone down, it will always be your fault, whatever the circumstances. Animals are also a potential threat. Camels in particular, with their noses high in the air, seem blinded to other road users by their own apparent self-importance.

Although many main roads are mostly good, there is always the threat at any time of large, unmarked pot-holes; even uncovered manholes aren't totally unknown and surfaces can be suddenly rough. With so many different road surfaces, gravel tracks, sandy pistes and muddy holes, driving in Africa can be great fun. But don't get carried away by the thrill of the moment; Africa will punish you severely. Always drive with great caution.

Keep to a moderate speed on the open road. We never drove anywhere over 80km/h (50mph); at this speed you can anticipate and react to obstacles and bad sections of road. A slower speed also helps to reduce wear and tear and is more economical on fuel. In sand and on bad roads or tracks, it is preferable to coax the vehicle to go in the right direction rather than to fight the wheel and risk damage. Take it easy; be vigilant.

Become familiar with the 4x4 capability of your vehicle. Does it have permanent or selectable four-wheel drive? Does it have differential lock (diff lock), and how can this be used to your advantage? Does it have free-wheel hubs? All this information will be in the vehicle handbook; it is essential knowledge that will help to prevent you getting stuck in difficult terrain.

The benefits of walking through an obstacle before driving through should never be underestimated, particularly when faced with deep soft sand, water, mud holes and rocks. The chances of getting stuck or causing major damage because of an unseen object can be greatly reduced. Finally, keep your thumbs out of the steering wheel rim on rough roads, because hitting even small objects can make the steering wheel kick back, enough to bruise or even break them.

The three main conditions you will face are sand, mud and corrugations. Each requires a different technique and presents its own problems. Many main roads in Africa are not in such a bad condition (with the exception of much of central Africa). Going trans-Africa you will inevitably encounter one or all of the following situations:

SAND Driving on sand can initially be daunting, but within a short time you will be able to pick out the different types of sand. It can be hard packed, quite fast, smooth with some resistance, or seriously soft and deep. In between are countless variations. Sand can change abruptly; be very careful until you get a feel for it. Driving across sand dunes is potentially dangerous and needs extreme care. Vehicles can easily roll over in dune country. Never drive on a dune at any angle other than straight on and straight down. They have a habit of forming hollow zones that cannot be seen. Do a reconnaissance walk on any daunting sand dune sections.

Most main desert routes avoid dunes of any significance. If you intend to follow sandy pistes for several days, let some air out of all your tyres. With flatter tyres a greater surface area exists, enabling the vehicle to float more easily above the sand. The effect this has on your mobility is immediately noticeable. Make sure your tyres are built for this, and have a gauge handy to check the pressure. Most dual-purpose tyres can be run around 1.5 bar (approximately 21psi) in sand. Keep a check on tyre temperatures frequently in sand if the pressures are low. Try to run them with the highest practical pressure for the conditions, unless there is no choice.

It's amazing how well a 4x4 vehicle copes in most sand. The key is momentum. Using high-range 4x4 is generally more appropriate for most desert crossings. We used low-range only when we could see a particularly soft patch ahead or were already stuck. It varies with the vehicle you have. A big throaty Toyota is less likely to get bogged. When you see a section that you feel needs low-range, give yourself plenty of room for the approach. Try to get into a suitable gear, probably low-range third, before you hit the soft sand. This will give you the momentum you need; try to change down smoothly to avoid losing it. Changing gear too suddenly in soft sand can bring you to a stop as quickly as braking. Changing gear successfully retains the momentum and prevents you getting stuck. It takes some practice, though. After a while it becomes a bit of a challenge trying to avoid getting bogged, especially if you are in convoy with experienced Sahara drivers, including the locals.

Try not to use the brakes, as you will build up a wall of sand in front of your tyres, making it harder to get moving. If you have to stop, look for a harder area and just take your foot slowly off the accelerator. If you feel yourself getting stuck, try 'waggling' the steering wheel from side to side; this helps to reduce the build-up of sand. When you do come to a halt, drop the clutch immediately and check the situation. Sometimes reversing out back to solid ground is possible and sufficient. Using excess power to get moving could seriously damage your vehicle, even snapping a drive shaft. In any case, too much wheelspin will just make the situation worse, getting you bogged even more deeply.

Once bogged, you have more strenuous options. Often scooping away the sand from in front of and around the sides of all the wheels will be enough to get started. If not, and your vehicle has diff lock, then engage it, select your low ratio, first or second, and try to engage the clutch smoothly, edging forward until you gain momentum. Sand should also be removed from anywhere underneath if the vehicle is very deeply dug in.

If this fails, then it's out with the sand ladders or sandmats. Two will often be enough, but they must be well dug in and as level as possible. Placing them in front of the rear wheels is usually best. Watch out behind, as ladders can be pushed forcibly backwards once motion is gained. Having your better half, whoever that may be, add some weight by pushing will also help, but they must be prepared to leap quickly out of harm's way as soon as you start to move. Sand ladders can disappear below the surface of the sand, leaving no trace on top. If this is the case, it is obviously useful to have a person there to tell you where to dig for them! If you are unfortunate enough to be stuck in soft sand on an upward slope, you may be in for a long slow session using your two ladders, or more if you have them. Once moving, don't stop until you are on a harder surface or on a downward slope. Don't forget to walk back and retrieve your sand ladders and significant pusher!

Driving on a good sandy piste is a rare experience these days, and one to be enjoyed. Just avoid becoming overconfident, enjoy the adrenalin rushes and highs of desert driving, and act carefully; you'll have endless fun!

MUD Mud can be worse than sand and, on a very bad section, hours can be spent extracting any vehicle except a bicycle, and your shoes too! Avoiding the main rainy seasons generally means avoiding the worst mud sections. However, be very careful driving on damp mud roads, particularly those in tropical rainforests that have exaggerated cambers. It is all too easy to start sliding sideways towards often deep ditch areas. Take these sections very, very gently, probably in your lowest gear.

A number of mud roads in Cameroon, CAR, Congo and DRC have quite steep hills, and going down these when sticky can also be a little hair-raising. Again use a low gear and crawl down. Always drive into a slide; turn the wheel into the wayward direction.

When you see a muddy section ahead, stop and engage 4x4. Select the appropriate gear before hitting the bad section. For vehicles with large engines, third-gear low-range or first-gear high-range is appropriate, and for smaller engines second-gear low-range. Don't head off thinking your speed will do the trick: this is just going to make things worse in most cases. Avoid wheelspin; it will make you bog down deeper. When the wheels start to spin, ease off the accelerator until you pick up more traction, then accelerate gently, trying to avoid more wheelspin. Once you appear to be stuck, you'd better get out and assess the situation.

So now what? You could have a cup of tea if it's bad. Initially you could try reversing slightly. If you are not badly bogged, this might work. If not, then it's out with the shovel. Digging tropical mud can be rather tiring, so that tea may well be needed. There are no quick ways out of this predicament. You need to clear away as much mud as possible. This can mean crawling about underneath to cut away compacted mud and even removing higher central mounds of the road itself. Using your sand ladder, jacks and wooden blocks may all be necessary, as well as utilising available resources like logs, rocks and bits of plank. You might have to fill in the road here and there, using whatever materials are to hand. Fortunately most muddy sections don't go on for many miles, except in the Congo. Ho ho ho!

When you encounter a water-filled bog hole, or even long sections of flooded track, always stop. Walk through the hole first, and locate any logs or rocks that are often put in by other drivers. These can do serious damage to the underside of your vehicle. Nine times out of ten it is better to drive through the middle of deep bog holes rather than to try to skirt round them. It is often muddier on the edges. You could end up sliding sideways into the hole, get stuck or, even worse, overturn. Mud can be fun, but it can also be dangerous in certain situations.

CORRUGATIONS Corrugations are probably the most irritating and most common driving obstacle in Africa. Many roads have been basically carved out of the existing terrain by grading machines. Some are excellent, but many more have not seen a grader since the day they were made or the last colonial left. Some are gravel, some hard-packed laterite (the red, dusty ones); some are black murram, which is dreadful after rain. All these sorts of roads can develop corrugations: continuous ripples on the surface. They can occur after a soft section, where previous vehicles have taken the opportunity to speed up. Unfortunately they can often go on for hours at a stretch and can shake a vehicle to pieces. Invariably there is no ideal way to approach these frustrating sections. Sometimes there are other tracks beside the main route that are better.

With fairly regular corrugations, there seems to be an optimum speed at which to drive. This can often be disconcertingly fast and is potentially very dangerous. Beware! The vehicle tends to float over the bumps, doing immense damage to the suspension and also making the steering very light. It is very easy to lose control and clatter off the road. Sometimes the nature of the corrugations changes, and the vehicle vibrates alarmingly, shuddering to a halt with tremendous shaking. In fact it's sometimes hard to slow down, as the vibration is so intense. Under these circumstances there is nothing to do but crawl along, hoping the torment will end soon. Going slowly will probably save time in the end, as speeding over corrugations invariably causes your vehicle to retaliate by breaking a spring or something else.

Once in the Cameroon jungle our engine stopped abruptly. No, it wasn't fuel problems, or any of the obvious problems, but a hidden, loose electrical connection on the injector pump solenoid, shaken apart by the corrugations.

RIVER CROSSINGS On most trips having to drive through very deep water is not very common. That said, a flash flood in the Sahara or a raging torrent in the mountains can be encountered. The first thing to do is nothing. Park your vehicle well back and assess the hazards; crossing any torrent is potentially a very real risk. Invariably with seriously deep water the only action is to wait. Have a few cups of tea; maybe even wait overnight for the water to subside.

Assuming it's safe and not too deep, walking through the water first is a must. Check for variable depth, large rocks and soft areas. If the depth of water is below the level of your radiator, fan and alternator, you can fairly safely proceed slowly, trying to avoid creating any big waves as you go. Always keep a constant speed and do not change gear; correct gear selection before you enter the water is essential. Don't stall the engine. If you do, attempting to restart it could cause even more damage. Water and mud may have been sucked into the engine via the exhaust, which means you have a major job on your hands. So basically don't take the risk in the first place.

Recovering from this mess will probably involve other vehicles, unless you have the luxury of a winch. In deeper water you could take off the fan belt to prevent damage to the fan blades. At worst the fan can be smashed by small stones and churned-up gravel and the radiator might object as well. Another suggestion, which we have not tried, is to place a foot mat over the radiator. This is said to create a larger bow wave and larger draw down in the engine bay, hopefully keeping more of the engine out of the water.

The best options, if they exist, are to find another way or wait, unless you have any serious reasons for rushing on. We once waited three days for a river to subside, so have enough food and water on board in case. Don't even consider driving into deep water if you haven't prepared your vehicle properly (see *Chapter 3, Vehicle selection and preparation*). You will literally be landed in even deeper water.

RECOVERY TECHNIQUES

With luck and sensible driving, you may not need to use recovery techniques much. Some of the recovery methods have already been touched on briefly in the driving section above. Getting stuck invariably happens when it's hot, windy or raining. Having the right equipment can make it easier. But taking every conceivable aid may in the end be the cause of your getting stuck in the first place, because of the weight factor. Extracting your vehicle from a tricky spot depends on what you are stuck in, your equipment and what is available locally (manpower, other vehicles, logs, etc). The availability of any anchorage points needs to be considered. In almost every situation digging, common sense and hard work will be required.

SAND LADDERS Sand ladders or sandmats are most often used to get out of soft sand, but can also be used in mud, as a jacking plate for high-lift jacks and for repairing holes in damaged bridges. First remove the sand from around all the wheels, and from the chassis if the vehicle is grounded. The mats should then be placed as flat as possible in front of the wheels with the least traction. Drive on to the mats and try to get as much speed up as possible. Do not stop until you are on a firm surface again. Sandmats can also be very useful when negotiating rotten log bridges, but again ensure they are secured in place before making any tentative advances.

HIGH-LIFT JACK Although we have not carried a high-lift jack, many strongly recommend it to save time and energy. Always remember to use a jacking plate under it before jacking in soft ground conditions. This could be a sandmat or pieces of wood. Two useful ways to recover a vehicle with a high-lift jack are 'jack and pack' and 'jack and push'.

In 'jack and pack', the high-lift jack is used to lift the wheels clear of the ground so that material such as rocks, wood or sand ladders can be packed under the wheels to increase traction. This method is useful when the vehicle is bogged up to its chassis in mud. The 'jack and push' method involves jacking the vehicle from the front or rear, so that both the wheels are off the ground. The vehicle is then pushed sideways off the jack. This method is useful when the vehicle is stuck in deep muddy ruts or grounded on a central ridge.

The high-lift jack can also be used as a winch, but it is limited to a pull the length of the jack before the whole assembly has to be reset. With all high-lift jack operations, it is important to remember always to leave the jack with the handle in the upright position when unattended. If you do not have a high-lift jack, you can use your hydraulic jack, jacking plates, blocks of wood, spare wheels and any materials found around the site. Good luck!

WINCHING There are few situations in which using a winch is the only solution. A winch could be useful in the Congo, where there are trees and some roads have steep gradients and nasty, car-eating deep ditches. Winches are not much use in sand. When thinking about winching, you need to consider suitable anchoring points.

A natural anchor is anything strong enough to take the strain – trees, large boulders or rocks. Making your own anchors, from spare wheels or sand ladders stuck vertically in the ground, should only be considered when nothing else is available, as they can be potentially quite dangerous. These methods usually require a lot of effort. The spare wheel or sand ladder must be very well dug in. Be careful how you attach the anchor strap. Try using a bar behind the tyre or sand ladders. Cable eye clamps are another method. The direction of pull needs to be as straight and as low to the ground as possible; you might need to dig a trench for the strap to lie in.

A snatch block is another winching accessory. It is a heavy-duty, single-line pulley and can be used to double the pulling force by attaching it to an anchor point, then passing the winch cable through the snatch block and back to the vehicle. A snatch block can also be used to change the direction of pull when using another vehicle to winch you out.

Winches can be dangerous; always ensure that the cable is securely fastened at both ends and all onlookers are well clear. This is very important in case the cable snaps or your anchor breaks. One person should co-ordinate the recovery and operate the winch and everyone else should stay well back while the cable is under tension. A heavy mat or blanket can also be placed over the cable to help stop it lashing if it snaps.

USING ANOTHER VEHICLE If you are travelling in convoy, many of the obstacles can be surmounted rather more easily. Using a cable between vehicles is the main method, but again beware of snapping cables. Anchor points must be carefully considered, to limit any breakages. Also be very careful when using cables in mud, and especially if any local heavy truck needs help.

MAINTENANCE, BREAKDOWNS AND REPAIRS

Remember: 'regular maintenance prevents breakdowns.' This cannot be stressed enough. Dusty conditions, extreme temperatures, contaminated fuel and bad roads all take their toll. Consult the manufacturer's handbook for service intervals as a start, and then consider the adverse conditions. More frequent checks will be necessary. In the desert, air and fuel filters will get clogged more quickly. If you do a lot of wading, gearbox and differential oils will become contaminated and you can pick up a tank of dirty fuel just about anywhere in Africa.

The box on page 150 can be used as a guideline for maintenance and inspection intervals. Changing all filters more often will help prevent breakdowns. It may seem like overkill to suggest checking something like the wheel nuts every day, but the constant vibrations from corrugated roads means that they can loosen themselves at a frightening rate. These things happen!

REGULAR MAINTENANCE You should get into the habit of checking certain things every day. Start by looking at oil and water levels, keeping both topped up without fail. Check the levels of hydraulic fluid for the brakes and clutch. Any noticeable drop will tell you that a problem may be developing. As you go around the vehicle, look at the wheel nuts, suspension fixtures, nuts, bolts and springs. Watch for any telltale drops of oil and hydraulic fluid around the wheels. It pays to crawl underneath at least once a day and look for any changes: things coming loose, exhaust, wires, fractured mountings, fuel pipes touching and wearing. Water leaks often show up in the morning. Put a spanner on all the vital steering and suspension nuts regularly and fix any minor problems immediately.

After a while you will be able to spot any potential problems far more quickly and easily. Toilet stops and lunch breaks are a good time to have a quick walk-around and carry out the following checks:

- Check underneath for signs of leakage and loose nuts.
- Visual check of hubs for signs of oil or brake fluid leakage.
- Feel wheel hubs for abnormally high temperature – could indicate a worn bearing.
- Feel the tyres for abnormally high temperature – could indicate low tyre pressure.

COMMON PROBLEMS

Vibration damage It may seem obvious, but inattention to the small things leads to bigger difficulties and potentially serious problems. With continually rough roads, the effects of vibrations are the most common problem. Nuts and bolts need constant attention. Take time to check after continuous vibration.

Leaks Leaks are invariably an effect of vibration; watch for weeping water hoses, brake pipes and fuel lines. Keep a screwdriver handy for loose jubilee clips. More seriously, watch for leaks from the radiator and hoses.

Suspension Suspension problems are an ever-present threat on poor roads. Careful driving and constant vigilance can reduce breakages. Fitting new springs on older vehicles before you set out is a good idea. Vehicles with coil springs are generally less trouble than those with leaf springs.

The chassis could crack if it was not in a good condition before leaving. Older models are more prone to this. A chassis in good condition should be fine if you take it steadily. It shouldn't be necessary to strengthen the chassis; this can distort things if not done professionally.

Many suspension problems can be prevented by careful maintenance. Check your suspension nuts are tight. Loose U-bolts can lead to the leaf springs slipping against the axle and eventually to a broken centre-bolt. When this happens the axle can then move fore or aft relative to the chassis and serious damage may follow.

ANOTHER PUNCTURE IN SUDAN

At the least our punctures meant interaction with the local people. Normally it's quite easy to breeze by, clinically isolated and cocooned in your own vehicle, passing villages and people whose lives are so different. Every time we stopped to repair our tyres, someone would ask us many things; sometimes we were offered cold drinks. In Sudan especially, people have retained their humour and sense of self-respect; there's no hassling, just a gentle friendliness and curiosity.

6

You will see a high number of local trucks and buses 'going sideways' as a result of a skewed rear axle. Africans rarely worry over such matters.

Tyres Tyres are a considerable expense. Punctures are inevitable, but tyre damage is also a constant threat in Africa. Be vigilant when running your tyres at lower pressure, when they are more prone to damage from rocks in sand. Stay away from sharp rocks, sticks and particularly the acacia thorns found under shady trees. Once back on a hard surface, be sure to pump them up or they'll rapidly overheat.

Keep a watch for tyres going down slowly. Punctures are the main hazard. Be careful to ensure the vehicle is stable before removing wheels; use wooden blocks. It's an obvious point, but in the heat of the moment things happen. Some can be repaired locally, but keep a careful watch on the job; some are done well, others very badly. If in doubt, do it yourself. You need at least two levers for this. When deflating a partially soft tyre, be careful to stop the valve flying into the sand or mud; they have minds of their own.

Breaking the bead between the tyre and the metal rim is the worst part. Soapy water can be used as a lubricant on stubborn tyres when levering. One way to break the bead is by jacking the tyre down away from the rim using the front bumper, if it's solid, or part of the chassis, as the top jacking point. Be careful not to damage the tyre; use a wooden block if necessary. Africans often drive over the tyre to break the bead, but this can cause damage.

If repairing a tube, be sure to scratch and roughen the tube well, using a hacksaw blade. Once the repair has been done, take great care not to trap small stones, sand, grit or flakes of rust between the tube and tyre, otherwise another puncture could result very soon. A good dusting of talcum powder between tube

INSPECTION SCHEDULE

On an old vehicle some of these may need to be looked at more often!

DAILY INSPECTION BEFORE STARTING ENGINE
Check for fluid leaks on the ground
Check for oil leaks around the engine
Engine oil level
Radiator water level
Brake- and clutch-fluid levels
Fan-belt tension
Spark plugs leads secure
Tightness of wheel nuts
Tyres, visual check
Check for fluid/oil leaks around the wheels
Suspension – look for loose nuts and bolts
Shock absorbers, visual check
Check for any other obvious loose nuts
General inspection of undercarriage and springs (daily when on rough roads)

After starting, check:
Water temperature
Oil pressure

and tyre can help lessen the friction between the two and reduce further troubles. It also pays to use graphite around the rim/tyre seal when installing new tyres before departure.

Be careful not to stand over a tyre when it is being blown up, in case it does not bed in properly. Carry a comprehensive selection of patches and repair material. It is also worth having tyre (rather than tube) patches to repair any large holes in the tyre itself. Tubeless tyres need special repair plugs. Old tubes can be cut for use as temporary liners if the tyre has sustained internal damage.

Fuel The poor quality of some fuel means your fuel filter is likely to get blocked more often than normal. It is a good idea to rinse the fuel tank before leaving, to get rid of any sludge that may be in the bottom, and flush the filter at the bottom of the pick-up (if fitted). This may not be necessary if your vehicle has been driven solely in countries with good fuel.

While on the road, clean out the sediment bowl regularly and change filters at the first sign of spluttering or loss of power from the engine. Filter your fuel through a fine gauze or cloth when filling the tank if you suspect it might be dirty.

If you have an apparent blockage in the fuel line, you can disconnect the pipe before the lift pump and blow through it. An obstruction can be located in this way; a short length of slightly larger pipe may be of use to avoid getting the fuel near your mouth. Keep an eye on the fuel lines; they can wear quite fast on bad roads. Also ensure that you can repair sections if necessary by taking spare pipe and joining links with ferals. In the event of a serious fuel feed problem in the lines or a leaking/damaged tank, a temporary fix can be made using your spare fuel lines fed from a jerrycan or small plastic container.

EVERY THREE OR FOUR DAYS These items should be looked at more frequently when on rough roads, and less on good roads:

Engine mountings
Exhaust system
Tyre pressures
Clean air filter – dust bowl or pre-filter if in dusty conditions
Drain plugs – check they're not loose
Spring U-bolt/nuts and spring centre bolt
Any movement between spring leaves
Cracks in coils or leaf springs
Rubbing of main leaf against the hangers
Check for any rubbing fuel lines, pipes and wires

WEEKLY
Battery acid level and corrosion of battery leads
Gearbox, transfer box and differential oil levels
Check steering-box oil
Check swivel housing oil/grease level
Steering damper
Air-cleaner oil bath – clean when in constant sand and dust
Brake cylinders and brake hoses

Electrical faults Electrical faults can be more puzzling than mechanical failures. All electrical systems involve a complete circuit for the flow of power. A logical analysis needs to be made before any drastic action is taken. The problem with wiring is that many wires are well hidden, in looms, and difficult to access. Vehicle wiring is exposed to extremely unfavourable conditions: heat, vibration and chemical attack. Look for loose or corroded connections and broken or chafed wires, especially where the wires pass through holes in the bodywork or are subject to vibration. Fuses often blow as a result of such problems.

All vehicles have one pole of the battery 'earthed' and connected to the vehicle bodywork. Nearly all modern vehicles have a negative (-) earth terminal. Electrical current flows through the component and back to the battery via the metal bodywork. If a component mounting is loose or corroded, or if a good path back to the battery is not available, the circuit will be incomplete and malfunctions occur. The engine and/or gearbox are earthed by means of flexible metal straps to the body or subframe. If these straps are loose or missing, problems may result: the starter motor may not turn sufficiently, ignition may fail and the alternator may not recharge the batteries. Sometimes the straps do not make good contact with the chassis; then the contact points need cleaning with emery paper. Various other electrical components – wiper motors, bulb holders, etc – are also earthed directly by their mountings.

Assuming that the earth return is satisfactory, electrical faults will be due either to component malfunction or to defects in the supply wires. For example, if the starter is faulty the cause could be the solenoid, the brushes inside or the wires linking it to the ignition, or even the battery leads. Broken or cracked wires internally can result in an incomplete circuit. Sometimes wires become bare and the current is earthed on to the bodywork, resulting in a short circuit and a blown fuse. If the fuse did not blow, the result could be burning of the wire insulation, more short-circuiting or, at worst, a fire. That is why it is inadvisable to bypass persistently blowing fuses with silver foil or wire. A good way to check out elusive problems is to bypass the suspect wire or component temporarily, using a length of wire with a crocodile clip or suitable connector at each end. A 12V test lamp can be used to verify the presence of supply voltage at various points along the wire so that the break can be isolated.

TACKLING HIDDEN PROBLEMS With so many moving parts and extra strain, your vehicle will be very lucky to escape all mechanical difficulties. Some failures are obvious and can be located visually: oil leaks, water leaks, brake-pipe fractures, cracked exhaust, loose wheel nuts and so on. Some problems can be investigated by smelling or listening: hot rubber, piston rings or broken valve springs clicking, exhaust loose, etc. The worst problems are the hidden ones: hot engine, squeaking brakes, wheel noises, knocking suspension noises and other mysterious rumblings.

Try to think through exactly what's happening, then attempt to isolate the problem with a few checks if possible. For example, jump up and down on the front bumper or a rear step and listen for any taps to locate suspension knocks. Check the vehicle manual to see if the symptoms are described. Squeaking brakes might be worn pads or, quite often, grit in the brake drum/disc. It could be the wheel bearing too, but touching a hub to see if it's hot may help to decide this. Some noises are worse on bad surfaces; others vibrate intermittently, suggesting less serious snags. Clutch and gearbox noises are very hard to isolate; often little can be done but to soldier on.

With any new noise that is constant, diagnose the problem as soon as possible. Engine noises and overheating are of prime concern.

With an overheating engine there is an obvious symptom, but the cause may be due to a number of defects.

For example, the water temperature light comes on; your engine is overheating not long after starting off. You need to understand what is happening so you can start eliminating possible causes:

- The engine is hot. Too much heat is retained or not enough lost, maybe both.
- Heat goes into the engine through burning fuel and friction from moving parts.
- Heat leaves the engine from the radiator via the cooling water, exhaust, oil and airflow over the engine.

The most likely cause is connected with the radiator and water system: a failure to lose heat. Water leaks are the first problem to look for and the easiest. The fan belt may have broken, although you can usually hear this happen. Is there an oil leak from the engine? Can you see oil weeping from gasket joints? If none of these seem to be the cause, it could be the heat sensor; even a wire problem is a remote possibility. Investigate the following:

MAINTENANCE SCHEDULE

Check the manuals for your particular model first.

Item	Maintenance Interval	
Diesel engine oil	6,000km (4,000 miles)	More frequently if doing a lot of low-range driving, as mileage ceases to relate to engine hours
Petrol engine oil	9,000km (5,500 miles)	
Diesel oil filters	5,000km (3,500 miles)	
Petrol oil filters	9,000km (5,500 miles)	
Diesel fuel filters	5,000km (3,500 miles)	Loss of power can be due to clogged filters from bad fuel
Petrol fuel filters	9,000km (5,500 miles)	Loss of power can be due to clogged filters from bad fuel
Sediment bowl	10,000km (6,000 miles)	On diesels inspect regularly
Air filters	10,000km (6,000 miles)	Oil-bath and reusable types, clean with every oil change
Gearbox and transfer-box oil	15,000km (9,000 miles)	
Differential oil	15,000km (9,000 miles)	
Set tappets	10,000km (6,000 miles)	See manuals; it may be a longer distance
Set timing	10,000km (6,000 miles)	See manual
Change spark plugs	20,000km (12,000 miles)	
Greasing	Every two weeks or after every wade	
Injector pump	See manual, as some need small top-ups	
Windscreen	Washer reservoir – as needed	

- Less airflow over the engine – a defective fan or a clogged radiator – or even the vehicle moving too slowly in the wrong gear.
- Reduced cooling from the radiator – water leaks, cracked rubber hoses, faulty thermostat, blocked radiator pipe, low coolant, faulty water pump.
- Check that it isn't simply a faulty radiator cap. Unimogs in particular have a complicated cap pressure system.
- Reduced cooling due to blown head gasket, or worse, cracked head.

Sometimes when a vehicle is ploughing through soft sand for long periods, the engine will get hot because it's doing a lot more work at slow speed. Friction can be generated because of insufficient oil. A low level of oil reduces its cooling ability. Oil more normally used in cold climates may be too 'thin' for hot parts of Africa. Using heavier-duty (thicker, more viscous) oil in hot places may be preferred, but be sure to warm the engine up before driving off.

GENERAL FAULT DIAGNOSIS Most common faults are caused by bad maintenance, bad lubrication, blockages, defective parts, poorly installed parts – and sometimes just plain bad luck. In general, if a vehicle is thoroughly prepared beforehand, most troubles develop as a result of outside factors. Things shake loose, things touch moving parts, items get too hot and so on. In general, things do not suddenly fail. Many problems that develop take time to become obvious, eg: a wheel bearing overheated by a sticking brake shoe. Major mechanical failures in particular are usually preceded by characteristic symptoms over hundreds of kilometres; for example, a badly set-up or worn thrust bearing in the gearbox will sound slightly different. Components that do occasionally fail without warning are often small and easily carried in the vehicle, such as the thermostat or the ignition solenoid. Of course larger items – the starter, the lift pump or the alternator – do wear out; it's best to get new ones before you leave, but also carry spares.

Often it is clear where to begin the investigation. Sometimes a fault can be cured, only to recur. Often the key is observation, seeing a problem before it becomes serious, and checking afterwards to make sure it has been fixed. Daily inspections can reveal potential hazards ahead. Sit down, have a cup of tea, smoke if you need to; a calm and logical approach is far more satisfactory in the long run. Take into account any warning signs or abnormalities that may have been noticeable in the period preceding the fault – power loss, high or low gauge readings, unusual noises or smells, etc – and remember that the failure of components such as fuses may point to some other underlying fault.

Whatever the fault, certain basic principles apply:

- Verify the fault. This is simply a matter of being sure that you know what the symptoms are before starting work. Don't rely on other people's assessments.
- Don't overlook the obvious. For example, if the vehicle won't start, is there fuel in the tank? If an electrical fault is indicated, look for loose or broken wires before digging out the test gear.
- Cure the disease, not the symptom. Replacing a flat battery with a fully charged one will get you back on the road, but if the underlying cause is not attended to, the new battery will go flat too.

Take nothing for granted. A 'new' component may itself be defective (particularly if it's been rattling round in the back for months), and it's a mistake to leave components out of a fault diagnosis just because they were recently fitted. When you do finally diagnose a fault, you will probably realise it was there before the problem.

Below is a series of suggestions for fault-finding. Similar troubleshooting lists can be found in most manuals. The following are some of the more likely problems:

Starting problems These include any problems when starting, and also a partial or complete failure to turn the engine:

- Flat battery: recharge, use jump leads or push start
- Flat battery caused by loose fan belt: re-tension
- Flat battery caused by loose or faulty alternator
- Battery terminals corroded or loose connection
- Battery earth to body defective: could be engine/starter strap
- Starter brushes, solenoid fault or loose or broken wiring
- Ignition/starter switch faults
- A corroded main earth lead: needs cleaning
- Insufficient power transmitting: engine fails to turn over
- Starter motor pinion sticking
- Flywheel gear teeth damaged or worn
- Starter motor mounting bolts loose

Fuel supply problems These include when the engine turns over but fails to start, fails to run cleanly or runs briefly before cutting out:

- No fuel in the tank
- Lift pump failure
- Air in the line due to leaks and damage
- Blocked fuel filters
- Blocked outlet in the tank: blowing down the line might clear this
- Fractured fuel line joints
- Blocked air breather hole in fuel tank filler cap
- Injector pump failure: oh dear, seek specialist advice

Main engine problems These include when the engine turns normally but will not start, an engine that will not run properly and cuts out or overheats:

- No fuel in tank
- Other fuel system fault: air leak
- Fuel starvation: engine fires but will not run cleanly; blocked filters
- Injector pump fault/leaking pipes/broken injector nozzle
- Poor piston chamber compression
- Ignition warning light illuminated (no charge)
- Air leaks at inlet manifold
- Major mechanical failure, eg: camshaft drive, timing chain, head gasket
- Serious overheating; engine cuts out, as above, radiator, etc
- Overheating, slack or broken fan belt: adjust or renew

Other engine problems If there is a whistling or wheezing noise:

- Leaking manifold gasket
- Blown or leaking head gasket

6

- Leaking air pipes or air compressor
- Cracked exhaust pipe or leaking joints

If you hear any tapping, rattling or knocking sounds from the engine itself or close by:

- Incorrect valve clearance
- Valves and camshaft worn
- Worn or stretched timing chain
- Broken piston ring (usually a clicking or ticking noise)
- Inappropriate mechanical contact (eg: fan blades)
- Worn or loose fan belt
- Peripheral component fault, ie: generator, water pump, etc
- Big-end bearings worn (a regular heavy knocking, may be less under load)
- Main bearings worn (rumbling and/or knocking, may be worse under load)
- Piston slack in chamber (often more noticeable when cold)

Note: Do not add cold water to an overheated engine, as damage may result.

Ignition and warning lights If the oil gauge reads low, or the warning light is illuminated with the engine running, it may be one of the following problems. A low oil-pressure warning in a high-mileage engine on tick-over is not necessarily a cause for concern. However, a sudden pressure loss at higher speed is far more significant. But it could be the gauge or warning light sender, and not the engine itself.

- Low oil level
- Incorrect grade of oil
- Oil filter clogged or bypass valve defective
- Oil-pressure failure valve defective
- Oil light/bulb defective
- Oil pump loose
- Oil pick-up strainer clogged
- Oil pump worn
- Defective oil gauge or sender unit
- Wire to sender unit earthed
- Overheating engine
- Worn main or big-end bearings

Other warning lights are illuminated
- Low oil level
- Coolant loss due to leaking, internal or external, damaged hoses
- Low brake/clutch fluid
- Defective thermostat
- Binding brakes
- Clogged radiator, externally or internally
- Flat or non-charging battery/alternator fault

Other faults – clutch, brakes and axles, etc
- Clutch slipping: worn clutch plate or weak pressure-plate springs
- Clutch erratic or heavy: master cylinder or slave cylinder rubbers worn
- Clutch failure: fluid loss from master or slave cylinder, or pipes
- Wheel noise: worn or damaged bearings, brake drum grooved, loose wheel nuts

- Squealing brakes: brake pads worn or damaged
- Squealing or grating noise from wheel: grit or small stones trapped in disc brake
- Soft brake or clutch pedal: air in hydraulic fluid, hydraulic fluid leaking
- Deep grinding axle noises: low differential oil
- Knocking driveshaft: defective or worn UJ, or loose nuts
- Hot brakes: badly adjusted, worn pads or loose brake shoes
- Hot wheels: badly adjusted or worn bearings, leaking hub seals
- Poor braking: badly adjusted brakes
- Poor braking: hydraulic fluid or hub bearing oil seeping on to brake pads
- Steering knocks: loose or worn track rod ends, bent track rod
- Steering erratic: loose wheel nuts, worn ball joint bearings/kingpins
- Loud exhaust: loose nuts on exhaust joints, hole in the silencer, loose manifold
- Sagging springs: cracked leaf spring/s
- Loud knocking from suspension: worn or damaged shock absorber rubbers
- Other suspension noises: damaged shock absorbers, loose nuts
- Skewed motion: broken spring centre bolt
- Driver's backache: driving too far or too fast, or old age!

Electrical faults
- Battery/ignition faults: as above under engine
- Lights fail: blown fuses, bulbs blown, loose wiring
- Indicator lights: bulbs, loose wire, fuses
- Engine cuts out: loose wiring on injector pump solenoid
- Any failure of electric units, wiper motor, horn, etc: fuses, loose wires
- Starter motor jams on: disconnect battery leads immediately and repair/replace starter motor
- Petrol engines' electrical faults: condenser, points, distributor cap and plugs
- Too much static electricity: driver's hair standing on end from African road users!

ROADSIDE REPAIRS Sooner or later African gremlins will decide it's your turn for a spot of bother and, of course, you may be a long way from the nearest help. This is the time for inspirational initiatives and inventive attitudes.

Invariably some improvisations will not work or will work only partially, but patience and thinking around a problem will usually bring a viable solution, whether permanent or temporary. Keep ideas simple. Assuming that you are carrying most or all of the items listed below as sundry accessories, you can often fix some quite daunting problems. Sometimes it is better to bypass the main problem and work on a simpler solution, one that can be sorted out later where facilities exist.

A good example is where you have a brake problem. The wheel cylinder is leaking brake fluid and needs to be replaced or have new rubbers. It's late afternoon, you can't camp anywhere and this could be a long job. You might encounter difficulties removing a tight brake drum, or perhaps the nuts holding the wheel cylinder are corroded and refusing to undo. Better then perhaps to disconnect the brake pipe leading to the mischievous wheel cylinder and block it off.

This could be done in quite a few ways, using jubilee clips, spare fuel line joints, clamps on the rubber section, other miscellaneous plastic pipe, even a fuel line nut and some old tube rubber cut to act as a seal and then screwed on to a jointed part of the line. Once you reach somewhere to park up for a while, you can fix it properly yourself with parts, or try the local mechanic. African bush mechanics have some amazing tricks up their sleeves.

Here are some useful tips and suggestions:

Starter failure Pushing is the obvious choice, but there may not be any or enough pushers about. If there is an ignition/starter electrical problem, it's possible on some starters to shortcut the ignition/starter pre-solenoid by using a screwdriver across the terminal of the starter. Be careful though, as it can spark a lot if the connection is not right, and at worst the screwdriver might try to weld itself to the terminal. If the earth is poor, you can also use jump leads from the battery to another earth point.

Some very old vehicles still have starting-handle holes behind the number plates (now we show our age!). If your vehicle has a starting handle, you've probably been stuck in Africa for 20 years! Starting handles used to backfire and break your arm at worst. It is also said that you can jack up a rear wheel and, using a length of rope wrapped around the wheel, pull this to rotate the wheel. We have never tried it. It sounds rather hard and won't work on vehicles with permanent 4x4. Try it if you're bored of waiting for help to arrive.

Damaged rubber suspension/shock absorber bushes These could be replaced by using an old tyre tube cut into many small discs with a hole punched or cut out. Add as many discs as necessary. Africans sell strong bushes made of old

---

MISSION IMPROBABLE

The following anecdote is taken from Bob's diary in 1976, from an overland trip on which he was a client. This extract was originally written while travelling through the Central African Republic.

BAHR AL GHAZAL, SOUTHERN SUDAN, 26 JANUARY Left Bangui then spent three days in Bangassou with brake trouble and officialdom delays. Drove on to Obo, road shocking; it's really an overgrown track and ferries not working. Delayed by a broken back spring. Next day a tooth came off the crown wheel on the back axle and made a neat hole in the diff cover.

Just past Obo the second diff blew. With the rest of the party setting up camp in the bush for some time, the driver, Nick, Dave and I set off to look for parts in Wau, 300 miles further on in Sudan. No traffic at all, so we had to walk the 40 miles to the border, mostly in the cool of the night until some villagers warned us about frisky animals with big hungry mouths and fluffy manes. Ate stale bread and shared some tins of fish. Spent the second night in a village – invited to stay in their little thatched mud house. It was quite something – we were offered food and some straw matting; such hospitality, a pity about the bugs in the night, though.

Hitched from the border to Wau on the top of an old Bedford truck, overloaded with a boisterous host of passengers clinging to sacks of grain over every bump of the dirt road. It was hell under the burning sun, stomach cramps threatening at any moment. (A great story to relate from the comfort of leafy England later – you know, great white ashen-faced hunter explores the Sudan by exotic lorry.)

WAU, SUDAN, 27 JANUARY Dave took Nick, who was very ill, off to Khartoum by plane. I found a complete axle in the customs house, but they weren't going to part with it. A few haggard-looking travellers arrived on the train from Khartoum, a five-day trip. Slept in the police station courtyard with other travellers. No beds, just sand and no spare parts.

tyres; they last much longer than the genuine spares. They won't pass an English MOT test, though. Temporary fixes can be done using string wrapped around damaged bushes to get a tight wad.

Leaking water hoses These can be temporarily fixed with wire/duct tape reinforced with old tube rubber and large jubilee clips. But you ought to be carrying spare hoses anyway.

Broken throttle cable or pedal Tie a piece of cord or electrical wire around the injector pump or carburettor arm and pass it through the window. We once did this on an Indian motor-rickshaw on the way to Delhi Airport and managed to co-ordinate the gear changes with the large Sikh driver. After we'd barely made it to the airport in time, the flight was then cancelled anyway!

Loose exhaust, broken mounts or holes Wire can be used to secure a loose exhaust pipe and make temporary mountings on to a suitable anchor point on the chassis. A hole in the exhaust can be patched from old food cans and wire or jubilee clips. Dum-dum exhaust paste is a good standby; it hardens quickly.

TUESDAY, 3 FEBRUARY Back at the stricken truck the locals had been bringing food; water was found a mile away. The camp was set out with loos, a cold store on the evaporation principle, a summerhouse with mosquito nets all round, and a shaded area of poles and leaves. Early next day, Aussie Dave and Kiwi Mike set out to walk to Obo, where a mission was rumoured to exist. Next day they arrived back with a big Unimog from the mission, proposing to tow the truck there.

THURSDAY, 5 FEBRUARY An amazing day – replaced the old Bedford axle with an abandoned Mercedes one. Had to replace one bearing; luckily the truck's one was exactly the same. The mission people welded the truck propshaft on to the new axle with the only electricity and welding gear between Bangui and Juba. The brakes didn't really work and we had to put four discarded bald Land Rover tyres on the wheels. The girls kept us all plied with great fruit salads, pineapples, papaya, bananas and lemon juice.

EN ROUTE, **10 FEBRUARY** Departed from the mission, full of trepidation. Nearly came off the road where some terrible rock steps in the track barred the route. Had to camp and use rocks next morning to build the road up under the truck. It took six hours to get 50 yards. Had a puncture afterwards, but got the tyre off using a screwdriver, hammer and jack handle. Used one of the two patches left and later got stuck in a mud hole for hours. Met some tourists going west; our notoriety has spread along the bush telegraph – 'So you're the lot who've been stuck for weeks.'
Crossed into Sudan, all the officials were most helpful; they could hardly believe their eyes, with the truck a good two feet lower at the back than the front. Had another puncture; we seem to be on three rear wheels longer than four.

NAIROBI, KENYA, 24 FEBRUARY Finally pulled into the big city. Ate almost continuously for three days; mostly bacon and eggs at Brunners and cake at the Thorn Tree Café.

Broken radiator cowling Wire can be used to secure a loose or broken cowling mount, but take care that the fan does not touch.

Radiator holed or damaged Soap, softened with a little water, will temporarily fix the leak. Other methods are to put an egg into the radiator water, but it's better to use proper Radseal, available from any motor factor trader. Araldite can be used to seal a badly leaking radiator with limited damage. In cases of severe damage, it is possible to block off any leaking channels or part of the radiator that is damaged.

Cracked or leaking fuel tank Fuel tank leaks can be reduced or cured using plastic padding or Araldite. The tank needs to be drained first to ensure the surfaces are dry and free from oily diesel. Fuel lines are best repaired properly with the necessary pieces and joints; carry spares.

Broken main leaf or coil spring Insert one or more wooden blocks between the axle and chassis. They need to be securely held in place with rope, etc. Any largish lump of rubber might do the trick – always assuming that you can find a largish lump of rubber in the first place. Whatever is used, make sure it's well away from brake lines, propshafts and other moving parts. Where some leaf springs have broken, you can insert small wooden blocks, bits of flat metal or any other suitable filler, and then bind the springs up as tightly as possible with thin nylon rope.

Damaged propshaft or UJ Best to have a spare UJ. Otherwise remove the broken shaft and continue in 4x4. Take care, as all the torque from the engine is now being transferred through one shaft that is not designed for this. It's fine on part-time 4x4 vehicles only. On permanent 4x4 vehicles it may not work where there is a transfer box differential. Using the diff lock will overcome this problem, but don't drive fast or for too long without releasing the wind-up by jacking the vehicle up periodically.

Clutch not functioning Start the engine in the lowest gear and change gear by matching the engine and road speeds. Otherwise crawl on using whatever gears you can get moving in.

Differential or pinion broken On some vehicles the front and rear differentials and pinions are interchangeable. Check your workshop manual to see if it's the case with yours. If they are interchangeable and your rear is damaged, swap the front units to the back to maintain rear-wheel drive. This is advised only as a last resort. You need to reset the crown-wheel and pinion backlash and interface gaps. Normally this is done using a special gauge, but it's possible to get a reasonable match using instant gasket squeezed on to the pinion interface gear. Rotate the pinion; it will leave marks on the crown-wheel. Some older manuals have a sample diagram showing the pattern required.

Sticking thermostat Remove the thermostat, but let the engine warm up for longer.

Leaking heater hoses You can use another piece of hose and jubilee clips to isolate and bypass the troubling leak.

Sump or differential holes Use plastic padding, Araldite or epoxy metal glue and, if necessary, a small sheet of metal for repair. All surfaces need to be free from oil before starting the repairs.

Track rod sheared Sounds unlikely, but it happened on a Bedford truck in Amboseli National Park in Kenya. Bind the rod up using any clamps, jubilee clips, nylon rope and a length of piping or a strong metal bar, and hope that the nearest welder is close by. Bent rods should be hammered back as well as possible.

Damaged bolt or nut threads All stripped bolts are best replaced if accessible. Try Araldite where possible as a temporary fix. Nut threads on such things as clutch slave cylinders are prone to damage and can be awkward to fix. Threads on exhaust manifold nuts and studs often strip easily because the nuts are softer. Try metal epoxy glues, or use wire as a quick fix.

Piston ring breaks/damage God forbid, but a known suggestion that has worked in remote areas on an ancient six-cylinder Bedford Truck is to remove the damaged piston and seal the piston chamber with a very tightly fitting, fashioned piece of wood. This blocks oil from the sump. The injector pipe to the affected chamber needs to be disconnected, as you don't want diesel in the oil system. This can be re-routed using a plastic pipe into a reservoir, or diesel will spray everywhere. We haven't actually tried this and it can only be a desperate last resort!

We did once have a truck aluminium piston welded and turned down with new ring grooves in Turkey. The welder was amazingly skilled.

Tyres damaged When the last spare has blown and you are desperate, it is said to be possible to fill a tyre with sand for a limited distance. Otherwise you can use old tubes to line damaged tyres. Africans even stitch up old tyres or bolt them together and use them again. There are no vehicle safety regulations; if it works it's OK!

Extreme heat It is possible to do a limited number of repairs using heat and your battery. Apparently, in a worst-case scenario, you can use your battery and arc-welding rods to effect simple repairs. We haven't tried it. Repairing metal brake pipes or loosening press-fitted parts can be done using an air pump or compressor to super-heat charcoals. Pump air down a metal pipe into the fire to generate the higher temperature a repair might require. However, none of these techniques should necessarily be your first course of action. Keep it simple. Normally it's better to effect a temporary cure and get along to a decent workshop if you can.

Degreasing A 50/50 mixture of diesel and washing-up liquid makes an excellent degreaser for pre-cleaning very dirty areas – rinse off with water after several minutes.

Old oil It is prudent to keep old oil both for extra insurance against sudden loss through damage and for ecological reasons. In the worst case, it can be filtered and re-used until a new source is found.

Suggested bush spares See *Chapter 3*, page 87 for a list of suggestions.

MOTORBIKE DRIVING HINTS AND REPAIRS

David Lambeth and Alex Marr
Once on the road, the two most important things are undoubtedly keeping your air filter clean (in very dusty conditions this can be necessary every day) and performing regular oil changes (around every 3,000km/2,000 miles). Foam air

6

filters can be washed in petrol/diesel (wear your nitrile rubber gloves), dried, soaked in air filter (or engine) oil and the excess squeezed out.

Other frequent checks should include chain tension; spoke tension and tightness of nuts and bolts. Always use self-locking nuts and threadlock fluid.

Even in dusty or sandy conditions, a chain will always last longer if lubricated. The rubber X rings in a modern chain need to be kept moist to be able to seal the internal lubricant. When run dry, a chain can get very hot, and the rings can dry out and split. Sand can also be very salty and lubricant can help to protect the chain and sprockets from corrosion.

RIDING IN DIFFICULT CONDITIONS

Sand Reducing tyre pressures considerably – as low as 8psi – increases the surface area of the tyre in the sand and makes riding a lot easier. However, if the sand is in stretches alternating with rocky terrain, do not reduce tyre pressure too much, as you risk a puncture on the rocks. In really deep sand which has been rutted by other vehicles, it can be easier to move through at walking pace, paddling with your feet until you feel in control enough to ride properly. If you feel the rear wheel getting bogged down, it is best to dismount immediately and push, simultaneously applying gentle engine power. If you get completely bogged down, slowly start moving the bike from side to side until it is free enough to be lifted out of the hole. This may require removing the luggage and, if it happens often, a sense of humour is very helpful!

Mud A real nightmare with a heavy bike, deep mud can mean you lose almost all grip and control. Stop before really bad sections and choose the best route;

KHARTOUM

And so to Khartoum. We camped at the Blue Nile Sailing Club, basically a large car park next to the river. The shower worked, and after days in the desert that was truly essential. There was also a pleasant green lawn with shady trees, where we met some travellers who were planning to cycle across Africa over a period of two to three years. They must be a little crazy, even crazier than us, we thought!

Then another white man arrived with just a tiny bag of personal possessions. He was in the process of shipping his vehicle from Aqaba to Port Sudan to avoid getting a carnet for Egypt. He planned to drive his almost-new Land Rover into the desert and make a film following the progress of some Sudanese nomads. On the vehicle, at least when it left Aqaba port, was all his expensive camera equipment, not to mention sleeping bags and other essentials for life in the desert. How much would remain when it arrived in Port Sudan? His girlfriend was due to fly out to Khartoum at the weekend, then they would take the weekly public bus to Port Sudan and wait for the ship to arrive. To get back to Europe, he was planning to ship the vehicle to Jeddah in Saudi Arabia, but, not being married to his girlfriend, she could not get a visa to travel through Saudi with him, so would have to fly to Aqaba and wait for him there. The whole thing sounded far too much hassle...

Mirror, mirror on the wall,
Who is the craziest of them all?
Cyclists, motorcyclists or car drivers?

sometimes there is an easier way round the edges or side. Check the depth of water-filled sections before riding through.

River crossings The golden rule is to walk through first, checking the depth and the state of the bottom. Riding on large, rounded mossy rocks in deep water is going to have only one result.

In high-risk situations it is better to push the bike through, taking the luggage off first if necessary. If the bike is going to fall over in the water, make sure you switch the engine off first.

Punctures Everyone should know how to mend punctures. It is not difficult, but does require technique and practice – make sure you do the practising at home before you leave. Using heavy-duty inner tubes significantly reduces the chance of punctures. Check regularly for thorns, nails and sharp stones in the tyre carcass even if you don't have a puncture. Get them out as soon as possible so that there is less chance of them slowly working through to the inner tube.

BICYCLE TROUBLESHOOTING

Generally it is very clear when you have a major malfunction on a bike, but minor and subtle problems can sometimes be more difficult to decipher.

- Numb hands – should this happen, check the angle of the tilt on your seat or the direction of the bend of your handlebars and adjust as necessary.

Faced with unexpected noises, try the following:

- Click (only when pedalling) – make sure crank arms and pedals are screwed on tight. Make sure crank arms are not hitting the front derailleur cage, the wire on your front derailleur, or kick stand. Check that the derailleurs, chain and gears are all aligned.
- Click or rubbing sound (even when you don't pedal) – check that everything attached to the rack is free from the wheel; check for deformed rim hitting brake pad or mudguard; check for broken spoke or broken axle.
- Rattle – check for loose screws all the way around on racks, water bottle cages or other screw-on accessories.

6

7

Day-to-Day Issues

However hard life is, approach it with humour and courage.
Sign on the wall at the immigration shed in Assamaka

BUREAUCRACY

Bureaucracy proliferates around the world and our own country is no exception. In fact, given that it was the British who perfected the art of bureaucracy which now persists in its ex-colonies, who are we to blame the Africans? However, bureaucracy in Africa can sometimes be encountered at its most intense.

There are a few golden rules to remember: be patient, stay calm and keep smiling. There will be times when this is easier said than done; hopefully you have time on your side. Make a cup of tea for yourself, and offer one to the officials, too. This will make them realise that you're not in a hurry and are less likely to be pushed into a corner. Keep a spare cup or two available for such an eventuality.

African red tape is something that may drive you crazy in the short term, but after the event you'll have a wealth of good stories to enliven your dinner-party conversations for years to come. Travelling with a vehicle or motorbike, you are almost certainly going to have to deal with officialdom and talk your way through

DJIBOUTI – A BORDER CROSSING

Just before the border with Djibouti, the road suddenly cascaded down a fantastic volcanic wall, the remains of a long-extinct caldera with sombre, brooding lava cliffs above a brilliant white-and-pink dried-out lakebed. This salt lake stretched into the dark, almost blue, mountains beyond. It was lunchtime at the border, even though it was now well past two o'clock. The Ethiopian immigration officers were very helpful, but the customs inspectors were nowhere to be found. Eventually a soldier sheepishly took us to one of many rusting cabins, old cargo containers and railway carriages. Here in air-conditioned comfort sat the elusive customs crew, cross-legged and chewing qat to take their minds off the sweltering heat outside.

Qat is a plant that resembles a privet hedge from an English country garden. That's how every guidebook describes it, and we cannot better the description. As the sun hits its strongest period, that is the time for the whole of the Horn of Africa and neighbouring Yemen to start the daily ritual of munching and chewing qat. Nothing can disturb this ritual; well, almost nothing. Exceptions are apparently made when a foreign tourist appears on the scene, such a rare occurrence is this.

Africa. African bureaucrats are no different from any others, in that they will not want to lose face. Always be patient, friendly and polite, even when you feel you are getting nowhere. Be rude or aggressive and you may spend the night there.

BORDERS AND POLICE CHECKS

Borders and police checks vary from country to country. Some border crossings will take hours, with a tedious amount of paperwork, while others have an easy and convenient system that's surprisingly fast. Never underestimate the systems of African border posts; always allow enough time to cross from one country into another. Sometimes things move faster when they are about to close, and you can often park safely at the customs post for the night, so that you're ready for a quick getaway in the morning.

It is worth seeking advice from other travellers who have recently crossed a specific border. Most border crossings will involve first immigration and then customs, where your vehicle or bike will be cleared; your carnet will be stamped in or out, and your international vehicle certificate and driver's licence will be checked. Vehicle insurance usually needs to be purchased, and there may be a police or military check on the vehicle. In Libya and Egypt you have to have local number plates attached, and of course you have to pay for these. In fact in Egypt they even crawled around under the vehicle looking for the chassis number, which is engraved into the chassis next to the front wheel. We didn't know where it was until they showed us. Luckily it was the same as on the carnet, otherwise perhaps we'd still be there! There may also be an import tax or fuel tax to pay. But with a carnet you don't have to pay import duty, so don't let anyone talk you into doing so. Keeping on top of all this can become a major occupation, but remember – be patient, stay calm and keep smiling!

Police or military checks are usually near border crossings, but also on the outskirts of towns and sometimes in the middle of nowhere. The officials may just want to relieve the boredom and say 'hello', or they may insist on seeing everything you have, but the latter is rare nowadays. We personally had no serious problems at any border posts on our last three trips, but there are always stories of over-zealous officialdom and delays. In Nigeria, which has a terrible reputation for police corruption, we were stopped at nearly every roadside check-post, but they simply said 'Good morning mister, how are you? Do you speak English? Safe journey.' If you can get a receipt for any roadside 'administration fee', the request is probably genuine.

Once near Arlit in Niger we had to pay a road toll for the first tarmac road we had been on for days. After our experiences at the Assamaka border and then the police station in town, we said we were not going to hand over any more money, but the policeman looked at us very apologetically and said 'It's not for me, sir, it's for the road,' as he gave us a genuine receipt. We felt very embarrassed at not having trusted him.

The best advice we can give is to play it by ear. It is up to you how to handle it if you are asked for money. Sometimes a cigarette (buy some to give away even if you don't smoke) or a pen and a smile is enough – sometimes a smile alone will suffice. It's hard for travellers to know how much to hand over. Some officials now expect that you will pay or give a gift.

In more remote areas the police and military may not have been paid their salaries recently. Some of them also perform important services, for example restricting access to dangerous or remote areas. They may be totally dependent on donations from tourists as well as the local community, so don't always just refuse to pay; consider their situation and be fair. Assamaka (Niger) is a particular case in point.

VISAS

Whenever you arrive in a large African town, particularly a capital city, you will probably have a long list of things that need doing: fixing the vehicle, buying spares, changing money, getting visas, sending and receiving emails, replacing food supplies, etc. These will probably take longer than you think!

Visa applications can be a waiting game, taking from 24 hours up to three days (the exception is a Sudan visa – it took us six weeks in London, the previous authors three months! On our second visit it took only one or two days in Cairo).

See *Visas* in *Chapter 5* (page 118) for more information.

Once in Africa you are dependent on the capital cities and the embassies represented there. Not every country has an embassy in every African country, but with some planning, depending on where you want to go next, you'll be able to get your visa within a day or two. Try to get your visas wherever it is the least hassle, perhaps when you are staying somewhere for a few days anyway. It is best to apply for a visa as soon as you arrive in town; it may take longer than expected for it to be issued.

Filling out the application forms can be time-consuming and involve lots of paperwork. Most embassies have specific opening times for visa applications, so

THE MEN OF THE NIGHT

South of Tamanrasset and the broken rocky remnants of the Hoggar Mountains, the road was open desert, with many pistes. The track crossed plains dotted with isolated craggy outcrops of boulders, destroyed by heat and cold, smashed by gripping winds and sandstorms, slowly decomposing to sand.

We camped close to the border with Niger. On the roof of the vehicle, we slept intermittently. A cool breeze rustled the plastic bag behind our pillows, while a billion stars sparkled above our open eyes. A massive tower of rock, erupting from the warm sands, cast a large eerie shadow. Sentinels of similar rock towers marched across the desert in the black of the night. Suddenly the headlights of a car brushed the Land Rover, and a convoy of two vehicles came to a halt some short distance away. Too stunned to be afraid, we peered out from below the bedding, not daring to breathe. A group of men in turbans got out of the vehicles. Leaping around and shouting, they seemed to be arguing. Then another car came past us. This was it; bandits, kidnappers, smugglers, whoever they were, we were sitting ducks.

After what seemed like an eternity, they drove off into the darkness of the night, leaving us waiting for our hearts to slow down again. Perhaps our crummy old Land Rover wasn't worth the bother.

At In Guezzam, the Tabaski festival was underway, the diesel station was closed and everyone was dressed in their finest robes and colourful *cheches* (turban-style colourful headscarves). Sheep were corralled nervously in pens awaiting their fate. 'We cannot find the fuel pump man; he is with one of his wives!' While waiting, we were invited to partake in the celebrations at the police station. After much delay, large plates appeared loaded with freshly grilled lamb and salad. All we could offer in return was a McVitie's chocolate cake, which went down very well with the local officers.

'What about the men we saw last night?' we asked. 'Oh, they're just smugglers – cigarettes, you know. We don't have any bandits here; you are quite safe.'

check beforehand. Some embassies demand a letter from your embassy, called a 'letter of introduction'. This is literally a form of introduction from one embassy to another, a totally unnecessary form of bureaucracy, since your passport proves your nationality. These letters usually take 24 hours to process and vary in price, costing anything between US$20 and US$100, depending on the embassy. Sometimes your own letter typed on official-looking letterhead notepaper may suffice.

Photographs – one, two or three depending on the country – need to be attached to the visa application. Passport photos are useful not only for visa applications, but also for other documentation that you may need for a specific country, such as photo permits.

When you apply for a visa it is useful to know the name of a hotel in the country you are proposing to visit. It may help if you can say you're staying at the Sheraton or another respectable hotel, rather than a backpackers' hostel or campsite. Visa costs can vary from US$20 to US$150, depending on your nationality and the country you are visiting.

PANTOMIME SEASON IN ASWAN

Sunday morning in Aswan. Oh yes we can, oh no we can't. The ferry goes on Monday, but will there be enough space? Wait until Monday.

Monday morning bright and early we arrived at the high dam. Four hours later we were still at the high dam, nervous with anticipation. We were dealing with Mohammed, but there were several Mohammeds. Yes, there is enough cargo; no, there isn't enough cargo. There aren't any other foreign devils with cars, so it's not looking too optimistic. We sit and sit. How much are we willing to pay for this once-a-week mayhem? Can we consider coming back next week? What about driving back to Cairo? No, please, not that! It's going to be pay up, Wadi Halfa or bust.

The Sudanese cargo manager, Mahmoud, seems to be the one who pulls the strings, although he claims he is consulting with a higher authority in the building conveniently out of sight. More cargo arrives and it looks promising. It's all an illusion, but it's conducted with a great air of honourable pretence on both sides. They say they really are sorry that there isn't enough cargo and we'll have to pay more. Of course we are totally over a barrel, and pretend that it's really too much, we'll have to drive all the way back to London. What a shame.

By 14.00 a deal is done. Come 16.00 and we are still waiting to be loaded. There is so much cargo that there is barely room for the Land Rover. A barge crammed with potatoes, tomatoes, cans of cooking oil and much else is lashed to the side of the main ferry. Finally we drive the Land Rover up two wobbly planks on to the deck of this narrow barge, without driving straight off the other side. The brakes mercifully stop us ploughing into the lake. They take us proudly to our cabin... What a heap of... and this is the new ferry. The communal toilets have already overflowed and are awash with eight inches of water, or whatever. In order to use them, you must stay above floor level on raised bulkheads and stand in the dark, hoping that your aim is straight and accurate. Judging by the state of the paintwork around the hole, the men are not very skilled.

The last time we took this ferry it was much more orderly with pre-payments and no bargaining.

Visa requirements for different countries and nationalities change regularly, and it's unlikely that they'll all remain unaltered throughout the life of this book. Always check beforehand. Some east African countries will issue visas at the border, but in much of Africa you almost certainly need to obtain one before you arrive. If in doubt, get it in advance. Your embassy or other travellers can give current advice.

The same applies to most ex-French colonies. Visas for these could once be obtained easily from a French embassy, but it's getting rare now, so check in case it's still possible. These countries once included: Benin, Burkina Faso, Cameroon, Central African Republic (CAR), Chad, Congo, Ivory Coast, Gabon, Mali, Niger, Senegal and Togo. Several of these have embassies or consulates in the UK; for others you might have to send your passport to Paris or get the visa *en route*.

Some border guards will ask to see a receipt for the visa. It may simply be an excuse to ask for money. Try to get a receipt from the embassy.

MONEY

> Finance is the art of passing currency from hand to hand until it finally disappears.
> Robert W Sarnoff

Visiting a bank can take a whole day. Changing travellers' cheques has become a nightmare in most countries (impossible in Sudan). Cash and ATMs are king now.

CURRENCY DECLARATION FORMS Fortunately these are rare now, but some countries require you to fill in a declaration on entering, saying exactly how much foreign exchange you are bringing in and whether it is in cash or travellers' cheques. If so, all your money might be counted out in front of you and listed on the form. You cannot change any money at a bank without this form. On leaving the country your leftover money, exchange receipts and declaration form should all tie up – don't get caught out.

Make sure you have already hidden some money in a safe place, so you can change money even if there is no bank around or open. This can often happen. Finding somebody to change hard currency is hardly ever a problem. Lebanese shop traders are often accommodating.

CASHING MONEY ON THE ROAD The best option is to take a mixture of euros, pounds sterling and US dollars, in small and large denominations. For more information, see *Money* in *Chapter 5* (page 121).

Changing money, like visa applications, can be time-consuming and filled with paperwork. Some banks are computerised while others need to go through all sorts of hassles before you see the cash. Always check opening and closing times of banks and leave plenty of time to change money, particularly in Arab countries where the opening hours vary. Remember that Friday is usually a holiday in Arab countries. Although banks may be open from 09.00 to 12.00, it is better to go earlier rather than later, even if you do have to wait for the attendant to have tea and say good morning to everyone.

Rates and commissions vary widely (from 1% to 10%) from bank to bank, so it is worth shopping around to ensure you get the best rate. It is also advisable to check where your next bank will be and change enough money accordingly. In Sudan it is only possible to change US dollars cash. Banks almost never change money in Nigeria, so you should look for a moneychanger or use an ATM if you can find one.

Credit and debit cards are now a better option for obtaining local cash. That said, there can be vast areas without ATM or credit card facilities, so you really do have to have wads of cash. In southern and east Africa, ATMs are now fairly widely available in larger towns and you can get your cash on the spot, but some countries have few or almost no facilities for plastic cards.

WHERE TO STAY

Also see general information under *Accommodation* in *Chapter 5*.

HOTELS Although hotels are plentiful in most parts of Africa, many of them do not come close to what we would call a hotel. But then nor do the prices. In some places they are run by the local community with no star structure at all, while elsewhere 1* to 5* accommodation can be found.

In many African countries, and particularly in the capitals, you will find a Hilton or Sheraton, a temporary escape from the Third World to the First. Such hotels can be a great place to relax and recover your energies when you have been on the road for some time. They usually offer all sorts of amenities, normally at roughly European rates.

'Hotels' in African terms can often be just the bare minimum, so always ask to see the room and negotiate the rate before booking yourself in. If you have your own vehicle, make sure that the hotel has a secure parking area; some hotels will allow guests to keep motorbikes in their rooms.

In many of the French-speaking countries along the west coast, you will struggle to find campsites or hostels, particularly in the larger towns, and you may have to depend on the kindness of a hotel manager to use his parking lot and perhaps the hotel for shower and toilet facilities. Sometimes the fact that you are driving across Africa will invoke such incredulity that it may land you a room in a posh hotel. However, we were lucky in Djibouti, when the manager of the Sheraton offered us a room for only US$50 after we'd been looking for a camping spot for hours. We used every minute of our air-conditioned comfort before checking out the next day.

BED AND BREAKFAST These are found mostly in southern Africa and along the east coast. Often quaint and family-run, they offer a wonderful opportunity to relax and get the latest information. They are usually reasonably priced, around US$20–40 for a double room. Tourist information offices should be able to supply you with a list of bed and breakfasts in the area and relevant prices.

PENSIONS AND AUBERGES Perhaps if you're driving across wildest and deepest, darkest Africa, you won't be in need of a *pension*! But let's be serious. Similar to bed and breakfasts, pensions are specific to the French-speaking countries such as Chad, Ivory Coast, Mali and Niger. They are often family-run and are abundant in Morocco. Most pensions are economical, clean, well run and informative, costing between US$25 and US$50 for a double room.

MISSIONS Throughout Africa, missions, hospitals and aid organisations will sometimes let you camp in their grounds or even offer you a room. Some will expect a small fee, others a large one – either way, a donation based on current camping rates is always welcome. Missions can be found in nearly every country in Africa. Most missions adhere to strict rules and regulations in terms of curfews, shower time, kitchen and leisure time. If you don't want to keep to such rules, find alternative accommodation.

YOUTH HOSTELS Located in the larger cities, they are often the cheapest places for a lone traveller, but two people travelling together can usually get a double room for the same price elsewhere. Some are spartan, with night-time curfews, daytime closing and no cooking facilities, often lacking in privacy. Others, however, are conveniently located and hassle-free, offering a wonderful opportunity to meet other travellers.

BACKPACKERS' HOSTELS Found mostly in southern Africa and along the east coast, there are occasional ones dotted along the west coast and in north Africa. They are economical, ranging from US$10 for a dorm bed to around US$25 for a single room, and often you can camp in the courtyard or garden. They offer a huge variety of information on what to do around town, and are a good place to meet up with other travellers.

CAMPSITES You will often find that your afternoon revolves around finding a good spot to stay. Along the more frequented Africa overland routes, there are campsites at fairly regular intervals. Major towns and out-of-the-way places will often have a site, but, if you're intending to do a loop around west Africa, you may struggle to find any at all. Campsites are not common in Libya, Sudan, Ethiopia, most of west Africa, Nigeria, Cameroon, Gabon, the two Congos and Angola. Sites vary in quality and prices will usually vary from US$5 to US$12.

Campsites give you the opportunity to meet other travellers, do some maintenance or repairs to your vehicle and catch up on all the other odd jobs that you might have been neglecting. Campsites are often a great source of information regarding vehicle repairs; where to go and who to see. Sometimes they even have their own individual mechanic, a sort of Mr Fix-It and perhaps an ex-driver for one of the tour companies. Information on campsites is included under individual countries in *Chapter 9*.

BUSH SLEEPING Don't miss sleeping out in the bush, listening to a million cicadas and other mysterious creatures of the night. Sleeping out in the desert, in the stillness of the night, is wonderful. Looking up, watching the stars and pondering the immensity of the universe, you can almost hear your own heartbeat.

MONKEY BUSINESS

South of Addis a good road drops down from the highlands into the Great Rift Valley of east Africa. We passed a lone Japanese cyclist on the road. The lakes of the Rift Valley are famous for their birdlife. We were surprised how dry the area just out of Addis was, with dusty plains of acacia and bush. Awasa is one of the more developed towns, with a superb hotel on the lakeside. Massive shady trees offered a cool retreat in the gardens, while flocks of colourful birds skimmed low over the lake. Vivid blue-bottomed monkeys looked inquisitively at the discarded icing off our last remaining piece of Christmas cake; the icing had become discoloured with dust, which gets everywhere, but the cake itself was still delicious! And the monkeys seemed to enjoy the icing too. So much so that we had to keep the windows of our room firmly shut.

7

For your own security, the less visible you are from the road, the better; you don't want the wrong kind of person to find you alone in an isolated spot. But trying to steer away from prying eyes can often prove difficult. Find a spot earlier rather than later, as problems tend to multiply once it gets dark; then you can't see where you're going, while others can see your headlights for miles. Having spotted a suitable area, ideally park up before others have noticed. This is easier said than done, as people seem to be in every corner of the bush these days.

Respect the bush and be aware of the fragile environment. If the area is particularly dry and there is a gale, don't light a fire. It would in any case make you extremely visible from miles around. Leave only your footprints – bury only biodegradable products. Do not bury any goods in national parks. Animals will usually dig them up and could injure themselves. It's best to carry all your rubbish with you until you find an appropriate place to discard it.

In Congo, Gabon or any other tropical rainforest area, bush sleeping can be very difficult, with solid vegetation right up to the sides of the road and wild animals on the prowl at night. One option, often the only one, is to find one of the 'gravel pits' that are found along the roads. Such pits often contain large pools of water, making a mosquito net absolutely essential. You are also almost guaranteed to have visitors, as these pits are frequently sited close to a village. It can also be hard to find a spot for bush camping in South Africa, Botswana, Namibia or Zimbabwe, where much of the land is fenced off. In north Africa you can occasionally camp in palmeries (palm groves), but as these are privately owned you should ask permission.

THE TAMBERMA IN TOGO

For those of you heading into northern Togo or Benin, be sure to detour to the Tamberma settlements (in Togo) or the Somba (in Benin) for an amazing experience.

The houses are not set in villages, but are found isolated across the savanna. The two- or occasionally three-storied, mud-walled circular buildings are like mini-fortresses. Each is a family unit and is 'guarded' by fetishes. Superstition is still rampant here, so it's definitely necessary to go with a local guide or you risk offending. A small fee is requested for the guide, who in turn interacts with the villagers and makes appropriate donations. Interesting fetish-style figurines are for sale here as well as other small local crafts, but it is all very low-key with few visitors.

The lower part of the structure acts as a defensive entrance, with hidden chambers for residents armed with poisoned arrows. Fetishes are again prominent. Climbing up round rough steps to the next intermediate level, you reach the kitchen or cooking area. Yet further on, you normally come round on to the roof terrace. Various different small, round chambers here provide living areas and sleeping places. Most are extremely low, better suited to pygmies. In particular, there is a low-roofed room where a woman must live when giving birth. She is not allowed to go downstairs until some time afterwards; she must wash on the roof and the water runs off through a channel. The men's room up here is significantly higher.

It is extraordinary to see people living like their ancestors, with few items of the modern era, but no-one could say that these people were down at heel or in real poverty. Their vibrancy is a testimony to the human spirit of self-sufficiency and proud independence.

VILLAGE STAYS Another choice is to ask the headman of a village if you may camp there. Staying in a village is one way of getting to know the people and culture. It is all too easy to forget that we are guests in the communities through which we are driving. Where there are a few roads or tracks, the population is likely to be concentrated along them. A small gift of appreciation such as a bottle of Coke, pens or cigarettes, is often welcomed. Even empty plastic water bottles are useful. Villagers are by nature curious, as we are of them, and you may feel a little intimidated by ogling adults and children. Mostly they are just friendly, though, and would like to communicate with you.

Remember that the vast majority of people in the world are friendly; if you didn't believe that, you would have stayed at home. You can have a fantastic experience out in the bush.

EATING AND DRINKING

Going local is inexpensive and can be great fun. All of Africa's countries have their own unique meals and local brews. Some can be an acquired taste, others will be something you might soon crave, and a few you will hope never to taste again. For the local flavours of the day go to the markets, street vendors, restaurants or local cafés. But do be cautious about the standard of hygiene. Avoid fresh uncooked salads and fruit that you haven't prepared yourself. You can't always choose where to stop the car in an emergency!

Most African countries have their own beer, brewed and bottled locally. In addition to this, you'll find fermented rice water, honey beer, millet beer and all sorts of other local delicacies brewed up 24 hours a day. In some Muslim countries, alcohol is prohibited, so be careful about this.

In most African cultures, people eat with their hands. If you are invited into a home, they will often offer you whatever cutlery is available. If this does not happen, there is just one golden rule you need to remember; always eat with your right hand. The left hand is used for all other, dirty business. If you are unsure about how to react, watch what others do. In some cultures, they will only begin eating once you have started. Ask to wash your hands before a meal. Often your insecurity and any mishap in eating with your hands can break the ice; it's your turn to be the entertainment.

In much of Africa you'll have no problem finding local produce at markets or from street vendors. Onions, garlic and tomatoes are nearly always available. Goat, mutton and chicken are also readily available, and fish is plentiful near rivers and on the coast. Many other fruits and vegetables can be found according to the country's economy and the season. However always make sure you have some emergency supplies of tinned/dried food with you. For example, in some parts of Ethiopia we found only garlic for sale.

In the markets, it can be great fun haggling and bartering your way through the smiling vendors, each protesting that their produce is the freshest, tastiest and cheapest. Visit a few stalls and ask around, so you can get a feel for prices, but always keep in mind the average local income. Sometimes you will be ripped off, but if you are happy to pay the price asked, then pay it.

SUPERMARKETS Most capital cities in Africa have a supermarket or two, from well stocked to nearly empty. West African capitals all have expensive supermarkets with French products. Local shops, often only a hole in the wall or a table set up on the pavement, have basic goods like toothpaste, toilet paper, margarine and other odds and ends. One hole-in-the-wall shop in Omdurman, Khartoum, had

No matter how much food you take or what you can find to eat, there's always some item that you crave. Chocolate melts, bacon is taboo in Muslim countries and bread with bananas can get tedious every day. If you can have yoghurt on cereals every day or with curries, your day is sure to go well! But you can't store a yoghurt for every day – and it just isn't found in many shops. A solution is, however, at hand.

It took a rather eccentric former American missionary to teach us a thing or two about Africa. His recipe below for making your own yoghurt on the road was a winner for us and may be for you too.

UTENSILS

1 small measuring cup, espresso size or similar
2 empty jam jars, thoroughly cleaned with boiling water
Saucepan for stirring in (optional: you can just mix it in the jam jar once you're experienced)

INGREDIENTS

2 cups of 'cold' water at 'room temperature'
2 cups of milk powder
1 cup of live yoghurt
2 cups of boiling water from the kettle (leave to cool just slightly)

METHOD Put the two cups of 'cold' water in the saucepan and mix with two cups of milk powder. Stir well to dissolve the powder as much as possible.

Add one cup of ready-made live yoghurt, which you can probably buy from the hotel or campsite you are staying in, or try a supermarket. Or if this is your second or more attempt, you already have it! Stir again gently.

Now add two cups of almost-boiling water and stir again gently. Don't worry if it is slightly lumpy.

Pour into the two heated and cleaned jam jars.

Wait and watch. If the ambient temperature is right, the yoghurt will start to set in less than one hour.

Leave it covered with a damp cloth overnight, and in the morning it will be fresh and cool.

Et voila! Next morning you have a delightful breakfast feast.

Don't forget to save a little to make more for the next day, then it will go on and on. Ours lasted all the way from Aswan to Durban, even surviving several days on the Wadi Halfa ferry crossing.

Sadly this method does not work very well in cold places, so added heat may be necessary. If the outside temperature is too cold, you can try leaving the yoghurt in the cab or near the engine, so long as it's not an oil-covered Land Rover block! But that's where the difficulties arise, as it sometimes ends up as 'lassi' – a yoghurt drink found in India – or it may separate into semi-solid cottage cheese and whey. At least it always seems edible, in whatever form.

Bon appetit! Enjoy your experiments.

an amazing array of goods, which we browsed through while our punctured tyre was being fixed next door. Orange juice, Egyptian fava beans, clean loose sugar …

For more luxurious items such as fresh cheese and chocolate, you will need to shop in large supermarket chains, like Nakomat or Uchumi in Nairobi, which are found in most east African countries. Morocco now also has several chains of European-style supermarkets, including Marjane.

INTERNATIONAL RESTAURANTS Perhaps there is a special occasion on the horizon, or you are tired of eating locally or cooking for yourself. Cuisine from all over the world can be found throughout Africa, particularly in the capitals, from Chinese to Italian, Indian to Lebanese, pizzas to hamburgers. The restaurants cater to every need and every pocket. Ask other travellers or wherever you are staying for advice on restaurants in the area.

WATER There is a saying in Agadez, Niger, that once you have tasted the water you will always want to return. In Agadez, the artesian wells are thousands of years old and the water is pure, coming deep out of the ground. It is checked regularly, too. But this is not always the case everywhere, and it's better to be safe than sorry; better to spend time purifying the water than be sick for days in your vehicle, or worse, on your bicycle.

You must respect local water sources. Water, especially clean water, is one of the most important commodities in Africa. Never do anything to a well that might contaminate it, such as throwing anything into it, or washing yourself or your clothes close by. This is particularly important in Arab countries, where water is also used for prayer.

Obtaining water and the amount you need to carry depends on the time of year you are travelling, where you are and how dedicated you are to washing yourself and your clothes. Obviously drinking is more important than washing when water is scarce or unavailable. Remember also that your radiator may be thirsty or spring a leak. Never waste water, especially when you're on the road.

In the desert at the hottest time of year you should allow six to eight litres a day intake per person, and even in January or February you will easily get through two or three. It is absolutely vital to drink as much as you need. If your urine becomes concentrated in colour, you could be heading for trouble. A good guide is that you should urinate often and it should be clear.

IT'S A GOAT'S LIFE

It was a fairly typical scene: a long line of vehicles stuck at the side of the road awaiting who knows what. We got out to investigate. Various police or army personnel stood officiously controlling the traffic, ie: blocking the road for no good reason other than that the president's house was nearby and he might come out at any moment … or not.

We waited. In front of us was a flashy car full of men in smart suits. After a while, one of the men got out and crossed the verge into the long grass, where he started to gather it up. What could a man in a snazzy suit be doing with his arms full of grass?

He opened the boot … a goat sat behind the spare wheel, resting his tired head on the tyre. His spirits lifted as well as his head when the delicious grass was placed in front of him.

Cyclists will face the greatest difficulties in terms of how much they can carry, and motorcyclists will also be restricted by weight. It is best to stick to the more major desert routes, where water is more likely to be available. Cyclists will need a good filter,

SOME LOCAL DELICACIES – TO TRY OR NOT TO TRY!

Charlie Shackell and Illya Bracht

EGYPT
Stella Local beer.
Alwa turki Turkish-style coffee – a great energy booster with lots of sugar.
Molokhiyya A soup made by stewing leafy vegetables with rice, garlic and chicken or beef broth. Do not be put off by its appearance.
Grilled samak (fish) Served by the kilo, it usually includes salad, bread and dips like tahini (sesame spread with olive oil, garlic and lemon) and baba ganoush (a mix of aubergine and tahini).
Gibna beyda White cheese like feta.
Gibna rumi Hard, sharp yellow-white cheese.

ETHIOPIA
Tej A very potent honey beer that you will either love or hate.
Coffee ceremony A must; be ready to experience a caffeine overload.
Shiro wot Vegetable stew eaten by Ethiopians during religious fasting.
Doro wot Hot chicken stew served on the famous *injera* bread.
Injera Flatbread, generally made to cover a table. Food is placed on top for communal meals. Not to everyone's taste; can be quite sour.
Kitfo Raw meat with yellow pepper (*mitmita*).
Coffee shops Serve fresh coffee, fruit juice and cakes.

GHANA
Apateche Traditional firewater found everywhere. Try it.
Star Local beer.
Shitor din Traditional dark chilli *sambal*.
Palava sauce *Palava* means 'trouble'; this is a variation of vegetable and meat stew.

IVORY COAST
Attiéké Grated *manioc* (cassava) served with fish and pepper sauce.
Maquis Chicken with onion and tomatoes.
Rice and offal balls A great delicacy.

KENYA
Tusker Local beer.
Irio Corn mash and maize which most Kenyans think is dull, but it's worth a try.
N'dizi Swahili for bananas, wrapped in groundnut.

MOROCCO
Green tea Very sweet, served with fresh peppermint leaves.
Tagine With chicken and prunes: a stew cooked in the traditional tagine bowl and said to be one of the oldest recipes in Africa.

because they are less able to carry supplies of good water and will be more likely to rely on poorer sources. If water is not clear, filter before purifying it. We drank either bottled mineral water, or boiled water that locals would drink straight from the tap.

NIGER
Green tea Traditionally brewed by Tuaregs over an open fire in tiny teapots.
Fresh camels' milk Like a warm milkshake and not to everyone's taste.
Goat's cheese A Tuareg delicacy; should be accompanied by dried prunes.
Tuareg bread Baked in the sand.

NIGERIA
Lager Star Local beer.
Gari foto Based on the root vegetable of the African diet.
Gari Like rice, the base for many dishes.
Okra soup Looks like slime, but never say no to a new experience!
Kyimkying West African kebabs and great street food.

SOUTHERN AFRICA
Castle Local beer.
Red wines From Cape Town.
Amarula A liquor made up from the amarula tree, which bears a fruit that elephants particularly like to eat.
Biltong Dried game, not to everyone's taste.
Bobotie A Malay dish served in southern Africa.
Boerewors A type of sausage, delicious grilled over an open fire.

SUDAN AND SOUTH SUDAN
Guava juice Freshly squeezed, served out of enormous cooler boxes.
Fuul Fava beans with oil, lemon, salt, meat, eggs and onions.
Ta'amiyya Deep-fried ground chick peas.

TANZANIA
Amstel Local beer.
Chapati ya n'dizi tamu Banana fritters, common throughout Africa.
Chilled banana cream Good, depending on its freshness.
Mboga ya maboga Pumpkin leaves and flowers in cream.
Plantain or banana chips

TUNISIA
Brik A thin, crisp, pastry envelope filled with egg, cheese or meat. If you choose egg, bite carefully – the yolk may spurt out.

ZIMBABWE
Black Label Local beer.
Nhopi dovi Like pumpkin.
Sadza Like the west African *banku*, the east African *ugali*, Zambian *ntsima* or South African *mealie-meal*, *sadza* is a stiff, steamed dumpling made from white maize flour. It is regarded as Zimbabwe's national dish.

In general, wherever there is a village you will find a source of water. Open bodies of water, streams, lakes, etc are probably contaminated and should be treated with caution. If you take water from an open source, always purify it, preferably by boiling. Water from the tap can vary in quality; the best advice is to ask the locals if they drink it straight. Then purify it anyway just in case. When faced with a village well, use some common sense. If people are washing nearby or the toilets are close by, then don't trust it. Even if you are at a remote desert well which is covered, you should still purify the water before drinking it; there may well be a dead goat down there.

For more information see *Water and water purification methods* in *Chapter 3* (page 77) and *Health* in *Chapter 5* (page 122).

SOFT DRINKS, BEER AND SPIRITS A cold, refreshing beer under a fading African sky is bliss after a hot day on the road. Except in north Africa, beer and local spirits are generally easy to find. Local bottled beers at local prices are excellent and have varying levels of alcohol. Imported spirits can be found in most capital cities at European prices. In Arab countries, where alcohol is often banned, don't try to smuggle any in. You could end up in prison, or worse. Soft drinks can be found almost everywhere and Coke or Pepsi is always available.

SHOPPING

Wherever you travel in Africa, the following are some of the local products and crafts available: weaving and cloth; sculpture; masks; silver crosses from Agadez, Niger; other jewellery; wood carvings; papyrus paintings from Egypt… enough to inspire the most reluctant consumer or, conversely, to keep the most ardent shopaholic occupied, while contributing directly to the local economy. See also *Cultural interaction and respect* in *Chapter 8*, page 188.

COCA-COLA   *Charlie Shackell and Illya Bracht*

Coca-Cola can be found wherever you go. In the middle of nowhere, desolate and isolated, without doubt there will be a hut selling Coca-Cola. It's not only good for tummy upsets or dehydration, but also great for cooking. If you have a very tough piece of meat, boil it up in Coca-Cola for an hour or so and it will become tender.

Part Three

THE GUIDE

8

Background

GEOGRAPHY, VEGETATION AND CLIMATE

In this section is a brief outline of the main physical features of Africa. All of the north, from the Mediterranean to 25°N latitude, is **desert**. It is amazingly varied and includes the mountainous areas of the Hoggar, Tassili, Tibesti and Ennedi. South of the desert is the transitional zone known as the **Sahel**. This is a region of hardy fine grasses, sandy sparse scrub, acacia trees and limited low tree cover. Moving south, these scrub areas become steadily thicker bush, with very striking baobab trees. This whole transitional area is known as **savanna**, a wooded zone with tall grasses that becomes steadily denser. Finally, around the Equator are luxuriant thick **rainforests** with tall trees and dark undergrowth. Heading into the southern hemisphere, the vegetation has similar patterns in reverse, but the desert is confined to the western region of Namibia. South Africa is generally classified as a Mediterranean climatic zone, but with variations depending on altitude. East Africa and Ethiopia present the other main variations, where the altitude is the dominant influence on the landscape and vegetation.

Africa's climate has gone through many changes. It is thought that most of Africa and indeed Europe had a wet and warm period between 13000BC and 9000BC. After this the climate became drier, but there is strong evidence from rock art that most of the Sahara was fertile, with herders and some sedentary groups. Some of the rock art seen on the Tassili Plateau in Algeria/Libya and in the Tibesti and Ennedi mountains in Chad is thought to be as much as 7,000 years old. The desertification of the north to form the Sahara steadily expanded from around 3000BC. Climatic changes are still in progress in Africa today, as the Sahara moves steadily southwards. The continuing droughts bear witness to this.

NATURAL HISTORY AND CONSERVATION

Detailed examination of this vast topic is beyond the remit of this guide. Suffice to say that any extended trip across the continent will encompass all the major natural features it has to offer. Apart from the well-known safari parks in east and southern Africa, there are many new and amazingly diverse additions to the conservation list. Almost every country in Africa, whether desert, savanna, rainforest or mountain region, has set aside areas of significant natural habitat, many with attendant wildlife. Increasingly Africa is embracing the new forms of tourism: ecotourism, wildlife preservation and conservation, cultural tourism and village development through small tourist initiatives. Botswana, Namibia, Tanzania, Kenya, Uganda and Gabon in particular have made great efforts towards conservation. It is no longer enough to chase around game parks or climb high mountains without giving something back. Endangered species are now at the forefront of conservation. That said, there are still serious problems. The most intractable are along the DRC/Ugandan/Rwandan border, where political instability and saving the mountain gorillas are in conflict. In years to come, the need to preserve the continent's natural attractions will always be tempered by the need to eradicate poverty and increase economic development. Protecting nature will hopefully be seen in future as a means of protecting the planet and aiding human development.

HISTORY

It is generally agreed that human development began in Africa. Recently the oldest remains were found in Chad, 300km north of N'djamena, pre-dating the hominid, Lucy, found in Ethiopia's Danakil region. Dated at just over three million years old, these remains confirm the existence of transitional humanoids that were neither apes nor fully developed humans.

DJIBOUTI – LAND OF EXTREMES

In the morning, bleary-eyed and tetchy from the long drive, we head for Lake Assal. Though the heat is already stifling by 08.00, the scenery is stunning. The road snakes over broken lava fields and past currently dormant volcanic cones. Most are not large, but the sheer number of old cones is breathtaking and somewhat sinister. Lake Assal, although only ten miles from the sea, is below sea level and separated from the sea only by the lava fields. The walls of this ancient crater are multi-coloured, but mostly dark and jagged. Along the shoreline of the brilliant blue lake is an almost fluorescent white collar of brilliant crystalline deposits. The road descends into this vast cauldron of colour and seemingly dead wasteland.

Yet life is found here too. Small antelopes hop agilely across the rough landscape, tentatively watching the intruders. Distant flamingos gather around the shore. Down by the lake's edge are amazingly shaped crystals and rare volcanic rocks, halite being the strangest, with its hollowed-out rugby-ball shapes and brown crystals locking into each other. Brilliant yellow sulphur crystals grow from the water's edge. This is not a place to walk around carelessly without a guide. Here is the birthplace of a new ocean, where Africa is being ripped apart along its famous Rift Valley. Somalia and most of Kenya will be cut adrift by the forces from below the earth of Djibouti.

Suddenly a thunderous, deafening, screeching roar breaks the silence of the desert. We jump out of our skins in fright. The French are playing soldiers in the desert, and their air force is terrifying everyone with its low-flying supersonic fighter jets. The noise is enough to awaken the demons of the dormant cones and send their boiling bellies of molten lava into crescendos of explosive rage.

The road east holds more surprises: massive dried-out whirlpools of solidified lava, where hardy scrub acacias are trying to stay alive. The Land Rover can barely cope with the gradients and the gearbox sounds noisy. The views south of the narrow Bay of Ghoubbet are stupendous. The waters are almost cut off from the Red Sea. The mountains to the north are stark and rugged. Towards Tadjoura the greenery increases, and soon we can make out the Forêt du Day, a small zone of intensely forested hills: a freak of nature, born from the sea mists and very infrequent rains.

Tailor made

self drive safaris

Botswana | Namibia | Zambia | Zimbabwe

Tel: +44 (0) 161 408 4316
Fax: +44 (0) 161 880 2414
Email: info@drivebotswana.com
Web: www.drivebotswana.com
facebook.com/drivebotswana
Skype: drivebotswana

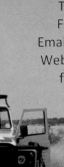

Extensive knowledge of their environment helps the San
people to survive in the arid Kalahari (AVZ) page 188

above left	Remote village in the mountainous part of South Sudan (JW/S) page 303
above right	Once the capital of Ethiopia, Gondar is home to the church of Debre Birhan Selassie, which boasts some of the finest murals anywhere in the country (AVZ) page 237
below	People offload fish from pirogues at the fish market, Tanji, the Gambia (AVZ) page 242
bottom	Fès is the oldest of Morocco's imperial cities and contains a vast medina with tanneries that have been in operation for centuries (J/S) page 273

above Aromatic spices are displayed in precariously balanced towers in souks all over Morocco (FC/S) page 273

right *Injera*, a spongy flatbread, is a staple in Ethiopia, where it is served with several types of stews and meat (D/S) page 176

below Baking bread in a traditional oven, Timbuktu, Mali (AVZ) page 266

above El Djem, Tunisia, has some of the most impressive Roman remains in Africa, including an amphitheatre dating from the 3rd century AD
(P/S) page 317

left The massive rock temples of Abu Simbel are a spectacular sight at dawn
(CJP/S) page 232

below With a Mediterranean climate, Stellenbosch is one of South Africa's prime wine-growing regions, and its wine route is justly popular
(JB/S) page 300

above The Dadès Gorge, Morocco, offers up spectacular views with its Berber villages against the backdrop of the Atlas mountains (J/S) page 273

above right Great Zimbabwe was once a royal palace for the Zimbabwean monarch, and is one of many monumental, mortarless sites spread across southern Africa (AVZ) page 328

below right An expedition to the Crabe d'Arakao, Niger, provides a wonderful introduction to Tuareg culture (SPJ & BG) page 284

below Climbing Kilimanjaro makes a great diversion for those with the inclination and fitness (AVZ) page 313

above   Recently discovered, the complex of caves at Las Geel, Somaliland, contains some of the earliest known cave paintings in the Horn of Africa (AVZ) page 298

left   Children paddle in a dugout canoe at Karonga, Malawi (AVZ) page 263

below   Fish River Canyon, Namibia, is the largest in Africa, at 550m deep in places (TH) page 280

above left   Erta Ale Volcano, in the Danakil
Depression, Ethiopia, is constantly
active (SPJ & BG) page 109

above right   Elephant (*Loxodonta africana*),
Okavango Delta, Botswana
(JG) page 213

right   Wind erosion and rainfall have
created a stunning, almost lunar
landscape at the Miradouro da
Lua, near Luanda, Angola
(PCS/WC) page 208

below   Lesser flamingos (*Phoeniconaias
minor*) at Lake Magadi, Ngorongoro
Crater, Tanzania (AVZ) page 310

Returning through Asia

Shipping your vehicle to Mumbai, India, and returning to Europe overland through Asia is a fantastic option for those who are keen to do an even longer trip (page 50)

There is evidence to suggest that five main ethnic groups existed in Africa. There were the Nilotic peoples, generally tallest in stature. In the north were people from whom the Berbers have descended. In the west were stocky black people. In central areas were the diminutive pygmies and in the east and south were the San, who are now known as the Bushmen of Botswana. A date for the emergence of these groups is around 100,000 years ago. The Egyptians seem to have developed later, before or around 6000BC, and separately from these groups. The Egyptian civilisation was at its zenith after 3000BC. It finally died out after being engulfed by the Nubians around 300BC. Then the Nubians too were overrun, by the Assyrians and Persians. Meanwhile, from central and east Africa, the Bantu people spread south between 100BC and AD200–300.

The next great civilisations to impose their will on north Africa were the Greeks and the Romans. The great cities of Carthage, El Djem, Sbeitla, Leptis Magna, Sabrata, and Apollonia arose. Further south another great kingdom, possibly with a Jewish connection, arose in the 4th century: that of Aksum in Ethiopia. Christianity spread into the empire, but in the face of the new religion, Islam, it was driven up into the highlands, where it continued to flourish. Perhaps the greatest change in Africa occurred with the rise of Islam, from its beginnings in Arabia in the mid 7th century. Arab traders and slavers moved down the coast of east Africa, where the Swahili language developed. Arab zealots moved swiftly across north Africa, the Sahara and deep into west Africa.

Way to the south, the only significant civilisation to develop in the rest of the continent was centred on Zimbabwe. Its famous ruins date from the 11th century. In west Africa three great civilisations or empires arose, mainly with the development of cross-Sahara trade routes using camels. The earliest was the Ghana Empire. It existed from AD700 to approximately AD1000. This was not centred on the area known as Ghana today, but located in southeastern present-day Mauritania. Later the Mali Empire arose, around AD1200, lasting until AD1500. This was a great period of wealth and trade, with the cities of Djenné, Mopti and Timbuktu at their zenith. Finally the Songhai Empire gradually developed, taking over from the Mali Empire, with its centre around Gao.

Slavery, which had already existed since the Arabs arrived, increased with the coming of the seafaring Europeans. The Portuguese began the process in 1450. Officially it was abolished in 1870, but it did not completely die out. In fact, tendencies towards slavery have not long been discontinued in Mauritania. The great wave of European expansion and subsequent colonisation began around the 1850s. By 1884 the great colonial powers were in such conflict over the territories that a meeting was called in Berlin to delineate the boundaries of the various countries. The British and the French took most of the continent, with Germany, Belgium and Portugal occupying much of the rest. Spain got Western 'Spanish' Sahara and Rio Muni/Fernando Po, modern Equatorial Guinea. Ethiopia remained virtually independent, but the Italians had some of its territory, as well as Libya.

After World War I, Germany lost Tanganyika and parts of Togo and Cameroon, but remained influential in Namibia. Independence finally arrived, from the early 1950s onwards. Libya was one of the first to become independent, in 1951, followed by Ghana in 1952, after agitation by Nkrumah. Many countries gained independence in the 1960s, including most of east Africa, Nigeria and the French and Belgian colonies or protectorates. The last were the Portuguese colonies, Guinea Bissau, Mozambique and Angola, finally succeeding in the years of 1974–75. In southern Africa different problems existed. Zimbabwe became independent in 1980, after a protracted period under the Smith government and various interim arrangements. Namibia was the last country here to gain its independence. It had been under South African administration, which had long been separated from the British yoke, but retained its unique racial separation with apartheid. South Africa finally became a multi-racial democracy in 1994.

AFRICAN EXPLORERS Today we can pore over glossy maps and calculate travel times and distances in Africa with ease. However, the early exploration of Africa was a haphazard affair. Some adventurers had official backing, others explored clandestinely; some were fanatical missionaries while others travelled with a deep faith in their hoped-for discoveries. Most set forth in the footsteps of Arab traders and slavers. An overland journey today follows these illustrious adventurers, but does not need to be so haphazardly planned.

One of the first African explorers was **James Bruce**, who set out for Ethiopia in 1769, ostensibly to find the source of the Nile. His journey took him into the highlands of the country, from the port of Massawa on the Red Sea. Climbing on to the high plateau, he first visited Aksum then headed south across the Simien Mountains to the capital, Gondar. After an epidemic of smallpox in Gondar, Bruce was briefly appointed court physician to Ras Michael, but became bewitched by one of his wives. After much drinking of honey wine at a wedding, he took his leave and travelled to Lake Tana and the Tissisat Falls on the Blue Nile. Avoiding the various intrigues of power in Gondar, he eventually made his way home via Sudan and the Nile. On his return in 1773 his exploits were doubted, although his books prospered. He received no acclaim until after his death in 1794.

The Scotsman **Mungo Park** was another adventurer to be sent out to find answers to African geographical mysteries. Heading inland from Gambia, he passed Segou but got no further than Silla in his quest for the route of the Niger River. This was in 1795. After recovering in England, he returned to Africa in 1805. This time his progress was better and he followed the river through Mali, Niger and Nigeria. He was killed at Bussa in Nigeria before completing his mission.

Three strong-minded but incompatible adventurers, **Oudney**, **Clapperton** and **Denham**, crossed the Sahara in 1822 from Murzuk to Bilma and Agadez. They eventually reached Lake Chad, seeking routes to the Niger River. Oudney died

A FARM IN TANZANIA

Just south of Iringa is Kisolanza Farm. This cool haven of peace sits at over 2,000m. As we drove in, two young white women came across and said in perfect Sussex accents, 'Do come and have a cup of tea.' The campground was very well organised and the food was tremendous. For less than a pound we gorged on best fillet steak, so tender it could be cut with a butter knife. A party of four South African vehicles and their ageing occupants shared the camp. The evening was spent exchanging stories. Where did you break down? (We all had Land Rovers!) How is your vehicle going? What sort of engine do you have?

The farmhouse stands on a hill not far from the camp; the roof is thatched, the walls of local stone. Such a magnificent house could easily fit into a Dorset village. The farm had run down during the socialist years of Nyerere, when landed gentry were considered undesirable in a left-leaning Utopian regime. New but admirably set bungalows have now been added to encourage ecotourism, the new byword in development in modern-day Tanzania.

Timbuktu is a city of explorers, mysterious blue men of the desert, fairytale mud mosques and stories of former untold wealth. It hosts the tangible melancholy of a former glory, its quiet decay arrested by modern infections. Timbuktu today is an enigma; the incessant wind blows plastic bags across a sand-laden street, grubby children follow the tailcoats of a stranger and modernity still struggles to impose its antiseptic character. Timbuktu does not disappoint.

Alexander Gordon Laing, Heinrich Barth and René Caillié all reached the city of Islamic learning, mostly in disguise, at great personal cost and a great deal of physical discomfort. Laing was the first, but he was killed on his journey home. Caillie made it back; Barth stayed for years and survived his journey. The houses of these great adventurers, where they hid or lived, still exist within the sandy old city. Why would anyone, particular an 'infidel' want to come to Timbuktu?

Having first reached the city in 1978, Bob was apprehensive about our impending return. Familiar sights remained, though – the impressive Djinguerey Mosque now given a new paved access path, the Sankore Mosque extended in tasteful style and the house of Laing still signposted but with at least 1m of sand removed from the street.

Where the early explorers awaited uncertain fates on their return journeys, those reaching the fabled city of the Mali Empire now have a good chance of getting back home afterwards. The internet of course has arrived in Timbuktu, but overland access is still rough, wild, lonely, rugged and, yes, achieved with a significant degree of physical discomfort.

Long may it last!

NOTE Visiting Timbuktu at the time of publication is a risky affair, so check locally in Mopti before travelling.

in Nigeria and only Clapperton succeeded in making any significant journeys, reaching Kano and Sokoto. In 1825 he again set out with **Richard Landers** to find the route of the Niger. It was left to the Landers brothers to solve the mystery of the Niger and its mouth in 1830.

Stories of great wealth and gold lured others to Timbuktu. **Alexander Gordon Laing** was one such explorer. He travelled across the desert via Ghadames and the Fezzan. Having once been left for dead after a Tuareg raid, he reached the fabled city and lived there in a house that can still be seen today. He never returned alive though, being killed by Tuaregs in 1826. The Frenchman **René Caillié** reached Djenné and Kabara by canoe, and arrived in Timbuktu in April 1828. He returned to France alive, crossing the Sahara to Morocco.

In 1850 **Heinrich Barth** and **James Richardson** left Tripoli southbound across the Sahara. Despite hostile Tuaregs, Barth succeeded in being the first 'infidel' Christian to reach Agadez. Richardson later died, but Barth continued to explore the area of Nigeria, Cameroon and travelled west to Timbuktu before returning alive to Germany in 1855. The Swiss explorer **Johann Ludwig Burckhardt** learnt Arabic and made a daring visit to Mecca, having travelled across Egypt and Sudan. Another adventurous German, **Gustav Nachtigal**, explored the Sahara and in particular the unknown Tibesti Mountains. He was lucky to escape from the

Background HISTORY

8

fiercely independent and unfriendly Tubu tribes of those mountains. Even today the Tubu only just tolerate outsiders.

In 1854 **Richard Burton**, having studied Somali customs, made a daring visit to Harar in Ethiopia, a city of devout Muslims where infidels were not allowed. But survive he did, being welcomed by the Amir. On a further expedition to Somaliland, Burton travelled with **John Hanning Speke**. In 1856 Burton and Speke were sent by the Royal Geographical Society to discover the source of the Nile. Having caught yellow fever, both were holed up in Zanzibar until June 1857. Travelling inland, they made it to Tabora and on to Lake Tanganyika. Here they split up, with Burton continuing to look for the source of the Nile in the area, while Speke headed north to a large lake, Lake Victoria, from which he came back convinced it was the source of the Nile.

Back in England, the debate between Burton and Speke continued acrimoniously. In 1862 Speke returned to Lake Victoria with **James Grant**. They explored the western shore, found a river and waterfall at Jinja, headed to Lake Albert and then continued up the Nile to Khartoum. However, they did not actually follow the river from Jinja for its entire course. Burton and others, with some justification, still doubted the assumption that this was the true source of the Nile. Around this time, an adventurer, **Baker**, and his former slave girlfriend met Speke and Grant in Gondokoro. Baker and his girlfriend continued south, exploring Lake Albert and locating the waterfall later called Murchison Falls. But still the absolute facts were not settled.

After Burton returned from another journey to west Africa and Gabon in 1865, a debate was organised between Speke and Burton. Unfortunately Speke shot himself dead, apparently accidentally, just before the meeting. His death, however, did not once and for all solve the mystery of the source of the Nile.

David Livingstone, part explorer and part missionary, arrived in southern Africa in 1835. After a series of expeditions into the Kalahari and the interior, he discovered Victoria Falls in 1855. Livingstone's exploits and exploration in Africa brought him acclaim in England, but the death of his wife affected him deeply. Then, in 1865, the Royal Geographical Society asked him to seek out the source of the Nile for final clarification. Livingstone was of the opinion that the river rose well to the south of Lake Victoria, possibly in Lake Bangweulu. After a series of fruitless journeys characterised by ill health and hostile tribes, he finally arrived at Ujiji on Lake Tanganyika. This was in 1869. Joining Arab traders, he sought out the Lualaba River for the next two years. The famous meeting with Stanley occurred in Ujiji in 1871. Revived somewhat, Livingstone travelled north with Stanley up Lake Tanganyika, but the source of the Nile eluded him. He died in 1872, heading south again.

Henry Morton Stanley, though born in north Wales in 1841, was an American citizen. He was quite a different character from the stiff-upper-lipped British explorers, yet he had as much grim determination as any of his predecessors. In 1874 he set out to explore Lake Victoria fully. He then attempted to check out Lake Albert, but warring tribes prevented this. He set out for Lake Tanganyika and then, having ascertained that it had no outlets, he headed west to the Lualaba River, which he followed. Continuing west, he discovered a larger river and the falls, which became known as the Stanley Falls, near modern-day Kisangani. Without knowing where his journey would take him, he finally arrived at the sea. But it was the Atlantic Ocean he found; he had followed the mighty Congo River to Boma. The mystery of the Nile had been solved, and it was Speke's original theory that was proved correct.

Stanley continued to explore Africa with the celebrated **Tippu Tip** and a massive retinue for protection, finally mapping out the remaining geographical conundrums of the great central African lakes. After his death in 1905, the colonial scramble for Africa began.

PEOPLE

Africa has a very diverse cross-section of people. In the far north are the Arabs, who migrated and brought Islam from Saudi Arabia. They mixed with the indigenous Berbers of the Maghreb. Further south are the famous nomads of the desert – the Tuareg and Tubu people of Algeria, Libya, Mali, Niger and Chad, who probably developed from the Berbers. The Moors of Morocco spread along the Atlantic coast to Mauritania. Much further to the east are the Nubia and Dinka of Sudan and the Amharic-speaking groups of Ethiopia. West Africa is well known for its diverse peoples, and it is they who add such colour and interest to trips in the region. The Fulani or Peul are the famous cattle herders. Other major west African groups are the Wolof, Bambara, Malinke, Songhai, Mossi, Bobo, Djerma, Bozo, Dogon, Hausa, Ibo and Yoruba.

In central Africa, pygmies are still found in Cameroon, the two Congos and Gabon, where the Fang are also found. Some of the Bantu-related groups in east Africa are the Buganda, Kikuyu, Masai, Rendille and Samburu. In Rwanda and Burundi the two main ethnic groups, who have been bitter enemies, are the Hutu and the Tutsi; the pygmoid Twa are only a small minority. Across southern Africa the following make up most of the people: Shona, Ndebele, Himba, Herero, Ovambo, Makua, Chewa, Basotho, Zulu and Xhosa.

DOWNTOWN DJIBOUTI – A MELTING-POT OF TRIBAL PEOPLE

The old colonial quarter of town has some picturesque buildings, many with arched façades that give much-needed shade to the vendors and pedestrians. There are street cafés and ancient tamarisk trees. Well-dressed businessmen mingle with entrepreneurial ladies dressed in amazingly colourful attire, laughing and gossiping over strong coffee. The African quarter and market area is totally absorbing. Shopkeepers and street vendors promote their wares; groups of men sit beside the old whitewashed mosques smoking hookah pipes and cigarettes. The women in the clothes market are deep in animated conversation. We, of course, are probably the source of most of their laughter and humorous gossip, but no-one is threatening. We drink tea; it's the milky Indian-style tea, which is a big surprise, as there aren't many Indians about. There are lots of Somalis, Ethiopian truckers, Eritrean refugees, Afar and Danakil tribals, Yemenis and Arab traders, but no white faces in the markets. Djibouti City is a fascinating place.

Check-out time in our own 'Paradise' Hotel is 14.00. We savour the cool luxury, watching the television. Our world is one of make-believe, cocooned in this small place where we can travel in time and space. We are transported back to little England. The budget is being discussed – we don't know if it's over or due next week; the weather forecast is for rain and the cars are expensive on *Top Gear*. Down in the car park the Land Rover is cooking, the steering wheel is too hot to touch and the guards are half-asleep in the great fog of humidity.

Finally, set apart from these Bantu peoples, are the San, who are the original Bushmen, the people who inhabited Botswana and parts of South Africa before retreating.

CULTURAL INTERACTION AND RESPECT

Africa has such a rich cultural heritage that you will only be able to scratch the surface. An understanding of local culture and history will go a long way towards enriching your experience.

The more you learn in advance, the less likely you are to disrupt local culture and the more you will get out of your trip. Travelling carries responsibilities as well as bringing pleasure – dress in a manner to suit the different cultures; respect people's dignity and wishes, particularly when taking photographs; respect religious sites and artefacts; keep the environment clean by burning your rubbish wherever possible; and do not encourage dependence by casually handing out gifts, unless some small service has been rendered.

Africa is home to myriad diverse peoples but has common themes across its vast expanse. Distinct tribal groupings cut across the illogical borders that the modern world ascribes to the continent. It is impossible to learn the spoken word of so many different groups, but any usage of even the most basic words will open doors and enable greater interaction. Most guidebooks give a few common greetings and phrases in the local language.

Despite the cultural divide, most Africans are welcoming, interested and lively. Many African societies have very elaborate greeting rituals from person to person that seem to go on and on. Some rituals amongst the nomadic peoples involve lengthy tea ceremonies but not much actual tea drinking. A simple handshake will, however, suffice for the rest of us.

One of the subjects most guaranteed to cause inadvertent offence or misunderstanding is that of traditional Islam in Africa. The nature of Islam in black Africa is generally more tolerant than that in the Arab regions. This does not mean, however, that one should act in a more liberal way, particularly regarding dress. Clothing, together with general appearance, is the one thing that defines your approach and can have negative as well as positive impacts.

RELIGION

ISLAM Apart from the well-known countries along the north African coast that adhere to Islam, a surprising number of sub-Saharan countries also have substantial numbers of their population, if not all, observing the religion. Islam spread south across the Sahara with the caravan routes from Egypt, Libya, Tunisia, Algeria and Morocco after its founding in the middle of the 7th century in Saudi Arabia. On the southern fringes of the desert, places like Agadez, Gao, Djenné and Timbuktu – the most mysterious of all – became rich and powerful. The empires of Ghana (not the current state), Mali and Songhai accumulated vast wealth. With the coming of ships, much of the trans-Saharan trade declined and the cities were eclipsed. By now the Islamic faith had become well embedded in the populations of much of west Africa. Countries like Guinea have surprisingly large numbers of devout Muslims, as do east African coastal districts. Swahili is a modified form of Arabic; the word Swahili is derived from the word for 'coast' in Arabic.

There are five main pillars of Islam. These are:

- Witness (*shahadah*): submission to God (Allah) and acceptance that Muhammad is his prophet.
- Prayer (*salat*): five times a day, at sunrise, midday, afternoon, sunset and evening. Before praying, Muslims must wash their head, hands and feet. They can pray in any place that is clean and not polluted, and they must face Mecca. On Fridays at midday, it is more beneficial to pray collectively at a mosque. Otherwise they may pray alone, wherever they may be. Men and women pray separately.
- Almsgiving (*zakat*): according to the Koran, faith in God should be expressed by doing good to others. A devout Muslim should, once a year, give 2.5% of his money to others in need.
- Fasting (*sawm*): the month of Ramadan is a holy month, when all Muslims must fast from dawn till dusk. If they are ill or travelling, or if they are pregnant women, they are permitted to postpone the fast until they are well. Elderly people and young children are excused from the fast. The purpose of the fast is to teach discipline to the soul. Eid al-Fitr is when the fast ends and all Muslims celebrate with a great feast – sheep and goats are not lucky, as hundreds of them are ritually slaughtered on this special day.
- Pilgrimage (*hajj*): At least once during his lifetime, it is a sacred duty for every Muslim to go to the Ka'aba, the sacred mosque in Mecca. This should be done ideally between the seventh and tenth days of the month of Zuul-Hijja, the 12th month of the Muslim year. This is usually between March

THE ROCK-HEWN CHURCHES OF TIGRAI

Glowing a deep crimson at sunrise, the jagged outcrops and sheer walls of the Gheralta massif hide some surprising sights. From Megab, two dramatically located rock-hewn churches can be visited. Maryam Korkor is the easier, but still challenging, choice, closest to the village and new Korkor Lodge. Initially we crossed quiet fields dotted with picturesque stone farmhouses shaded by acacia, cactus and the extraordinary *euphorbia candelabra*. The ascent began with a dramatic climb up a narrow crack barely 3ft wide, exciting and exacting. Emerging briefly on to a small flat area, we passed a small abandoned church. A seemingly impossible vertiginous section followed, up and across a colourful rock face and along precarious ledges — a 400m ascent in all. The atmospheric church of Maryam Korkor has a complex design, with some well executed paintings of biblical figures and horses.

We edged around the corner, following a narrow ledge 300m above a sheer drop to the valley below, to the small church of Daniel Korkor. The entrance to this domed sanctuary is barely 2ft wide and 3ft high, with more colourful paintings inside. From this lofty perch, panoramic views extend in all directions.

The nearby church of Abuna Yemata Guh is a much more serious challenge to reach, with some exposed climbing necessary. It has a sheer drop on the final approach. Also close to Megab are the rock-hewn churches of Debre Tsion and Dugem Selassie, but public transport is non-existent.

Expect tough climbs and rough routes when visiting the Tigrai rock churches. Around 20 significant sites are on offer to overlanders, but those travelling on public transport will end up doing a lot of legwork to visit just a few of these magnificent monuments. Entry fees are currently 150 birr (US$8) per person per church, and a guide might try to extract anything from 150 to 400 birr.

Background RELIGION

8

and July, depending on the moon. The hajj includes, among other things, the *tawaf*, seven anticlockwise circuits of the Ka'aba, prostrations at the site of Abraham, and the sacrifice of either a sheep or a camel, depending on one's wealth. This meat is given to the poor. The pilgrimage ends with another feast, the Eid al-Adha, after which the pilgrim must visit the tomb of the prophet in the holy city of Medina.

Some more tenets of Islam are: the Koran is the word of God; Muhammad is his prophet; the Sunna is the right way of life, which represents everything that the prophet Muhammad did or said. The books of Hadith record the Sunna, the way to live. Note that the Sunna is the guidance given by Muhammad; it is not the same as the Koran, which is the direct word of God. The Koran and the Sunna together are known as the al-Asl, the foundation of Islam. A *madrasa* is an Islamic school.

Muhammad's daughter was Fatima. Ali was his cousin. Muhammad favoured Ali as his successor, and married Fatima to Ali. Those who follow Ali are known as Shi'a Muslims.

CHRISTIANITY The colonial expansion across Africa that began in the mid 19th century brought with it the missionaries, explorers and traders who sought to exploit Africa for its natural physical wealth as well as its people. Slavery, long endemic in the continent, had already expanded to provide cheap labour for the Arabs and later the American colonists.

Christianity found favour with the peoples of the sub-Sahara, often where slavery had its prime locations. The west African coastal people suffered the greatest impact of slavery. These areas are now some of the main heartlands of the religion. The religious divide in the countries of the Sahel, particularly Nigeria, Chad and Sudan, has been the source of communal tensions and periodic violence that continues to this day. The Coptic Christian movement found homes both in Egypt and in the isolated highlands of Ethiopia. Further south, Christianity is the dominant faith. As with most things African, the energy and vibrancy of the people manifests in its faiths, with lively and robust forms of preaching and worship.

TRADITIONAL RELIGION Although less common, the practices of Africa's original animistic beliefs are still to be found almost anywhere except the north. Along the coast of Togo, voodoo has survived and retained its traditions. Its followers worship the cult of ancestors and fetishes. Most African animistic ideas incorporate such ideas. The Dogon people of Mali have retained their ancient beliefs. Their traditions are linked to the stars, sun and moon through their god.

FESTIVALS

West Africa has a number of colourful and vivid festivals. In Mali there is the annual Cattle Crossing at Diafarabe, which takes place in December. This festival is when the Fulani herders reunite with their families. The famous Dogon of the Bandiagara Escarpment in Mali have colourful masked dances and ceremonies, usually from March onwards after the harvest. In recent years a desert music festival has been taking place north of Timbuktu in Mali, subject to security factors. In Niger is the famous Cure Salée around In Gall in September. It involves young men dressed and made up to impress and woo partners. The Bianou festival in March is another spectacle in Niger, with Tuaregs riding camels into Agadez.

Across north Africa and amongst all the Muslim communities are the normal Islamic holidays and fastings. Tabaski, the most important festival, involves the eating of sheep and goats in large quantities and is a time when people dress in their finest clothes, particularly in places like Mali and Niger (the dates for this festival vary). Eid al-Fitr is the day that celebrates the end of the month-long fast of Ramadan. Eid al-Moulid is celebrated as the Prophet's birthday.

Timkat is probably Ethiopia's most colourful festival. It is the celebration of Christ's baptism. Across all of Christian Africa, Palm Sunday is a particularly colourful time for processions and gaiety. Versions of the carnival or Mardi Gras are celebrated, mainly in the ex-Portuguese colonies. There is a biannual film festival in Burkina Faso, and the Fêtes des Masques in Ivory Coast in November.

Not so much a festival, the annual dusty raid in the Sahara of the Paris–Dakar Motor Rally has been abandoned after terror threats. The 2008 rally, which would have been the 30th Paris–Dakar rally, was cancelled completely. Nowadays the 'Paris–Dakar' rally is held in South America (Buenos Aires–Chile–Buenos Aires).

DATES FOR 2014–17
Ramadan 28 June 2014, 18 June 2015, 6 June 2016, 27 May 2017
Eid al-Kebir (Tabaski), Eid al-Fitr and **Eid al-Moulid** see www.when-is.com

ARTS AND ENTERTAINMENT

Discovering all things African – religions, music, literature and history – is fascinating. The visual arts are closely tied to the craft traditions of carving and weaving.

ARTS AND CRAFTS
Sculpture Wherever you travel, you are sure to come across wonderful sculptures and art forms, distinctive to their own particular region. Of course, the main tourist areas are swamped with souvenir reproductions of little merit, but take the trouble to visit the many national museums in Africa and you will discover a treasure trove of astounding proportions.

To get a flavour for African sculpture before you go, check out the museums. A comprehensive guide to African sculpture (for England and Scotland) is *African Assortment* by Michael Pennie (Artworth, 1991). It discusses and illustrates works on display in 34 separate museums.

Nigeria/Benin The famous 10th-/11th-century Benin bronzes of southern Nigeria are some of the finest artworks that west Africa has produced.

Tanzania The famous Makonde are often remarkable works of art carvings found along the coast in Kenya and Tanzania.

Zimbabwe Zimbabwe has gained a particular reputation in the world of sculpture, with some experts claiming that the country has no fewer than six of the world's top ten stone sculptors. A visit to the Chapungu Sculpture Park in Harare is an absolute must.

Masks Masks are another art form, many designs and styles having their origins in the ancient animistic beliefs. Mali, Burkina Faso and Ivory Coast are well known for their masks and Togo for its fetishes.

8

Weaving and cloth The astonishing array of colourful materials in almost any market is overwhelming. Although increasingly made locally, a lot is still imported, much of it from Holland. Ghana has a thriving textile industry, mostly village-based around Kumasi. Kente cloth is its most famous product. Elsewhere most of the material is produced on a small scale. Indigo cloth is produced in north and west Africa, and is widely used by the Moors and Tuareg people, as well as other nomadic tribes.

Miscellaneous Egypt is famous for its papyrus paper and delicately painted images, while in Niger Agadez has its silver crosses. There are myriad local crafts.

MUSIC Music is the heartbeat of Africa. Africans love to talk about their favourite artist. The continuing interest in modern African music is refreshing and means a vast catalogue of material is now available. The variety of African music is amazing. Most good music shops stock a reasonable selection of African CDs. Below is a list of musicians to look out for; some are dated but represent the birth of African modern music, while others are more recent. See also Putomayo World Music (*www.putomayo.com*).

Algeria Souad Massi is known for her acoustic folk songs with socially conscious and outspoken lyrics. She had to move to Paris after being too outspoken.

Benin One famous artist is Angélique Kidjo (*www.angeliquekidjo.com*), who has successfully hit the European market. Her albums include *Ayé* and *Fifa*.

Burundi After her childhood dreams in Burundi, Khadja Nin's big break on to the music scene came after her move to Europe. Her song 'Sina Mali, Sina Deni' is an adaptation of a Stevie Wonder song, speaking of spiritual liberation.

Cameroon Having moved from Cameroon to Paris at the age of 13, Kaissa Doumbe has performed with many great musicians, including Salif Keita and Jean-Michel Jarre. Her music has its own flexible style. 'To Ndje' is a nostalgic song about her homeland.

Cape Verde Cesaria Evora is undoubtedly Cape Verde's most famous musician. The music of her goddaughter Maria de Barros, although she was born in Senegal, is strongly influenced by her parents' native land of Cape Verde, and its melancholic songs of longing.

Democratic Republic of the Congo (DRC) You will hear the sounds of *soukous* across Africa, with its infectious jangling guitar lines and sweet vocals. The king of *soukous*, Franco died in 1990. For a taste of his best listen to the 1985 release *Mario* and his 1950s classics *Originalité*. Franco's band, OK Jazz, was for many years effectively a training school for all of the greats of DRC music. Thankfully, they continued after their leader's death, immediately recording the impeccable *Champions Du Zaïre* (they were rejoined for this album by former member Ndombe Opetum, whose solo albums were a delight).

One former member of OK Jazz, Papa Noel rarely receives the praise he so richly deserves. Two albums, *Nono* and *Ya Nono*, are still popular. Franco's great rival over many years was Tabu Ley, who has a similarly large catalogue of releases. Check also his protégés Sam Mangwana and top female vocalist Mbilia Bel.

The 1980s saw a shift in the music of the DRC (then Zaire), with the rise of new stars preferring to leap straight into the faster dance sections of the *soukous* style and dropping the traditional ballad themes. Top of this group of musicians included Kanda Bongo Man – look out for *Non Stop Non Stop*. Other bands of this new wave include Pepe Kalle's Empire Bakuba, Zaiko Langa Langa and Papa Wemba.

Gabon The *soukous* band Les Diablotins were known for their albums recorded in Paris in 1983 – *Les Diablotins à Paris Volume 7*.

Ghana One musical contribution from Ghana was 'highlife' – the dance band music that has developed with its synthesis of African and Western styles. Look out for the compilation of E T Mensah's 1950s hits, *All For You*. Also look out for Daddy Lumba, Highlife 2000, entitled *Aben Woaha*. A compilation of early 1960s highlife hits is *Akomko*. It featured tracks from the Black Beats, Stargazers Dance Band and Red Spot. For a taste of other music from Ghana, the *Guitar And The Gun* compilations are memorable.

Guinea Guinea shares the *griot* traditions of Mali and many musicians move between the two countries. Guinean *griot* Mory Kanté, for example, replaced Salif Keita in the Malian Super Rail Band. Mory Kanté is now the best-known musician from Guinea. His breakthrough album was *Akwaba Beach*, but he also appears with Kanté Manfila and Balla Kalla on the rootsy *Kankan Blues* – a much rawer sound recorded at the Rubis Nightclub in Kankan, Guinea.

For many years, the national band of Guinea was the Beyla group Bembeya Jazz, who used modern electric instruments to interpret traditional themes. They have long since disbanded, but some of their recordings are available. One of Guinea's most popular performers of semi-acoustic Manding music is Sekouba Bambina Diabaté. The all-woman equivalent band was Les Amazones. Two of its members, Sona Diabate and M'Mah Sylla, released an excellent album called *Sahel*, featuring acoustic instruments.

Ivory Coast Dobjet Gnahore received her early musical training from her father. She moved to France in 1999. Her music is the lively result of a variety of influences from different African countries. She sings in local languages Beta, Fon, Baoule, Lingala and Malinke. 'Abiani', a plea for positive thoughts in the face of death, is one of her well-known songs.

Kenya and Tanzania East African music is dominated by three main styles – a local version of the DRC *soukous*, the unique sound of Swahili Taarab music and the big-band sound of Tanzania. For *soukous* try Orchestra Virunga or Orchestra Maquis Original. For the Swahili sound there is Black Lady and Lucky Star Musical Clubs' *Nyota: Classic Taarab from Tanga*. Of the Tanzanian big band stars, the all-time great was Mbaraka Mwinshehe. By the time of his death in 1979, he had recorded dozens of albums such as the *Ukumbusho* series.

Mali The traditional music of Mali is dominated by the *griots* – singers who have been charged through history with maintaining the oral literature of the area. Their pure voices combine with two beautiful instruments – the 21-stringed *kora* and the *balafon* (xylophone). Mali has produced a number of tremendous and quite distinctive large bands. Its music typically integrates traditional patterns and styles with modern instruments. Several former *griots* have made the transition.

8

One of the country's most successful musical exports has been Salif Keita, a great singer. If you like your music filtered through modern Western pop, then solo albums like *Soro* and *Ko-Yan* are worth a listen. But if you want to hear Salif Keita at his best, look for the albums made before 1984 with Les Ambassadeurs (such as *Les Ambassadeurs Internationaux*).

One classic album from Mali was by Salif Keita's former group, the Super Rail Band. He left in 1973, but it was not until 1985 and the band's first UK release, *New Dimensions in Rail Culture*, that it achieved international success. This album features the voices of Sekou Kanté and Lanfia Diabate. The Super Rail Band was based in Bamako, but the second-largest town in Mali, Segou, was home to the excellent Super Biton Band. Their best album is simply called *Super Biton de Segou*.

The classic-sounding Ali Farka Touré is still one of the most accessible to Western tastes, even though his music is traditional. The 1994 release of *Talking Timbuktu* reached an even wider audience, recorded with American guitarist Ry Cooder. More recently female artists have become popular, like Nahawa Doumbia's *Didadi* and Oumou Sangare with *Bi Furu*. Ramatou Diakite was part of the group Kulanjan and later released *Gembi* in Bambara language. Moussa Diallo is a prominent singer releasing *Chiwara* in 2003 before *Maninda*. Other noted releases are from Habib Koite and Bamada (*Kanawa* and *Saramaya*), Idrissa Soumaoro (*Oulii Ka Bo*), Tinariwen, a Tuareg band (*Amassakoul N Tenere*), Keletigui Diabete (*Koulandian*), Tom Diakite (*Fala*), Boubacar Traore (*Kanou*), Issa Bagayogo (*Bana*) and Mamou Sidibe (*Bassa Kele*).

Niger Worth looking out for is the Guez Band from Arlit. This is the new style of the Sahel.

Nigeria Nigeria has the most developed music industry. Its best-known musical style is *juju* – typically guitar-based bands, weaving melodies around a core of talking drums. Main exponents are Ebenezer Obey, King Sunny Ade and Segun Adewale (*Ojo Je*). No account of Nigerian music would be complete without Fela Kuti, whose politically charged 'Afro-beat' music ensured conflict with the authorities – he was even jailed from 1984 to 1986. His son Femi Kuti continues the family tradition.

Senegal Another very famous artist to hit the European market is Youssou N'Dour from Senegal. His albums feature a few solo hits and some with his band, the Super Étoile.

South Africa Paul Simon may have popularised the music of southern Africa with his *Graceland* album, but check out the singing by Ladysmith Black Mambazo. The Women of Mambazo was founded in 2001 by Nellie Shabalala, whose husband was leader of the Ladysmith Black Mambazo. She was shot dead outside her home in May 2002 after a joint performance some days earlier. The song 'Vimba' is dedicated to her memory. South African music is incredibly varied, from traditional music to township jive, and some of the best jazz. Two compilations are of note: *Zulu Jive* and *The Indestructible Beat of Soweto*. Johnny Clegg has recorded various albums. More traditional and with a Mozambique influence is Steve Newman and Tananas. The exiled Miriam Makeba and Dollar Band (*Abdullah Ibrahim*) are South African and worth a listen. Long-time star Dorothy Masuka (*Mfan Omncane*) was exiled from South Africa to Zambia and Zimbabwe years back but made a comeback after returning in 1992. More recent female artists include Judith Sephuma (*Le Tsephhile Mang*) and Sibongile Khumalo (*Mayilhome*).

Zimbabwe The modern music of Zimbabwe has been popularised in the West by the Bhundu Boys and the Four Brothers. Also listen to Oliver Mtukutzi (*Shoko*) and Thomas Mapfumo (*The Chimurenga Singles*), two of Zimbabwe's former number-one singers and bandleaders. A great introduction to the music of Zimbabwe is heard in the compilation of various artists on *Viva Zimbabwe*. The live music scene in Harare used to be one of the best in the world.

Record stores and websites Much of the above music can be found and bought locally in Africa. Always check the CDs if you can; some will be of dubious quality, but that's part of the fun. Better-quality recordings can be found outside Africa. If you would like to get a feel for African music beforehand, try the Africa Centre in London or www.africana.com and www.putumayo.com.

LITERATURE Modern African literature has linked the oral traditions of the past with the alien Western traditions of the novel and theatre. A good starting point for anyone interested in the whole range of contemporary African writing is the anthology *Voices From Twentieth-Century Africa – Griots And Towncriers* (Faber and Faber, 1988). Edited by African poet Chinweizu, it is a collection of the more popular writers of the continent. *The Traveller's Literary Companion to Africa* by Oona Strathern (In Print Publishing, 1998) takes readers on a country-by-country literary tour.

The following are the more familiar writers to look out for.

Chinua Achebe His two novels are highly recommended. They were written 30 years apart and reflect on different periods in Nigeria's history. The effect on African society of the arrival of Europeans is the subject of *Things Fall Apart* (Heinemann, 1958). In *Anthills of the Savannah* (1987) the subject moves on to the problems of corruption and governing modern Africa.

Ayi Kwei Armah Ghanaian novelist, much influenced by black American writers. Novels include *The Beautyful Ones Are Not Yet Born, Why Are We So Blest?* and *Two Thousand Seasons*.

Sembene Ousmane The Senegalese writer and film director is best known for the novel *God's Bits of Wood* (Heinemann). This vividly tells the story of the great strike on the Bamako-to-Dakar railway.

Stanlake Samkane Zimbabwe's best-known novelist and historian. His classic novel *On Trial for my Country* puts both Cecil Rhodes and the Matabele King Lobengula on trial to discover the truth behind the 1890 invasion of what became Rhodesia.

Wole Soyinka The prolific Nigerian playwright and poet was awarded the Nobel Prize for Literature in 1986. *The Man Died* (Arrow) is a vivid account of the two-and-a-half years he spent in prison during the Nigerian civil war in the late 1960s. *A Dance in the Forests* is one of his most ambitious plays, steeped in the beliefs and background of Yoruba heritage.

Ngugi Wa Thiong'o Kenya's greatest writer has been highly critical of his homeland, leading to many conflicts with the authorities, including time in jail and in exile. Earlier books concentrated on the struggle against colonialism, but he then moved on to criticise post-colonial Kenya in the classic *Devil on the Cross* (Heinemann).

Es'kia Mphahlele The South African critic, novelist and short-story writer is reckoned to be the father of serious study of African literature. His book *The African Image* was the first comprehensive work of African literary criticism.

NON-FICTION In *Land, Freedom and Fiction* (Zed) David Maughn-Brown successfully weaves together the history, literature and politics of Kenya, discussing the distortions and reworking of history by writers about the Mau Mau struggle that led to independence.

Long Walk to Freedom is the autobiography of Nelson Mandela and should be part of any reading on South Africa.

Not by Africans, but about Africa, is a book by Peter and Beverly Pickford. Their *Forever Africa* is a visual feast of sepia and colour photographs, depicting the people, landscapes and wildlife seen on their journey from Cape Town to Tangier.

See www.africanwriter.com and *Appendix 5, Further information* for more books.

TRAVELLING POSITIVELY with Janice Booth

Wherever you travel in Africa, you are bound to see poverty, urban squalor and occasionally genuine hunger. Life for the poor in both cities and rural areas may prove harsher than you'd imagined. Your reaction may well be a mixture of sadness, perhaps shock and often a feeling of guilt. The imbalance seems unjust, and the scale of the problem daunting. Why do some have so much when others do not? The reasons are complex, rooted partly in culture, partly in ignorance and poor education, partly in foreign exploitation – and these are only the more obvious causes.

African tradition has cast women in the role of workers, fetching water, looking after the children, cooking and washing. Men were traditionally the hunters. In rural Africa it is very common to see men sitting under trees, apparently deep in thought or conversation but otherwise inactive. As the continent becomes more urbanised, so they have needed to become more industrious and many have enormous reservoirs of energy and initiative. Still tradition dies hard, and 'development' often requires painful compromises. As choices increase, so do pressures. Adapting to the pace and the advanced technologies of the 21st century isn't necessarily easy.

So, where can we fit in? Isn't it enough that we've shopped in local markets, paid local mechanics, stopped at some local campsites and used local ferries? Aren't the big charities and governments dealing with development? Do we as individuals have anything to offer (apart from our hard-earned cash, which we don't want to throw away into such a bottomless gulf of need)? How can we really make a difference to this vast, teeming, vibrant, contradictory, maddening and stunningly beautiful continent?

LOCAL CHOICES Of course, shopping locally and using the services of local people are ways to contribute. Buy souvenirs from the craftspeople who seem to have made them rather than via middlemen who will siphon off profits, and patronise small street vendors rather than big supermarkets. Don't bargain to a price below what is reasonable; the difference may be the price of a drink to you but the price of a whole family meal to the vendor. Stay in small local hotels rather than foreign chains. Use the services of a local guide or a child who wants to help, and pay a fair rate. Bring with you only those supplies that you know you won't be able to find in Africa, and buy the rest in local stores and markets.

EDUCATION Education is the future of Africa. In many places you will see children dressed in smart, brightly coloured uniforms, bouncing along to school with great exuberance and energy. In others they may be ragged, crammed together on rickety wooden benches or grouped in the shade of trees, eyes fixed earnestly on the teacher and learning by rote because they have no books. Whatever the conditions, there is an insatiable wish to learn. If you have spent time in a village and made some contact with its inhabitants, why not consider donating some pens, crayons and notebooks to the local school? School equipment is easy to buy in local markets. Ask to be introduced to the schoolteacher, so that he/she can receive and officially distribute the gift. Offer to spend some time in the school, being questioned by the children about your home country. If an adult language or literacy course is running locally, offer to drop in on that, too. After all, knowledge is about stretching horizons and learning new things, which is just what you're doing by travelling, so why not make it a two-way process? Anyway, it's fun!

If you have contact with schools back in your home country, consider setting up a link, especially if the internet is available. When you get home, if you feel able to undertake the sponsorship of an individual child or older student in Africa, the big international organisations offering this can be found on the internet. Education is a gift for life.

NB: Travellers often collect pens/biros at home beforehand, but do check that they work and have plenty of ink before donating them. To an impoverished rural child, a new pen is a huge and thrilling gift. He/she is so proud and happy and then so bitterly disappointed when it stops working after only a few hours. It would have been better never to have had it.

IN THE VILLAGE As you pass through – or stay in – small towns and villages, you'll come across missionaries, expatriates, aid workers and various development projects. If the work that they're doing interests you, make a note of their contact details. Once back home, you may be able to organise fundraising or other support. This is development 'on a human scale' – a well, a school, an orphanage, a village hall, a water pump, a plot of farmland – so the local organisers will appreciate your individual interest as much as you enjoy being personally involved.

While you're driving, you may also spot wooden signs beside the road advertising small development projects – housing schemes, irrigation, co-operatives, agriculture – and giving a contact address or phone number. Jot them down: you never know what may be useful later.

If you felt drawn to a village or a community but didn't manage to get details of any current activity there, it's worth trying an internet search for its name when you get home – try various spellings, just in case – as this sometimes produces unexpected contacts.

VOLUNTEERING If you want to return to work as a volunteer in Africa and have some relevant skills ('relevant' covers a wide range), start by checking out Voluntary Service Overseas (*www.vso.org.uk*) or Earthwatch (*www.earthwatch.org*). VSO also welcomes donations, from small amounts up to the cost of maintaining a volunteer in a developing country. An internet search for organisations using volunteers will provide many more possibilities, including ones specialising in shorter projects, which may involve anything from teaching English to manual labour. If teaching English appeals, why not take a short course in TEFL (Teaching English as a Foreign Language; (*www.tefl.com*). An internet search will reveal various colleges; one where you can learn at a distance by post or email is Global English (*www.global-english.com*). UK-based, it has students from as far apart as Thailand and the USA.

A way to volunteer without leaving home is via the Online Volunteering Service (*www.onlinevolunteering.org*), managed by the United Nations Volunteers Programme (UNV), which is the volunteer arm of the United Nations. Volunteers need reliable access to a computer and the internet, and some relevant skill or experience. Via the OVS they undertake a variety of computer-based assignments for organisations in developing countries: for example translation, research, web design, data analysis, database construction, proposal writing, editing articles, online mentoring, publication, design, etc. Also check out Mercy Corps (*www.mercycorps.org*) and see Peter Lynch's *Wildlife & Conservation Volunteering: The Complete Guide* (Bradt Travel Guides, 2012).

BIG INTERNATIONAL CHARITIES The big international charities are colossal, and it's sometimes hard to remember that their work does reach down to benefit the poorest at grass-roots level. It's particularly hard to believe, although it's true, that they need our small donations. Most of them don't deserve their poor reputation

VOLUNTEERING IN IVORY COAST   *Aline Catzeflis*

This was the first time that my feet had actually touched the soil of Africa. For a long time I had dreamed of this journey. It was neither a visit to friends nor adventure tourism that attracted me to this continent, but the opportunity to participate in a humanitarian aid project. Ivory Coast offered me this possibility.

On arrival in Abidjan, I avoided the sprawling city, preferring to head off to my destination. Man is a frontier town in what is known as a 'free zone'. The description is misleading; it is not a zone without government or administration, it has former rebels. Even though these rebels have been integrated into the government and surrendered their arms, there are still micro-groups who look after road traffic, for example. Travelling in a car marked 'Mission Catholique', we passed through checkpoints with relatively few problems. If there were, a few sachets of Swiss instant coffee would do the trick. However, public transport buses and share-taxis had to go through time-consuming procedures and added taxes!

The roads leading north and west from Abidjan were in a good state of repair, but there were numerous wrecked buses and trucks. Vehicles are heavily loaded and often tip over. Tree branches strewn across the road mean a broken-down vehicle or recent accident ahead. The trucks are going to or from Sierra Leone, Mali or Guinea; often carrying huge tropical tree trunks, which hopefully are not protected species. After six hours on the road, 'my' town appeared dramatically among the hills. It is called 'Man of the Eight Mountains', even though most of the summits are no higher than 500m. The Dent du Man (Tooth of Man) dominates, its abrupt face composed of pale, clear rock that can be seen for miles.

I visited in August, the rainy season. The sky was veiled by heavy clouds and loaded with rains that fell every afternoon. The streets were covered with a light, bright orange mud, which enhanced the colours of the papaya, banana and other trees that lined the roads surrounding the town. No amount of rain could stop the breathless rhythm of the traffic. The streets were animated by an otherworldly dynamism. It's not that the people moved any faster than in Switzerland; it's simply that their sheer numbers gave the sensation of something far more intense. Around the edge of the markets the pervasive aroma of frying drew us for spending too much on administration, and they respond magnificently to disasters such as the 2004 tsunami in Asia and the 2008 earthquake in China. If you want to make a general donation 'for work in Africa', you could do far worse. They advertise extensively, so check their ads and their websites to see which comes closest to your interests. If it's wildlife that appeals to you, then you'll already know about the Worldwide Fund for Nature (WWF) (*www.panda.org*) which works just about everywhere and has had some remarkable conservation successes.

SMALLER CHARITIES Nowadays the smaller international charities are amazing in their range and variety; whatever you want to support, you'll find it somewhere. The handful of lesser-known ones listed below are small enough to have a personal approach but large enough to make a useful impact. This is only a tiny sample of the many available; you'll certainly come across others in the same or different fields.

Firelight Foundation www.firelightfoundation. org. This US-based organisation works through local people & groups, & currently supports projects in Cameroon, Ethiopia, Kenya, Lesotho, Malawi, Rwanda, South Africa, Tanzania, Uganda, Zambia & Zimbabwe. Its remit, which is interpreted

in to taste the *alloco* (fried plantain). It was just not possible to visit a local bar without tasting *atcheke*, the national dish (manioc reduced to a fine semolina), served with either fried fish or roast chicken and accompanied by a spicy tomato-onion sauce.

I was staying in the Mariapoly Vittoria, a centre directed by the Focolare Movement. There had been a small dispensary here for a couple of years. I had come to work in the dispensary for three weeks. My job was to write down all the particulars of the patients who came to visit: their names, age, address, illness and medicines/treatment prescribed. In principle, it should not have been complicated, but problems arose when the answers were unknown. I would ask a mother for the date of birth of her child and she would reply simply, 'During the rice harvest'. This was the magic of Africa: a quite different concept of time, of rules of life. The names attributed to the children certainly bore no resemblance to those with which we are familiar. One day I had the honour of registering an Emile Zola!

People's relationships were marked by an apparent coldness, though after a while it became clear to me that there was nothing nasty about it. One morning, in the polite European way, I asked a patient to go and wait outside for his medicines. He looked at me without moving and showed not the slightest intention of moving. I then asked my colleague to tell him in the local language, thinking that he didn't understand French. My colleague said to him abruptly in French, 'Go outside and wait there!' I was shocked by his tone of voice, but clearly the patient was not surprised; on the contrary, he went outside, relieved finally to be finished with this dumb conversation.

We must forget our codes, rules and conventions to be receptive to these new exchanges, and take it upon ourselves to try to understand another way of life. Africa allowed me to rediscover the truth about our relationships with other people, other things, and to face up to the most important problems, security, food, money, interests that we have completely forgotten in our developed societies.

very broadly, is 'to support & advocate for the needs & rights of children who are orphaned or affected by HIV/AIDS in sub-Saharan Africa & to increase the resources available to grass-roots organisations that are strengthening the capacity of families & communities to care for children made vulnerable by HIV/AIDS'.

Good Gifts Catalogue www.goodgifts.org. This novel idea enables you to support development schemes while remembering friends & family at anniversaries, Christmas, etc. For example, you can buy a 'Goat for Peace' for your aunt's birthday; it'll be delivered to one of the goat schemes in Africa, & you'll get a card for your aunt explaining the gift. As the brochure says: 'This is no ordinary goat: this is a revolving goat. Where communities are slowly rebuilding themselves, a revolving goat (with the aid of a revolving ram) starts families. Kids go to restock families without goats and so on. A goat is a milk & fertiliser factory and goes a long way to improving the local diet; a 4-legged step towards self-sufficiency.' The goat is only one of a huge range of gifts – look at the online catalogue at the website above.

Practical Action www.practicalaction. org. Originally founded in 1966 by the radical economist Dr E F Schumacher, this charity works on the principle that a small-scale approach can bring results that benefit whole communities long into the future. Practical Action enables poor communities to discover how new technologies, adapted in the right way, can provide lasting, appropriate solutions to poverty.

Send a Cow www.sendacow.org.uk. Based in the UK, this small charity provides not only cows but also goats & chickens on a self-help basis to impoverished families & individuals (widows, orphans, etc) so that they have a means of livelihood & hope for the future. It gives training in livestock rearing & organic farming, & access to low-cost veterinary & advice services. Projects are in Ethiopia, Kenya, Lesotho, Rwanda, Tanzania, Uganda & Zambia.

War Child www.warchild.org. War Child works with children suffering the effects of conflict. Current African projects are in Angola, Burundi, DRC, Ethiopia, Eritrea, Rwanda, Sierra Leone & Sudan.

Water Aid www.wateraid.org.uk. Dedicated exclusively to the provision of safe domestic water, sanitation & hygiene education to the world's poorest people. In Africa, it works in Burkina Faso, Ethiopia, Ghana, Malawi, Mali, Mozambique, Nigeria, Tanzania, Uganda & Zambia.

BEGGING There's no way you can escape beggars in Africa, and how you handle the problem is a very personal matter. Remember that the 'visible' misery of those thrusting their hands out to you as you pass is not necessarily any worse than the 'invisible' misery of those suffering silently at home; a donation to a relevant charity (for the homeless, or the orphaned, or the disabled, or the abandoned) is likely to mean that your money is used more effectively. But sometimes it's hard to walk on by.

STUFF YOUR RUCKSACK – AND MAKE A DIFFERENCE

www.stuffyourrucksack.com is a website set up by TV's Kate Humble which enables travellers to give direct help to small charities, schools or other organisations in the country they are visiting. Maybe a local school needs books, a map or pencils, or an orphanage needs children's clothes or toys – all things that can easily be 'stuffed in a rucksack' before departure. The charities get exactly what they need and travellers have the chance to meet local people and see how and where their gifts will be used.

The website describes organisations that need your help and lists the items they most need. Check what's needed in the countries you are visiting, contact the organisation to say you're coming and bring not only the much-needed goods but an extra dimension to your travels and the knowledge that in a small way you have made a difference.

A DOG NAMED HOPE

From Guinea's bustling capital city Conakry, we were keen to explore the offshore islands. We took the ferry past rusting wrecks in the harbour and across a clear blue sea, with tropical islands dotted in the distance. Gradually our destination came closer, and soon we stepped off on to a remote beach. 'Just follow that path through the forest, and you'll reach the other side of the island in three or four minutes,' our boatman said. As we arrived, a gorgeous golden retriever appeared, with two young foreign travellers. 'He'll follow you everywhere,' they said. 'We're going back to the mainland on the boat you just came on.' So we were alone again, but for the dog.

Our room was a beautiful straw chalet overlooking a deserted beach. Later we walked along the smooth sand. The dog ran up to greet us, our own personal bodyguard. 'What's his name?' we asked the man at the restaurant.

'Espérance,' he replied. That means hope. In such a poor country it seemed a fitting name.

'Where are you from?' we asked. 'You speak very good English.'

'I am a refugee from Sierra Leone,' he replied. 'I speak English, so I persuaded Madame to give me a job here for board and lodging only. She said she can't pay me anything because business is bad, but I am happy because I have food and a roof over my head, and, above all, I am safe here. But I hope I will be able to go home soon.'

He probably has by now, we hope. As we left for the ferry the next day, Espérance sprang along the path to see us off. Hope springs eternal in Africa.

If you decide to give cash on the spot, then do look the person in the eyes, smile and say an appropriate 'Good morning'; being given a coin is probably far less of a novelty to him or her than being treated like a human being. (And prepare for the onslaught as others nearby spot that you're a soft touch and suddenly materialise.)

Just occasionally you can turn begging into an encounter that's pleasurable for you both. Many children do it from habit and would much rather be playing, so if you turn it into a game, they'll remember the fun of it far longer than the handing over of a coin. Also try learning 'What is your name?' in a few appropriate languages – perhaps French, Arabic and Swahili. The effect is astonishing on someone, whether child or adult, who's used to being ignored or pushed aside. Even if you learn only their name, tell them yours and then say goodbye; you've lifted them several rungs up the scale of humanity and that's what they'll remember. Or if you're refusing to give, then use their name politely as you say 'No'. In fact this is a great way to connect with children at any time; by using their name, you give them dignity and they respond.

Again, do bear in mind the damage you can do by giving little gifts (sweets, pens, biscuits or whatever) to a child or youngster who comes up and begs, however cutely. If the begging bears fruit (and if the gift isn't immediately grabbed by a bigger child), he/she will start to pester all visitors, some of whom may react aggressively or unpleasantly. However, it's fine as a 'payment' for genuine helpfulness.

WHEN YOU LEAVE Here's a final chance to be useful to Africa. Don't take home that T-shirt you probably won't wear again, that almost-full bottle of baby lotion, that soap, pen, pad of paper, that length of rope, torch, batteries, those duplicate tools… instead, collect them up and give them to a local charity. Organisations looking

8

after the homeless or running children's homes can turn pretty much anything to a good use. As an added bonus, you'll have more space in your vehicle for all those bulky souvenirs that you couldn't resist.

TOURISM IN GENERAL Obviously responsible tourism is vital to the future of interethnic relations and cultural interaction. The actions of the visitor today are the seeds of the reaction to the visitor tomorrow. Tourism can offer Africa another source of employment, a tool for development and a direction for understanding. Ecotourism is a new word and concept in Africa, but one that will develop with greater education. It is incumbent on us to keep Africa as we found it in most aspects, and maybe somehow in other aspects to leave it a better place.

However we travel in Africa, we are always going to be seen as rich people, but it is still a source of surprise how little this can matter sometimes. Interaction between peoples is the only way of developing greater understanding, and at least in that, if in nothing else, we may be seen to be doing some good.

A–Z Africa Country Guide

This section gives a brief introduction to each country, listed in alphabetical order. Those contemplating crossing Africa with a tour company or on public transport may also find this overview useful for planning.

WHICH COUNTRY?

Africa is too vast for one trip; you'll just have to go back again … and again … Each country has its own unique unmissable 'something': deserts, culture, people, wildlife, beaches, mountains and even rainforests with mud roads. Any combination will immerse you in stunning landscapes, national parks and fascinating culture, but it is invariably the vibrant people and colourful characters you meet who make the trip truly memorable.

Most African countries are not currently at war, but some are racked with internal dissent, such as the DRC, Congo and, less so, western Sudan. Also note the impact of the Arab Spring on Tunisia, Libya, Egypt and Syria. Apart from Ethiopia and Eritrea, there are few contentious border disputes. However, be prepared for some information in this book and on the internet to be out of date. Keep abreast of any new information as you go. There are numerous detailed guidebooks available for many of the countries covered here – check the selection on offer from Bradt (*www.bradtguides.com*).

For wildlife we would suggest visiting southern and eastern Africa, where the majority of the large national parks are located – Kruger National Park (eastern Transvaal – South Africa), Umfolozi (Natal – South Africa), Kalahari Gemsbok Park (border of Botswana and South Africa), the Okavango Delta (Botswana), South Luangwa (Zambia), Lake Kariba (Zimbabwe), Masai Mara (Kenya) and Ngorongoro, Serengeti National Park (Tanzania). For culture and people you could visit the Himba in Namibia, the San people in Botswana, the Masai in Kenya, the Turkana of Lake Turkana (sometimes referred to as the Jade Sea), the Omatic tribes of southern Ethiopia or the Tuareg of the desert.

Of course, we haven't quite visited every country in Africa on our last four trips, and no doubt things will continue to change. So you will need to be flexible and keep up-to-date through websites and fellow travellers.

NOTES ON THIS PART OF THE GUIDE

Currency rates and fuel costs are as accurate as possible as of February 2014.

CURRENCY RATES Rates can sometimes fluctuate wildly and suddenly. www.oanda.com and www.xe.com/currencyconverter are helpful for finding the latest exchange rates.

RED TAPE The sections on red tape cover specific issues related to that country, such as special permits or taxes.

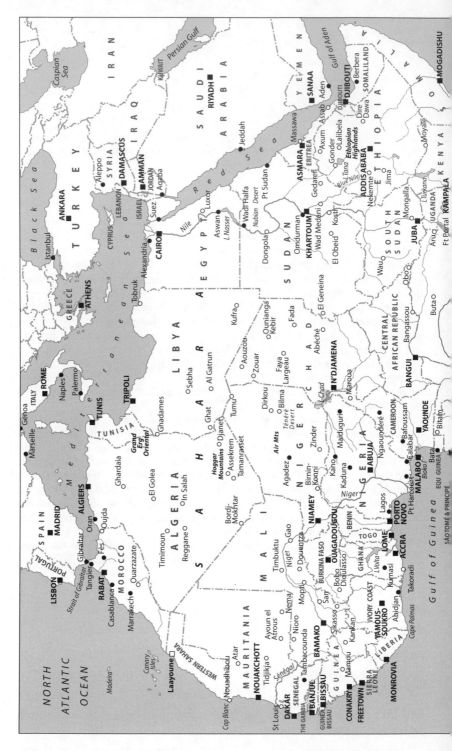

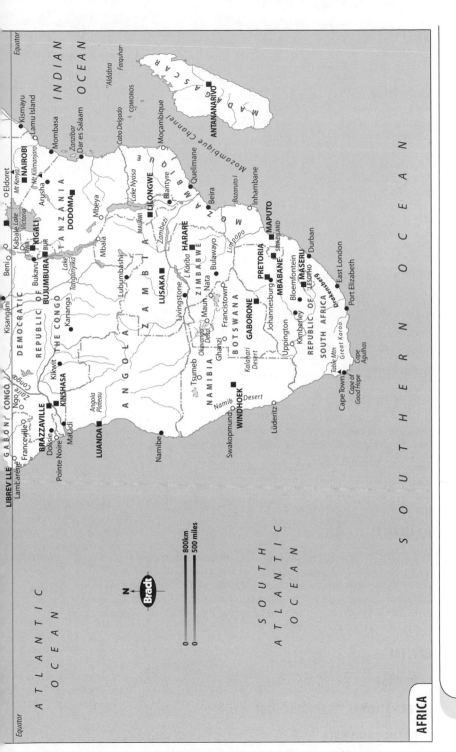

AFRICA

Visas Prices will vary according to nationality and have a habit of increasing steeply. Visa costs tend to be cheaper *en route*, but this is not always the case. Some visas need to be obtained in your 'home' country.

Embassies Previous editions of this guide listed embassy addresses in the capitals for other African countries, but addresses change so frequently that it's better to consult local people and the internet, although you should be cautious with the latter as some sites are out of date. Some useful websites for tracking down embassies are:

http://embassy.goabroad.com
www.embassyworld.com
www.embassypage.com
www.embassy-finder.com

Nationals of countries who have no embassy in a given country can try an embassy from a neighbouring country, eg: Brits can check at French embassies, etc.

DRIVING AND ROADS Driving information relates to specific issues and an overview of road conditions.

Fuel Prices are given as a relative indication only, since the cost of a barrel of oil fluctuates and oil prices are quoted in US dollars with very variable exchange rates. Check out www.mytravelcost.com.

HIGHLIGHTS These sections give useful information about what to see *en route*.

WHERE TO STAY We have listed most of the camping places/hotels that we have used, or have been told about recently. It often helps and saves time to have an idea of where you can stay. Of course, some places shut down, grow grander or become less attractive. Some useful websites are www.hostels.com, www.tracks4africa.co.za and www.caravanparks.com.

GPS GPS is recorded in different ways, as anyone with a GPS device will be aware. We have done our best to be as accurate as possible where GPS locations are given.

ALGERIA

WARNING! Having been off-limits for several years, overland travel in Algeria was again possible in the early 2000s, but is currently not safe because of the kidnapping of 32 foreign tourists in 2003 and the attack on the In Amenas oil installation in 2013. Groups linked to al-Qaeda are believed to be operating in the area. Seek sound travel advice if you do intend to visit.

CAPITAL Algiers

LANGUAGE Arabic. French is widely spoken too.

INTERNATIONAL TELEPHONE CODE +213

CURRENCY AND RATE Algerian dinar (DZD); US$1 = DZD78.64

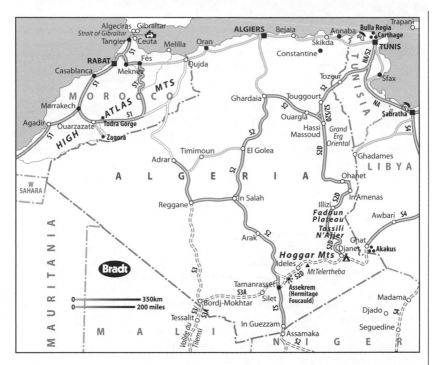

RED TAPE The carnet is not accepted and a laissez-passer will be issued at the border. Insurance must be purchased at the borders or nearest town. Currency declaration forms may need to be filled out on arrival and shown on departure, though they may not be checked. If you are checked, it may be thorough. All non-declared money found could be confiscated. Ensure that you get valid receipts when changing money at a bank, although the black market is thriving, particularly in euros. Remember that your declaration form needs to tally with bank receipts. But it may be that you cannot find a bank when you need to, and are forced to change money on the black market. Put some aside (hidden) for this eventuality. Also be aware that it is almost impossible to change travellers' cheques anywhere in the country. Take enough cash.

Visas Visas are required for all except Moroccan and Tunisian nationals. Visa costs vary depending on the country of application. You will also need three photographs, an invitation from the agent who is hosting you in Algeria, and an introduction from your embassy if you are not getting the visa in your home country. Double-entry visas are available. Visas are not issued at the border.

African embassies
http://embassy.goabroad.com/embassies-in/algeria
www.algerianembassy.org.uk
www.algerianembassy.org

DRIVING AND ROADS Drive on the right. There are good surfaced roads throughout the north and most of the way to Tamanrasset, and now to In Guezzam. Eastern roads are also sealed to Djanet. There are many desert pistes of varying quality.

Fuel costs Diesel: US$0.17; petrol: US$0.28 per litre.

CLIMATE The best time to visit the desert is December to March. October, November, April and May are hotter but just about bearable. Avoid the desert from June to September.

HIGHLIGHTS The main highlight is the Sahara: Timimoun, Ghardaia, Tamanrasset, the volcanic Hoggar Mountains, the hermitage of Père du Foucauld, Djanet, the Tassili N'Ajjer Plateau with its prehistoric art and fantastic rock towers, and the remote Tassili du Hoggar in the far south. The black Tademait Plateau south of El Golea and the Arak Gorge are stunning, and there are beautiful sand dunes across the desert. The Kasbah in Algiers is also a highlight and along the coast are Constantine, Djemila and the Kabylia Mountains.

WHERE TO STAY Sleeping out in the open desert was wonderful. If it becomes possible again, make absolutely sure you are well out of sight of the road or piste. Basic accommodation costs between US$15 and US$40. Algerians are extremely friendly and will go out of their way to help you, sometimes even offering accommodation. You can also ask to camp in the back yard of some hotels.

Ouargla The **Hôtel Tassili** allowed parking/camping behind the hotel. It is north of the main road.

Ghardaia Try either the central **Hôtel El Djenoub**, with secure parking nearby, or the **Hotel Rym**, which has underground parking.

El Golea There was a nice but sandy campsite in the palmeries on the way south out of town; look for the camping sign on the gates. The central **Hotel Boustane** also had parking.

In Salah The **Hôtel Tidikelt** allowed camping outside in the garden area.

Tamanrasset The **Hôtel Tinhinane** in the old main street had economical rooms with safe parking. There were two campsites east of town. Try the **Hôtel Tahat** for a splurge.

Djanet In the centre of the town is **Camping/Hôtel Zeriba,** a pleasant retreat.

OTHER Trekking tours are still possible in the Tassili N'Ajjer and the Hoggar.

FURTHER INFORMATION
Sahara Overland Chris Scott (see *Appendix 5*, page 364)
Algeria Jonathan Oakes (Bradt Travel Guides)

ANGOLA

WARNING! Although the civil war in Angola finished ages ago, there are still unexploded mines littering the countryside. Do not head off any road to camp; use the roadside quarries.

CAPITAL Luanda

LANGUAGE Portuguese

INTERNATIONAL TELEPHONE CODE +244

CURRENCY AND RATE Angolan new kwanza (AOA); US$1 = AON97.61

RED TAPE Expect some checkpoints along the roads. You might have to register with the police in any main settlement. The few travellers who have managed to get into the country from the DRC have said that the Angolan officials have often been most helpful.

Visas Visas are required for all. Obtaining an Angolan visa is currently extremely difficult. Applications can be attempted directly by contacting the Ministerio de Hostelaria Turismo Angola office (*2 Andar, Palácio de Vidro, Largo 4 de Fevereiro, Luanda;* \+244 2 338 625). Good luck!

Visas are not issued at the border and are supposed to be obtained in your country of origin. *En route* overlanders were trying in Lomé, Abuja, Yaoundé, Libreville, Brazzaville, Kinshasa and when desperate in Matadi in the DRC. The consulate here has sometimes given five-day transit visas.

African embassies
http://embassy.goabroad.com/embassies-in/angola
www.angola.org.uk/embassies
www.angola.org

DRIVING AND ROADS Many of the main roads are being reconstructed by the Chinese. Some routes that used to take days can now be done in a few hours. Look at the internet for the latest travellers' reports. There are patches of tar between Luvo and Mbanza Congo and then new tar for 200km towards Tomboco, with a reasonable surface as far as N'zeto. Mussera is two hours south on a bad road. The road is being worked on before Caxito and then it's fine to Luanda. There is a ring road around Luanda if you need to avoid costly accommodation

– signed *autoestrada*. Follow motorway signs to Cabolombo if you want to try the coastal route. It's a new toll road for 600km to Benguela via Porto Amboin, Sumbe and Lobito. Between Benguela and Cacula the road should be complete, but south to Humbe work continues (2013). Humbe to the Namibian border is fine. There's new tarmac between Luanda, Huambo and Benguela on the inland route.

Fuel costs Diesel: US$0.53; petrol: US$0.81 per litre.

CLIMATE Angola has a varied climate with rains inland from October to May. The dry season is from June to August. The south coast is drier.

HIGHLIGHTS South of N'zeto are turbulent rivers, savanna, jungle and some beautiful rock formations, all close to the sea. The Ponta das Palmeirinhas south of the capital offers a viewpoint where some unusual rock formations are seen. In the southwest there is an extensive mountainous region inland from Namibe. Lubango is likely to become *the* tourist destination of southern Angola, as more people discover its long-unexplored delights. Outside Lubango is the Tunda-Vala volcanic fissure gorge with 1,000m cliffs, all viewed from a panoramic platform. In the far south are the Quedas do Ruacana waterfalls, when flowing, on the border with Namibia.

 WHERE TO STAY Finding places to stay in Angola can be a problem. Try missions, half-open national parks, roadside quarries and hotels with secure parking. Hotels in Angola are very expensive, ranging from US$80 to US$100 for tiny rooms to over US$360 for international standard in Luanda. A few more camping options are developing, usually in conjunction with hotels. As a last resort, try police stations.

WARNING! Crime levels in **Luanda** are high, so beware. Security issues here are paramount but you might be able to park near the Hotel Panorama around the bay or at the **Clube Nautico** (yacht club) in Luanda on the Ilha (basic conditions).

Parque Nacional da Quicama South of the capital, this may have camping options.

Cabinda Some overlanders have stayed at the Catholic mission by the church near the immigration office, where registration might have to be done.

M'banza Congo Try at the church, where the French priest has been helpful to travellers.

N'zeto Look for camping along the coast, south of N'zeto. Try at S 07° 20.093, E 12° 56.471.

Caxito No recommended options, so if desperate stay near the police station.

Quedas De Agua Da Binga The falls are off the main road, with bush camping and a toilet almost at the falls.

Benguela Hotels are expensive, so it's back to the bush or the bush quarries.

Lubango There might still be a campsite in Lubango near the botanical gardens. There is also a quarry about 30km south of Lubango on the route to Namibia that may be suitable for bush camping. **Casper Lodge** (S 14° 55.906, E 13° 28.158) has camping as does **As Mulembas Guesthouse** on the road to Tunda-Vala. (The Shoprite store has come to town!)

Namibe There is a campsite just before the **Diversi Lodge** on the promenade. **Flamingo Lodge** (*www.aasafaris.com*) is another possibility on the south side of town. Camping is around US$20 per person.

South of Chibia There is a quarry on the RHS (S 16° 05.330, E 14° 12.526) near the junction signed to Kavalawa.

Namakunde Look for a sandy track approx 15km north of town (S 17° 10.070, E 15° 46.968).

Ruacana You can camp at **Osheja Guest House** or on the Namibian side at **Hippo Pools Camp** (S 17° 24.318, E 14° 13.022).

FURTHER INFORMATION
Angola Mike Stead and Sean Rorison (Bradt Travel Guides)
www.angola.org

BENIN

CAPITAL Porto Novo

LANGUAGE French

INTERNATIONAL TELEPHONE CODE +229

CURRENCY AND RATE West African franc (CFA); US$1 = CFA478

RED TAPE Of little significance in Benin, except visas.

Visas Visas are required for all except nationals of the Economic Community of West African States (ECOWAS). They are normally available at the borders of Benin for 48 hours' transit only, costing around US$45. You will need two passport photos. Yellow fever vaccination certificates are also officially required, but not often checked.

African embassies
http://embassy.goabroad.com/embassies-in/benin
http://embassy-finder.com/benin_embassies
www.embassyinformation.com

DRIVING AND ROADS Drive on the right. Most roads in Benin are paved and even those that aren't are in good condition, with only a few pot-holes.

Fuel costs Diesel: US$1.51; petrol: US$1.30 per litre.

CLIMATE Humid everywhere, with steady temperatures around 27°C. The dry season is from December to April. Northern Benin, being part of the Sahel, is less humid but very hot during March and April. Its dry season lasts from November to May.

HIGHLIGHTS The capital city of Porto Novo is a sleepy town with some interesting buildings and markets. Ganvié, a village built on stilts

in the middle of a lagoon and accessible only by dugout canoe, is near Cotonou. The voodoo museums of Ouidah, Grand Popo and the coastline are worth a visit. Inland are the historic palaces of Abomey. The three-storey houses of the Somba/ Betamaribe people around Natitingou are worth seeing and, in the north, the Parc National du W. The railway, one that still works, is a fine way to travel.

WHERE TO STAY

Cotonou Finding secure parking is a big problem. It might be more pleasant and safer to avoid Cotonou and stay in Ouidah to the west, where a couple of cheap beach resorts exist. If you have to stay in Cotonou, try the **Hôtel de la Plage** near the beach; it had parking but the area was not that safe. It would be better to first try asking to park/camp at the **Hôtel Aledjo** east of the city on the beach. Further out is **Auberge au Large**; it may allow parking/camping along Route des Pêches. The **Guesthouse Cocotiers** is another option, but secure parking would need to be sorted out. It is located in Haie Vive near the Africare NGO.

Porto Novo The choice is bleak; suggested is the **Hôtel Beaurivage**, where rooms are expensive but the view is pleasant.

Ouidah Try the **Hôtel Jardin Bresilien** in the beach area. Rooms from US$14.

Grand Popo The L'Auberge de Grand Popo has been modernised. The hotel has a superb restaurant and campsite with a view of the ocean in an extremely beautiful setting. Also look for **Awale Plage Camping**. Another spot to aim for is **Victor's Place** near the Protestant church.

Abomey A little way from the town centre, **Chez Monique** has a shady tropical garden and straw-roof restaurant. You can camp at the back of the hotel. The voodoo festival is entertaining if one is in progress. Around US$6/7 per person.

Dassa The **Dassa Motel** (Auberge de Dassa Zoume) is on the west side of town, past the dramatic rocks near the ring road. Parking is available here, with rooms from US$28.

Parakou The run-down but atmospheric **Hôtel de la Gare** had large rooms and good parking (it may be called Buffet Hotel now). Nearby, just 4km away on the road to Natitingou, on the *barrage* (dam) by the Voie de Djougou, a fish farm may offer accommodation overlooking a series of beautiful lakes.

Natitingou It might be possible to park in the grounds of the **Hôtel Tata Somba**. Another hotel option might be the renovated **Auberge le Vieux Cavalier** east of town, where trips to the villages can be organised. Other B&Bs are **Ma Case Au Benin** and **Hôtel Bourgogne**.

Kandi Look for the **Motel de Kandi** north of town. In town is the pleasant **Auberge la Rencontre** with a roof terrace.

Parc National de la Pendjari You can stay at the **Campement de la Pendjari** where camping costs about US$7–10 per person. Bookings were possible through Hotel Tata Somba in Natitingou. **Hôtel Baobab** and **Auberge Camp Numi** are reported to allow camping.

OTHER Taking of photographs is permitted, but be respectful, especially when visiting fetish temples and shrines. Crime in Cotonou has increased significantly.

FURTHER INFORMATION
Benin Stuart Butler (Bradt Travel Guides)
www.hotels-benin.com is a good website for finding accommodation.

BOTSWANA

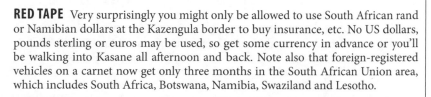

CAPITAL Gaborone

LANGUAGE English and Setswana

INTERNATIONAL TELEPHONE CODE +267

CURRENCY AND RATE Pula (BWP); US$1 = BWP8.91

RED TAPE Very surprisingly you might only be allowed to use South African rand or Namibian dollars at the Kazengula border to buy insurance, etc. No US dollars, pounds sterling or euros may be used, so get some currency in advance or you'll be walking into Kasane all afternoon and back. Note also that foreign-registered vehicles on a carnet now get only three months in the South African Union area, which includes South Africa, Botswana, Namibia, Swaziland and Lesotho.

Visas Visas are not required for nationals of the USA, UK, most other Commonwealth countries, or most of western Europe, as long as the stay does not exceed 90 days. Entry permits for 30 days are issued at the border.

African embassies
www.gov.bw
www.botswanaembassy.org
www.embassyworld.com

DRIVING AND ROADS Drive on the left. There are good surfaced main roads but the rest are merely tracks and pistes. Road mostly OK to the border at Martin's Drift. Fuel stations in the north are unreliable; top up wherever possible.

Fuel costs Diesel: US$1.20; petrol: US$1.15 per litre.

CLIMATE It is hot in the daytime throughout the year, but between July and September temperatures at night can plummet to near freezing. The main rainy season is from December to April.

HIGHLIGHTS The Okavango Delta, Moremi Game Reserve and Chobe National Park are obvious highlights. Maun has various campsites and organisations that arrange tours into

each of these areas. The Kalahari Desert, with its vast open spaces, Kgalagadi Park and Central Kalahari Game Reserve, is worth a visit, as are the Makgadikgadi and Nxai Pans (only with 4x4 and in the dry season, April to December). Only use well-marked tracks on the pans, or your vehicle will sink. It is advisable to go with another vehicle. The Tsodilo Hills hosts ancient San paintings.

WHERE TO STAY
National parks' entry permits and campsites must be pre-booked. Most campsites have been privatised. Entry permits may be obtained at park offices in Gaborone, Maun or Kasane.

Gaborone With only a few cheap hotels in town, try camping in the **Mokolodi Nature Reserve** (US$25 for two). The **Testimony Guest House** in Mogoditshane Gaborone has been mentioned. **Beams Campsite** is another central place, costing around US$10 per person.

Francistown With a large attached campground, **Hotel Murang** is spacious, shady and relaxing. It's out of town to the east. Camping is US$20–25 all in.

Makgadikgadi and Nxai Pans Camps in these areas are expensive, but there are campsites in both national parks. Outside the parks, look at **Planet Baobab** near Gweta, or **Nata Lodge** in Nata. In the Nata Sanctuary camping is allowed at basically serviced designated places, US$5 per person.

Kanye The **Hotel Motse** is delightful and you can camp in the orchard behind. It's rather hard to find, but is on the north side of town; ask at the fuel stations. It costs US$15 (car plus two).

Kang Just about the only place on the trans-Kalahari road between Kanye and Ghanzi with a motel, shop and fuel. Secure parking.

***En route* to Nata** About 200km north of Nata is **Panda Rest Camp**, near Pandamatenga. You may see elephants and other game along the way, so watch out.

Nata Look for **Maya Guest Inn** and **Nata Lodge**.

Central Kalahari region There are a few basic camping areas within the vast region.

Ghanzi Try the **Kalahari Arms Hotel** or the **Thakadu Camp**.

Maun A good choice is available: **Andi Camp, Old Bridge Backpackers, Crocodile Camp, Island Safari Lodge, Maun Rest Camp, Okavango River Lodge** and **Sitatunga Camp** all offer basic camping facilities from US$7. See the latest on www.maunselfdrive4x4.com.

Okavango Delta No stay within the Okavango Delta (or any national park in Botswana) will be cheap, but the delta is a unique attraction. Most 'camps' in the delta area are luxury-style but Moremi Game Reserve (see below) and the Panhandle, fringing the northwest side have more choice.

Moremi Reserve There are several options here: try **Khwai Campsite** at North Gate, **Xakanaxa Campsite, Third Bridge Campsite** or **South Gate Campsite**.

These are inside the park, so the costs will be higher. Allow about US$50 per person including entry, camping and vehicle.

Panhandle At the foot of the Panhandle, **Sepupa Swamp Stop** offers camping for around US$6 per person. Further north, established options with campsites include **Guma Lagoon Camp**, **Nguma Island Lodge**, **Shakawe River Lodge** and **Drotsky's Cabins**.

Kasane/Chobe National Park A popular area is along the Chobe River around Kasane, west of Kazungula. The **Ngina Safari** camping is basic; **Kubu Lodge** has camping options, as does **Toro Safari Lodge**. Nearer Kasane is **Thebe River Lodge** (*www.theberiversafaris.com*) – nice if not flooded, US$12 per person; closer still to the national park is **Chobe Safari Lodge**. Away from the river are **Luyi Campsite** and **Senyati Safari Camp**. Further south in the national park itself is **Savuti Campsite**.

Tsodilo Hills Getting to the Tsodilo Hills, a World Heritage Site, is now easier with road improvements, and is worth the effort. There are new community campsites near the hills at US$15 per person. It should be possible to bush camp *en route*.

OTHER Importing of meat is prohibited, with frequent checks.

FURTHER INFORMATION
Botswana – Okavango Delta, Chobe, Northern Kalahari Chris McIntyre (Bradt Travel Guides)
www.botswananet.org

BURKINA FASO

CAPITAL Ouagadougou

LANGUAGE French

INTERNATIONAL TELEPHONE CODE +226

CURRENCY AND RATE West African franc (CFA); US$1 = CFA478

RED TAPE Things are generally relaxed across the country.

Visas Visas are required for all foreigners. They are normally, and more cheaply, issued at the main borders, but check at the closest African embassy. The *Visa Touristique Entente* intended to cover Benin, Burkina Faso, Ivory Coast, Niger and Togo seems to be unavailable these days. In countries where there is no representation, the French consulate may handle Burkina visas. Vaccination certificates for yellow fever may be checked.

African embassies
http://embassy.goabroad.com/embassies-in/burkina-faso
www.embassypages.com

DRIVING AND ROADS Drive on the right. Main routes have mostly good surfaced roads. Secondary roads are quite reasonable, with some maintenance.

Fuel costs Diesel: US$1.59; petrol: US$1.79 per litre.

CLIMATE The cool dry season is from November to mid-April and the rainy season from June to September. The north has less rain and is hotter.

HIGHLIGHTS Although the 'Grand Marché' in Ouagadougou is no more after a huge fire, the area is still a shopping zone. Ouagadougou is a food connoisseur's delight, known for its variety of restaurants ranging from African and European to American. Banfora is excellent for cycling, and the surrounding area. Bobo Dioulasso, with its mud mosque, has long been a favourite. As well as the mud mosque, the biggest attractions are the Bobo (local tribe) houses, distinguished by their tall, conical roofs, in the surrounding countryside. The Sultan's Palace (Na Yiri) at Kokolongho, 45km west of Ouagadougou, is a worthwhile stop *en route*. Built in 1942, it is the home of Naaba Kaongo. The small town of Bani, near Dori, has some amazing mosques. In the north, a melting pot of people gathers in the market of Gorom Gorom every Thursday. The Parc National du W is another attraction.

WHERE TO STAY

Ouagadougou The best and most secure place is at the **Mission Catholique**, within the compound near the cathedral. Try the sisters (Les Sœurs Lauriers) or the brothers (La Fraternité). You are not allowed to sleep in your car; rooms are compulsory, but very cheap. Otherwise try at **Hôtel Les Palmiers**, which has parking. If you prefer to stay well out of town, look for **Campement Phargon**, 12km east on the main highway to Niger. There is also a *campement* at **Rapadama**, 53km east of Ouaga.

Bobo Dioulasso The best option is **Casa Africa**, with shade, camping, cheap rooms and a restaurant. It's southwest of town across the railway. Nearby is **Campement le Pacha**, another option with a shady garden, but they seem to be discouraging campers. Near the Grande Mosque is **Hôtel Les Cocotiers** with hot but cheap rooms and some parking without shade. It's popular with backpackers. For a big splurge try the **Hôtel Les 2 Palmiers** near Le Pacha. It's a good place for a drink in any case.

Boromo About halfway between Bobo and Ouaga, centrally in town on the south side of the road, is the **Campement Relais Touristique**, a great stop for a drink and/or snack, where rooms are US$25/35 with fan/air conditioner.

Banfora The **Campement Baobab** is 4km from town near the Domes of Fabedougou, with a great atmosphere, thatched huts and camping options. Allow around US$6 per person. If you want a hotel, try the atmospheric **Hôtel le Comoé**, on the southern edge of town; they may allow camping in their courtyard for a minimal fee. Equally charming but more expensive is the **Hôtel Canne à Sucre** (*www.banfora.com*). **Grand Hôtel Banfora** has good parking. Close to Banfora are the unusually shaped hills of the Pics du Sindou. You can stay in the Sindou village at **Campement Djatiguiya**.

Oronawa West of Bobo Dioulasso in this small town is the delightful **Hôtel Le Prestige**. Internet café here.

Ranch de Nazinga A quiet French retreat (*www.ranchdenazinga.com*).

Dori/Bani The **Camping de Djomaga** about 7km out of Dori is a good option, around US$5 per person for camping. **Hebergement Le Nomad** can set up dune trips from Bani.

Gorom Gorom Try **Le Campement Rissa,** a decent option where camping costs US$5 per person. Also here is **Campement Hôtel Gorom Gorom**, a quiet place with a rocky outcrop. Oursi, with a lake and dunes nearby is a gem; stay at **Campement Aounaf**.

Tenkodogo On the way to Togo is the great **Hôtel Laafi** with good parking inside, garden and restaurant. It's on the west side of the road. You can camp or have a room with air conditioning for around US$26.

Fada N'Gourma The **Belle Etoile** is a cultural experience as well as a place to stay. From US$10.

OTHER Photographic permits are no longer required, but be careful taking pictures and remember that photos of government institutions are completely forbidden. For repairs and parts check Burkina Motors in the centre of Ouagadougou.

FURTHER INFORMATION
Burkina Faso Katrina Manson and James Knight (Bradt Travel Guides)

BURUNDI

CAPITAL Bujumbura

LANGUAGE French and Kirundi

INTERNATIONAL TELEPHONE CODE +257

CURRENCY AND RATE Burundian franc (BIF); US$1 = BIF1,540. There may not be any moneychangers at the Rwandan/Burundian border.

RED TAPE You can expect an occasional roadblock.

Visas Visas are required for all visitors. You will need two passport photos. Visas are issued at the airport and recently at the main Rwandan/Burundian land border, but check beforehand.

African embassies
http://embassy.goabroad.com/embassies-in/burundi
www.embassyinformation.com

DRIVING AND ROADS The main road between Bujumbura and Kigali is quite acceptable, with a spectacular drop into the Rift Valley of Lake Tangyanika. The

9

road south to Nyanza (115km) is mostly OK with bumps and short, unmade, poor sections. Uphill from Nyanza-Lac town, the road is good to Mabanda. Turn right on to a dirt road for the Tanzanian border. Customs and immigration are here, well before the border, just 50m to the right off the 'main' road. The last 20km between borders is pretty dreadful, muddy and difficult if wet, but great fun!

Fuel costs Diesel: US$1.77; petrol: US$1.79 per litre.

CLIMATE The climate is varied. The general rainy season is from November to May. A dry period lasts from June until October, but seasons are not clearly defined.

HIGHLIGHTS Bujumbura has an attractive setting and some old colonial buildings. Other sights are the Parc National de la Kibira with its rainforest, the Parc National de la Rurubu, and the waterfall, Chutes de la Kagera, near Gitega.

 WHERE TO STAY

Bujumbura We stayed at **Hôtel Le Rift**. Head for Museum Vivante, turn right at the USA University – dirt lane here, take the second left and the hotel is on the corner. Also not far from La Pirogue bar on the lakeside, left – right – left off main road, rooms from US$25. Ask someone in the bar to show you the way! There is an internet café in town along the Sage Hotel road. There's also **Hôtel le Doyen** and camping might be a possibility out of town at a former colonial place called **Safari Gate** on the lakeside.

Lake Tangyanika The **Lake Tangyanika Bluebay Resort** is 40 miles south of Bujumbura. Also at 73 miles is a beach area with a mini-resort. South before Nyanza-Lac town is the **Hôtel Nyanza-Lac Makamba** on the right, on the lakeside with rooms for US$26/35.

FURTHER INFORMATION
http://allafrica.com/burundi

CAMEROON

WARNING! Avoid the far north close to the Nigerian border, owing to kidnapping threats.

CAPITAL Yaoundé

LANGUAGE French and English

INTERNATIONAL TELEPHONE CODE +237

CURRENCY AND RATE Central African franc (CFA); US$1 = CFA478

RED TAPE You will be stopped sometimes for passport and vehicle checks. Beware of accidentally driving on the President's road in Yaoundé!

Visas Visas are required for virtually everyone. Getting a visa in advance in your own country is often very expensive, with all manner of paperwork. Visas are not issued at the border. *En route* you could try in Dakar, Lagos or Calabar, Nigeria. One has to wonder if they really want any tourists.

African embassies
http://embassy.goabroad.com/embassies-in/cameroon
http://cm.embassyinformation.com

DRIVING AND ROADS Drive on the right. Road surfaces range from exceptionally good tarmac to diabolically corrugated dirt, with all variations in between. North of Ngaoundéré or south and west of Yaoundé are some fairly good tarred roads. Otherwise there are some reasonable dirt roads that are closed when it rains, plus a few awful stretches of corrugated dirt – best not dwelt on. There are some new road projects, so the situation is improving. The border road from Mamfe to Nigeria is one of these. A better road from Bertoua to Yaoundé is via Abong-Mbang. The road to Gabon is good. For a big, dry-season adventure, you could try heading southeast from Bertoua to Yokadouma and on through the jungle to Sokamba. A route is said to lead into Congo, to Quesso, but we don't know if the barges can carry cars across the rivers!

Fuel costs Diesel: US$1.36; petrol: US$1.49 per litre.

CLIMATE Coastal Cameroon is very wet almost all year. The north is hot and dry, with a long rainy season from May to October. The south is hot and humid, with a short 'dryish' season from December to February and rains from March until October, with a less wet period in July and August away from the coast.

HIGHLIGHTS Climb Mount Cameroon, west Africa's highest mountain at 4,070m; visit the Benoué national parks. The beaches at Kribi are excellent. If safe in the north, explore the villages and markets around Maroua, and hike in the Mandara Mountains, including Roumsiki.

Southern Cameroon has some spectacular hill regions with the last of the Pygmy tribes, but they are extremely difficult to reach; you could join an organised expedition with a volunteer organisation in Yaoundé. The Lobeke National Park can be reached via Yakadouma, but the roads are often impassable, especially after rain.

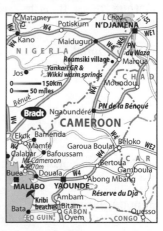

⌂ WHERE TO STAY
Yaoundé Finding a reasonably priced hotel with parking in the capital is difficult. **Hôtel Meumi** is convenient but its rates are increasing.

The **Foyer Internationale de l'Eglise Presbytérienne** is situated near the water tower and Carrefour Nlongkak; it has been used by overlanders. It's all right for US$6–7.

Douala Best avoided, but if you have to stay, try the **German Seamen's Mission** in the Akwa district. Despite its name, it's popular, and costs US$30+.

Mamfé We stayed at the **Heritage Inn**. We were told, 'Sorry, we have only the most expensive room left. It's US$12.' This was a suite with air conditioning, sofas and a huge bathroom. We didn't mind at all! Don't plan on getting fuel here; it's close to the Nigerian border and fuel shortages are frequent.

Buea The town is on the slopes of Mount Cameroon and is also its base camp. You must have a permit and guide to climb the mountain; both are available in the main street in town. Climbing Mount Cameroon can take three or four days. In Buea is the **Hôtel Mermoz**, where a double room costs from US$16. The Presbyterian church used to allow camping.

Kumba The **Azi Motel** is one parking/camping possibility, especially if you have dinner in the restaurant.

Limbe In town try at the **Park Hotel Miramare** behind the botanical gardens. Camping may be available at the 6 or 8 Mile Beach area. The **First International Inn** has bungalows.

Kribi Stay at **Tara Plage** with a good restaurant, from US$7 per person for camping.

Ebolowa Try a hotel with tennis courts on the edge of town.

Bamenda There is the **Baptist Mission Resthouse**.

Foumban The town is rich in historical sights. Try staying at the **Catholic Mission**, which has a nice garden.

Maroua Try at **Hôtel le Sare** or **Hôtel Sahel**. There is a campement called **Boussou**, which is cheaper.

Waza National Park Camping is possible at the **Centre d'Accueil de Waza** for around US$7. Check the latest security situation with regard to the Boko Haram Islamists.

Roumsiki This is a hill retreat with good trekking and outer villages where it is possible to stay. In 'town' you could stay at **Kirdi Bar**, a cheap option for camping, or at **Auberge Le Kapsiki**.

Garoua Try the plush hotel, **Relais St Hubert**. It has air-conditioned rooms and secure parking. Camping might be allowed and a double room costs US$40.

Benoué National Park About 30km from the main road at Banda. There is camping at the **Campement du Buffle Noir**.

Ngaoundéré On the south side of town, try **Hôtel Transcam**, which has secure parking. Southeast of town, about 35km away, **Ranch de N'Gaoundaba** has been mentioned as a good option in the hills, near a volcanic crater lake.

OTHER Photographic permits are not required, but many officials will tell you that they are. Crime is on the increase, particularly in Yaoundé and Douala. Don't drive on the President's unmarked private road, a large roundabout area in central Yaoundé; it could be a costly error.

FURTHER INFORMATION
Cameroon Ben West (Bradt Travel Guides)

CENTRAL AFRICAN REPUBLIC (CAR)

WARNING! Owing to the ongoing civil disturbances and remnants of the LRA rebels in the Central African Republic, we advise against overland travel into the country. It could improve with a new regime in place – again! Seek sound travel advice if you do intend to visit. Some information listed is likely to be out of date.

CAPITAL Bangui

LANGUAGE French

INTERNATIONAL TELEPHONE CODE +236

CURRENCY AND RATE Central African franc (CFA); US$1 = CFA478

RED TAPE Avoid all military personnel and try not to stay too long in one area.

Visas Visas are required for all and costs are unknown after the latest coup. Two photos, two application forms, a yellow fever certificate, a letter from your company stating that the applicant will resume work on returning and a return ticket were all required. Visas are not issued at the border. Visas may only be given for short stays, requiring extensions in Bangui.

African embassies
http://embassy.goabroad.com/embassies-in/centralafricanrepublic
www.embassypages.com/car

DRIVING AND ROADS Drive on the right. There are sealed roads to the northeast and northwest of Bangui for a limited distance, but closer to the borders of Cameroon, Chad and South Sudan, roads are in very poor condition, particularly during the rainy season.

Fuel costs Diesel: US$2.10; petrol: US$2.13 per litre.

CLIMATE It's hot and humid in the south, drier in the north. The rainy season is from March to October, starting later and finishing earlier the further north you go.

HIGHLIGHTS The rolling savanna forest across the border from Cameroon gives a feeling of vastness. The Chutes de Boali north of Bangui are spectacular, particularly during the rainy season. Also worth seeing are the Kembe Falls east of Sibut, and the remote forests beyond. In Bangassou you could take dugout canoe rides along the river in search of hippos. The Dzanga-Sangha Nature Reserve has some great wildlife, including lowland gorillas. The Worldwide Fund for Nature is involved.

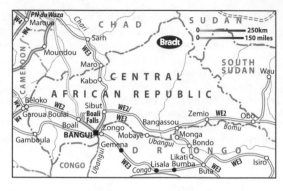

WHERE TO STAY

Bangui Recent reports suggest the **Karakandji Guest House** is a possible place, as is the **Iroko Hôtel** in the Quartier Castors, rue Yakité. Apparently it's friendly, which makes up for the bucket shower option, and is reputed to cost US$30 double with breakfast. The parking situation is unknown. Overlanders used to go to the **Centre d'Accueil Touristique Dalango** (US$5 for camping). It's located in the African Quarter, on Avenue Boganda, 1.5km to the west at Km5. It is still apparently open, but then again how safe is Bangui?

Bossentélé The **Auberge Sous Manguiers** is clean. It apparently boasts shared toilet and bucket showers for US$5. Find it south of the Bouar road down a small lane – ask the locals.

Bozoum If anyone ever manages to drive to this isolated town, watch for the **Mission Catholique** that sits on a hill. For US$14 you get the school grounds for free.

Bayanga Built by the Worldwide Fund for Nature (WWF) with aid from Germany, the **Doli Lodge** is a remote and rustic eco-lodge. Tour operators and researchers use it as a base for trips into the Dzanga-Sangha Nature Reserve.

Boda A bit off any obvious route, but if you land up here look for the **Auberge Atlantic** (behind the hospital, in the centre). It's clean with shared toilets and bucket water, US$4–5.

Obo The Obo Mission allowed camping and had a very well-equipped workshop some years ago (see page 158). It apparently now has an airstrip.

OTHER We would suggest that your camera stays out of sight in Bangui. Ask people in the countryside for their permission, as some in the Central African Republic are extremely sensitive about photography.

FURTHER INFORMATION The WWF (*www.panda.org*) currently has conservation, health and education projects in the CAR, so their website has relevant information.

CHAD

Chad is currently the brightest hope for a big adventure in the Sahara with a foreign or local tour operator. Go while it lasts, to the Ennedi and even perhaps Mount Emi Koussi in the Tibesti region.

CAPITAL N'djamena

LANGUAGE French and Arabic

INTERNATIONAL TELEPHONE CODE +235

CURRENCY AND RATE Central African franc (CFA); US$1 = CFA490

RED TAPE The eastern border with Sudan may be on the verge of reopening, but check before planning. Poorly paid officials can be hard to deal with. When we travelled to the Ennedi Plateau in a local agent's cars, our drivers always tried to avoid police check-posts, suggesting that the situation is not much different elsewhere in the country.

In theory a carnet is not required, but some adjacent countries will need them anyway. For those without a carnet, a *Laissez-Passer pour Vehicules* will normally be issued at all custom border posts for a hefty fee. Travelling outside N'djamena requires an *Autorisation de Circuler* from the Ministry of Tourism.

Visas Visas are required for all Westerners. Yellow fever vaccination certificates may be checked on entry. Visas are not issued at the border. It was possible to get an invitation by email from a local tour operator and have a visa issued at the airport on arrival by air.

African embassies
http://embassy.goabroad.com/embassies-in/chad
www.embassypages.com/chad

DRIVING AND ROADS Drive on the right. There are short sections of tarred road northeast of N'djamena and the road via Mongo to Abeche has been sealed. A new road has accompanied the oil discoveries from Bongor to Moundou and the Cameroonian border. As roads improve with Chinese help, buses are operating between N'djamena, Mongo (US$15) and Abeche (US$30), for those on local transport. The rest are either sandy desert tracks in the north or very bad mud roads in the south.

Fuel costs Diesel: US$1.63; petrol: US$1.64 per litre.

CLIMATE The desert climate in the north is very hot and dry all year round. The heavy rains are from June to September in the south.

HIGHLIGHTS The bustling Grand Marché in N'djamena is colourful. The Tibesti Mountains in the north will be a highlight when they are safe. The region has fantastic volcanoes, isolated villages and the Trou du Natron crater to savour. The Ennedi Plateau, including the Guelta d'Archei, is usually more easily accessed with a local guide; it offers stunning desert scenery with natural arches, freshwater crocodiles and prehistoric rock art. Ounianga Kebir, Ounianga Serir and the northern lakes are amazing, as is the Depression du Mourdi area.

WHERE TO STAY

N'djamena There are several hotels in N'djamena and you may be able to park in their yards (**Aurora** or **Sahara** perhaps). We stayed at the centrally located but now pricey **Hôtel Sahel**. Or ask at the **Novotel** – formerly Hôtel Tchadienne – if you can camp in their grounds. If you're lucky, you may be allowed to use the staff showers and the hotel's pool. Otherwise suggested are the **Auberge Lenderguigui** in the Moursal area, but the parking situation is unknown. It charges US$20 with an hourly rate if you need it! More sedate (perhaps) is the **Mission Catholique** in the Kabalayé area for about the same cost.

Mongo The **Camp de Passage Ouada Moun-Kara** is a clean spot with doubles for US$10–15. The **Pam Guesthouse** charges around US$25. Elsewhere the **Mission Catholique** south of the bus station will do you nicely for US$17–30.

Abéché This is not a very large town and the surrounding area is typical Sahel. We would suggest bush camping if the region is open again. Otherwise in town is the **Mission Catholique** (opposite the church of Sainte Thérèse de l'Enfant Jésus). Rooms have en-suite bathrooms for US$15.

Faya The **Hotel Restaurant Emi Koussi** was the only choice during our visit, but now you can look for the **Boubouk Hotel** located close to the airfield. Point Afrique charter groups use it. Prices range from US$20 to US$30, but they could rise rapidly if tourism continues to develop.

Fada We camped at our driver's cousin's house – the toilet was just outside in the street. Another hotel called **Boubouk** has apparently opened.

Ennedi The Ennedi Plateau is a beautiful desert area, similar to the Tassili du Hoggar in Algeria. But it is equally wild and we do not suggest going there alone. Travel with a local agent to avoid the risk of landmines remaining from the civil war. Wild camping is the delightful norm.

Tibesti Mountains Bush sleeping is the only option and a travel permit for the area is required. After the border dispute between Chad and Libya, mines remain. A tour of the Tibesti is definitely not for the faint-hearted. In fact we do

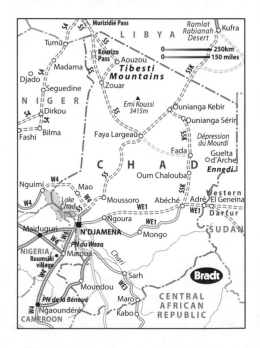

not recommend you to go there at all at the moment until local operators begin trips (check *www.point-afrique.com*). If it becomes safe, you would need enough fuel, water and food supplies for approximately 1,000km (600 miles). Obtaining permission to travel in the area will probably be rejected.

OTHER A photographic permit is said to be required, but can take up to a week to issue, so most travellers don't bother. The answer is not to take any pictures, or be extremely discreet when you do. Out in the desert this is not a problem, though you should always ask if photographing people. The Tubu people are particularly averse to having their photo taken.

If the route between Chad and Sudan (Adré border) is deemed safe with improvements in Darfur, be sure to have sufficient supplies of fuel and food.

FURTHER INFORMATION
www.expeditionworld.com

DEMOCRATIC REPUBLIC OF THE CONGO (DRC)

WARNING! Owing to the civil war in the eastern Democratic Republic of the Congo, the situation is unclear. Seek sound travel advice and, depending on the state of the country, travel in convoy if possible. The western areas are currently safe.

CAPITAL Kinshasa

LANGUAGE French

INTERNATIONAL TELEPHONE CODE +243

CURRENCY AND RATE Congolese franc (CDF); US$1= CDF919

RED TAPE Officials of the DRC are known for their corruption and drunkenness (from palm wines). Avoid them when possible. Never drive at night. You should register with local police in every town you stay in. Keep a copy of your passport details – in fact, dozens.

Visas Visas are required for all and costs vary depending on where you get the visa. Normally the visa has to be obtained in your country of residence. You will also need three to four photographs and possibly an introduction letter from your embassy. Vaccination certificates are obligatory. Visas are not issued at the border.

African embassies
http://embassy.goabroad.com/embassies-in/congo-democratic-republic-of
www.embassypages.com/congodemocratic

DRIVING AND ROADS Drive on the right. There are not many good stretches of road in the DRC; they become a sea of mud during the rainy season. Expect road 'taxes' occasionally. There are some sealed sections on the Kinshasa to Matadi road. A high fee for the Congo bridge can be anticipated. From Songololo, the road to the Angolan border at Luvo is poor. The truck-swallowing mud holes and roads of the northeast used to be fun. Trying to drive between Kinshasa and Lubumbashi

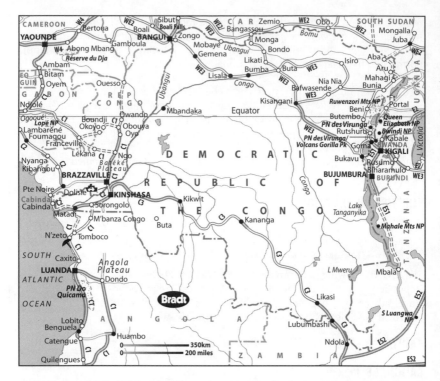

via Kikwit and Mbuji-Mayi is still an adventure too far for most, but apparently not impossible. Motorcycling the route is probably the better option.

Fuel costs Diesel: US$1.04; petrol: US$1.57 per litre.

CLIMATE It is impossible to summarise the climate for the whole of the DRC, as it is such a huge country. Along the northern route (the one formerly taken by most travellers), the only time of year it is likely to be fairly dry is from December to February. If travelling from Gabon to Angola through the two Congos, after May can sometimes be better, but since rain is possible at any time, avoiding wet conditions cannot be guaranteed.

HIGHLIGHTS Crossing the Congo River from Brazzaville and experiencing Kinshasa. In the east is the Parc National des Virunga, known for its gorilla trekking and volcanoes (although access has been affected by the civil war). Climbing the Nyiragongo active volcano is spectacular. The Epulu Reservation for the mysterious okapi is open to visitors. Mount Hoyo offers a cool respite and numerous caves and interesting rock formations, but check with local officials on rebel activity in the area. Don't forget the music of the DRC. And if it becomes safer, there are even worse roads to test your driving skills, your vehicle and your staying power.

WHERE TO STAY Because of the dense forest it is hard to get off the 'road', so sleeping/parking/camping in disused road quarries will be the best option. Travellers used to stay at the various missions dotted around the country; this is one of the few reasons why certain roads are still driveable. The current state of the missions is uncertain, even if the state of the roads and bridges is predictable.

Kinshasa The city is a vast sprawl. It's worth checking the missions in town, because there's little else on offer without blowing a hole in the budget. **Mission St Anne** has been recommended. **Sunny Day Guest House** is listed by www. hostelworld.com. **Hôtel Phênix** on Avenue Flambeau is a larger place, but there may or may not be parking available.

Muanda It might be worth checking at the **Convent School** near the hospital or the **Catholic Mission** for US$5 each plus car. Otherwise try at S 05° 52.729, E 12° 20.702 down an oil drill track (on the left going south).

Boma About 20km before town is a cattle ranch that might allow bush camping.

Matadi There is a convent beside a truck park, which offered some security for a fee; there several hotels have opened in recent years which can offer secure parking. Ask at the **Catholic Mission** if stuck. Otherwise look for a budget hotel such as **Auberge Lisanga** with parking or **Hôtel Equinox** well out of town.

Luvo (Lufu) Border (S 05° 49.900, E 14° 04.513). Camping is possible on the grass beside the Customs/Douanes building. Police hold passports for the night.

Goma Two campsites were open before the troubles: one was close to the Rwandan border, the second was behind the Chez Kamanza supermarket. Another option is the **Colibri Hotel**, where camping is allowed for US$5 per person; rooms here US$15+.

Kisangani The latest Bradt guide suggests **Hôtel Rimka**, and there are others, including the centrally located **Guest House du Canon** near the post office.

Nia Nia In case the security issues improve, you could try the **Hôtel Escale** – it has reasonably clean rooms and bucket showers, and costs US$10 for a double room.

Parc National des Virunga (*www.visitvirunga.org*) The park was closed from 1997 until 2004, but most of it is now open and ready for tourists. There is an office in Goma for information. Entry permits and gorilla-tracking permits are paid for at the headquarters in hard currency. Climbing Nyiragongo is also organised from here. In the park there are basic camping facilities at **Bukima**, **Djomba** and **Rwindi Lodge**, but check in Goma whether they are open.

Bukavu Bukavu is seeing a resurgence in hotels and restaurants thanks to numerous aid workers in the region, and the nearby gorilla reserve of Kahuzi-Biega is a popular stopping point for visitors. Parking may be possible at **Hôtel Belle-Vue**, **Hôtel Riviera** or **Hôtel Lolango**.

Lubumbashi The **Mbala Hotel** is around US$50 for a double room. The **Grand Karavia Hôtel** and **Guesthouse Resource** both have secure parking. Excluding the visa issue, getting this far from Zambia is easy, but getting anywhere further towards Kinshasa is not!

OTHER Photographic permits are required, but are only valid in the region of issue. Try in Kinshasa, Kisangani and Lubumbashi or, easier perhaps, don't get caught taking pictures. The cost is dependent on the official. There were also special requirements for travel in the mining regions in central DRC. These permits were only issued in Kinshasa and could take up to two weeks. Most travellers bribed their way through these areas. Anyone contemplating taking the Congo River boat between Kisangani and Kinshasa should have at least three months spare!

FURTHER INFORMATION
Congo and Democratic Republic of Congo Sean Rorison (Bradt Travel Guides)

REPUBLIC OF THE CONGO

WARNING! More overlanders are visiting Congo. The main problems of the past were with Ninja rebels in the regions west of Brazzaville along the road to Dolisie, but they have not been a concern for several years. Trains run between Pointe Noire and Brazzaville. Check the latest security situation. The road north of Brazzaville that heads to/from Franceville is currently safe.

CAPITAL Brazzaville

LANGUAGE French

INTERNATIONAL TELEPHONE CODE +242

CURRENCY AND RATE Central African franc (CFA); US$1 = CFA478

RED TAPE The country is much calmer now, but try to avoid all military personnel and don't drive at night.

Visas Visas are required for all. They are not issued at the border. There are embassies in Cameroon and Gabon.

African embassies
www.embassypages.com/congorepublic

DRIVING AND ROADS Drive on the right. Roads are improving. Coming from Ndende in Gabon, the road is immediately awful after the border. Allow six hours for the next 150km via Kibangou. After two hours of grim road, a new tarsealed road continues to Dolisie – wow! It's a super toll-highway from Dolisie to Pointe Noire, and fine to the border of Angola/Cabinda. From Franceville/Leconi a narrow, sometimes sandy, and bad route goes to Okoyo. The road to Boundji is bad, but then sealed to Obouya. The northern 'highway' from

Brazzaville to Quesso is mostly good, but from Owando north to Quesso is bad. Apparently the driving time for the Société Océan du Nord bus between Brazzaville and Quesso (US$50) is around 16 hours.

Fuel costs Diesel: US$1.57; petrol: US$1.59 per litre.

CLIMATE The climate is mostly hot and humid. The main drier season is from May or June to September.

HIGHLIGHTS Brazzaville is a lively place. Congolese music and food are well-known bonuses of a visit here. Then there are the beaches around Pointe Noire and the nearby Jane Goodall Chimp Sanctuary. In the north, close to Gabon, isolated in dense rainforest, is Parc National de Odzala, known for its gorilla trekking. Close to the CAR border, in the far north beyond Quesso, and adjacent to the Dzanga-Sangha reserve is the Nouabalé-Ndoki Park. It's not a cheap experience – US$1,600 for five days. This should include shared transport from Quesso to Bomassa and to the different sites in the park, accommodation, food, guides and entry taxes. The bad roads of Congo are another highlight if you like that sort of thing!

WHERE TO STAY

Brazzaville Brazzaville is expensive and it is difficult to find camping accommodation here. Highly recommended, with glowing reviews, is the **Hôtel 8 Novembre** near the Hippodrome; ask for Olivier. There is a Chinese restaurant here. You could try either of the Catholic missions in town – **Eglise Sacré Cœur** (Avenue Maréchal Foch, behind the Méridien Hotel) or **Eglise Kimbanguiste** (Plateau de 15 Ans, near the Hôtel Majoca).

Pointe Noire Most accommodation is along the Cité. Campers can try **La Requième** on the beach and use the shower and toilet at the back. The shabby-looking **Yacht Club** (S 05° 52.729, E 12° 20.702) also has camping for US$6–7 per person.

Jane Goodall Chimp Sanctuary Bush-style camping is available at the sanctuary; ask for Victor.

Border near Nyanga There is a small overgrown quarry close to the road (S 03° 46.778, E 12° 28.784). 'No other options before or after. Pretty awful spot really,' as described by Princess and Nev, so be warned!

Kibangou South Quarry Camp On the right-hand side, this is a great spot (S 03° 46.778, E 12° 28.784).

Dolisie No good spots, as the Catholic Mission is probably not an option. Try the lousy vacant lot opposite the hospital, just past the Total servo/Catholic Mission. A super new train from here to Brazzaville is now operating.

OTHER
Parc National de Odzala Extremely difficult to get to, but very rewarding for those who do make it; the amount of wildlife here is astounding. For further information contact WCS in Brazzaville (*www.wcs.org*).

A photographic permit is not required, but be extremely cautious when taking photos and stay clear of all government institutions. Drivers can expect a fee of US$100–150 for the ferry between Brazzaville and Kinshasa.

FURTHER INFORMATION
Congo and Democratic Republic of Congo Sean Rorison (Bradt Travel Guides)

DJIBOUTI

CAPITAL Djibouti City

LANGUAGE French and Arabic. Afars is also spoken.

INTERNATIONAL TELEPHONE CODE +253

CURRENCY AND RATE Djibouti franc (DJF); US$1 = DJF180

RED TAPE None of any significance, except visas.

Visas Visas are required for all. They are valid for one month and cost around US$90. They are not issued at the border. In Addis a visa may cost as much as US$150. There are not many embassies; in Europe there is one in Paris.

African embassies
www.myembassy.net
http://dj.embassyinformation.com

DRIVING AND ROADS Drive on the right. The main roads to Ethiopia and Tadjoura are generally good; off the main routes, it's desert tracks and piste. Be very careful if going to Lac Abbé; take a guide to avoid quicksands and getting seriously lost.

Fuel costs Diesel: US$1.03; petrol: US$2.02 per litre.

CLIMATE The climate is generally very hot and humid on the coast, with a cooler season from November to mid-April and occasional rain during that period.

HIGHLIGHTS Djibouti City has some colourful markets, old colonial buildings, tea shops and old mosques. You could take a boat trip across the Gulf of Tadjoura, but driving there is very spectacular, with black lava flows and volcanic cones. Lac Assal lies below sea level, with amazing brilliant-white salt, sulphur and halite crystals. The Forêt du Day, a small zone of luxuriant growth, is accessed by a shocking rocky track. Randa is a nearly defunct retreat, but a pleasant drive. Lac Abbé is known for its birdlife. Enjoy the flamingos and natural chimneys formed by the escape vents of underground steam dotted along the foreshore.

 WHERE TO STAY
Djibouti City Try the **Sheraton**; it has secure parking. In town try the **Auberge Sable Blanc** on Boulevard de la République (N 11° 36.058, E 43° 08.876); it may still have parking/camping. In the African quarter there is some budget accommodation available, but no obvious secure parking.

Tadjoura With superb coral reefs 10m from the shore, this is a great place for a stopover. Bush sleeping well outside the town is one option. Try **Hôtel Le Golfe** or the hotel opposite nearby, which have parking.

Randa Look for **Campement le Goda** just before town.

Forêt du Day Try **Campement de Dittilou**, but getting there is shockingly rough.

Dikhil Try the **Hôtel le Palmerie** on the main road. Camping is not encouraged.

Lac Assal Bush sleeping is not recommended; stay close by at **Le Plage du Goubbet**, with camping and small thatched huts.

Lac Abbé Lac Abbé can only be reached by 4x4 and requires at least two days, including a guide. Bush camping is possible, but beware of quicksands, or better, try the new **Campement Asbole**.

Border: Galafi We camped/parked here close to customs on our way back into Ethiopia.

OTHER Photographic permits are not officially needed, but officials particularly may act petulantly, and in any case people in Djibouti are not happy to be photographed, so beware! Djibouti is an expensive country.

FURTHER INFORMATION Lonely Planet has a dated Ethiopia and Eritrea guide that includes Djibouti. *Petit Fute* produces a guide in French.

EGYPT

WARNING! Following the unrest after the change of government in 2013, the situation is unpredictable. It should get safer with the increased military presence.

CAPITAL Cairo

LANGUAGE Arabic

INTERNATIONAL TELEPHONE CODE +20

CURRENCY AND RATE Egyptian pound (EGP); US$1 = EGP6.97

RED TAPE The roads south of Aswan and Ras Banas have been closed for years by the military, but recent news suggests some possible changes. Convoys are sometimes in operation between the Red Sea resorts and Luxor and Aswan. At the time of writing, Egypt had a temporary import ban on 4x4 vehicles in the Sinai, and ports were liable to be closed at short notice.

Visas Visas can now be obtained at airports and at some borders. For those entering by road, it is better to get it in advance.

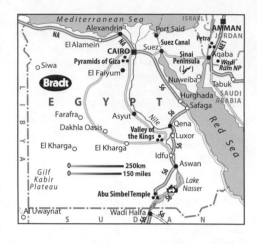

African embassies
http://embassy.goabroad.com/embassies-in/egypt
www.embassypages.com/egypt

DRIVING AND ROADS Drive on the right. All the main routes are well surfaced. Outside the major routes you will find road signs in Arabic only. To exit Cairo for the White Desert Oasis Route, go back on to the ring road and take the exit to the Pyramids on a dual carriageway. Then take El Fayoum road motorway marked as 'Western Desert Road'; this is not the road to the oases of the Western Desert but a new motorway south to Luxor! To go to the White Desert, turn off at a signpost to '6th October City, 221, Al Wahat' route. After 10km to the end of 6th October City, follow signs 'Al Wahat el Bahariya'. There's no fuel for 340km from here. It's seven hours' drive to Bahariya Oasis.

Fuel costs Diesel: US$0.46; petrol: US$0.60 per litre.

CLIMATE Egypt is hot and dry for most of the year, except for the winter months of December, January and February.

HIGHLIGHTS Of course you can't miss the Pyramids of Giza. Also in Cairo are the Tutankhamun treasures and, close by, the Pyramids of Sakkara, including the newly discovered 4,300-year-old tomb. The Coptic monasteries of St Paul and St Anthony are further south, close to the Red Sea coast. Along the Nile are the temples of Karnak and Luxor, plus the Valleys of the Kings and Queens in Luxor. Kom Ombo and Idfu are worth stopping at on the way to Aswan. Aswan has the Philae Temple and a pleasant riverside environment. Abu Simbel is spectacular if you have the time and money to go that far. The Sinai has its own highlights of St Catherine's Monastery, climbing Mount Sinai and the fantastic snorkelling and diving along the coast. The Red Sea has the popular resorts of Hurghada and Safaga. Finally, the Western Desert has the oases of Kharga and Siwa, and the incredibly beautiful formations of the White Desert.

 WHERE TO STAY

Cairo The **Motel Salma** (*Sakkara Rd, Harania village, Giza (N 29° 58.217, E 31° 10.617);* m *0104871300, 0122774042 or 0122704442;* e *salma.camp@yahoo.com; www.facebook.com/salmacamping.salma*) is located near the Wissa Wassef Art Centre just south of Giza on the Sakkara road. There's lots of space but little shade, and camping will cost around US$5–7.

Bahariya There are various camping places around, but none so great. Seek out **Hotel New Oasis**; turn right at the police station along a narrow road to the palmeries. There's good parking, US$13 B&B. **Garden of the Moon** camp is 30–40 minutes south of Bahariya on the right.

Al Kasr The **Bedouin Oasis** may have camping *en route*. It is approximately 90km to the White Desert region from here via the Black Desert.

White Desert (*Entry US$5 pp & E£10 to camp anywhere*) At 87km from Bahariya on the right are some fabulous outcrops, where you could camp. Also near the main entrance area are some amazing mushroom rocks which would also be suitable.

Farafrah Expensive, but stop at the **Hotel Al Badawiya** for tea.

Dakhla/Mut The **Nasr Hotel and Camp** has a pool but little shade, US$7. The Citadel has a parking lot.

Brown Desert You might be able to get into the hills on the left to camp, but beware of any military, around Km115 on the left. Heading to El Kharga, watch out for signposts concerning the 'Paris' turn-off area. Go left when you see a sign indicating 245km to El Kharga.

El Kharga Camping is permitted at **Hotel Kharga Oasis** near the Tourist Office. Go left into town, then ahead, right at a Y-junction and it's on the left among palm trees; it costs US$8. South of El Kharga is **Nasr Camping** on the right near some dunes/oasis.

St Anthony's and St Paul's monasteries These monasteries do not allow camping. Do not go there expecting to be allowed in to stay the night.

Luxor The **Rezeiky Camp** is very pleasant, with some shade. Coming from El Kharga, the signs are confusing and it's tricky to find the Nile bridge crossing. After the Desert Highway road, turn east to a check-post, left at a T-junction, 8km to a sign for Luxor, right to cross the Nile, then left for 10km to town. Go left at the airport sign, 1km+ into town, look for Rezeky Camp and Hotel (Karnak is some way right of it). Camping costs US$11 and rooms US$25.

Hurghada Try **Hotel Snafer**; parking will be sorted out with the police for security reasons. It costs US$20–25 for a double room.

Safaga Camping at **Sun Beach** is the only option as far as we know. It's pleasant with a beachside tent bar. US$10 for a car plus two people.

Aswan The first visit we stayed a mile or two south of the very swish Old Cataract Hotel at the pleasant **Hotel Sara**, with safe parking and good rooms, all negotiable. Some way north of Aswan is **Camping Ashraf**. There's no shade but a nice ambience and good showers. Groups sometimes come here for traditional dinners. It's across the Nile on the west bank. Go 10km north of the town to a bridge. Turn left after the bridge; go south for 7km, then right at the second mosque, which is blue. Go up through narrow streets, passing a modern walled complex. Then go left, passing a white building, to the dunes at the end of the road. Around 15 minutes from town, it costs US$8 all in for camping for two people in your own vehicle.

Between Libya and Alexandria We did not find anywhere, and the military does not allow desert camping. There are plenty of expensive hotels near El Alamein.

Between Alexandria and Cairo Try the **Fisherman's Village**, a local mini-resort in a quiet spot west of the main highway.

Sinai Nuweiba has a couple of camping places. One is five to ten minutes north of the port, called **Soft Beach** (*www.softbeachcamp.com*). Huts go for US$12 and camping is negotiable. **Pigeons House** in Na'ama Bay, Sharm el Sheikh is another option. It had comfortable huts with fans, and served breakfast. Accommodation costs from US$20.

OTHER There is a ferry service to Port Said from Iskendrun, Turkey.

The Sudan embassy may need a letter of introduction from your own embassy if you do not have an Ethiopian visa or a work employment letter already. Visa cost is US$100. No double-entry visa given. The address in Cairo is 8 El Sherbinu Street, Dokki, but do check that it hasn't moved again.

Baksheesh (tipping) is widely expected. Haggling is an art form in Egypt and, whether it be for accommodation or curios, be aware of local prices and never quote a price you are not prepared to pay.

Exit from Egypt Leaving Egypt can be complex. First check in with Mr Salah at the Nile Navigation Company (📞 +20 (0)1283160926; e *takourny@gmail.com*) for ferry availability; it could be full for a week or more. Passenger tickets are sold here. A 'first class' cabin costs EGP485 for a bed; a second-class seat costs EGP307; and a vehicle less than 5m high costs EGP2,012. Large vehicles can expect a long wait before they get a place on the big barge. The smaller normal barge takes four vehicles plus motorcycles, which cannot normally go on the main passenger ferry – we don't see why not, as bicycles can do this.

You also need to visit the Court Police to obtain clearance to leave the country (N 24° 03.693, E 32° 53.153) and the Traffic Police to surrender your Egyptian number plates (N 24° 05.043, E 32° 54.502), before the ferry sailing day.

Sailing day Go to the port south of Aswan, it's not well signposted, but is generally south of the Traffic Police area. Allow time for this and get there early. It's much easier here now as the price is fixed, so there are no *baksheesh* negotiations. Pay at least E£2,000+ for your vehicle. Pay stamp duty of E£2 at the office on the right through the gate near the parking area. Customs tax is E£25. Passports are done next, then you wait by the ship. Loading the vehicles comes next and hopefully the passenger ferry will depart around 17.00. Take bedding, tent, water and food, especially if on deck. Take food in any event – the ferry food is very dubious.

Abu Simbel is often passed at dawn around 06.00 – a spectacular sight.

Latest reports There are indications that the road between Aswan and Wadi Halfa may be derestricted soon. Toll fees and taxes might be as high as US$3000 for up to three cars, but look at the positives — it'll be a faster option, because the ferry may sometimes only go once a month.

FURTHER INFORMATION
www.touregypt.net
www.cairo.com

EQUATORIAL GUINEA

CAPITAL Malabo

LANGUAGE Spanish

INTERNATIONAL TELEPHONE CODE +240

CURRENCY AND RATE Central African franc (CFA); US$1 = CFA478

RED TAPE The police are said to be a little pushy, but if all your paperwork is in order there shouldn't be a problem. You might be allowed to cross the border for a brief visit from Cameroon, for a small fee.

Visas Visas are required for all. Visas are not issued at the border, but you could ask near Ebebiyin on the northern border with Cameroon.

African embassies
http://embassy.goabroad.com/embassies-in/equatorialguinea
http://gq.embassyinformation.com

DRIVING AND ROADS Drive on the right. Roads are mostly very poor, but new oil wealth should change this one day.

Fuel costs Diesel: US$1.40; petrol: US$1.60 per litre.

CLIMATE Equatorial Guinea has a wet tropical climate, with a drier spell from June to September on the mainland. December and January are driest on Bioko Island.

HIGHLIGHTS Malabo, with its old Spanish architecture, and Luba's nightlife on Bioko Island with beautiful beaches. There's a Bioko Biodiversity Protection Programme underway (*www.bioko.org*). The rainforests of the mainland are mostly pristine for the most part.

WHERE TO STAY
Ebebiyin If you visit Equatorial Guinea at all by road, it will be through the border here. Try the hotels, eg: **Hotel Mbengono**.

Bata Finding any secure parking would be difficult in Bata. **Hotel Yessica** might have parking.

OTHER Photographic permits are essential, so check out the procedure at the border. These used to be obtained from the Ministry of Culture, Tourism and Francophone Relations. Do not take pictures of any government organisations.

FURTHER INFORMATION
www.guineaecuatorialpress.com

ERITREA

WARNING! It is currently impossible to drive into Eritrea from Ethiopia and Sudan. Crossing into Djibouti is also virtually impossible, since Eritrea and Djibouti also dispute some areas. Good luck if you manage to get here, but you may not get out again!

CAPITAL Asmara

LANGUAGE Arabic and Tigrinya

INTERNATIONAL TELEPHONE CODE +291

CURRENCY AND RATE Eritrean nafka (ERN); US$1 = ERN10.47. Avoid the black market. Currency declarations are rigorously enforced.

RED TAPE It's currently necessary to obtain travel permits for destinations outside of Asmara. Check security issues before heading into the Danakil areas.

Visas Visas are required for all and should be applied for in your home country. Visas are hard to obtain at present. Visas are not issued at the border. Make sure you have a valid yellow fever vaccination certificate.

African embassies
http://embassy.goabroad.com/embassies-in/eritrea
www.embassypages.com/eritrea

DRIVING AND ROADS Drive on the right. Roads are in good condition on most major routes, deteriorating as you get off the beaten track. The road south from Massawa to Assab is substantially improved now and possible with a well-equipped vehicle. Security issues are still a concern. Hard information about this route is difficult to find.

Fuel costs Diesel: US$1.10; petrol: US$2.50 per litre.

CLIMATE Eritrea has a varied topography, so the climate is different in each of its main zones. In the highlands temperatures vary from freezing in December to 30°C in May. Short rainy seasons are in March and April; the main rains are from late June to early September. Daily temperatures range from 20°C to 35°C in winter to up to 40°–50°C in summer along the coast.

HIGHLIGHTS Asmara is known for its pleasant ambience, Italian buildings and cool climate. The dusty alleys of Massawa are being restored, across the first causeway on Taulud Island. Keren is a predominantly Muslim town and has a colourful daily market, renowned for its silversmiths' street, and the livestock market every Monday. There are churches and monasteries close to the Ethiopian border and Qohaito has Axumite remains. The Danakil Desert is an incredibly remote area, sparsely populated by the Afar nomads.

WHERE TO STAY Good-value accommodation was available when we last visited. You will need to shop around for safe parking if you have managed to get your vehicle into the country in the first place.

Asmara There are quite a few *albergos* (inns) to be found along Liberation Avenue. For camping, try the **Africa Pension**, an old converted villa. The **Hotel Sunshine** and **Hotel Khartoum** may be possible places to park.

Massawa Massawa does not have any campsites, but does have accommodation on the mainland and on Taulud Island. Ask at the **Gurgussum Beach Hotel** if parking is possible; it's north of the old city area.

Keren Try the noisy **Eritrea Hotel** or the nicer **Hotel Sicilia**, with shady courtyards.

Agordat Try at the **Alwaha Oasis Hotel** a bit out of town.

Barentu On the way to Sudan is this small off-limits town. **Hotel Selam** is recommended.

OTHER There are uncharted mines throughout Eritrea, so stay on the main roads rather than off the beaten track, and always ask the locals for route advice.

FURTHER INFORMATION
Eritrea Edward Denison (Bradt Travel Guides)
www.asmera.nl (this is not a typo; it is asmera)
www.travelhouseeritrea.com

ETHIOPIA

CAPITAL Addis Ababa

LANGUAGE Amharic

INTERNATIONAL TELEPHONE CODE +251

CURRENCY AND RATE Ethiopian birr (ETB); US$1 = ETB19.27

RED TAPE None of any significance. Ethiopians are generally pleasant, if more than a little inquisitive! Insurance that covers most of east and southern Africa can be obtained from the Ethiopian Insurance Corporation in Addis near Wim's and the station. Also, for Ethiopia only, they have a branch in Gondar opposite the castle near Western Union.

Visas Visas are required for all except nationals of Kenya. Yellow fever vaccination certificates are mandatory. Visas are not issued at the border. Recently a new rule was introduced making it necessary to obtain a visa in your own country, meaning either a rush to get to the country, or posting passports back by DHL to a visa agency in your own country – things can only get more complicated these days it would seem! Be sure to get a double-entry visa if planning to visit Somaliland. Currently it is not possible to obtain an Ethiopian visa in Hargeisa.

African embassies

http://embassy.goabroad.com/embassies-in/ethiopia
http://www.embassypages.com/ethiopia

DRIVING AND ROADS Drive on the right. Many main roads in Ethiopia are now tarmac or under construction. With increased risks along the Marsabit road from Ethiopia to Kenya, many overlanders now go via Arba Minch to the Kenyan border at Banya Fort and on to Lake Turkana. From Arba Minch to Nanyuki, allow five days on rough roads.

Fuel costs Diesel: US$0.97; petrol: US$1.14 per litre.

CLIMATE The main rainy season is from June to September, with lighter rains from February to April. In the lowlands it can get extremely hot from April to June, while the colder season in the highlands can be very cold.

HIGHLIGHTS The northern historical route includes Gondar, for its castle compound, and Bahir Dar beside Lake Tana, source of the Blue Nile, and goes close to the Blue Nile Falls. The route also includes the Simien Mountains and Axum, plus the famous rock-cut churches of both Lalibela and Tigrai. South of Addis are the lakes of the Rift Valley and the Omo region, with its traditional village life and culture. East is the Danakil desert, and *en route* to Somaliland is the ancient walled city of Harar. Ethiopian cuisine (memorable to say the least) and the elaborate coffee ceremony are a must, as well as the traditional music and dance.

WHERE TO STAY

Addis Ababa In Addis **Wim's Place** (N 09° 00.589, E 038° 45.325) (*www.wimshollandhouseaddis.nl*) is the only place to camp (US$8 per vehicle). It also has one en suite room (US$16) and a good restaurant. Go straight up to the old railway building, past all the buses, then go left and then second left. If Wim's is full, try the nearby **Buffet de la Gare** (US$13 for a double), with parking, or the **Pension Baro in the Piazza** (parking and simple rooms US$16 for a double).

Gondar The **Terera Hotel** has a view of the royal enclosure – it is located just to the north. Camping costs US$3–4 per person. Behind the Hotel Terraza is **Hotel Belegez** with a small

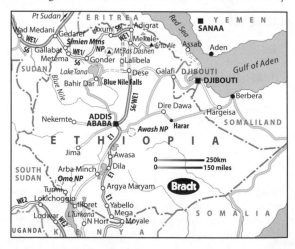

yard (camping US$5, double room US$10). Gondar often has a shortage of water and getting a shower can be a little frenetic.

Lake Tana In Gorgora, on the shores of Lake Tana near Gondar, **Tim and Kim Village** (*www.timkimvillage.com*) is highly recommended for travellers, including overlanders in their own vehicles and backpackers without a tent. Stunning location, good food and cold beer.

Bahir Dar We camped in the exotic lakeside garden of the **Ghion Hotel**. Camping cost US$6, rooms US$12–15. Nearby is the **Hotel Bahir Dar Pension**. Tyre repairs are available 1.5km west along the dual carriageway road by the hotel. When leaving for Addis, go south of the hotel to a dual carriageway and turn right to the west. It's about 260km to Debre Markos (four or five hours).

Debre Markos Try the **Hotel Shebele** (US$8) or **Hotel Tadeli Getahurs** (US$7), both with parking. It's a cool town at 2,500m about 90km before the Blue Nile Gorge. Mixed surface road with some gravel. Degen is a town at the top of the gorge, which is nearly 30km across by road. The road is decent to Fiche.

Debre Libanos The **Top View Resort** has a parking/camp area on the turnoff before Debre Libanos monastery. Entry and guide cost birr100, plus a tip.

Axum Try the **Africa Hotel** or the **Axum Touring Hotel**, suggested as being pleasant watering holes.

Mekele There's parking at the atmospheric **Abraha Castle Hotel** (US$16–30 for a double).

Megab/Korkor Overlanders can enjoy excellent camping facilities at **Korkor Lodge** (N 13° 55.917; E 39° 22.917) (e *info@korkorlodge.com; www.korkorlodge.com; US$10–15*) in the shadow of the Gheralta massif. Luxury eco-chalets will also be available.

Wukro There's good parking at the **Top View Hotel** in a quiet location above the town. Rooms US$10.

Lalibela We once camped in the driveway of the **Seven Olives Hotel**; ask if it's not very busy. There's a nice view and enough room to spread out. The food is traditional; try *injera wat* in the restaurant. Camping costs US$7–9 per person. The **Hotel Roha** to the west of town also offers camping at US$7.

Woldiya The **Lal Hotel** allows camping in its back yard; it has a bar, comfortable lounge and rooms. It also has an amazing vegetable and fruit orchard. They will sell you some of the produce straight from the ground or tree. There's also a bread shop on site. Camping is US$7 for two.

Kombolcha The **Hotel Tekle** is good value, with pleasant rooms, restaurant and parking on a hill. A double room costs US$10. **Hotel Sunny Side** is another option.

Ziway The **Hotel Bekalaa Mole** on the left comes with powercuts, but has a nice garden. US$6 for a room.

Awasa On the lakeside try **Hotel Woye Shebele**; it's shady and the gardens host lots of birdlife. Watch out for the monkeys! Camping costs US$6 for two and a room will be around US$12.

Dilla There is **Hotel Degam** and a couple of others.

Harar There is good parking at the **Harar Ras Hotel**, where old rooms cost US$17. **Heritage Plaza** also has parking, but rooms cost US$40.

Yabello On the main road, the **Yabello Motel** is a great place, with en-suite and more basic rooms, parking and a nice garden. There is a small garage next door. A double room costs around US$12.

The Omo region The best bet here is to bush camp. If you decide to stay in Arba Minch, stay at **Roza's Place**, where camping is allowed in the courtyard and she reputedly makes the best fish cutlets in all of Ethiopia! It makes a great break from *injera*.

OTHER Keep all bank receipts. For high fliers, try www.abyssiniaballooning.com. If you have vehicle trouble, ask at Wim's for Ron. If he's not there, go to the following garages: **Land Rover** (*Ethiopian Lakes Garage;* ✆ *11 443 1493/4/5; www.ethiolakes. com*) and **Toyota** (*GMC Anware Rd;* ✆ *11 123 5336/7/8;* e *gmc@ethionet.et*).

THE JULIAN CALENDAR AND 12-HOUR CLOCK Ethiopians use the Julian calendar, which means that their year falls seven or eight years behind the European calendar, and there are 13 months in the calendar of the Orthodox Church. Ethiopian time is also measured in 12-hour cycles, starting at 06.00 and 18.00. In other words, their 19.00 is our 13.00 and vice versa. Be very aware of this when booking a bus or flight, and double-check departure times! Most banks and other such institutions have both Western and Ethiopian calendars and times.

FURTHER INFORMATION
Ethiopia Philip Briggs (Bradt Travel Guides)

GABON

CAPITAL Libreville

LANGUAGE French

INTERNATIONAL TELEPHONE CODE +241

CURRENCY AND RATE Central African franc (CFA); US$1 = CFA478. Gabon is expensive.

RED TAPE Some officials are suspicious of foreigners, so approach with care.

Visas Visas are required for all. To get one in Africa, you may need a letter of introduction from your embassy and a yellow fever vaccination certificate. Visas are sometimes issued at the border, but it's risky. Coming from Cameroon, Bitam is the main formalities post.

African embassies

http://embassy-finder.com/gabon_embassies
http://ga.embassyinformation.com/

DRIVING AND ROADS Drive on the right. Roads are a mixture of good, new tarmac interspersed with some poor, corrugated dirt. North of Ndjolé there is still one short bad section. Libreville to Lambarene is good but quite hilly. To Réserve de la Lopé, the road is narrow, remote and very hilly and about four hours from Ndjolé. To Franceville sections are being slowly worked on, with tarmac between Lastoursville and Franceville. There is a train between Libreville and Franceville. The route from Lambarene to Mouila is new (two hours' drive), but the road from Ndende is bad.

Fuel costs Diesel: US$1.00; petrol: US$1.10 per litre.

CLIMATE The climate is hot and humid, with the dry season from May to September and another short drier spell in mid-December.

HIGHLIGHTS In Libreville are extensive local markets, and a few resorts along the ocean as far as the beach at Cap Estérias. Lambarene is set on the beautiful banks of the Ogooué River, with the Albert Schweitzer Hospital and Museum. Gabon has extensive virgin forest covering very hilly country, which can be seen by visiting the various reserves. The parks are host to lowland gorilla, forest elephants and chimpanzees. The most famous is the Réserve de la Lopé, where one can go in search of lowland gorillas. Tours are expensive; two days with one night here costs US$400. For the Moukalaba-Doudou National Park, a three days/two nights tour costs US$400. The remote Ivindo National Park (including Kongou Falls) can be visited for three days/two nights for around US$600.

WHERE TO STAY

Libreville We stayed at the **Hôtel L'Alize**, Michèle Marine, which is one of the cheaper places but still expensive. Camping may be possible in the parking area, but rather unpleasant with very high humidity. The **Hôtel Tropicana** resort, near the airport, is a more pleasant and cheaper option used by expatriates. It has a beachside café-restaurant, but check that the overnight parking is secure; accommodation costs from US$45 for a double. The **Beach Club** (N 0° 28.507, E 09° 23.778) is another option. It has been free in the past! Parking is on the courts around the back, with camping on the grass. This is a posh place where the wealthy bring their kids to swim. The pool costs CFA5,000 each for the day, with expensive beers, clean toilets and showers. Camping was possible in Sablière Beach, a suburb just out of the centre near the airport, but with dubious security.

Cap Estérias Cap Estérias is just north of Libreville and very pleasant. Camping is possible at **L'Auberge du Cap**. It also has rondavel huts and a restaurant. Also suggested is **La Marina**.

Lambarene We parked for free in the grounds of the **Ogooué Palace Hotel**, which is on the river to the north of town near the church and

mission. The clean mission **Sœurs de la Conception**, the red-brick complex on the nearby hill, is not that cheap and does not allow camping; rooms are available for US$20 with Wi-Fi. Another suggestion is **Le Petit Auberge**, two blocks southeast of Bar Dancing Le Capitol, but camping facilities would need to be negotiated. It could be noisy.

Réserve de la Lopé (S 0° 30.000, E 11° 30.000) If you take the train, this is the easiest national park to get to and has abundant wildlife. In your own vehicle, be prepared for a remote drive. *En route* are various quarries (S 0° 06.850, E 11° 19.955). Camping is not allowed inside the reserve. The **Hôtel Lopé** is very expensive. It might be possible to stay in cheaper lodgings in the village, but come well prepared; try **Casa de Passage** for around US$10. **Lopé Motel** run by Patrick could be another option. The super **Motel E Mbeyi Annexe** is near the water tower (S 0° 06.457, E 11° 36.625). Camping costs US$6 per person, including water usage. The park action comes at a hefty price: CFA30,000 per person per activity. Hikes to Mount Brazza are possible.

Bitam Try the **Hôtel Escale**, which has parking and a nice restaurant.

Oyem South of town on the west is the **Oyem Motel** with parking and cheap rooms at US$12. Otherwise try the occasional quarry south of town. One is at N 01° 09.167, E 11° 41.908.

Ndjolé An oasis of comfort in a sea of wild jungle, the amazing **Auberge St Jean** could well be on the banks of the Loire in France.

Lastoursville Try a hotel or head south to find a place in the jungle.

Franceville Check if you can camp at the **Hôtel Masuka** or stay at **Hôtel Apily**. Camping is possible in the Lekoni canyons, but check security in Franceville first.

OTHER Be wary of taking **photographs**, as the Gabonese are quite touchy about it and your camera could be confiscated. Mitzic has a well-stocked **supermarket**. Those trying to get **public transport into Congo** from Franceville could pay US$100 each for the rare transport to Okyo (four to six hours) in the dry season.

FURTHER INFORMATION
Gabon, São Tomé & Príncipe e-book Sophie Warne 2003 (Bradt Travel Guides; see www.bradtguides.com)
www.wcs.org for information on national parks in Gabon

GAMBIA

CAPITAL Banjul

LANGUAGE English

INTERNATIONAL TELEPHONE CODE +220

CURRENCY AND RATE Dalasi (GMD); US$1 = GMD38.09. ATMs are hard to find outside Banjul.

RED TAPE Roadblocks can be tiresome, with some officials surly at the best of times. The Undercover Narcotics Brigade might search your vehicle for drugs. They can be pretty thorough. Make sure you have all the prescriptions to hand for any medication you are carrying. The Gambian–Casamance border at Soma is easy. The Gambian immigration, police and customs are all in the town, by the junction of the South Bank Road and the Trans-Gambia Highway. Make sure they stamp your carnet in the correct place. 'Fees/taxes' amount to 300 dalasi (for two).

Visas Visas are not required for most nationalities, but US citizens should check. Ensure that your passport is valid for six months or more. Yellow fever certificates are obligatory.

African embassies
http://embassy.goabroad.com/embassies-in/gambia
www.embassypages.com/gambia

DRIVING AND ROADS Drive on the right. Roads along the coastal strip and the airport road are good, but inland expect some deteriorating surfaces.

Fuel costs Diesel: US$1.53; petrol: US$1.63 per litre.

CLIMATE Cool dry season from December to April followed by a warmer dry season and rains between June and October.

HIGHLIGHTS Visit the mysterious Wassu Stone Circles, Take a trip in a local boat up the Gambia River and admire the birdlife. Relax on the Atlantic beaches and visit the market at Basse Santa Su. Banjul should be seen for its run-down ambience.

WHERE TO STAY There are not many campsites; try www.visitthegambia.gm.

Banjul Banjul town is not suitable for camping.

Serekunda/Bakau The obvious choice is **Sukuta Camping** (*www.campingsukuta. com*). It's advertised on various rock outcrops all the way from Laayoune to Nouakchott, so you don't miss it. Camping costs about US$15 (car plus two).

Fajara You will have to shop around for camping, but try at **Fajara Guesthouse** south of Kairaba Avenue or **Dutch Compound**, for which you will have to ask directions. Camping costs US$7.

Sanyang Down the coast two places offer basic African cultural experiences – **Sanyang Nature Camp** and **Rheakunda Camp**, with a dancing and drumming school.

Gunjur There are some pleasant, restful locally run spots, like **Gunjur Guesthouse** (good parking), **Rasta Kunda Beach Camp** and the **Balaba Nature Camp**. Prices are around US$10 per person.

Kartong South of Banjul near the Senegalese border, try the **Boboi Beach Lodge** (*www.gambia-adventure.com*), where camping is US$10 per tent. Also here is

Country Edge Lodge with camping; **Tamba Kruba**, a cheaper option at US$4 each; and a new place, **Kartong Tesito Ecotourism Camp**.

Tendaba Camp One of the most popular nature areas, with bungalows from US$10 per person.

Assau Stone Circle Camping may still be possible at **Village Camp** for US$6 per person.

Janjangbureh (formerly Georgetown) There are various camps set up here, primarily for birdwatching. Look for **Baobolong**, **Dreambird Camp**, **Alakabung** and **Bird Safari Camp** (*www.bsc.gm & www.hiddengambia.com*). Prices are reasonable, from US$6 per person upwards. **Janjangbureh Camp** (N 13° 32.592, W 14° 45.304) (✆ *9816944; www.gambia-river.com*) has shade, a riverside bar and restaurant, cold showers and clean toilets. It is run by a friendly woman manager and has 'excellent security guards in the form of a pack of ten dogs'. The camping might come free for those indulging in the excellent and inexpensive restaurant.

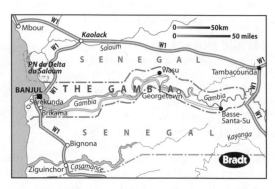

Albreda The **Kunta Kinte Roots Camp** (N 13° 20.051, W 16° 23.243) (✆ *9905322*; e *baboucarrlo@hotmail.com*) has cold showers, clean toilets, good security, shade and views over the River Gambia. It's close to village shops and has a bar and restaurant. The generator is reported to be noisy. Camping costs US$5 per person; bungalows are US$17.

Farafenni Try **Eddy's Hotel and Bar** (N 13° 34.295, W 15° 35.802) (✆ *7621197*). It's convenient, secure and has a bar and restaurant area. Powercuts included. Moses, the manager, is very helpful. The camping spot has absolutely no shade and costs US$10, while rooms cost US$15.

OTHER Banjul is seeing an increase in **crime**. Do not walk on your own at night along the beaches of Bakau and Fajara. There have also been many complaints about beach boys, known as 'bumsters', who offer you anything and everything. Motorists may be fined for strange infringements!

The Barra–Banjul **ferry** is reported to be erratic. The one at Bansang (cost GMD60) is recommended. The one at Janjangbureh may be expensive.

For a **mechanic**, Moudou Gaye in Barra has been recommended (*N 13° 29.085, W 16° 32.689*; ✆ *7081919*). Land Rover parts are available in Banjul.

FURTHER INFORMATION

The Gambia Linda Barnett and Craig Emms (Bradt Travel Guides)
www.gambia.com

GHANA

CAPITAL Accra

LANGUAGE English

INTERNATIONAL TELEPHONE CODE +233

CURRENCY AND RATE New cedi (GHS); US$1 = GHS2.49

RED TAPE There are occasional roadblocks; just ensure all your paperwork is in order. Touts can be a nightmare at the border between Ghana and Togo. Politely ignore them.

Visas Visas are required for all foreigners and are not issued at the border. Yellow fever certificates are obligatory. Previously on arrival you might have been asked how long you intended to stay. Whatever you say could be written in your passport and you won't be able to stay for longer, despite what your visa indicates, so always state the entire duration of your visa.

African embassies

www.ghanaweb.com
http://gh.embassyinformation.com

DRIVING AND ROADS Drive on the right. The coastal roads are excellent, but as you move further north they get a little patchy.

Fuel costs Diesel: US$1.02; petrol: US$1.04 per litre.

CLIMATE Hot and dry in the north and humid along the coast. The rains arrive in late April and last intermittently until September.

HIGHLIGHTS The coastline from Accra to Dixcove has former gruesome slave forts along the coast at Elmina and Cape Coast. Inland is the ancient Ashanti capital, Kumasi, known for its massive market and Kente cloth-weaving villages nearby. The Kakum and Mole national parks are worth a visit. The coast has some good beaches – Kokrobite, Busua, Dixcove and Axim – with improving facilities.

WHERE TO STAY

Accra We don't know of any obvious place to camp in central Accra, but you might try the **Crystalline Hostel** which has rooms around US$20, or the **Amomomo Beach Garden**. Nearby, east of Accra at Coco Beach, is **Akwaaba Beach Guesthouse** (*www.akwaaba-beach.de*) which may have been renovated. **Accra Camping and Carpark** 20km towards Kokrobite is another spot.

Kokrobite About 25km west of Accra. A very popular place here is **Big Milly's Backyard**.

9

Meals are also available just outside on the beach; you can get a fine toasted egg fry with a taste of the local firewater, *apatechi*. US$4–5 per person for camping. Kokrobite is renowned for the Academy of African Music and Arts (AAMAL), with live music, drumming and dancing every weekend. A new resort has been opened here; rooms are US$15.

Anomabu 20km east of Cape Coast is **Anomabu Beach Resort** (*http://anomabo2.digitafrica.com*), with camping for US$6 per person.

Cape Coast Try the **Oasis Guest House**, with double rooms for US$8–15. Also suggested is **Ko Sa** on the beach towards Busua.

Elmina The **Almond Tree Guest House** (*www.almond3.com*) is recommended. Also try the camping at **Stumble Inn**.

Busua Suggested is **Alaska Beach Resort** with camping, rooms US$10–15.

Dixcove Options here include **Hideout Lodge** (*www.hideoutlodge.com*), close to Butre. Camping and bungalows on the beach cost US$5–6. The **Green Turtle Lodge** (*www.greenturtlelodge.com*) also has camping from US$4 per person; and for eco-luxury, there is **Safari Beach** (*www.safaribeachlodge.com*). All are to the west of Dixcove.

Kumasi The **Presbyterian Guesthouse** is one place you can camp. It's a beautiful place with huge shady trees, located close to the city centre; cost is around US$5. **Rose's Guest House** might be a possible alternative. **Kumasi Catering Resthouse** has shady grounds but is often full.

North to Burkina There is plenty of savanna forest where you can camp wild.

Bolgatanga The **Sand Gardens Hotel** is pleasant at US$10 a room.

Mole National Park This is in the northwest of the country. Try the new national parks campsites, priced at US$3 each. The **Mole Motel** may let you camp for around US$4 per person.

OTHER Accra is the place to get a **Land Rover** fixed. Seek advice before diving into the ocean, as Ghana is plagued with **dangerous currents**. In general, **taking photographs** of people is not a problem, but always ask beforehand and do not photograph near government institutions.

If you're keen to learn the African beat, the social enterprise African Footprint International (*www.africanfootprintlegends.com*) is a **drum and dance workshop** located near Cape Coast.

If you need a mechanic in Accra, Roger (Nana) and Godwin (❋ *028 213 803;* e *rogerko2001@yahoo.com*) have been recommended.

FURTHER INFORMATION
Ghana Philip Briggs (Bradt Travel Guides)
www.ghanaweb.com

GUINEA

WARNING! Check the travel advice in case there is a resurgence of past unrest.

CAPITAL Conakry

LANGUAGE French

INTERNATIONAL TELEPHONE CODE +224

CURRENCY AND RATE Guinean franc (GNF); US$1 = GNF7,020

RED TAPE A few police manning roadblocks at night might hold your papers until you pay a bribe. In other words, don't drive at night. You shouldn't pay more than US$5 as a bribe. During the day there are very few checks. The Kandika border (Guinea-Bissau–Guinea-Conakry) is said to be easy and friendly, with taxes about CFA2,000 to the Guinea Bissau customs. The piste on both sides of the border is apparently rather challenging.

Visas Visas are required for all. They are not issued at the border. Depending on which country you are in, the Guinean embassy may ask for a letter of introduction from your own embassy. In Bissau you will need a photocopy of the ID pages of your passport, yellow fever certificate, two photos and, oddly, the Guinea Bissau visa and entry stamp. It is at Rua 12 opposite 'Bissau Electronica', east of the central stadium (N 11° 51.617, W 15° 35.075) (☏ *3201231;* ⏰ *08.30–15.00 Sat–Thu, 08.30–13.00 Fri*). It may be issued on the spot or on the same day. This costs US$130–180.

The visa can also be obtained from the Guinean embassy in Freetown (*111 Jomo Kenyatta Rd, New England;* ⏰ *09.00–15.30 Mon–Thu, 09.00–13.00 Fri – maybe same-day service*). The visa costs US$100 for citizens of the UK, USA and Australia, €60 for Europeans, US$50 for citizens of China and Brazil, and is free for Malaysia and Cuba!

African embassies
www.embassypages.com/guinea
http://gn.embassyinformation.com

DRIVING AND ROADS Drive on the right. The main road from Conakry to Bamako is generally not too bad, but elsewhere the roads are poor and those that are paved are usually pot-holed. The road to Dalaba and Labé is not too bad. After Labé it is rough into the higher country, but is being worked on. The last 120km to Senegal and on to Tambacounba is new. In the east, roads are exceedingly variable. The road to Sierra Leone from Coyah to Pamalap has been sealed. The road is patchy and pot-holed from Mamou to Faranah but then new to Kissidougou. From here to Gueckadou is bad, then it's good as far as Lola. Guinea does have some fun sections of dirt road for those

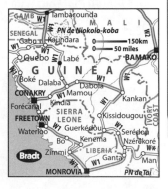

yearning for the old days. There is a good piste from Forecariah to Moussaya and then on to Kindia, however from Kindia to Télimélé and then directly north to Gaoual is terrible. The dangerous, steep, bendy and washed-out piste/road from Gaoual to Koundara is paved after Boumenal.

Fuel costs Diesel: US$1.40; petrol: US$1.70 per litre.

CLIMATE Guinea has a tropical climate, with a lengthy rainy season between May and October determined by altitude and location.

HIGHLIGHTS Conakry has some pleasant leafy areas and markets. There are beaches on the Iles de Los, Iles de Roume and Iles de Kassa. Most can only be reached by pirogue (a small river craft of various sizes). Iles de Los has a mini-resort. You may even get a spontaneous musical performance. Some local outfits teach tourists about the music and you can learn to play the *kora* here. Inland is the Fouta Djalon Plateau with short treks from either Dalaba, a pleasant hill resort, Labé or Pita.

⌂ WHERE TO STAY

Conakry The best place with parking is the **Hotel du Golfe** (N 19° 34.124, W 13° 39.670) (*Quartier Minière, in the Rogbane area;* ☏ *64 25 94 78;* e *hoteldugolfedeguinee@ yahoo.fr*). Rooms are clean with en-suite shower and toilet, and breakfast is included. Double rooms cost GNF400,000. In the northern area, try **Hôtel Kaporo**. In town is the **Hôtel Niger**, a seedy but cheap place without parking.

Dubréka near Conakry There is a watering area on the river Soumba with little shade but 'a good breeze does blow and the frogs croak heartily' (N 09° 53.302, W 13° 29.111). People come to collect water, swim and wash clothes throughout the day.

Koundara There are two places where you can park and camp. **Hôtel Gagan** is the quiet one a little further out east, costing US$4. **Hôtel Niafay** is friendly with more space but more noise. Both are reached down a tiny track from the central empty fuel station.

Dalaba The **Pension Tangama** is a relaxing place with parking. Up the hill overlooking the valley is the more upmarket **Sib Hôtel du Fouta,** Quartier des Chargeurs, Dalaba (N 10° 41.334, W 12° 15.917) with camping (US$7+) in the garden and great panoramic views across the rolling hills.

Fouta Djalon Plateau With rolling green hills and a cooler climate, the excellent hiking is a must-do. Stay with local people in traditional village huts and preferably have a local guide to translate.

Chutes de Ditinn Campement Solidaire, Fouta Trekking Aventure (N 10° 49.481, W 12° 11.643) (☏ *060 57 02 79/0622 91 20 24/0662 94 07 17; www.foutatrekking. org*) is friendly and secure with lots of space, privacy and shade to set up camp overlooking the river (and the monkeys). Toilets, bucket showers and water for washing up are provided. The walk to the waterfall takes 20 minutes. The nearest village is an hour away, but it has a shop that sells bread and other provisions.

Labé Try the wonderful, efficient and friendly Hotel Tata, Quartier Pounthioun (N 11° 18.753, W 12° 17.497), with thatched huts in the garden and some parking places. Delightful Madame Raby runs the place. Rooms cost from US$20 and camping is possible, but there's little shade.

Around 80km north of Labé In the forest off the N5 (N 11° 39.097, W 12° 42.178) welcoming people nearby will come for a chat as they pass by while collecting palm wine and hunting.

Mamou Look out for **Hôtel Baly** with a courtyard.

Kindia On the way out of town on the east side, but not signposted unless you are going north, is the **Hôtel Flamboyant**. This is a great retreat with extensive gardens. Camping is allowed, or take a room. Let us know if the pool has been filled!

Télimélé Télimélé has a hotel, Le Petit Palais, which is signposted from the road and lies on the right-hand side as you drive through from south to north.

Foulayah Try **Campement Solidaire** (N 09° 56.906, W 12° 52.892) (*Eaux de Kilissi;* ⟍ *0622 13 35 65;* e *amtendances@yahoo.fr*).

Wild camps There are wild camps between **Télimélé and Gaoual** (N 11° 01.476, W 13° 05.198) and **South of Koundara** 35km off the N5 (N 12° 14.500, W 13° 06.757).

Kankan The **Hôtel Bate** has good secure parking and the lively markets are not far away. It's a quiet retreat with a bar and restaurant. The annexe is cheaper (US$24) and the air conditioning works at times. Beware of hidden one-way street signs near the hotel.

Malian border There is **Relais Tata** on the Guinean side.

Kissidougou On the road out west towards Faranah is the pleasant **Hôtel Savannah** with parking in a yard opposite, where you can cook and probably camp if you wish. We witnessed Guinea being thrashed by Ivory Coast here after Guinea had beaten Morocco in the Africa Cup of Nations. We could have watched Portsmouth v Arsenal in a shed with television and generator in a village 20km out of town.

Macenta Look for **Hôtel Bamala**.

Nzérékoré The cramped but secure **Hôtel Chez Aida** is in a quiet area northwest of the markets, up a little hill.

OTHER Guinea is a great country for outdoor enthusiasts, particularly **cyclists and hikers**, and is also well known for its music. The Fouta Djalon is the most obvious option; remember to carry adequate water and food with you. The eastern forest area is remote and there are still areas of dense rainforest with narrow muddy roads that are passable in the dry season. There is also the great biking/hiking Pita–Télimélé route, which was part of the Paris–Dakar rally in 1995. Hotels are still excellent value, so it's not necessary to rough it all the time.

FURTHER INFORMATION
West Africa (Rough Guides)
www.guineenews.org

GUINEA BISSAU

WARNING! Things are much better now but check for the latest advice after the insurrection of 2012.

CAPITAL Bissau

LANGUAGE Portuguese

INTERNATIONAL TELEPHONE CODE +245

CURRENCY AND RATE West African franc (CFA); US$1 = CFA478. ATMs are only found in Bissau, including one at the Banco da Africa Occidental on the Rua Gerra Mendes.

RED TAPE You may find intermittent roadblocks, but locals are friendly. The border at São Domingos is generally easygoing. Taxes are around CFA2,000 for the Senegalese customs and CFA6,000 for the Guinea Bissau customs. For vehicle insurance, Carte Brun, see under *Senegal*, page 291. There are a lot of police checks, especially on the way in to Bissau. There are a surprising number of female police, who are usually friendly and not really bothered about seeing any documents.

Visas Visas are required for all foreigners. They cost around US$50 and are valid for one month. Visas are not issued at the border. They can be obtained from the quiet, shady and friendly consulate in Ziguinchor at 250 rue Santiaba (N 12° 34.834, W 16° 16.061). Take one photocopy of the personal details and photo page of your passport and one photograph (not necessary if you have colour photocopies of your passport). The cost is CFA20,000 for a 30-day double-entry visa and it may be issued on the spot.

African embassies
http://embassy.goabroad.com/embassies-in/guinea-bissau
www.embassypages.com/guineabissau

DRIVING AND ROADS Drive on the right. Generally main roads are quite good, with few pot-holes. Other roads are usually pot-holed. The road is good from Bissau to Mampata Forea. The piste to Jemberem in the south is fairly comfortable until the turn-off at 36km from Jemberem. Then it gets narrower, bumpier, more overgrown and eroded, as well as being more frequented by cyclists.

Fuel costs Diesel: US$1.50 per litre; petrol: US$1.60 per litre.

CLIMATE The hottest months are April to May, with the coolest months from December to January. Rains are from July to September.

HIGHLIGHTS Explore the Portuguese colonial areas of Bissau. In the north are the coastal mangrove swamps around Cacheu, with its tiny ruined fort. More offbeat is a visit by boat to the Bijagos Islands. In the south is the rainforest habitat of the Jemberem, Parque Nacional de Cantanhez.

WHERE TO STAY Organised campsites are a rarity and there are few favourable wild camping opportunities.

Bissau Finding somewhere to park or camp will be difficult. Try asking at one of the hotels, perhaps the top-end **Hotel Bissau** or maybe **Hotel 24 de Septembro** out of town. Try **Caritas** at **Avenue de 14 Novembro** (near Hotel Libya) (N 11° 51.479, W 15° 37.162). The site boasts good security, showers and

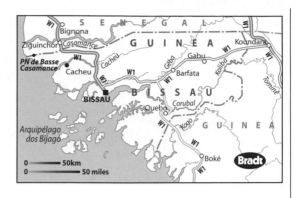

toilets, shade, peace and space in beautiful gardens. Shops are ten minutes away; the Guinea embassy is 40 minutes away in town. The welcoming people who run this place also operate the adjacent Roman Catholic seminary, nunnery, community centre for meetings and sales of non-pharmaceutical medicines. It also has a mechanics' workshop.

Bafata The **Hotel Maimuna Cape** has good standard rooms for US$20. It has power and running water eventually, but poor security.

Gabú The **Hotel Visiom** (N 12° 16.745, W 14° 12.993) (☏ *6866699*) is five minutes' walk to the centre of town, with its huge market and many shops. It is very welcoming with a cooking area, bar, TV and secure parking for US$20.

Cacheu Try the **Hotel Baluarte**, where the rates for camping accommodation will need to be negotiated.

Jemberem, Parque Nacional do Cantanhez Look for **U'Anan Camp** (N 11° 14.101, W 15° 12.300) (☏ *6060019/6637263*). It is situated within the village of Jemberem (where you can find a nightclub, bars, restaurants and shops) and has a bar and restaurant. The area has space adjacent to rainforest and frolicking monkeys. There are facilities with 'purple soap'. Ask for Porno, who offers a warm welcome to this female-initiated and run co-operative. Some days there is a stall selling local non-pharmaceutical medicines and honey. Cost for two with a vehicle is around US$10. Guides also operate from the camp and will escort you on early morning trips to see chimpanzees enjoying their breakfast.

Pousada do Saltinho (N 11° 37.070, W 14° 41.229) (☏ *5900693*) has a bar and restaurant, security but little shade. There are toilets but no showers and hammocks with views over the waterfalls. Cost is around US$13 for two.

Bijagos Archipelago These are a group of islands off Guinea Bissau. Assuming you can find secure parking for your vehicle, the best bet is to pack an overnight bag and head over to one of the following two islands, which have some accommodation. **Bolama Island** is the closer to the mainland, but accommodation is basic. **Bubaque Island**, at the centre of the archipelago, is one of the easiest to reach. Praia Bruce Beach on the southern end of the island has some places to stay. Ask other travellers about any new developments.

OTHER Apparently Dutch-made dog food is available from Supermercado Mavegro, Rua Eduardo Mondlane, just below the British and Dutch consulate!

FURTHER INFORMATION
West Africa (Rough Guides)

IVORY COAST (CÔTE D'IVOIRE)

WARNING! We strongly advise you to check all sources of travel advice before entering the country. The political situation is still fluid, so expect security issues travelling overland for a while hence. Parts of Abidjan are notorious for crime, with rogue elements.

CAPITAL Yamoussoukro (Abidjan remains the commercial centre).

LANGUAGE French

INTERNATIONAL TELEPHONE CODE +225

CURRENCY AND RATE West African franc (CFA); US$1 = CFA478

RED TAPE Expect some hassles throughout the country.

Visas Visas are required for all non-Africans. Vaccination certificates are obligatory. Visas are not issued at the border.

African embassies
http://embassy.goabroad.com/embassies-in/ivory-coast

DRIVING AND ROADS Drive on the right. Good surfaced roads on main routes did exist but some are now pot-holed in places. The state of dirt roads elsewhere is not known. Apparently the road from Guinea to Man via Danane is OK, with pot-holes.

Fuel costs Diesel: US$1.61; petrol: US$1.58 per litre.

CLIMATE There are two climatic regions. In the south, the temperature remains at a steady 30°C all year round but rainfall is heavy at times. There are four seasons: a long dry season from December to April; a long rainy season from May to July; a short dry season from August to September; and a short rainy season from October to November. The north has a broader temperature range, with a rainy season from June to October and a dry season from November to May.

HIGHLIGHTS Grand Bassam, with its colonial-era buildings, once had a stretch of bustling beachfront cafés and entertainment. Abidjan offers contrasting affluence and poverty. It had a huge market for secondhand spares, plus great supermarkets with goodies such as imported cheeses – costly but worth it. Yamoussoukro is full of fascinating contrasts, with quiet streets, concrete structures and eight-lane highways lined with thousands of lights ending abruptly in the jungle. The Basilique de Notre-Dame de la Paix, which resembles St Peter's in Rome, is the white elephant of Africa, built by President Houphouët-Boigney at a cost of a mere US$300 million in 1983. Upcountry, Korhogo, the capital of the Senoufo, is famous for its wooden carvings and Korhogo cloth (mud-coloured designs painted on fabric). In December there are several festivals. Try to visit the pottery and blacksmith quarters, with temples for each of the crafts. Also visit Komoé National Park. Man has fantastic scenery, with the Cathedral and Grand Mosque side by side.

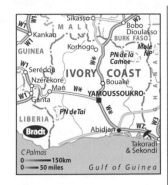

WHERE TO STAY

Abidjan Abidjan has six sections – Plateau, Treichville, Marcory, Adjame, Cocody and Deux Plateaux. Camping is not a safe option anywhere near town; it's best not to stay in Abidjan for those with wheels. Try asking at the expensive **Hôtel Golf** east of the centre along the shores of the Ebrie Lagoon. In town two places have been mentioned: **Le Prince** (*Av 24*), has a room with fan for US$12/14 and the **Abobo Hôtel** is around US$10, parking status unknown.

Grand Bassam Grand Bassam is frequented mostly by expatriates during the weekend, so visit during the week. Camping is not safe as crime is rampant, so look around the hotels for a place to park. Try **Taverne la Bassamoise** or **Hôtel Boblin la Mer.**

Assini One place has been suggested – **Jardin d'Eden**.

Man The **Hôtel Amointrin des 18 Montagnes** (◝ *33792670*) is next to the Bethany Centre; also **Hôtel les Cascades.**

Yamoussoukro There is no camping in Yamoussoukro and you will have to ask one of the hotel managers if you can stay in their courtyard.

Korhogo There is no camping, but budget accommodation is available. It's just a matter of finding secure parking for your vehicle.

OTHER A **photographic permit** is not required, but be very careful until the political problems have calmed down. **Camping accommodation** is hard to find.

FURTHER INFORMATION
West Africa (Lonely Planet)

KENYA

CAPITAL Nairobi

LANGUAGE English and Swahili

INTERNATIONAL TELEPHONE CODE +254

CURRENCY AND RATE Kenyan shilling (KES); US$1 = KES86.35

A–Z Africa Country Guide   KENYA

9

RED TAPE You may need a foreign road permit if you stay more than a week: US$2–US$30 for one month and US$100 for three months. It might be charged at your exit border if coming from Moyale.

Visas Visas are required by most visitors but everyone should check, as changes have been made. Getting a Kenyan visa in advance in Tanzania, Uganda or Ethiopia is simple and hassle-free. Costs vary from US$45 to US$90. It may still be possible to get visas at the border if coming from Tanzania or Uganda, but check beforehand.

African embassies
http://embassy.goabroad.com/embassies-in/kenya
www.embassyworld.com
www.yellowpageskenya.com
www.embassypages.com/kenya

DRIVING AND ROADS Drive on the left. Many of the roads in Kenya are excellent, but some are deteriorating. The roads get worse the further north you go. Around Mount Kenya some sections are quite rough, as is some of the coast road to Mombasa. Watch out for some bad driving locally. To Marsabit from Moyale takes around 11 hours, or seven to eight from Sololo. Appalling corrugations and even flooding is possible. Avoid the wet season. There are a couple of police check-posts *en route* but security still varies this close to Somalia. There may be a system of convoys or escorts. South of Marsabit the road is again shocking for 90 miles. Expect new tarmac to Merille, 75 miles south of Marsabit, when the Chinese finish the road from Archer's Post to a mining area.

Fuel costs Diesel: US$1.22; petrol: US$0.95 litre.

CLIMATE Coastal areas are tropical and hot, but tempered by monsoon winds. The wettest months are April, May and November; the hottest are February and March; the coolest are June and July. The lowlands are hot and dry. Much of Kenya stands at over 1,500m (4,500ft) and has a more temperate climate with four seasons. There is a warm and dry season from January to March; a rainy season from March to June; a cool, cloudy and dry season from June to October; and a rainy season from November to December.

HIGHLIGHTS Visit the famous national parks including Masai Mara, Amboseli, Tsavo and Nakuru. Climb Mount Kenya and visit the different lakes: Naivasha, Bogaria, Baringo and Turkana. There are many good beaches and resorts between Mombasa and Lamu. Also watch out for the various colourful tribes: Samburu, Turkana, Rendille and Masai. Eating is a highlight, too. There is great ice cream, a cheese factory in Eldoret and superb bacon and eggs in Nairobi.

 WHERE TO STAY
Nairobi Most campsites have access to the city centre by public bus and *matatus*. For Nairobi eating, the most famous restaurant is **Carnivore**, specialising in all types of game meat, near Wilson Airport off Langata Road. For morning coffee, try the Thorn Tree Café at the New Stanley Hotel. For Land Rover repairs try the Impala and Royal garages. **Upper Hill Campsite** (S01°17.161, E36°46.387) (*Othaya Rd;* 0202500218; m 0721 517869; e upperhill_campsite@yahoo.co.uk; *www.upperhillcampsite.com*) is in a pleasant hilly area west of the city centre in Lavington. Ask for Jessie and Rich.

There's Wi-Fi and a new treehouse. Take bus number 46 from the bus stand near the Hilton hotel. Camping costs around US$6 and double rooms US$20.

Nairobi-Langata Popular with overlanders is **Jungle Junction** (S1° 21.767, E 36° 44.438) (*Kongoni Rd;* m *0722 752865*). Camp US$7 per person, rooms US$20–35. **Wildebeest Eco Camp** (*Mokoyeti Rd West;* ☎ *020 210 3505;* m *0734 770733;* e *info@ wildebeesttravels.com*). It has a laundry service, Wi-Fi, bar, snacks, burgers, sandwiches and juices. Dinner is a fixed buffet-style meal for KES800; camping is US$12 per person, dormitory US$15 and rooms range from US$32 to US$160. **Acacia Campsite** (*Magadi Rd, 2km from Langata*) has parking and a grassy area for camping. There are showers and a restaurant/bar. En-suite rooms are US$25–35, dormitories US$8 and camping US$6. Security has become an issue here, unfortunately.

Nairobi-Karen The **Karen Camp** (*Marula Lane;* m *0736 216822;* e *info@ countryhouse-inn.com*) has camping for US$7 per person, dorms US$15 per person and twin rooms US$40–50. The **Country House Inn** (*Ngong Rd*) has camping, bar and a restaurant with Wi-Fi.

Nakuru Look for **Backpackers Campsite** (US$10) and **Kembu Camping**, 20km from town towards Njoro and Molo. It has rooms, small cottages and a treehouse cottage, with camping from US$5. Also look out for **Acacia Cottages**, with camping US$3–4 per person. On the lake is **Mbweha Camp**, but it has gone upmarket. The **Punda Milias Campsite** (*www.nakurucamp.co.ke*) is 3km off the main road, about 15km from Nakuru, coming from Nairobi.

Lake Naivasha The lake area makes a good break from the chaotic lifestyle in Nairobi. Try **Fisherman's Camp** with huge, shady acacia trees, an incredible amount of birdlife, loads of water activities and a great bar. Camping costs about US$6 per person. Also look for **Camp Carnelly's**, **Top Camp**, **Crayfish Camp** and **Burch's Marina**. The **Fish Eagle Inn** (*www.fisheagleinn.com*) is near the lake (fenced in) with a nice grassy area – watch out for falling tree branches, though! Colobus and vervet monkeys tend to call by, so don't leave any food out. Rooms are available in the hotel if you want a luxury night. Camping costs US$7.

Eldoret The **Naiberi River Campsite** just outside Eldoret is good, and has the most comfortable bar imaginable. Camping costs US$6–7.

North of Eldoret The **Overland Camping** is on the left some way from town.

Ugandan border The **Emael Hotel** is at Malaba, on the Ugandan side.

Mount Elgon Camping is pleasant at the **Delta Crescent Farm**, 28km from Kitale near the park entrance, and costs US$5 each.

Turbo On the way to Uganda is the **Spring Park Hotel**, a nice local camp and hotel – very cheap, safe and clean. Camping costs US$4 per person, rooms US$11.

Kericho The **Kericho Tea Hotel** (̂ *052 30005;* m *0714 510824;* e *info@teahotel. co.ke*) has a restaurant, rooms and tea plantation tours from KES200 each. Camping US$6 per person. Hotels are quite good value, including **Kericho Garden Motel** and **Kericho Lodge**.

Lake Baringo Try **Robert's Camp** on the lakeside; camping costs about US$6 each.

Lake Bogoria Posh camping can be had at the **Lake Bogoria Hotel** for US$8 each.

Mount Kenya For information on Mount Kenya, go to the **Naro Moru River Lodge**, which also offers camping at US$6–7 per person. It is about 1.5km off to the left on the main Nairobi–Nanyuki road. In Naro Moru town there is **Mount Kenya Camping and Hostel** and the **Blue Line Hostel**, and it's OK to camp at the **Mount Kenya Guides** place. Four days' conservation fees for the park is around US$300.

Nanyuki North of Nanyuki is **Timau River Lodge**, which has cottages and camping; cost US$6–8 per person. Also look for the **Nanyuki River Camel Camp**.

Lodwar In town is **Nawoitorong Guesthouse** with cheap camping options. *En route* and north of the Marich Pass is **Mtelo View Campsite**, a nice retreat.

Maralal On the way to Lake Turkana, Maralal is high up in the hills and above the Lerochi Plateau. It is also famous for its Camel Derby in October. The best place to stay is the **Yare Safari Club and Campsite**.

Up to Lake Turkana Bush sleeping is the best option, but check the latest security warnings. The road up to Lake Turkana crosses volcanic outcrops, which means there are lots of sharp stones that make it slow going. On Lake Turkana, in Loyangalani, there were a number of campsites: **El Molo**, **Sunset Strip**, **Gametrackers** and the **Oasis Lodge**.

North Horr A community-based project for the Gabbra people is the Kalacha Camp – you can camp or stay in huts.

Moyale You can camp outside the friendly customs office. Ask the police or try the wildlife camp. You can stay on the Ethiopian side at the **Bekele Mola Motel**. Better to go on perhaps, as the road is shocking and very slow to Marsabit.

Sololo It is about 80km from Moyale and 6km to the right off the main, dirt road. Either turn off to the **Anglican church** on the right to camp, or go a little further to the **Mission hospital** grounds. Donations welcomed, but no fees.

Marsabit The national park campsite is very expensive and run-down. The best place in town is the **Jey Jey Motel**, with cheap, clean rooms and safe parking. It is just off the main road. They do a superb greasy egg and toast. Ah, those little pleasures! A double room costs US$6–8. Recommended for camping is **Henry's Camp**, out of town. Ask around for directions, as it's hard to find.

Isiolo There's **Rangeland Camping** on the main road uphill towards Nanyuki, on the right about 10km south of town. Camping is US$12, and it has good rooms.

Mombasa and the coast The options are endless, but not in Mombasa town. The problem is finding safe parking for your vehicle. Many people rave about Tiwi Beach, south of Mombasa. **Twiga Lodge Beach Camp** is an old favourite. There are also various beach bungalows offering accommodation; prices from US$6 to US$30 per person, depending on what you want. Diani Beach has **Diani Campsite and Cottages**.

Malindi Further north up the coast is **Silversands Campsite**. Also here is **KWS Compound** and **Malindi Marine Park Campsite**. Prices start at US$4 per person.

Lamu As this is an island, vehicles have to be parked at Mokowe – check security here – it's close to Somalia.

National parks Most of Kenya's national parks allow vehicles and have camping facilities. The cost of taking a foreign-registered vehicle into most national parks is high. It can cost you over US$100 per day per person (US$60–80 per person park fee and KES300 per day plus US$15–40 camping). Smartcard electronic ticketing is now used – tickets are usually on sale at the main gates, but allow time for the process. Another option is to organise a tour of the various national parks in Nairobi. Get some advice from Upper Hill Campsite regarding the most economical tours available. Also see www.kws.org for prices and information on the parks.

OTHER Nairobi has a poor reputation regarding **crime** and petty theft. Don't walk around with valuables and be very careful if you go out at night.

FURTHER INFORMATION
Kenya Highlights Philip Briggs (Bradt Travel Guides)
www.kenyalogy.com
www.worldtravelshop.biz/overland/kenya

LESOTHO

CAPITAL Maseru

LANGUAGE English and Sotho

INTERNATIONAL TELEPHONE CODE +266

A–Z Africa Country Guide   LESOTHO

9

CURRENCY AND RATE The Lesotho loti (LSL) is the local currency, but South African rand are universally accepted. The current rate is US$1 = LSL10.86.

RED TAPE None of any significance. Lesotho is within the South African customs area. Note that foreign-registered vehicles on a carnet now get only three months in the South African Union area, which includes South Africa, Botswana, Namibia, Swaziland and Lesotho.

Visas Visas are not required by citizens of the Commonwealth and South Africa. Other visitors should check.

African embassies
http://embassy.goabroad.com/embassies-in/lesotho
www.embassypages.com/lesotho

DRIVING AND ROADS Drive on the left. Many of the roads in western Lesotho are good and tarred, if a little narrow in places. The roads get worse the further you go from Maseru into the eastern mountain regions. Be warned, crossing the Sani Pass is only possible in summer and could be nerve-racking for some.

Fuel costs Diesel: US$1.34; petrol: US$1.20 per litre.

CLIMATE Lesotho has a varied climate affected by a wide range of altitudes. The dry season is June to August, with a wet season from October to April.

HIGHLIGHTS Lesotho is a mountainous enclave within South Africa. It shares the delights of the Drakensberg range, but is much more isolated. Hiking and horse riding are the main activities. Sani Pass is literally a high point. The culture is very strongly retained.

 WHERE TO STAY
Maseru Off Kingsway, the **Lancer's Inn** has some rondavels and good parking. The luxury **Hotel Lesotho Sun** on the hill above town may allow parking/camping.

Teyateyaneng Try the **Pitseng Guesthouse**. Camping costs US$9 for car plus two people. Also nearby is **Blue Mountain Resort**, a more upmarket establishment.

Malealea South of Maseru, camping is possible at the **Malealea Lodge**, which also has hiking options.

Sani Pass Backpackers and camping at/near the **Sani Mountain Lodge** (Sani Top Chalet) complex.

FURTHER INFORMATION
South Africa, Lesotho and Swaziland (Lonely Planet)

LIBERIA

Overland travel to Liberia is now possible. Due to the ongoing rebuilding of the country's infrastructure, it would be wise to check how things are, particularly if and when the UN troops leave.

CAPITAL Monrovia

LANGUAGE English

INTERNATIONAL TELEPHONE CODE +231

CURRENCY AND RATE Liberian dollar (LRD); US$1 = LRD86. US dollars are freely interchangeable in shops, hotels, fuel stations, etc.

RED TAPE Expect some roadblocks, where friendly UN troops will wave you on. The local police are also very friendly. Occasionally we had to fill in paperwork or hand over copies of passports, but everything was good-natured. There is no longer any need to report to immigration in Monrovia.

Visas Visas are required for all. Vaccination certificates are obligatory. Visas are not issued at the border.

African embassies

http://embassy.goabroad.com/embassies-in/liberia
http://embassy-finder.com/liberia_embassies
www.embassypages.com/liberia

DRIVING AND ROADS The road from Bo Waterside, the Sierra Leone border, is mostly very good to Monrovia. Heading upcountry, the road is generally in good shape to Gbarnga, but after to Ganta there are some poor sections. There are always isolated pot-holes, so don't take your eyes off the road. Elsewhere roads are not busy outside Monrovia, which has traffic jams at rush hour. The road east to Harper via Zwedru is still bad, and particularly awful in the wet season.

Fuel costs Diesel: US$1.19; petrol: US$1.22 per litre (note prices at pumps are quoted in gallons).

CLIMATE Liberia has a fairly wet climate, with the drier season from November to April.

HIGHLIGHTS Liberia has most of the last remaining concentration of wet tropical rainforest in west Africa. Monrovia is being slowly reconstructed and the beaches nearby are pleasant – Silver Beach, St Martin's and, yes, 'Thinkers' Beach! Firestone rubber plantations (some now up and running again) here were the largest in the world before the troubles. The remains of the jungle mansion of former

President Doe are near Zwedru. Harper is a beautiful spot, but getting there is not paradise. The people are some of the friendliest in Africa.

WHERE TO STAY

Monrovia With an influx of UN, NGO and development people, hotel prices are very high. At present camping is not a feasible option; parking in the grounds of a benevolent hotel might be worth a try. We were forced to splash out on an air-conditioned room at **My Hotel** (US$100+) in the centre mainly because it had a well-guarded parking area and a massive generator. There is nowhere to camp at the popular Mamba Point. **Kamoma Hotel** on the main road seven miles east of Monrovia is recommended for cheaper rooms and maybe camping. Even further out is the Red Light area (that's the name – really!) with cheaper local places, but safe parking is an issue.

Bo Waterside There is no town here, just the border village, with no accommodation. We camped at the police station east of the border and gave a donation so the boys and girls could pay for fuel for the generator in order to watch the football.

Robertsport The road is west of Monrovia and on the south side coming from the Bo Waterside border. There is a **community campground**, **Kwepunha Surf Retreat**, **Nana Lodge** and **Gurtrude's Oceanview Resort**.

Salala About 110km from Monrovia on the Gbarnga road is the small settlement of Salala. **Oasis Lodge** is a secure and friendly place with camping for US$25 in the grounds or a room from US$35.

Totota About 145km from Monrovia is the amazing **CooCoo Nest** at Tubman Farms, which has rooms, a café and a deserted zoo. It's something of an institution by reputation. The **Sata Guesthouse** is signposted along the road before Gbarnga.

Gbarnga We did not see any suitable place to stay, as it's off the main road, but there should be something available if you're stuck, because the town is fast developing and there are plenty of UN people about. **Hotel Ebony** has been suggested for US$15.

Ganta The town is more of a large village, but along the main road north before the end of it is the **Hotel Alvinos** on the 'Guinea road', where you need to turn off for Nzérékoré in Guinea.

OTHER You can find **car parts** in the Randall Street area of Monrovia and on the road from Bo Waterside on the way into town. Toyota is well represented here, but there are hundreds of secondhand-parts shops too. In the same area is Prestige Motors, the Land Rover dealer, but they don't hold much stock. The area around the US embassy in Monrovia may be blocked off.

FURTHER INFORMATION
www.lonelyplanet.com/liberia
http://wikitravel.org/en/Liberia
www.liberia101.com

LIBYA

WARNING! Libya had become an established tourist destination, despite its idiosyncrasies, but since the 'liberation' it has pockets of lawlessness. The border areas of Algeria and Niger host Islamists on the lookout for easy (and even hard) prey, so keep away from those areas of the country. Transit from Tunisia to Egypt may be possible within the lifetime of this guide. Seek up-to-date advice.

CAPITAL Tripoli

LANGUAGE Arabic

INTERNATIONAL TELEPHONE CODE +218

CURRENCY AND RATE Libyan dinar (LYD); US$1 = LYD1.24

RED TAPE Unknown at present, but before the troubles tourists in their own vehicles needed to travel with a guide or with a guide in his own vehicle. This could change in future, so check before travelling.

Visas Visas are required for all. Nationals of Israel or those with an Israeli stamp in their passport will not be admitted. When safe, tourists will probably have to travel with a Libyan tour company, meaning in convoy with the guide's vehicle. Visas are currently valid for one month (three-day transit might be possible, but it means a lot of driving). You may be required to register within 48 hours at the first police station you come across in Libya. Regulations are changing constantly, so check before travel. See also www.libya.embassyhomepage.com.

African embassies
http://embassy.goabroad.com/embassies-in/libya
www.embassypages.com/libya

DRIVING AND ROADS Drive on the right. The roads on major routes are good and the rest are desert pistes and tracks. Main roads are quite busy along the northern coast near Tripoli; driving standards are rather erratic, to put it mildly.

Fuel costs Diesel: US$0.11; petrol: US$0.10 per litre. Libya has the cheapest fuel available in Africa.

CLIMATE The best time to visit is during the northern spring and autumn months from October to early March, although you might come across the *ghibli,* which is a hot, dry and sand-laden wind that can raise the temperatures to 40°C or more.

HIGHLIGHTS Tripoli has a fascinating old city medina. The magnificent Roman ruins of Leptis Magna and Sabratha should not be missed, plus the ancient Greek cities of Cyrene and Apollonia. In the west are the old granaries at Nalut and the old mud city of Ghadames. The war graves at Tobruk are sobering. In the Sahara are the Dune Lakes close to Awbari and the Akakus Mountains near Ghat. Visit the prehistoric rock art and see the superb desert scenery, including some rock arches.

9

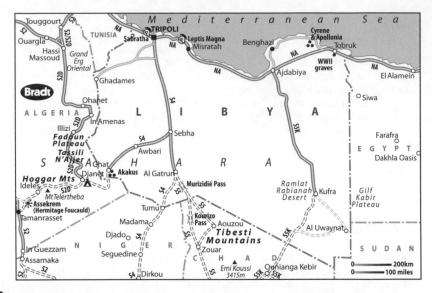

🏠 **WHERE TO STAY** Wild camping was the most pleasant option throughout Libya, and away from settlements this was not a problem when carrying adequate fuel and water. Even in the larger towns, it's best to park up for the day, do what needs to be done, and leave in the early afternoon to find a camping spot. There are hotels in most major cities, but prices are high and you might be charged in foreign currency.

Tripoli Rather difficult and expensive, so stay at Sabratha or camp on the beach at Zuara near the Tunisian border. The **Al Kabeer Hotel** (Grand Hotel) had a large garden and used to allow 'parking'.

Leptis Magna The **Tourist Village** with camping was just outside the entry gate to the ruins. Across the road to the west is a hotel with its name in Arabic. It also allowed camping.

Awbari In Awbari the **Africa Camp** was a pleasant place, right below the dunes.

Siltar Try to camp in the grounds with the Roman statues, which your guide will know about. Rooms were also available.

Ghadames On the road into town before the old city, the **Hotel Al Waha** had a secure compound.

Sebha The Fezzan Campsite may be closed now.

Tobruk There is a hotel with parking on the south side of town, overlooking the wide open area before the main business area. The guides know it.

OTHER Libya is a Muslim country, so dress and act appropriately, and remember, no alcohol whatsoever is allowed. Libyans are sensitive towards photography, so be careful what you photograph and never, ever take pictures of women. For an invitation from a Libyan travel agent, contact Abdel Doumnaji at Africa Tours in

Sebha (📞 + *218 71 637 600*; m *+218 92 513 2304*; e *africatours.ly@hotmail.com; www.africatours.ly*).

FURTHER INFORMATION
A Tourist in the Arab Spring Tom Chesshyre (Bradt Travel Guides)
Limited info at www.lonelyplanet.com/libya

MALAWI

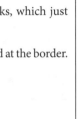

CAPITAL Lilongwe

LANGUAGE English and Chichewa

INTERNATIONAL TELEPHONE CODE +265

CURRENCY AND RATE Malawi kwacha (MWK); US$1 = MWK422

RED TAPE None of any significance. There are occasional roadblocks, which just check vehicle particulars and your travel itinerary.

Visas Most nationalities do not require visas. A visitor's stamp is issued at the border.

African embassies
www.wawamalawi.com/embassylist
www.embassypages.com/malawi

DRIVING AND ROADS Drive on the left. Roads throughout Malawi are generally in good condition, but there is surprisingly little traffic, especially in the north of the country.

Fuel costs Diesel: US$1.81; petrol: US$1.87 per litre.

CLIMATE The climate in Malawi is generally very pleasant. The rainy season is from November to March, when it can be quite grey and overcast some days.

HIGHLIGHTS The main highlight is of course the long lake, with quite a few pleasant beaches, specifically Chitimba, Nkhata Bay, Chintheche, Mangochi and Senga Bay. However, there is a very high risk of contracting bilharzia if you go swimming in its alluring waters. Close to the lake is the Nyika Plateau and colonial Livingstonia. Further south are the Zomba Plateau, Liwonde National Park with an array of wildlife, and Mount Mulanje.

WHERE TO STAY
Lilongwe The **Mabuya Camp** (e *bookings@mabuyacamp.com; www.mabuyacamp. com*) is a good place to meet other travellers and get a feel for what to see in Malawi. The cost is around US$6–12 per person. Also check out **Barefoot Safaris Lodge Campsite**, 10km from town, which costs US$10 per person. Other places are **Annie's Coffee Pot** and **James' Joint** backpackers.

Karonga On the beachfront is the large compound, with some shade, of the **Mafwa Lakeshore Lodge and Campsite**. Camping costs US$6.

Chitimba There are many places: **Hakuna Matata Campsite** (☏ *+265 881 262 338;* e *hakunamatata.chitimba@gmail.com*) is below the escarpment on the beach. It has sheltered cooking, light on the site and good grassy areas. Camping is US$9 per person plus vehicle, and the electricity charge is US$2 per night. **Chitimba Beach Campsite** (e *camp@chitimba.com*) is adjacent to Hakuna Matata. Facilities include potable water, bar, restaurant, internet, beach volleyball, a laundry service, an organised village walk with a visit to the witch doctor, wood carving lessons, pig farm visits and trips to Livingstonia. Camping is US$4 per person plus vehicle; upgrades to rooms or dorms are available. Other places include **Mdokera Beach**, **Namiashi Resort**, **Florence Resthouse** with camping, **Mayuni Safari Camp** and **Ngara Resort**, also with camping. **Sangilo Eco Lodge** is about 18km north of Chitimba but is really accommodation/lodge focused. To get to the Eco Lodge you have to follow the road through a small village and then head down a very steep hill; it's best to do it in low range gear. Camping is US$6 per person.

Livingstonia During the rainy season, the road up from Chitimba was bad. It is apparently better to get there from Rumphi from the south. The **Lukwe Permaculture Camp**, an eco-friendly campsite, is reported to be a good place to stay.

Nyika Park There is a camping area near the expensive Chelinda Camp chalet complex. US$6 per person.

Nkhata Bay Try **The Big Blue** for camping, also **Butterfly Lodge** and **Njaya Lodge and camp**. The **Mayoka Village** is a picturesque place with pleasant rooms.

Kasungu National Park Stay at **Lifupa Lodge** with camping for US$5 per person.

Nkhotakota In town the **Special Pick and Pay Resthouse** has camping; south of town are **Sani Beach Resort** and **Nkhotakota Safari Lodge**, both with camping. In the nearby wildlife reserve are **Bua River Camp** and **Chipata Camp**, and further south is **Ngala Beach Lodge**.

Chintheche Kande Beach has improved and become the **Kande Beach Resort** (*www.kandebeach.com*). There are beach chalets and en-suite doubles. Camping is US$5 per person. Others with camping include **Chintheche Rest Camp**, **Nkhwazi Lodge**, **Kaniya Cottage** and **Flame Tree Lodge**, **Sambani Lodge** and **London Lodge**. South are two excellent spots at **Nkhawazi Lodge** and **Makuzi Beach**.

Mzuzu The **Mzoozoozoo** is a pleasant hostel with camping. The welcoming **Pine Tree Lodge** B&B is 3km along the Nkhata Bay road, and has rooms from US$40. In nearby Nyika National Park camping is available at the **Chelinda Campsite**.

Salima Options here are **Steps Campsite** and **Hippo Hide Resthouse**.

Senga Bay Rather hard to find, but just before 'town', is **Cool Runnings**. It's signposted by a smiley-face logo in places and is a shady, grassy campsite with cottages if you prefer, and lakeside restaurant. There are several other places with camping, so take your pick from **Wheelhouse Marina**, **Carolina Resort**, **Baobab**, **Steps Rest Camp**, **Sangalani** and **Tom's Bar**.

Mangochi North of Mangochi are a number of places to stay. They include **Nkopola Lodge** and **Palm Beach Resort**.

Cape Maclear There is plenty of accommodation along the beachfront. Look for **Malambe Camp**, **Emanuel's**, **Fat Monkey**, **Gaia Lodge** or **Steven's Place**. For a quieter alternative, particularly if you are bringing a vehicle, try the **Golden Sands Rest Camp**. Camping costs US$4 per person. You should expect to party at Cape Maclear. Bilharzia and malaria are both rampant in this area.

Blantyre On Mulomba Place is **Doogle's,** a great place with a good atmosphere, bar, food and internet service; camping costs US$4 per person. The area outside is not safe at night, but there's no need to leave the premises. Otherwise try the **Limbe Country Club** further out to the east.

Liwonde/Liwonde National Park Near town is Shire Camp. Within the park, the best place to stay is **Chinguni Hills Campsite** for US$5 each. Otherwise there is the popular **Mvu Lodge and Camp** which has a restaurant and open-plan bar overlooking the river. Camping costs US$10 for two and they can also arrange boat rides on the river.

Zomba Plateau The Zomba Plateau is in the cooler highlands with great hiking opportunities. You will need to find secure parking if hiking up to the plateau. The **Chitinji Campsite** on the top of the plateau is run by the local community and will cost you next to nothing. Also try the **Forest Campsite** or **Zomba Forest Lodge** on the lower slopes, accessed by a dirt road.

Mount Mulanje Camping at the **Mulanje Golf Club**, if still possible, is about US$6 per person, or try the **Likhubula Forest Lodge**.

OTHER Long ago, if you were a long-haired man, it was sheared off at the border there and then. Fortunately Malawi is now a relaxed country in which to travel. Do not get caught with the local grass, known as 'Malawi Gold', as the police are clamping down on users and dealers. In some campsites you will find notes on signboards saying 'Hi, I am currently in jail for carrying drugs. I really just need somebody to talk to.' You have been warned.

Remember the **high risk of bilharzia** in the beautiful blue waters of the lake; be very wary of swimming. The lake areas are also **malarial zones**, so take precautions with nets and mosquito repellents; keep the tablets going and cover up fast after dusk!

FURTHER INFORMATION
Malawi Philip Briggs (Bradt Travel Guides)
More campsites at www.worldtravelshop.biz/overland/malawi-campsites-gps

A–Z Africa Country Guide   MALAWI

9

MALI

WARNING! Following the French 'rescue' of Mali, it is not known where a safe line can be drawn. We would guess that anywhere south of Mopti is OK, but of course random terrorist acts could persist. The north should be avoided and anyone wanting to get to Timbuktu (and back again!) should listen to local advice and travel warnings.

CAPITAL Bamako

LANGUAGE French

INTERNATIONAL TELEPHONE CODE +223

CURRENCY AND RATE West African franc (CFA); US$1 = CFA478

RED TAPE Tourism had become quite important to the economy in Mali and it is to be hoped that visitors will return to this fantastic country.

Visas Visas are required for all. There is no Mali embassy in Britain, so it is better to get the visa in Africa. Visas were being issued at the border, but you'd better check beforehand. Registering with the police does not seem to be necessary any more, but check the current status with other travellers. Vaccination certificates are obligatory.

African embassies
http://embassy.goabroad.com/embassies-in/mali
www.embassypages.com/mali

DRIVING AND ROADS Drive on the right. The main road between Bamako and Gao through Mopti is mostly good with a few variable sections. The exciting but very corrugated desert piste from Douentza to Timbuktu will shake your bones to bits! The very unsafe northern track to Gao is lonely and very sandy. The roads into Senegal and Mauritania are now finished and sealed. The last section to Kayes from Bamako is a bit pot-holed. The road south to Kankan in Guinea should be done!

Fuel costs Diesel: US$1.56; petrol: US$1.77 per litre. Carry extra supplies in case of shortages on desert routes, including to Timbuktu (fuel can normally be obtained in Douentza and Timbuktu itself).

CLIMATE Mali spans the desert and Sahel, creating differences across the country. The three main seasons are the rainy season from June to September/October, the cool dry season from October/November to February, and the hot dry season from March to June. The *harmattan*, sand-laden winds, blow from January through March.

HIGHLIGHTS Mali is one of the highlights of west Africa. It has everything that encapsulates Africa: colourful markets and people, deserts, mud architecture, river life and dramatic escarpments. Bamako has great bustling markets. Segou, Djenné and Mopti have traditional mud-brick architecture and mosques – the one at Djenné is particularly spectacular. The Bandiagara Escarpment in the Dogon country is a

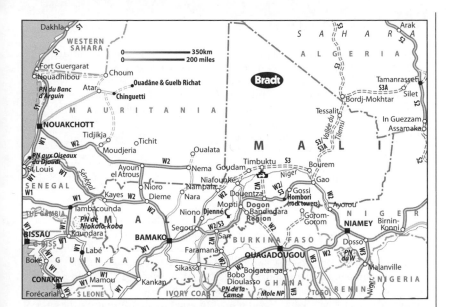

cultural feast, with some trekking. Timbuktu and Gao (if safe), on the edge of the Sahara, are famous for their history. Getting to Timbuktu and, unlike many of the early explorers, getting back again, should be a memorable journey, when safe again.

WHERE TO STAY

Bamako Just over the bridge to the south in the Badalabougou district of Bamako is the popular **Sleeping Camel Hotel** (↘ *78 17 53 65; www.thesleepingcamel.com*): camping US$6 per person, double room US$28. Camping at the **Auberge Djamilla** (*www.aubergedjamilla.com*) south of the river not far from the old bridge (to the south) in their pleasant garden is fine, but it's often noisy with 'car sellers', and costs US$12 for two.

Also south of the river on the way to Segou with a nice shady garden is **Hôtel Les Colibris** (↘ *20 22 66 37 or 20 23 76 43; www.hotelcolibris.com*) which charges US$45 or more for a bungalow.

A newish hotel along the river (also on the south side) is **Bamako Plage** (*www.hotelbamakoplage.com*). It has large grounds, an outdoor swimming pool, around 15 self-contained huts and plenty of parking space – give it a try.

If you're coming from Kankan late in the day and don't want to face the chaos in Bamako, there are now several campments in Sibi below some amazingly beautiful rocky outcrops. **Auberge de L'Arch** (↘ *76 29 06 37*) is one of the nicest.

The very pleasant **Campement Kangaba** is 18km from Bamako (*3e Pont (third bridge) Yirimadi*; ↘ *76 40 30 37/78 35 13 67; www.lecampment.com*). It is also a nice place for overlanders, but food and drink are a little pricey. Now that Bamako has three bridges over the Niger River, the campement is a lot closer to the centre. The turn-off is just before the police check (on the left) if you are going towards Segou. They are roughly 3–5km along this dirt road. US$14 for two.

Bougouni On the southwest side of town is **Hôtel Piedmont**. Head south along a good tar road from the roundabout with a fuel station; this is out of the town centre on the Bamako road. Rooms and sloping camping space here.

Selingue Look for **Hôtel Woloni** – around US$60 for a self-contained hut.

Segou The **Hôtel L'Auberge**, a popular watering hole in Segou, has parking in its annexe. They also run the **Hôtel de l'Independence** just out of town on the road to Mopti, which has secure parking, with camping possible (US$12 for two) and rooms from US$25. Also check **Hotel Djoliba** (✆ *21 32 15 72/080/659; www.hotel-djoliba-segou.com*) – it's a three-minute walk from Hotel L'Auberge.

Bla A small OK dirt road leads to a campement close to the Bani River.

San Camping is allowed at the **Hôtel/Campement Teriya** for US$6 per person. Also before town from Segou is the **Hôtel Santoro**, which has a pool and a little space to camp if you don't want a room.

Djenné The best and almost the only place to stay is **Hotel Djenné Djenno** (*www.hoteldjennedjenno.com or http://djennedjenno.blogspot.com*), at US$52 for a double room. It's not really aimed at campers, but overlanders can camp with limited facilities for US$6 per person. Campers are expected to eat and drink in the hotel restaurant and bar. Dinner is a fixed three-course menu for US$13, and breakfast with real coffee and homemade jams costs US$5. No cooking in the garden! You can also camp at **Chez Baba** near the main market for US$6, and on the roof of **Hôtel Faguibine** out of town.

Mopti Other than being an impressive town, Mopti is the gateway to the Dogon country. The old favourite in town, the **Campement Hôtel du Mopti**, is still there, but it's now smack in the middle of a noisy intersection area. It's the only real camping option if you want to be in town, though. There is also the **Hôtel Ya Pas de Problème**, but the on-street parking is not good. **Hôtel Kanaga** is the plush super-deluxe spot in town, with parking, and for more luxurious offerings there are **La Maison Rouge** (✆ *77 76 81 51; http://lesmaisonsdumali.com*) and **Hotel Ambedejele** (✆ *21 42 10 31; www.ambedjelehotel.com*). The latter is located between Sevaré and Mopti, but closer to Sevaré.

Sevaré Sevaré can be used as a base for Mopti. An excellent option for overlanders is the friendly **Hôtel Via Via**, with camping in a pleasant courtyard, rooms and a great restaurant.

Dogon country Following the recent security issues in Mali, check the website *www.dogoncountry.com* for the latest information.

Bandiagara Before town is the **Auberge Toguna** with camping from US$4. **Hôtel Le Village** also has space for camping. **Hotel La Falaise** is the nicest place to stay in Bandiagara and they also have a swimming pool (✉ *contact@hotel-la-falaise.net; www.hotel-lafalaise-mali.com*). They don't have much room for camping (only on the roof) but they have reasonably priced en-suite rooms with both fan or air-con (average price US$50) for two people.

Sangha Campement Also known as La Guina, the **Hôtel Sangha** is a relaxing place with a garden. The **Gîte de la Femme Dogon** is another pleasant spot. Le Grand Castor Dogon Auberge is also a possibility.

Bankass Look for the **Hôtel Les Arbres** with camping in the garden, as well as the **Campement Hogon**. The nicest place to stay is **Hotel Nommo** (✆ *79 25 60 86*). Rooms from US$25.

Koro There are said to be three different hotels/campements here according to the website *www.dogoncountry.com*. Check for the latest information.

Dogon trekking All fees, including accommodation, should be arranged with your guide beforehand. Meals are not included, but costs are minimal. Accommodation is a mattress on the roof, a wonderful experience as you hear the village sounds, or in village campements (US$3–5 plus tax of US$1). Sleeping fees depend on which campement you choose; the north (above Sangha) is typically more expensive than the rest of Dogon. Take some time in choosing your guide and in negotiating the fees. You will initially be hassled, but once a guide has been chosen, the rest should disappear. There is a guides' association in Bandiagara and Sangha (the association in Sangha is at the Sangha Campement, so not hard to find), with a list of qualified guides. Guide fees start from US$20 plus negotiable daily costs. For porters, allow US$5–10 per day.

Douentza Unfortunately, at the time of writing, Douentza is definitely a no-go area for travellers. For when things improve, **Chez Jerome** (N 15° 00.555, W 02° 56.777) was the most efficient place before the troubles, offering fixed nomad tents and camping, with good open-air showers, from US$12. Across the road was the **Auberge Gourma** with camping for US$6 per person. **Campement Hogon** was another possibility. The **Hôtel Falaise** west of town had a great garden for campers.

Hombori Also unsafe at the time of writing, the **Campement Tondako** had a pleasant compound, thatched huts and a restaurant serving excellent local food (camping US$6 for two). Others were **Campement Mangou Bagni** and **Campement Kaga Tondo/Chez Lelele**. They used to organise elephant-tracking safaris. Out of town 13km, below the fantastic Hand of Fatima outcrop, was the rustic **Campement Manyi**.

Gossi Gossi had the basic **Gossi Campement** for those hoping to locate the elephants of the Gourma area. The region is unsafe now.

Gao Before the Islamist invasion the following existed: Sahara Passion, Camping Euro, Camping Bangu, Campement Yarg, Camping Tin Fadimata and Campement Tila Fanso.

Bambara Maounde On the way to Timbuktu there was a rustic campement here.

Timbuktu The wonderfully renovated traditional **Auberge Le Caravanserail** had a sandy yard for campers (US$12 for two). It hopes to reopen soon. It's on the corner of rues 164/139, west of the road into town from the Niger ferry, a couple of sandy streets over and about 0.5km south of the post office. Suitable for all budgets and with safe vehicle parking, it also has beautiful rooms and a superb restaurant. If it's full you will probably have to try the **Hôtel Bouctou** for camping and a secure parking area. The hard-to-find **Sahara Passion** (*www.hotelsaharapassion.com*) is hiding in the back streets in the north of town. On the south side of the Niger River, about 35km south in Tiboraghene, is **Campement Ténéré**, for those stuck here after ferry hours. If you are camping in the bush, be sure to keep some distance from settlements, or the police may disturb you. Other more upmarket hotels in Timbuktu are **Hôtel La Maison, Hôtel Colombe** and **Hôtel du Desert** near the Auberge Le Caravanserail. **Campement Touristique du Mora** is apparently another choice, 5km west on the Goudam road.

Niono du Sahel The town lies in a risky area now. Previously for those coming from or going to Mauritania, this was the first or last chance for a beer. Well away from the scruffy centre, 2km west along the dusty sandy little road beside the hotel and across a riverbed, is the **Centre de Djamana** complex and radio station. Parking was outside in the street, but it seemed safe enough.

OTHER Sadly, armed rebels still hide out (after the French army arrived) in northern Mali, particularly in the Adra des Iforhas region north of Kidal. Timbuktu, Douentza and Hombori are unsafe at the time of writing. All the northern border areas are insecure, so find out what the latest status is. Bamako is a large place these days, with the usual petty crime, vendors, cars, people and animals using every part of the road and pavement. Ideally it's best to walk everywhere rather than drive, but distances are great. Don't expect to escape the attention of tourist guides, touts and onlookers these days. In town you should be fairly safe parking outside the Burkina Faso embassy north of the new bridge. If you need parts for your Land Rover, Prestige Motors is south of the river; it is partly signposted but you may have to ask the way and it may only have limited spares for older models.

For organised trips contact Karen at Toguna Adventure Tours in Bamako (m 02 29 53 66/69; m 06 21 50 79; e *togunaadventure@afribonemali.net; www.togunaadventuretours.com*) who keeps us regularly updated.

FURTHER INFORMATION
Mali Ross Velton (Bradt Travel Guides)
www.togunaadventuretours.com

MAURITANIA

WARNING! There is a risk to travellers of kidnapping, so keep abreast of the latest advice and travel websites. That said, there are numerous security check-posts on the one-day transit between Nouadhibou and Nouakchott. Perhaps the risk is worth considering, since the direct transit is short and it's the only serious problem between Tangier and Cape Town – apart from Angola visa issues. Avoid the region around Chinguetti now.

CAPITAL Nouakchott

LANGUAGE Arabic

INTERNATIONAL TELEPHONE CODE +222

CURRENCY AND RATE Ouguiya (MRO); US$1 = MRO291

RED TAPE You will probably have to buy insurance at the border, even if you have valid insurance for west Africa. Buy it in Nouadhibou if you can, as it is far less expensive than at the border. For ten days, insurance will cost around 9,500 ouguiyas. Customs will charge a 'tax', so have some small notes. Some of the desert settlements impose a 'right of passage tax' on visitors. Before crossing at Diama you will probably need to pay 4,000 ouguiyas to drive through the national park on the Mauritanian side. At the border you might get landed with a bill for 6,000 ouguiyas in taxes on the Mauritanian side. Alcohol is not permitted, except at expensive European restaurants in Nouakchott.

Visas Visas are required for all and are not available at borders. Going south, get the visa in Rabat, Morocco, at 6 rue Thami Lamdawar, Rabat-Souissi (N 33° 58.800, W 06° 49.900). The embassy is normally open five days a week and issues visas within a day. It might be necessary to arrive well before opening time (07.45) as doors close early (09.00). Visa collection is at 14.30. For added speed, consider using a Mr fix-it for MAD10. Visas cost of US$40 each for 30 days. You need two photos and one photocopy of your passport and entry stamp. There is also an embassy in Bamako.

African embassies
http://embassy.goabroad.com/embassies-in/mauritania
www.embassypages.com/mauritania

DRIVING AND ROADS Drive on the right. Roads are generally in good condition on all major routes. Deterioration has been reported in the south towards Senegal. Watch out for sand drifts over the roads. To avoid possible old landmines, keep on the south side of the railway tracks from Nouadhibou to Choum and Atar. Around Atar some tracks are very rocky. The Saharan pistes are very remote between Oualata and Tichit, Chinguetti and Tidjikja, so taking a guide is a good plan. Do not drive alone in these areas, even when it is considered safe.

Fuel costs Diesel: US$1.23; petrol: US$1.44 per litre.

CLIMATE Most of the country has a true desert climate, very dry and extremely hot throughout the year. The far south has occasional rains.

HIGHLIGHTS Most travellers cross through Mauritania from Morocco to Senegal direct or vice versa. The Parc National du Banc d'Arguin has spectacular birdlife. The best time to visit the park is during the nesting period from April to July and October to January. The park is quite hard to get to, but information can be obtained from the park's head office in Nouadhibou. You will need to take a guide. Also noted but **currently unsafe** is the Adrar region around Atar, with its rocky plateaux and the Terjit oasis. The Chinguetti and Ouadâne oases are beautiful and surreal, being partially abandoned. Further south and also in a remote, dangerous area are the old oasis towns of Tidjikja, Rachid and Tichit. Oualata, with its intriguing houses, was another exciting sight near the Malian border, but check the security situation before you go.

WHERE TO STAY Before the kidnappings, desert sleeping was the best option.

Nouakchott Convenient and pleasant is **La Nouvelle Auberge** (US$12 for two) west of the main street near a fuel station and roundabout. Camping is also possible at the **Auberge Menata** (N 18° 05.606, W 15° 58.634) in a quiet but central street, which has parking space. The shady Menata has hot showers and toilets but they aren't cleaned that regularly. There is a kitchen, a fridge-freezer, every utensil under the sun and resident cockroaches. There's also Wi-Fi and a shop next door. Security is good, but people come here to sell stuff or beg. Camping is US$17 for two plus a car. Former owner Olivia has sold the place. Her new *auberge* (B&B) is just up the road. This is not an overlanding place but a charming bougainvillea-filled

guesthouse with a restaurant – **Maison d'hôtes Jeloua** (*www.escales-mauritanie.com*). Also popular was the **Auberge du Sahara** (*www.auberge-sahara.fr*) east of the Stade Olympique on the road north to Nouadhibou. **Auberge Awkar** is another suitable place on offer nearby. All these places also have rooms.

Nouadhibou Well south past the main area of town is **Camping Chez Abba** (N 20° 54.524, W 17° 03.222). Be warned that the hot showers have toilets within. The kitchen is handy but not very clean. It's fairly secure, except for the fact that it is also an overnight stop for haulage trucks. It costs from US$6 per person. For a treat at a colonial-style retreat, try **Hôtel El Jazira**.

Gare du Nord At km240 between Nouadhibou and Nouakchott is a fuel station/tyre-repair restaurant/shop/mosque, with camping permitted if you have to stop.

Parc National du Banc d'Arguin The national park is great for wild camping, as it is generally deserted. Guides are optional. Make sure you get the 'Guide de voyage au Parc National du Banc d'Arguin' map/guide with GPS for the sights when you pay your entrance fee: 2,400 ouguiyas each to stay as long as you want.

Atar Sadly this is not safe these days. In case of miracles, we mention **Camping Bab Sahara**. Otherwise try the **Toile Maure Campement**, 2km or so out of town.

Chinguetti Before the threats, the **Auberge la Rose des Sables** was pleasant and had been going for years. Other places were **Auberge des Caravanes** and **Le Maure Bleu**.

Ayoun el Atrous Avoid this area until the situation is safe again. The same advice applies to Kiffa and Boutilimit.

Kiffa The friendly **Hôtel El Emel** had camping in its pleasant courtyard for US$13. It was just west of town on the road out. Rooms, meals and drinks were available.

Boutilimit The **Auberge Touristique** is a spacious, pleasant complex with bungalows under thatch on the east side of the main road northwards from the centre.

Wild camping Here are some recent suggestions from Simon and Kate and their dog Max. Remember the kidnap threats, though!

Off the road to Nouakchott Old iron ore workings (N 20° 53.474, W 16° 11.737). Fairly windy.

South of Tessot Le Parc National du Banc d'Arguin, (N 19° 37.454, W 16° 21.543). Lots of wildlife.

Baie Saint Jean Northeast of Mamghar, Le Parc National du Banc d'Arguin (N 19° 31.263, W 16° 17.215). Sheltered in the hills next to the bay.

Dunes off the beach road to Nouakchott Between Nouamghar and el-Mhaijarat (see R1 in the book *Sahara Overland* by Chris Scott) (N 19° 12.488, W 16° 23.154). Make sure you park quite a way off the road, as it is extremely busy when the tide is low.

Behind beach dunes There is a place where you can get well and truly stuck for a while off the piste to the Diamma crossing to Senegal, near Tiguent (N 17° 5.264, W 16° 14.761).

Off the N2 Camp among some acacia trees and camels about 50km from the border (N 20° 40.699, W 16° 03.611).

OTHER The clean Moroccan mechanic-staffed BMW/Land Rover dealer in the southwest quarter of Nouakchott is liable to overcharge. The sandy workshops in the Ksar area are probably just as good if you are desperate. Toyota has a centre near Camping Abba in Nouadhibou.

According to Simon, Kate and Max (the expert), dog food can be bought at the Mauri Centre, about 20 minutes north of the Auberge Menata at the junction of Avenue du General de Gaulle and Avenue du Palais des Congres. Librairie Vents du Sud on Avenue Kennedy is an excellent bookshop with a wide range of works by Mauritanian authors, books about Mauritania, the latest J K Rowlings in French, and newspapers, magazines, wrapping paper, cards and art materials.

Get at least 20 photocopies of personal details/photo page and your Mauritanian visa/entry stamp page of your passport to hand out to police.

FURTHER INFORMATION
There is dated info in *West Africa* (Rough Guides)
Check www.lonelyplanet.com/thorntree for travellers' updates.

MOROCCO

CAPITAL Rabat

LANGUAGE Arabic

INTERNATIONAL TELEPHONE CODE +212

CURRENCY AND RATE Dirham (MAD); US$1 = MAD8.18

9

RED TAPE Officials are often extremely helpful and kind. It is advisable to have several copies of the *Personal details* document in *Appendix 2*, page 346, plus copies of your passport, Moroccan entrance stamp and driving licence, as these are required at roadblocks in Morocco and Western Sahara. Alternatively, take a copy of your passport photo page, write all the relevant information on it, then make a multitude of copies of this.

Be sure to **STOP** at all police road check-posts at the 'Halte Gendarmerie' signs, or they may fine you. **Don't move on** until they wave at you to do so.

Visas Most visitors to Morocco do not require visas and can remain in Morocco for 90 days after entry. There are some exceptions to this rule (Israel, South Africa and others), so check before travelling.

African embassies
http://embassy.goabroad.com/embassies-in/morocco
www.embassyworld.com
www.embassypages.com/morocco

DRIVING AND ROADS Drive on the right. Roads are generally in good condition on all major routes, apart from the more remote desert tracks.

Fuel costs Diesel: US$1.10; petrol: US$1.53 per litre. In Tantan and further south, the fuel is almost half price.

CLIMATE Morocco has a variety of climates: Mediterranean in the north, Atlantic in the west, continental in the interior and desert in the south. The Atlas Mountains can get very cold for much of the year outside the summer months. Rain is likely in winter and heavy snow is probable in the mountains.

HIGHLIGHTS The Atlas Mountains are famous for their Berber villages and stunning landscapes, including the Todra Gorge. The historical towns are Tangier, Fès, Meknès, Chefchaouen and Marrakech. The famous Djemaa el-Fna, a huge square in the old city of Marrakech, comes to life in the early afternoon. Between Ouarzazate and Zagora is the Road of the Kasbahs, with fortified mud citadels. Check out the massive citadel of Ait Benhaddou. The fringes of the Sahara in the south offer good, if limited, off-road opportunities. The coastline includes the cities of Casablanca, with some Art-Deco buildings, and Rabat, famous for its magnificent architecture and lack of tourists. Essaouira and Taroudannt are two other places of interest.

WHERE TO STAY Sometimes it is more convenient to stay in towns than on the outskirts, where many campsites have retreated. There are hundreds of pensions available in all major towns; parking is the main snag as there are not so many guarded places. A double room will cost around US$20–40. Most serve breakfast. Another speciality of Morocco is the *riad*, a town house usually located within the old medinas. Rooms are invariably tastefully decorated around quadrangles and the owners are the congenial hosts. Again, parking is the main difficulty with these places. Country campsites are often reasonably convenient, though these days many of them have been invaded by white campervans escaping the winter cold in Europe. Check www.travel-in-morocco.com/modules/smartcamping for more information.

Tangier Look for **Camping Miramonte** in a pleasant green area about 3km west of town. There is a rumour, though, that it may be closed in winter.

Tetouan Near the coast at Martil you will find the pleasant **Camping Al Boustane**. It is just north along the coast from the centre; US$7 for two.

Chefchaouen Famous for its supply of hashish, this town in the Rif Mountains is a relaxing place. The town has a Hispanic look of whitewashed houses and tiled roofs. The only campsite is **Camping Municipal** about 3km from the centre; it has Wi-Fi, and costs US$10 for two. There are many budget hotels and most serve delicious green tea.

Ouazzane The **Motel Rif Camping** is on the east side of the main road near the town, 4km south.

Fès This is the oldest imperial city in Morocco. There are two camping options – **Camping Diamant Vert**, about 8km out on the south side, with a limited bus service into town, and the more expensive, but only 4km out, **Camping International**.

Meknès Look for **Camping Agdal** just near the Ville Imperial. It's convenient, quiet, secure and full of campervans. Volubilis, the old Roman ruins, are close to Meknès.

Asilah Campervans (and any other riff-raff like Land Rovers!) are allowed to park outside the city walls at a designated spot. A fee of US$3 is charged. The two campsites appear to be closed in winter. There are no toilet or washing facilities here, but there is a restaurant nearby.

Rabat Camping at Sale Beach has gone. **Camping Gambusias** at **Skhirat** (N 33° 53.239, W 7° 00.764) is a very pleasant, green, grassy campsite attached to a hotel on the way to Casablanca; no hot showers but really nice. The man at reception was a perfect gentleman as well. It costs US$11 for two. This place is a suitable base for getting the Mauritanian visas in Rabat. In town for a splurge, try the **Riad Dar al Batoul** (e *albatoul@menara.ma; www.riadbatoul.com*), but check that parking is safe.

Casablanca The only camping option was way out of town on the road to El-Jadida, called **Camping de l'Oasis**. Driving around here is a nightmare and most people continue on the motorway to Marrakech.

Atlas Mountains On the way across the mountains is Telouet, just east of Tizi-N-Tichka, where you will find **Camping Auberge Tasga**. On the southern side is the Dadès Gorge at Boumalne, with the **Auberge le Soleil Bleu**. There are many

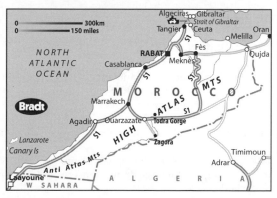

nearby Berber villages and a walk here is worthwhile. Along the gorge look for **Camping d'Ait Oudina**, **Camping La Gazelle du Dadès** and **Camping Berbère de la Montagne**. Try **Camping Taghya** in Dades Gorge (N 31° 32.976, W 05° 54.650); US$6. Camping in the gorges can be dangerous after rain and is not secure.

Tinerhir For Todra Gorge there is a good campsite at Tinerhir called **Camping Ourti**. Camping is also possible at **Camping Soleil** and **Auberge Atlas Camping** (N 31° 33.204, W 05° 35.007), one of the best campsites with friendly, helpful staff. It has hot showers, clean toilets (with toilet roll), a washing machine, washing-up area, proper enclosed waste disposal area and Wi-Fi. The quiet riverside setting next to the palmerie is superb. For a room, try the **Hôtel Tomboctou** (*www. hoteltomboctou.com*).

Marrakech About 10km out of town off the main road from Casablanca is **Camping Le Relais de Marrakech**. It has clean facilities that work, large nomad tents available, tasty food and a swimming pool. There's even a beauty salon and a doggie shower! It's off to the west of the main road; take the Safi road then turn off on a small road to the right. Close by, but right on the noisy main road, are **Camping Ferdaous** and **Camping International**. There are many *riads* in the old medina area and other cheaper hotels, but parking your precious vehicle in a guarded car park some distance away will be your main concern.

Essaouira On the south side are **Camping de la Plage**, **Camping des Olives** and **Camping Sidi Magdoul**. Further out, look for **Camping Le Calm**. Down the coast to Kaouka is **Camping Kaouka** (N 31° 21.061, W 09° 47.706), which comes highly recommended. There are decent-sized pitches bordered by rosemary bushes and trees, hot and clean showers and toilets, and a washing-up area.

Agadir The town's **Municipal Camping** site is popular with campervan retirees from Europe. It's OK, if a little crowded.

Ouarzazate On the road to Tinerhir is **Campsite Municipal** just outside town, east of the big kasbah but within walking distance. Camping costs US$7 per vehicle. There is also a place to camp 14km north of town near the Ait Benhaddou turn-off. Not cheap but with secure parking south of the oued (riverbed) is the amazing **Kasbah Dar Daif** (e *contact@dardaif.ma; www.dardaif.ma*). They are also very helpful if you need any vehicle repairs. From US$85 per double for a splurge.

Ait Benhaddo There are a couple of small sites for campers.

Taroudannt Riad El Aissi (✎ *0663 030792; www.riadelaissi.com*) is 3km from town.

Tata Try the **Municipal Campsite** in the centre, which is fine for US$6 per car. For a taste of luxury, take a room at the atmospheric **Maison d'Hôtes Dar Infiane**, south of town in a palmerie.

Akka There is a camping place, **4x4 Campers**, south of town on the west side.

Zagora There are several designated campsites here with shady palm trees. These include **Camping Auberge Prends ton Temps**, **Camping Auberge Les Jardins** and several others.

Agdz A superbly atmospheric place, the **Kasbah de la Palmeraie** offers not only camping in the palmerie but also rooms in the kasbah. It's north of the main plaza along a rough road.

Erfoud and Merzouga There is camping near the Oued Ziz, on the left before town if you're coming from Errachidia. For a big splurge, book into **Hotel Kasbah Tizimi** (*www.kasbahtizimi.com*), which has good food and costs upwards of US$50 for a double room. In Merzouga there are many places to stay, with a few offering fixed tents as well as rooms. Try **Kasbah Mohayut**, **Camping l'Oasis** or **Camping Ocean des Dunes** for normal camping.

Tiznit The town has a campsite on the north side.

Guelmime There is one campsite before town on the right if coming from Agadir.

Fort Bou Jerif (*www.boujerif.com*) This fabulous place is about 40km west of Guelmime, off the road south to Laayoune. Prices from US$13 with your own tent. Sample the camel tajine for a real treat!

For places further south, see *Western Sahara*, page 321.

OTHER To ease the hassle factor from the hashish touts, it is best to dress conservatively and respect the culture, although you will see tourists running around with next to nothing on. Hashish is illegal and the fines for being caught with it are heavy. Beware of car-based hash sellers who block roads. Campervans are absolutely everywhere.

And, to repeat, the Mauritanian embassy in Rabat is at 6 rue Thami Lamdawar, Rabat-Souissi (N 33° 58.800, W 06° 49.900). Get it here!

FURTHER INFORMATION
Morocco (Rough Guides)

MOZAMBIQUE

CAPITAL Maputo

LANGUAGE Portuguese

INTERNATIONAL TELEPHONE CODE +258

CURRENCY AND RATE New metacal (MZN); US$1 = MZN30.95. The plural of metacal is metacais.

RED TAPE Traffic officials at roadblocks in Mozambique were once on the make. We had no problems but were frequently asked if we had two warning triangles, which we did. More likely now is that officials at roadblocks want to practise their language skills and have a quick English lesson – 'Hello, how are you? Where are you going?'

Visas Visas are required for all except South Africans. You also have to pay a border tax of US$10. It is better to pay in South African rand if you are coming in that way, as it is cheaper than paying in metacais. Visas may be issued at the border, but don't bank on it.

African embassies

http://embassy.goabroad.com/embassies-in/mozambique
http://mz.embassyinformation.com

DRIVING AND ROADS Drive on the left. The main north–south highway through Tete, Beira and Maputo is mostly OK, but some sections are poor. The state of roads in the north is less predictable. There is very little traffic and there are not many fuel stations between the main towns. Carry enough fuel and water. (Make sure your vehicle insurance is valid; you will probably have to buy more at the border anyway.)

Fuel costs Diesel: US$1.07; petrol: US$1.38 per litre.

CLIMATE The dry season is from April to September, when it is cool and pleasant. The wet season is from October/November to March, when it is hot and humid. It is generally drier in the north.

HIGHLIGHTS Hectic Maputo still has some fine colonial buildings and good nightlife. There are some beautiful beaches on the southern coast close to Inhambane at Tofo, plus Vilanculos and the lovely islands of the Bazaruto Archipelago. The northern beaches, Pemba and Ilha do Moçambique, are more remote and less inhabited. In the central bushland is the once-popular Parque Nacional da Gorongosa.

 WHERE TO STAY

Maputo Try **Fatima's Place** (*1317 Av Mao Tse Tung*), where two vehicles can be parked in the garage, and there is a security guard at night. It costs around US$15 for a double room. Meals, drinks and loads of info are available. On the main road north of Maputo (on the west side of the road) is the spacious **Camping Casa Lisa** (*www.casalisa.co.za*). It has an excellent bar and restaurant. Camping costs from US$7 per person.

Ponta do Ouro to Belene There are a number of proper camping places along the southern coast: **Campismo Ninho**, **Ponta do Ouro Campsite**, **Ponta Malongane Resort**, **Jay's Lodge** and **Complexo Palmeiras** are some of them.

Xai Xai Camping by the beach is found at the **Xai Xai Caravan and Camping Park**; US$5 per person. **Paradise Magoo** is 35km to the north.

Inhambane Try the **Lighthouse Campsite**. Otherwise it is probably best to camp at the **Maxixe Campismo** place across the estuary on the main road. It is signposted. Ferries sometimes run infrequently, so check first.

Tofo There are quite a few places here, but access is tricky because of the rather deep soft sand around here. **Fatima's Nest** has a place with camping; it costs US$4 per person. Further along the beach is the sandy **Bamboozi 'Resort'** with camping, US$5 per person. Camping is also offered at **Turtle Cove** in Tofinho.

Vilanculos Close to the beach is the grassy, shaded **Camping Vilanculos**. It is popular with South Africans. It costs around US$8–9 per person. Another place with camping is **Baobab Beach Backpackers**. Vilanculos is a favourite spot for travellers. Day excursions can be planned to the Bazaruto Archipelago, where the diving is excellent.

Tete The best choice for camping/parking is the Indian-run **Motel Tete**. Camping costs US$6 per person. There are also some simple campsites on the north side of the river east of the big bridge.

Chimoio It's possible to camp at the windmill-style **Hotel Moinho**, which is popular for its restaurant and bar. It is out of town on the road to Beira. Camping costs US$6 per person. Also suggested is **Pink Papaya**.

Gorongosa National Park
This is beginning to redevelop and **Chitengo Safari Lodge** offers camping for US$6 per person.

Beira The only place for overland campers is the **Biques Campsite**, which charges US$4 per person.

Nampula The **Complex Bamboo** is one place to try to camp, otherwise rooms are costly.

Chocas The **Carrusca Mar** has been getting good reviews.

Ilha do Moçambique It is possible to drive across to the island, as there is a 3km bridge that joins it to the mainland. There are no camping facilities on the island, so ask one of the hoteliers if you can park in their yard. Camping is possible on the mainland at **Camping Casuarinas** at a cost of around US$4–5 each with your vehicle.

Pemba North of Ilha do Moçambique is Pemba, where you could stay for days. Try the **Nacole Jardim**, where camping is offered for US$10 each. At Wimbe Beach is **Russell's Place/Pemba Magic**. Camping costs US$6 per person. **Pembe Dive and Bush Camp** is another. Further up from Pemba, the roads become worse and the going is slow, but the whole northern area is wild and untamed.

Pangane A quiet place with camping, **Achimes Camp** and maybe **Camagamento Pangane** are pleasant. Nearby are a number of tranquil islands slowly being developed within the Quiramba National Park. Some islands have luxury resorts, while others offer cheaper places. On Ibo is **Casa Janine**; rooms cost US$15–20 and camping US$5–6, but be sure to find secure parking on the mainland.

OTHER Reports suggest that a Chinese-built bridge (known as the Unity Bridge) exists at the Mtambaswala border. Head west from Mtwara through Newala and Masasi, preferably in the dry season. We have no other information though, so before trying to take this coastal route, check the status of the border, road and bridge. This info was found on www.driveout.co.za/destinations/tanzania-mozambique.

FURTHER INFORMATION
Mozambique Philip Briggs (Bradt Travel Guides)

NAMIBIA

CAPITAL Windhoek

LANGUAGE English and Afrikaans

INTERNATIONAL TELEPHONE CODE +264

CURRENCY AND RATE Namibian dollar (NAD); US$1 = NAD10.87. The Namibian dollar has the same value as the interchangeable South African rand, which can be used for most transactions. It is best to use up Namibian dollars before leaving Namibia, because they cannot be used in South Africa.

RED TAPE Refreshingly little, but avoid the mining area around Lüderitz, as the police can be a bit overzealous. Note also that foreign-registered vehicles on a carnet now get only three months in the South African Union area, which includes South Africa, Botswana, Namibia, Swaziland and Lesotho.

Visas No visas are required by nationals of Australia, Canada, Ireland, New Zealand, South Africa, the UK, the USA, and most other southern African and western European countries.

African embassies
www.namibweb.com/namemb.htm
www.embassypages.com/namibia

DRIVING AND ROADS Drive on the left. The roads are in excellent condition except for parts of the Namib Desert, Kaokoland and Khaudum National Park. Most secondary roads are gravel/sand/dirt, but are well maintained and quite fast. Having said that, drive carefully – it would be easy to slide off if going too fast.

Fuel costs Diesel: US$1.07; petrol: US$1.04 per litre.

CLIMATE Overall the country is fairly dry. It gets quite hot in summer (October to April). Any rainfall occurs during the summer months. Winter is cool and the evenings can get quite cold. The coastal region of the Namib Desert is cool, damp and rain-free, with mist for much of the year.

HIGHLIGHTS Namibia has a long list of highlights, including Windhoek. The amazing orange/red dunes of the Namib Desert, seen at their best at Sossusvlei, are spectacular. Swakopmund and Lüderitz have relics of the German colonial period. In the northwest is Kaokoland, with its beautiful scenery and Himba people.

Then there are the national parks, including the world-famous Etosha, plus the Waterberg Plateau, the Skeleton Coast, Fish River Canyon, Kalahari Gemsbok and Namib Naukluft, all with varied wildlife. In the northeast, the Caprivi Strip strikes east across northern Botswana.

🏠 WHERE TO STAY

Windhoek A popular campsite is at **Daan Viljoen Game Park**, 18km west of town. You can pre-book at the NWR (Namibia Wildlife Resorts) in Windhoek, which handles all park bookings, or you can just turn up. Camping costs US$20+ per site. Alternatively, **Arebbusch Travel Lodge** in Olympia, on the road south to Rehoboth, charges US$10 per person to camp. In town are various backpacker/camping options, including **Cardboard Box** and **Chameleon**, which charges US$12–13 for camping and from US$20 for a double room. Other choices are **Rivendell Guest House** and **Backpacker Unite**. Out of town to the east is **Trans Kalahari Caravan Park** and to the northwest is **Elisenheim Guest Farm**. Also see www.caravanparks.com.

Swakopmund Although not as ethereal a town as Lüderitz, Swakopmund is attractive and interesting. In town try **Desert Sky Backpackers**, a well-organised place with parking. The **Amanpuri Travellers Lodge** is used by overland groups. Across the road from the Dunedin Star is the **Villa Wiess house/hostel** with a good bar. Just on the southern end of town there are **Tiger Reef Campsite** and **Alte Brücke Restcamp**. Out of town, try **El Jada Restcamp**. There are several other possibilities along the coast to the north.

Walvis Bay Camp at **Long Beach Resort** out of town to the north.

Okahandja The **Okahandja Lodge** offers campers a spot for US$7 per person. Nearby at the dam is the **Von Bach Campsite**, US$16 per site.

Spitzkoppe There is a proper site now with an ablution block. It's possible to camp amongst these amazing boulders and craggy peaks, not far north of the main Swakopmund road.

Skeleton Coast National Park/Henties Bay The **Bucks Camping Lodge** is a top-end option. There are other sites at **Mile 14** and **Jakkalsputz Campsite**. Heading north, you find **Mile 72 Campsite** and **Mile 108 Campsite**, US$10 per person. At Torra Bay is **Torra Bay Campsite** with standard rates around US$8 per site plus US$4 per person. **Springbokwasser Camp** at Springbokwasser Gate is basic but has beautiful views.

Kaokoland Facilities are developing rapidly in this region, with quite a number of good places. Brandberg, Uis/Ughab, the Organ Pipes region, Twyfelfontein, Khorixas and north along the C34 all have designated campsites and more expensive choices. Bush sleeping is, however, still a great option as you head north. At Epupa Falls you can sleep under the palm trees, or in the enclosed campsite. Owing to the influx of tourists, however, the Himba's lifestyle has been threatened. Although you may be asked for it, do not give them alcohol.

Khorixas The **Khorixas Rest Camp** can be booked through NWR, but it's not required. It has good facilities with hot showers, laundry tubs, a pool next to the bar and a restaurant that serves good meals (approx NAD80–120 for dinner). Chalets

and rooms are available. Camping is US$12–13 each. The **Aba Huab Rest Camp** is about 5km before Twyfelfontein if coming from Khorixas. It has an open sandy area for tents, a bar, hot showers and clean toilets. Camp Xaragu is another option, where camping costs US$15 per person.

Etosha National Park The gem of northern Namibia, Etosha offers lodges and camps at three main locations: **Namutoni**, **Halali** and **Okaukuejo**. The park entry fee is around US$10 per person for foreigners and US$6 per vehicle (entry to most Namibian parks costs around NAD80 per person). Camping costs US$30+ for a maximum of eight people. There are also options around the park itself to suit all pockets. Booking is advised. See also www.nwr.com.na and www.etoshanationalpark.org.

Grootfontein Look out for **Roy's Camp** out of town in a pleasant location. It's along the B8 then the D2885. Camping costs US$5–6 each. Farm walks, fresh meat and food are all available.

Ondangwa Around 10km out of town is the **Nakambale Museum and Restcamp**, a local project with cultural interest. At Ruacana Falls is the **Hippo Pools Campsite**.

Rundu You might try the **Sarasunga River Lodge**, which offers camping for US$5 per person. The **N'Kwazi Lodge** near Rundu has camping and trips across the river into Angola. Some 35km east is the clean, community-based **Mbamba Campsite** and another 50km east is **Shankara Lodge** with camping.

Caprivi Strip At Popa Falls there is camping at several places, including **Ngepi Camp** for US$7 per person, **Suclabo Lodge**, **N'Goabaca Community Campsite** and **Popa Falls Camp**. The area is developing fast and new places are being built along the strip. In the Kwando River zone are **Bumhill** and **Nambwa** campsites, **Mazambala Island Lodge** and **Camp Kwando**. Further east at Katima are **Zambezi River Lodge**, **Kalizo Lodge** and **Caprivi River Lodge** (Land Rover owners get a discount!). Finally, at the border is **Salambala Community Campsite**. For a full list, see www.linx.co.za/camps.

Gobabis The new **Goba-Goba Lodge and Rest Camp** overlooking the Black Nossob River charges around US$19 for a site.

Border with Botswana A new campsite, **Buitepos Camping/East Gate Rest Camp**, has opened on the Namibian side close to the border. It's particularly useful if you are coming from Ghanzi in Botswana, where there are no camping places, wild or otherwise, due to fencing.

Route C26 Conveniently placed are **Weissenfels Guest Farm**, where camping is US$14 per person, and **Hakos Guest Farm**, which is a cheaper option at US$7 each.

Naukluft Mountains About 10km from Bullsport on the D854 is the **Naukluft Campsite**. Another place is **Hauchabfontein Camping**, as well as more expensive rest camp options. There are various lodges such as **Capricorn** and **Kobo Kobo Mountain Lodge** for a splurge.

Namib Naukluft Park There are eight or nine designated camping areas for those who are fully independent. Book through Namib Naukluft Campsites (*www. nwr.com.na*).

Solitaire The one-horse/house town of Solitaire has a pleasant **campsite and lodge**. Their apple strudel is divine and the homemade bread superb. Camping costs US$15 for a car plus two people. Not far away, camping is also available at **Solitaire Guest Farm**.

Sesriem The **Sesriem Campsite** has some shade. It has hot showers, bar, restaurant, pool and small shop for around US$25 for a large pitch. Further out a newer option is the **Sossusvlei Campsite** and also **Footloose Camping**. Camping is not permitted at nearby Sossusvlei itself. Park entry is US$10 per person.

Aus Look for the **Klein Aus Vista and Campsite**. The campsite is about 800m further up the track past reception; there are hot showers and toilets and potable water. There are a few colour-coded walks from the campsite, and maps are available from reception. Beware of leopards and other wildlife; wear good shoes and long trousers against thorns and snakes. It's best to book in advance; contact Piet (☏ *+264 63 258116; www.klein-aus-vista.com*). Prices are around US$10 per person. The **Namib Garage Camping** is opposite the garage/shop. Ask for Karen. There's little shelter but a good size braai pit with electricity. It costs US$8 per person.

Lüderitz Lüderitz is a surreal German colonial relic set on the edge of the Namib Desert. The only place to camp is the windy **Shark Island Campground** north of town, which costs US$9 per site. Try **Lüderitz Backpackers** for less windy conditions.

Duwisib Has the castle and also the **Duwisib Campsite**; US$9 per site plus US$4 per person. **Duwisib Guest Farm** is another spot.

Helmeringhausen This is a charming one-horse/hotel town; the hotel is a great place to stop or stay, with more delicious apple strudel. **Camping** is possible here for US$20 for up to four people.

Betta Betta is also a one-house town. Coming on the desert road south from Sesriem to Helmeringhausen, there are many very expensive farm lodges. For a cheap option, try **Betta Camp**.

Keetmanshoop The town has the municipal Keetmanshoop Rest Camp, a caravan/camping park. **Quivertree Forest Restcamp** is out of town.

Grunau Camping at **Grunau Motors** is US$12 a pitch.

Fish River Canyon National Park The park has the very nice **Hobas Campsite**, costing US$20 for a site. Facilities include hot showers, good toilets, a small pool and a shop selling tinned food, snacks, bottled water, sodas and beer. Further south you can also camp at **Ai Ais Hot Springs** resort. The Fish River Canyon entrance is US$10 per person. See also www.namibian.org/travel/namibia/fish_river.html.

Close to Fish River Canyon Set amongst some ancient boulders and tastefully done is **Canyon (or Cañon) Lodge**. This is expensive and sheer luxury. More affordable is their place north of Hobas on the west side of the road, called **Cañon Roadhouse**, which has camping for US$15 per person. Another place nearby is **Koelkrans Campsite**.

OTHER Do not photograph anything remotely close to a government institution. Crime is on the increase in larger towns, but campsites have also been targeted; lock your valuables away at night.

FURTHER INFORMATION
Namibia Chris McIntyre (Bradt Travel Guides)
www.nwr.com.na

NIGER

WARNING! Tensions continue in the country, so check for the latest security information. Currently Niamey and the western areas are normally OK. East, beyond Birni N'Konni and possibly to Zinder, you will need to check. Agadez has been on the 'avoid list' but we hear that security is now a little better, so it may be worth a check, since it's a fabulous place to visit.

CAPITAL Niamey

LANGUAGE French

INTERNATIONAL TELEPHONE CODE +227

CURRENCY AND RATE West African franc (CFA); US$1 = CFA478

RED TAPE One of the friendliest countries we have travelled in, Niger has little red tape. However, if ever coming from Algeria, the border officials at Assamaka are prone to need a little something extra to do the paperwork; it is jolly hot work lifting a pen and disturbs the lethargy of the place! The old practice of getting the passport stamped in every town had all but finished, except in Arlit and places like Bilma. This is referred to as '*vu au passage*'.

Visas Visas are required for all non-Africans. They were easily obtained from the countries bordering Niger (though not perhaps Mali). You'll need one to four photos for each application. Visas could be obtained in Paris for those heading south. Vaccination certificates are obligatory. Visas are not issued at the border.

African embassies

http://embassy.goabroad.com/embassies-in/niger
www.embassypages.com/niger

DRIVING AND ROADS Drive on the right. Roads are generally in good condition, particularly along major routes: Niamey, Maradi to Zinder and via Tahoua to Agadez and Arlit. Remoter routes are desert pistes and tracks.

Fuel costs Diesel: US$1.44; petrol: US$1.34 per litre.

CLIMATE The climate is hot and dry, except for a brief rainy season in July and August. The coolest months are December to February, when the *harmattan* wind blows the dust off the desert.

HIGHLIGHTS The Grand Marché in Niamey, with market days in Filingué and Zinder being very colourful. Agadez is a fabulous place, with Tuareg markets and traditional mud architecture: the mosque, Sultan's Palace, Hotel de l'Aïr and Vieux Quartier in particular. Taking an expedition into the remote areas of the Aïr Mountains, Crabe d'Arakao, Adrar Chiriet, Temet and/or the Ténéré Desert with Fashi, Bilma and the Djado Plateau, was possible but expensive. For safety reasons, it was obligatory to have a guide with vehicle from a local tour operator and a travel permit for the area. When safe it is worth every penny, as it is an exceedingly stunning and beautiful area as well as being a wonderful introduction to the Tuareg culture. The Tuareg, the blue men of the desert, are a nomadic tribe famous for their camel caravans bringing salt from the Bilma and Fashi oases. These caravans continue to this day; trucks were tried but they kept breaking down.

🏠 WHERE TO STAY

Niamey The old **Camping Touristique** needed repair and may have had it by now or been closed down! It was west along Boulevard des Sy et Mamar. Try asking at the **Grand Hôtel** if you can park/camp; it has lots of space and is a great place for sundowners by the river. Also try **Hôtel du Sahel** further up the road. **Hôtel Maourey** is a good place in town, but it has no parking.

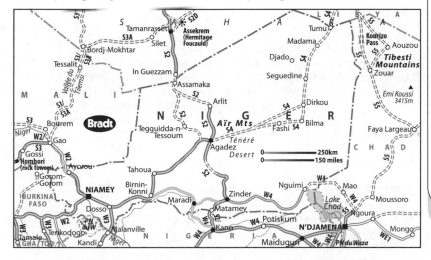

Dosso The best and most entertaining place is the **Hôtel Djerma**, with good parking, a pool, colourful ladies and a lively atmosphere. The steaks are great. Is the pool still empty?

Park du W The park has **Campement Nigercar, Campement de Boumba** and **Campement de Karey Kopto**.

Birni N'Konni Look for **Relais Camping Touristique** along the main road.

Zinder There is a campsite called **Camping Touristique** just north of town – ask locals for details. It is rumoured to double as a brothel! The **Hôtel Amadou Kouran Daga** may allow parking/camping. Close by is the **Auberge Mourna** if you want a room, or try **Hôtel Gamzaki**.

Tahoua Try the **Hôtel l'Amitié**. It seemed to be called **La Giraffe** as well.

Agadez The **Camping L'Escale** was a huge campsite 4km northwest of town, with lots of shade and great toilet and shower facilities, costing US$12 for two. It was also possible to park in the grounds of the classic **Hôtel de l'Aïr**, with its rooftop café and view of the mosque. If open, the **Hôtel Agreboun** can squeeze in one car. **La Tende** allowed camping; it was northwest of town.

Aïr Mountains Unsafe at present. **Campement de Timia** and **Campement de Tasselot** were around Timia. In the north at Iferouane are **Camping Oasis les Arbres** and **Auberge Tidargo** (Chez Sidi) all with camping choices.

Arlit It's anyone's guess whether Arlit will ever be safe for roaming tourists.

OTHER Do dress conservatively in this Muslim country. Always ask permission before taking photographs and stay clear of all government institutions.

FURTHER INFORMATION
www.expeditionworld.com

NIGERIA

WARNING! Recently the Islamist group Boko Haram has been kidnapping and attacking various targets across northern Nigeria, so it's best to keep south of a line just north of Abuja. There have been intermittent violent clashes between Muslims and Christians around Jos and Kaduna. Seek travel advice before entering Nigeria. Avoid the Niger Delta around Port Harcourt while low-key kidnappings of oil workers is ongoing (it's not low-key if it's you!).

CAPITAL Abuja

LANGUAGE English (main local languages are Hausa and Yoruba)

INTERNATIONAL TELEPHONE CODE +234

CURRENCY AND RATE Naira (NGN); US$1 = NGN163.05

RED TAPE Apart from getting the visa in the first place, roadblocks are evident throughout Nigeria, sometimes within 5km (3 miles) of each other. These are police, traffic police, forestry police, fundraisers (!) and military police. Apparently policemen and many government employees are often not paid for long periods at a time. Some may ask for a *dash*, a little 'gift' for services rendered. It's up to you to decide each case on its merits.

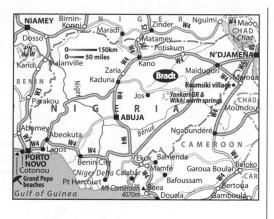

Visas Visas are required for all non-Africans. The cost depends on your nationality. You will also need two or three photographs and, if you get it in Africa, maybe a letter of introduction from your embassy. Even then you may only get a 48-hour visa to be extended in the country with yet more hassles. Yellow fever vaccination certificates are obligatory. Visas are not issued at the border. Getting one in your own country is strongly advised, but the procedure is expensive and far from simple.

African embassies
www.onlinenigeria.com/embassies
www.embassypages.com/nigeria

DRIVING AND ROADS Drive on the right. Main roads are generally in good condition, but once on side roads watch out for pot-holes and worse.

Fuel costs Diesel: US$0.95; petrol: US$1.34 per litre.
'At the time of writing there was no fuel available.' That's what Charlie and Illya wrote in the third edition of this guide and it still applies in many areas. Sometimes fuel is found in fuel stations, but often the only fuel available is hidden away round the corner on the black market. It's totally crazy when oil is Nigeria's major source of income.

CLIMATE The south is hot and humid, with a long rainy season from March to November. The north has far greater extremes of temperature, as a result of the Saharan influence. It can be blisteringly hot. The rains last from April to September, with a shorter wet season in the far north.

HIGHLIGHTS Most travellers enjoyed the north of the country until the kidnapping threats. Highlights included the Yankari Game Reserve and Kano (famed for its old city), Sultan's Palace, mosques, dye pits and the narrow streets lined by the remains of the old city wall. The rolling green hills of the Jos Plateau have a relatively cool climate all year round. The crime and heavy concentrations of the population in the south deter some, but there's little choice now. Benin City in the south is famed for its bronzes. In the far southeast near Cameroon is Calabar town, where many travellers 'relax' for a while, getting their visas and visiting the cattle-ranching area of Obudu.

⌂ WHERE TO STAY

Kano The only campsite was the **Kano State Tourist Camp**, just off Bompai Road; it was friendly, secure and helpful. Camping cost US$5 per person. Hussein or Mohammed used to fix any problems with vehicles or fuel supplies.

Sokoto Best avoided these days, but if you end up here, try the **Sokoto Guest Inn** with big chalets in a garden setting.

Jos Jos had no campsite, but the **Plateau Hotel** might allow parking for a night or two. Another was **Hill Station Hotel** with colonial charm in a leafy area.

Potiskum Best keep away at present – at the time of writing, there had been two recent attacks by Islamists in the town. If trouble has died down, try the **FNC College**. Double rooms were US$11.

Maiduguri There are a few hotels but the town is in the 'Boko Haram' zone. Try the **Maiduguri International Hotel**, which has parking in large gardens but quite expensive rooms.

Abuja We stayed at the **Hotel Luna** about 20km west of town near the main road junction. There's parking and it's friendly. A double room cost US$10 but it's sure to be more now. Some overland trucks have camped at the **Sheraton** near Wuse market. The **Lakeview** or **Lake Crescent Hotel** also allow camping with various forms of entertainment. For an excellent mechanic in Abuja, ask the hotel for Cyprian Ogbodo.

Lagos If you have to stay in Lagos, it's expensive, even for many of the grimmer places. It could be easier to stay at Eleko Beach, 60km east of town, where there are said to be beach huts.

Abeokuta If you have come through the Ketou/Meko border from Benin, you will pass this historic Yoruba town. Try **Mokland Inn** at 7 Oba Alake Road.

Ibadan Secure parking can be found at the **Plaza Park Hotel** near the university, just east of Oyo Road. Rooms cost from US$30 upwards.

Oshogbo For a quiet retreat, try the **Ambassador Guest House**, 6km west of town. It's not cheap, though. An alternative is the **Hotel Heritage International**.

Benin City There was parking of a sort at the **Central Hotel**. Otherwise there is the **Edo-Delta Hotel** with a church on site. Also suggested with parking is **Hotel Felona**, where the bacon and eggs may tempt you. Rooms are US$65. Ouch!

Calabar There is camping at **Paradise City Hotel**. The nearby sanctuaries for drill monkeys are worth a visit and it should be possible to stay at **Rhoko Camp**.

Yankari Within the park, roughly 45km from the gate, is **Wikki Camp** for about US$5 per person plus vehicle charge.

Obudu Cattle Ranch and Afi Drill Ranch These were two nice places to camp close to the Cameroonian border, but the access roads are steep and difficult in the rain. Obudu was expensive.

Gboko Try **Lemba Lodge** within a secure compound.

OTHER Ensure that all paperwork is in order and be patient. Do not photograph any government institutions. Dress conservatively, particularly in the northern Muslim areas.

Recent years have seen a significant rise in **room costs**, even if standards have not improved. Be aware that there are frequent and long-lasting power cuts throughout the country. So although you may have a suite of rooms (for US$15–30 or so) with a luxurious bathroom, you will probably have no water except in a bucket and no air conditioning except the breeze when you head outside to sleep on the roof of your vehicle.

Cameroon visas have so far been easiest to obtain in Calabar near the border, but check in Abuja if you are near the capital.

FURTHER INFORMATION
Nigeria Lizzie Williams (Bradt Travel Guides)

RWANDA

CAPITAL Kigali

LANGUAGE Kinyarwanda, French and English (English is less widespread outside Kigali)

INTERNATIONAL TELEPHONE CODE +250

CURRENCY AND RATE Rwandan franc (RWF); US$1 = RWF680.45. The official and private forex bureaux at the border only change cash – US dollars or euros are best. Moneychangers also operate at border crossings, but watch out for rip-offs before the deal. Elsewhere in the country you're also better off with cash.

RED TAPE There are occasional police checkpoints, but they don't seem to target overlanders. Your vehicle may be checked for roadworthiness – carry two warning triangles and a fire extinguisher. It's easy to exit into Burundi. You must buy separate car insurance at the border as you enter.

Visas At present visas are not required by nationals of the UK, Germany, Sweden, Canada, USA and South Africa for stays of under three months. For others they cost around US$50–70 and are currently obtainable at the border.

African embassies
http://embassy.goabroad.com/embassies-in/rwanda
www.embassypages.com/rwanda

DRIVING AND ROADS Drive on the right. There are many steep hairpin bends. Roads linking main cities and border points are generally surfaced and relatively good; some smaller roads are narrow and twisty, and may be muddy (or in some areas impassable) after rain. Ask local advice, particularly in the wet season. The road to Gitarama and on to Huye/Butare and the Burundi border is good, with views of Virunga. Also to Lake Kivu the road is good but typically twisting, slow and hilly. There is a new road direct to Ruhengiri and Kibuye; it is also hilly and twisting.

Fuel costs Diesel: US$2.01; petrol: US$2.02 per litre.

CLIMATE Rwanda is a high, hilly country and not too hot. Rainy seasons are March/May and October/November. The hottest months are August and September.

HIGHLIGHTS There are three national parks: the Volcanoes Park in the northwest (mountain gorillas, golden monkeys, Dian Fossey's grave, crater walks, trekking), Akagera Park in the east (hilly savanna, lakes, hippos, giraffe, elephant, antelope, fish eagles) and Nyungwe Forest in the southwest (chimps, colobus and l'Hoest's monkeys, orchids, birds). The National Museum of Rwanda in Butare is one of east Africa's best, with extensive displays on Rwandan history and culture. Visits to interpretive genocide memorials are possible. The tranquil lakeside towns of Kibuye and Gisenyi offer stunning views of Lake Kivu and boat trips to some islands.

WHERE TO STAY Rwanda is a very densely populated country and secluded spots are hard to find. All three national parks have basic (but not cheap) campsites nearby. In most towns there's a small hotel or guesthouse where you can ask to camp.

Kigali The **One Love Guesthouse** (*rue de Kinamba;* ☏ 575412) is on the east side of town down from the centre and main area past the Okapi Hotel, then right around the ring road; look out for it on the left. Camping costs US$7 each but facilities are basic. It was possible to camp at the **Episcopal Church Guesthouse** (*Av Paul VI;* ☏ 573219) or take their cheaper rooms.

Gisenyi Try the **Hotel Palm Garden Resort** on the shore of the lake or in rondavels at the **Paradis Malahide** in Rubona. Otherwise there is the **Methodist Church Centre de'Accueil** in a quiet location to the north.

Lake Kivu There was lakeside camping in Kibuye at the **Kibuye Guest House**. In Cyangugu you can stay at the **Home St François** for a budget option.

Musanze (formerly Ruhengeri) The **Hotel Ituze** is suitable for those with their own vehicles.

Parc National des Volcans Try at the **Kinigi Guest House** near the park or a campsite near the park office. Ask for more information at the main Rwandan Tourist Office in Kigali: ORTPN (Office Rwandais du Tourisme et des Parcs Nationaux).

Lake Muhazi Beside Lake Muhazi in the east there was camping near Gahini at the Seeds of Peace Centre and Jambo Beach (on the main eastern Kigali–Uganda road), and on the northern shore at some idyllic small bar-restaurants (accessed via the Byumba road).

Kibungo If you are *en route* to Kigali from Tanzania, you might need a place here. **Sunset Guesthouse** has been suggested.

Nyungwe National Park The park has the **Uwinka Reception Centre Campsite** in a forest setting with trails.

Butare The **Hotel Foucan** is pretty nice for US$30 per double room – a touch of relative luxury with safe parking. It's on the east side of the main street.

OTHER Be tactful about **photos** – always ask, always respect the answer. Supportive tourism is a way to help overcome the horrors of the past.

Permits to visit the amazing **mountain gorillas** (US$375–750 park fee per day, special permit) must be bought in advance from the Rwanda Tourist Office in Kigali (*Office Rwandais du Tourisme et des Parcs Nationaux (ORTPN); www. rwandatourism.com*).

FURTHER INFORMATION
Rwanda Philip Briggs and Janice Booth (Bradt Travel Guides)

SENEGAL

MILD WARNING! Periodic disturbances still occur in the Casamance region, so check before travelling there.

CAPITAL Dakar

LANGUAGE French

INTERNATIONAL TELEPHONE CODE +221

CURRENCY AND RATE West African franc (CFA); US$1 = CFA478. There are ATMs in every major town.

RED TAPE Roadblocks are frequent and not always marked; the police are sometimes overzealous if you are in a vehicle or on a motorbike. Always adhere to all the rules and try to avoid handing over original documents. Expect in the order of CFA5,000 'tax' to the Senegal police plus the CFA4,000 toll for the bridge on the Senegalese side. Some gift taxes should be ignored if possible. Expect a 'tax', say CFA5,000, at the Karang exit. The gendarmerie at the entrance and exit to Ziguinchor can be zealous as well as *en route* to Guinea Bissau. There are quite a lot of military and police checks on the road from Gambia to Bignona.

Car insurance Buy the Carte Brun covering all the ECOWAS countries (Benin, Burkina Faso, Ivory Coast, Gambia, Ghana, Guinea, Guinea Bissau, Liberia, Mali, Niger, Nigeria, Senegal, Sierra Leone and Togo); it lasts for six months. The Carte Brun can be bought in Senegal, Gambia, Niger and Mali. It costs roughly US$40 for two drivers. It's worth hunting down the insurance booth at the border rather than getting it in Saint Louis, because you will be stopped by the police, and they will ask to see your insurance. If you are refused the Carte Brun at the border crossing into Senegal (where it is overpriced), it is still worthwhile buying a little insurance here to cover you until you can get to a town to buy the Carte Brun, as the police will definitely stop you and fine you if you are without any insurance.

Visas From 1 July 2013, all EU nationals need a visa to enter the country. Since the rules may change without notice, please check the official website for the latest information: www.snedai. sn/en. Visa costs depend on your nationality and country of application. A yellow fever certificate is obligatory.

African embassies
http://embassy.goabroad.com/embassies-in/senegal
www.embassypages.com/senegal

DRIVING AND ROADS Drive on the right. Roads are generally in a variable condition, with pot-holes. Most are quite decent, but a few are a surprise. The Tambacounda road from Dakar to the Guinean border, which was once horrendous, has now been resurfaced. Tambacounda to Boundou is OK but then unpaved, corrugated and very slow going for the last 40km to the Guinean border.

Fuel costs Diesel: US$1.67; petrol: US$1.96 per litre.

CLIMATE Dry from December to May; hot, humid and wet from May to June. The dry season is shorter in the south and east.

HIGHLIGHTS Dakar has some beaches not far from town for lazing and good nightlife; be careful at night. Take a boat trip to the historic former slaving centre, Ile de Gorée. Ferries leave from the wharf area in Dakar every one or two hours. Hike in the Casamance region when it's safe and enjoy the beautiful beaches of Cap Skiring. Visit the Siné-Saloum Delta and the Parc National de Niokolo-Koba. Highlights of the north include the old town of St Louis and the magnificent birdlife of the area. Touba is a pilgrimage centre with massive modern mosques. Senegal is also famed for its musicians, such as Youssou N'Dour.

WHERE TO STAY In the 'old days' there were many tourist campements, but these are slowly evaporating or being upgraded. Finding good budget options is becoming harder and wild camping is very hard.

Dakar The options for budget rooms and camping are all miles out of town along the north coast. **Auberge Ma Petite**, close to the beach, is at Lac Rose, Rufisque (N 14° 49.833, W 17° 13.526) (✆ 77 511 2745; e mapetitecamargue@gmail.com). It's an excellent choice with space, shade, security, cold showers, loos, a bar and restaurant. It costs US$10 camping for two. For Wi-Fi head to Chez Salim (www.chez-salim.com) – they will give you the password if you have a drink at the bar. In town there is the **Hôtel Via Via Dakar** (e senegal@viaviacafe.com), a travellers' haunt, but it's not so cheap at US$40 double and safe parking could be the main issue.

Siné-Saloum Delta/Foundiogne The delta is often overlooked and is a wild, beautiful area of mangrove swamps, lagoons, forests, dunes and sand islands. In Palmarine is **Campement Villeois de Sessene**. North of the Saloum River is **Djidjack** (N 14° 01.452, W 16° 46.087) (☏ *33 949 9619; www.djidjack.com*). There is good security (two fierce dogs who don't like foreign dogs!), showers, toilets, bar, restaurant and bakery nearby. There is also a library with lots of books. Sporadic Wi-Fi. Camping from US$10.

Near Djiffer, camping accommodation was available on the western edge of the delta at the tip of a narrow spit of land called Pointe de Sangomar. **Le Gîte du Bandiala** is near Missirah. Pirogues can be hired to reach the beautiful islands of Guior and Guissanor. Foundiogne has a good selection of places to stay; **Baobab sur Mer, Foundiogne Hôtel, Indiana Club, Les Belongs** and **Saloum Saloum**.

Toubakouta South of the Delta. Neither option has shade but both are secure, convenient and have cold showers and clean toilets. **Camping Coquillages** (N 13° 47.247, W 16° 28.565) costs US$14. Also try **Keur Youssou** (N 13° 47.270, W 16° 28.435) (☏ *33 948 7728*) with bucket showers, US$12.

St Louis The **Zebrabar** is the overlander congregating ground here. It's near Mouit south of town on a road off to the right ahead and then down various small lanes. The camp is very pleasant, with beautiful surroundings, as well as a popular bar and restaurant with on-site mechanic. Follow the signposts (N 15° 51.827, W 16° 30.720) (☏ *77 638 1862; www.zebrabar.net*). It costs US$16 for a car plus two.

If you head south for 5km towards the Parc National de la Langue de Barbarie, famed for its birdlife, look for **Hôtel Dior** at the Hydrobase. Camping in town is not possible, but there are a number of hotels, including the famous **Hôtel de la Poste** (*www.hoteldelapostesaintlouis.com*).

Wild camp Found along the beach between Saint Louis to Dakar (N 15° 05.482, W 16° 58.928). Make sure you camp well back from the beach, as there is a lot of traffic at low tide.

Touba Try the **Campement Touristique le Baol**; it's 10km south of town in Mbaka. Watch out for the inquisitive goats. Mosquitoes come for free. Camping costs US$7, bungalows are also available, and there is a restaurant.

Koungheul *En route* to Tambacounda is the hunting retreat of **Campement Bambouck**, with camping and bungalows. It's a good spot to break for tea.

Casamance The best bet is to stay at one of the local campsites called **Campements Touristiques**, where prices are standardised at US$6–7 for a bed. Camping would need to be negotiated. Ask at **Elinkine** about village campements (Campements Villageois), and whether the basic campements are still operating on the Ile de Karabane.

Bignona Look for **Auberge Kayanior**, Quartier Chateau d'Eau (N 12° 48.487, W 16° 13.689) (☏ *33 994 3014*). It has a bar and restaurant with Wi-Fi. Normally no camping, but rooms are cool and large with en-suite bathroom with fan.

Ziguinchor Try the **Camping Casamance** (N 12° 34.271, W 16° 14.911) (☏ *77 735 3400/77 557 3108; www.campingcasamance.com*). It has a shady bar, restaurant and a treehouse area plus Wi-Fi. Breakfast is CFA1,500, lunch CFA1,000 and a large gin and tonic CFA1,000. Facilities are good, but don't leave things unattended; the site is surrounded by a palmerie frequented by people tending their crops. It's 40 minutes to town and five minutes from handy shops. According to Kate and Simon, 'Maëlle (French-speaking) and Pape (English-speaking Casamancian) are very attentive hosts along with their two children, resident sheep, chickens and parakeet.'

North of Djembering Wild camping is possible on the beach (N 12° 28.874, W 16° 47.424). Nearby is **Campement Chez Edy** (N 12° 28.300, W 16° 47.300) right on the beach, run by an Irishman who has his own bar and restaurant. Local musicians use his bar as a venue for spontaneous jamming sessions. Eddie has an in-depth knowledge of the local area.

Cap Skiring Has a couple of better campements and plenty of new good hotels. **Hôtel La Paillotte** (✆ *33 993 5151; www.paillote.sn*) in Cap Skiring offers excellent Wi-Fi with a beautiful view over palm trees to the sea. This hotel is at the entrance to Cap Skiring, opposite a petrol station and just before a military/police check-post.

Oussoye Has a couple of long-standing traditional mud-built and cool village campements.

Tambacounda There are two hotels out of town on the way in from Dakar. Camping may still be tolerated, but neither is cheap. For rooms **Relais de Tamba** is negotiable around US$35–60 and the **Oasis Oriental Club** is a bit more. Bush camping is better.

OTHER The beaches at Cap Skiring are some of the nicest in Africa. Watch out for the **police around St Louis**, who seem hell-bent on fining foreigners for anything, real or otherwise. The officials at the **border with Mauritania** are notorious for extra 'taxes'.

Dogs should note that food is available from all of the supermarkets in Cap Skiring and at the petrol station in Ziguinchor.

FURTHER INFORMATION
West Africa (Rough Guides)

SIERRA LEONE

CAPITAL Freetown

LANGUAGE English

INTERNATIONAL TELEPHONE CODE +232

CURRENCY AND RATE Leone (SLL); US$1 = SLL4,340. ATMs in main centres.

RED TAPE Customs are now issuing a SLRTA (Sierra Leone Road Transport Authority) **permit to drive**, which costs around US$25 (SLL100,000). When you apply for your visa, you should also apply for a **laissez-passer** for your vehicle at the same time. You cannot obtain this at the border. You need a laissez-passer even if you have a carnet de passage.

Following the civil war, there are very frequent police checks at the entrance and exit to every town and village. Some may ask you for a tip; others may want to search your vehicle. All of them find it very hard to believe that you are tourists without a 'mission', as they are so accustomed to the overwhelming presence of NGO personnel (in gleaming white chauffeur-driven Toyota Land Cruisers rather than dusty old Land Rovers). Kate, Simon and four-legged Max were chased by plain clothes immigration officers through the streets of Kabala on a scooter to check that they had not sneaked across the border!

Visas Visas are required for all. To be sure, obtain the visa in advance. Rumours suggest they may be issued at the border, but check beforehand; check also about the laissez-passer for your vehicle. There's no point in getting your visa at the border if they won't let your vehicle in!

African embassies
http://embassy.goabroad.com/embassies-in/sierra-leone
www.visitsierraleone.org

DRIVING AND ROADS Drive on the right. The roads are improving. Sealed roads now head east from the Guinean border at Pamalap to Freetown and all the way to Kenema. From Freetown to Makeni the road is in a reasonable condition. From Kenema to Zimmi remains awful but fun; expect an eight-hour rollercoaster. There are also a few sealed sections heading north towards Guinea. Elsewhere the state of disrepair is likely to be bad (such as from Kabala to Faranah in Guinea). The provincial roads and tracks in the Outamba-Kilimi National Park and the Loma Mountains are rutted, washed out and slow going.

Fuel costs Diesel: US$1.10; petrol: US$1.65 per litre. Sold and priced locally in gallons.

CLIMATE The main rainy season is from June to September, with the rest of the year much drier.

HIGHLIGHTS Sierra Leone once had a thriving beach-holiday tourist industry, which may soon be redeveloped Freetown, although formerly run-down and crowded, is beginning to experience a revival. Its often unlit, seedy streets have a certain vibrant charm. Close by are a number of good beaches: Lumley, Lakka, River No 2 and Tokeh. Banana Island and Bunce Island with its old fort may be revived. In the Loma Mountains is Mount Bintumani, the highest point in west Africa at nearly 2,000m, set in a forest reserve. Also, when things improve, there is the Outamba-Kilimi National Park. For something completely different, visit the central town of Bo, famous as a diamond centre. The road to Liberia is a highlight for those desperate to use their 4x4 capacity.

 WHERE TO STAY
Freetown Hotels are expensive here, probably due to too many expats hanging around. Out of town along Lumley Beach and with low-roofed

underground parking, try **Cockle Bay Guest House** (from US$35 for a double). You can just get a vehicle into the yard of **Franjia Guesthouse** (US$40) if pushed. Not far from Franjia is the **YSC Complex**, where there is internet and a café. It might be possible to camp, as there is a lot of secure space. Power cuts are frequent in Freetown, so air conditioning and fans are often superfluous. As things settle down, new places should open further down the coast – one day.

Freetown Peninsula coast There are a few options south of Freetown, but none are very developed and the road was shocking. **River No 2** is one of the best places and it's shady. Showers are open-air for bathers and it gets deserted after dark. Camping costs US$8–9; rooms are apparently US$50. **Lakka Beach** is seeing new developments. **Tokeh Sands Resort** has beach bungalows, otherwise try at (N 08° 19.445, W 13° 11.873). There is still no development here, but the security guards may let you camp near the beach. No toilet or shower facilities – US$5. **Bureh Beach** (N 08° 12.483, W 13° 09.329) is a stunning but little-developed location where you may be able to camp for free, with shower and toilet facilities, in return for buying dinner at the surf club. Unforunately it's marred by piles of rubbish everywhere, and in the nearby village. **Sussex Beach** is another possibility, but its access road is an obstacle course. It should improve. At **Kent** there is parking/camping, but it's all very primitive.

Kenema You can try **Eastern Motel** with parking. Heading south, Joru and Zimmi are just mud-hut villages, so don't expect to find a concrete building anywhere.

Makeni Look out for the **MJ Motel** (N 08° 53.045, W 12° 03.857) (*38 Azzolini Highway*) with excellent security and secure parking, 20 minutes from the town centre. Rooms have fans, air conditioning after 19.00, TV and en-suite bathroom. Full English breakfast is the high point here. Doubles are around US$60. Also try the **Multiple Guest House** (N 08° 53.229, W 12° 03.015) (*7 Lower Mathankoh St*). Good security with just enough secure parking for one Land Rover. It costs US$30 for two plus a car.

Bo Head east out of town to the relaxing and well-run **Countryside Guest House** with a pool and restaurant; it's also a good spot to catch up with your laundry and car washing.

Wild camping This is possible in the jungle, but there can be plagues of black flies who love to head for your eyes! See the following:

NE of Kambia On the road towards the Outamba-Kilimi National Park (N 09° 12.440, W 12° 51.756).

Outamba-Kilimi National Park In the Kilimi section (N 09° 37.449, W 12° 17.162) and in the woods south of Fintonia (N 09° 39.330, W 12° 13.176).

Kabala to Makeni In the woodlands off the road 15km south of Kabala.

Kabala to Koinadugu Again, a wooded area off the road (N 09° 33.083, W 11° 22.758).

Loma Mountains (East) Between Kayima and Kurubonla (N 09° 08.614, W 10° 57.824).

OTHER Be wary of the police, who can be intimidating. Try not to hand over any documentation to the police if you possibly can, as a few will try to conjure up any reason to 'fine' you.

There is a great Lebanese supermarket for food stocks/soups, etc next to the Malian consulate on Wilkinson Road, close to Franjia Guesthouse and above Cockle Bay. Dog food and other important accessories can be bought at the supermarket on Wilkinson Road (N 08° 28.987, W 13° 16.103). For motor parts, try MotorCare in Freetown. There's a mechanic with old Land Rover parts on the road into Makeni coming from Kabala (N 08° 53.830, W 12° 02.264).

When visiting Bo, the former RUF headquarters, exercise a low profile when taking photographs. Of course, it's tempting to take pictures of diamond shops, isn't it!

FURTHER INFORMATION
Sierra Leone Katrina Manson and James Knight (Bradt Travel Guides)
www.sierra-leone.org
Outamba-Kilimi National Park: http://outamba-kilimi.com
Loma Mountains Forest Reserve: www.visitsierraleone.org/attractions/nature-and-wildlife/Loma-Mountains-Mount-Bintimani-Bintumani.html

SOMALIA

WARNING! Sadly things have still not changed much in Somalia, although a tentative new government of 'almost' national unity backed by African Union troops is struggling to improve security, despite Al Shabab terrorists. Overland travel is not possible. Basic information has been included. Some embassies are opening, though!

CAPITAL Mogadishu

LANGUAGE Somali

INTERNATIONAL TELEPHONE CODE +252

CURRENCY AND RATE Somali shilling (SOS); US$1 = SOS1,199

RED TAPE Unknown, but who needs red tape with so many guns about?

Visas Visas are required, but with the state of the country anyone can probably enter without a visa, although it is not recommended.

African embassies
www.embassypages.com/somalia

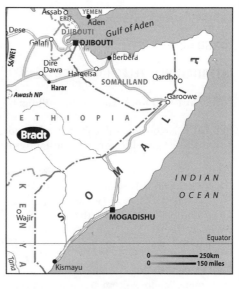

DRIVING AND ROADS Drive on the right. If the Michelin map is to be believed, the roads from Mogadishu to Hargeisa were relatively new just before the troubles.

Fuel costs Unknown.

CLIMATE Much of Somalia is hot and dry, but there are intermittent rains in the south from March to September.

HIGHLIGHTS Formerly parts of the capital, Mogadishu, were quite picturesque, but the city has suffered from the ongoing conflict. Many years ago, the people were noted for their friendly welcome. There must be hundreds of miles of attractive coastline, but there's little chance of anyone except pirates seeing them for the time being.

SOMALILAND

Unrecognised internationally as a separate state, Somaliland has functioned quite impressively as an independent democratic entity for over 20 years. In general, with some exceptions, Somaliland has been much safer than the south and it is possible to visit Hargeisa, Berbera, Burao and Sheikh with some confidence in the local security services. That said, it still rates as a troubled and risky place with terror threats/kidnapping on most travel advisory websites.

WARNING! It would be unwise (although possible) to try to get your own vehicle into the country, but a steady trickle of travellers have visited with often glowing reports about their welcome. Again, we can be under no illusions that all is completely safe – you take your own responsibility for any visit, of course.

CAPITAL Hargeisa (Hargeysa)

LANGUAGE Somali

INTERNATIONAL TELEPHONE CODE +252

CURRENCY AND RATE Somaliland shilling; US$1 = SOS6,800

RED TAPE No obvious difficulty for independent travel, although you may need to hire an armed guard. This rule is constantly changing.

Visas Visas are required and are available in Addis Ababa on the spot (US$45). They are also available in London from the Somaliland Mission (*www. somaliland-mission.com*). The online service is intermittent and unreliable.

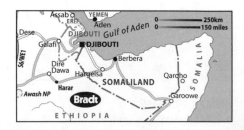

African embassies
www.somalilandpress.com
www.embassypages.com/
somaliland

DRIVING AND ROADS Drive on the right. The first 10km from the Tog Wajaale border is piste (road under construction). The rest of the road to Berbera via Hargeisa is mostly good tarmac, apart from the last 60km before Berbera, which has some short pot-holed sections. The road from Djibouti is a desert track until Borama.

Fuel costs Diesel: US$1.50; petrol: US$1.00 per litre.

CLIMATE Somaliland is mostly hot and dry – see also *Somalia*, page 297.

HIGHLIGHTS Apart from the colourful people, Hargeisa has little of specific tourist interest, but just being there is an exciting if slightly tense experience. Berbera has an old Ottoman-era historic area and Las Geel is a relatively recently discovered, unmissable ancient rock art site. Four to six days should suffice for a short visit. Meeting the Somali people is a real highlight.

WHERE TO STAY

Hargeisa The hotels **Ambassador** and **Mansoor** have parking but are expensive. In the centre is the excellent **Oriental Hotel** and **Dalmar Tours** (double room US$30). Other options include the **Al Jaziira**, **Imperial**, **Jirdeh** and **Safari**. Prices range from US$15 to US$80.

Berbera The out-of-town but expensive **Mansoor** has parking. Otherwise the **Yakye** (Yaxye), **Dahabshiil**, **Esco** or **Al Madina** are options without enclosed parking. Apparently some overlanders have shipped their car from Berbera to Salalah in Oman (see *www.ouradventurebug.com*).

OTHER Photography: people are generally very friendly, but taking photos may cause offence, particularly in Hargeisa, so always ask first.

Ethiopian Airlines (*www.flyethiopian.com*), the most reliable carrier, flies from Addis to Hargeisa. See also Daallo Airlines (*www.daallo.com*), African Express (*www.africanexpress.co.ke*) and Jubba Airways (*www.jubbaairways.com*). None of these three are particularly reliable carriers.

OFF THE MAP IN SOMALILAND

Following a failed attempt to go to Mogadishu in 1975, it was not until January 2014 that we finally made it to Somaliland... We flew into Hargeisa with some trepidation, but the friendly welcome at the hotel immediately put us at ease. However, we did require an armed escort for our 2-day tour. The bustling markets of Hargeisa are as colourful as any in Africa. Las Geel is a true revelation; its exotically shaped outcrops shelter stunning artwork dating from maybe 10,000 years ago. Brightly painted cows clearly illustrate the pastoral lifestyle of that time. Sleepy Berbera is a surprise, its old quarter full of crumbling Ottoman buildings and wide sandy streets. Despite being a historic port of some note, there is not yet much of a new quarter. It's a shame that the country has not yet received international recognition, but it is doing very well for itself without any official foreign aid.

Were we adventurous or simply stupid? Sadly there's no way of knowing how safe this revealing experience is.

Somaliland Philip Briggs (Bradt Travel Guides)

SOUTH AFRICA

WARNING! Crime is rampant.

CAPITAL Pretoria (administrative) and Cape Town (legislative)

LANGUAGE English and Afrikaans are the official languages, with another nine local official languages. Those spoken most are Zulu, Xhosa and Sotho.

INTERNATIONAL TELEPHONE CODE +27

CURRENCY AND RATE Rand (ZAR); US$1= ZAR10.87

RED TAPE The big change is that foreign-registered vehicles on a carnet now get only three months in the South African Union area, which includes Botswana, Namibia, Swaziland and Lesotho. So don't hang about! Those overstaying are liable to lose their carnet bond money or worse. You can apply for a vehicle entry permit for longer stays. If you are intending to sell your vehicle in South Africa, you have to discharge your carnet by officially importing the vehicle or bike. This is not as easy as it was before, so check the latest rules before the three-month period ends.

Visas Visas are not required for most holiday visitors. You'll be issued with an entry permit on arrival. Visas are not issued at the border. With overland travel you may have to convince the immigration officer that you have sufficient funds for your stay, but crossing borders is usually hassle-free.

African embassies
http://embassy.goabroad.com/embassies-in/south-africa
www.pretoria.co.za/directory/official/embassies
www.pretoria-south-africa.com/embassies-in-pretoria.html
www.embassypages.com/southafrica
www.saembassy.org

DRIVING AND ROADS Drive on the left. Most roads are in excellent condition. Watch out for car-jacking areas and don't stop on any highway lay-by away from settlements.

Fuel costs Diesel: US$1.24; petrol: US$1.33 per litre.

CLIMATE The climate is extremely varied and quite localised. The summer (wet season) is from September to April in the north. Winters can be cold, particularly at night. In Cape Town the winter months (May to August) are wet and it can be very windy along the coast. June and July are the best months for game viewing. The Indian Ocean coast is driest from June to September.

HIGHLIGHTS South Africa is such a vast country that (too many) months could be spent exploring it. Highlights include the Kruger National Park and

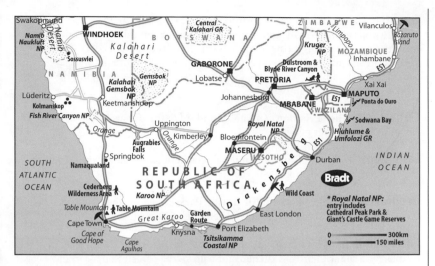

surrounding area, as well as Karoo National Park and Augrabies Falls. Of course Cape Town, Table Mountain, the Cape of Good Hope and the vineyards in the surrounding area, including Stellenbosch, should not be missed. East is the Garden Route along the southern coast, including Knysna, and for all surfers, Jeffreys Bay. Oudtshoorn has ostrich farms and the Kango Caves. In the great Karoo are quirky Matjiesfontein with its oddball Lord Milner Hotel and railway station, plus Graff Reinet and the Mountain Zebra National Park. Natal has lush green rolling hills and incredible beaches along its coastline. The Drakensberg Mountains are spectacular, with Giant's Castle and Golden Gate Park, as is the Cederberg Wilderness Area. Durban is known for its beaches and cosmopolitan flavour, and nearby is the wilder region of the Transkei.

⌂ **WHERE TO STAY** The options are limitless and the country is well set up for camping. Facilities are excellent. Costs are US$5–10 per person, depending on the site. There are also a lot of backpacker places where parking is not usually too difficult.

Cape Town The **Zandvlei Caravan Park** is a campsite at Muizenberg, south of town in the eastern beach area, on the way to the Cape. It costs US$5–6 per person. On the outskirts, **African Overlanders** (S 33° 52.177, E 18° 44.54) (see advert, page 20; ☏ +277 1521 9742; *www.africanoverlanders.com*) offers camping (US$6 per person), beds (US$9 in a dorm, US$32 for a double), vehicle storage and an all-in-one quote for shipping (US$3,200 from Cape Town to Tilbury).

Orange River The **Fiddlers Creek Campsite** (*www.bushwhacked.co.za*) has sites on dirt/grass, with a braai pit and a sheltered cooking area with electric points, running water and sink. It costs US$7 per person.

Springbok The **Springbok Caravan Park** is on the ring road just south of town. It has BBQ pits and good bathrooms, but little shade and it can be windy. There are powered sites, rooms and a small shop. Costs from US$6 per person.

Klawer Look for the **Oasis Lodge and Campsite**. Camping fees are based on four-person sites, only US$10.

Cederberg area Camp at beautiful and relaxing The Baths (*www.thebaths. co.za*). It's off the main road from Citrusdal and has a natural hot pool and tranquil surroundings. Camping costs from US$10. Also recommended is the **Ukholo Lodge** where camping is at the back of the house, with a fire pit and good-sized cooking shelter with electricity, hot showers and clean toilets. Camping US$7 each; ask for Edmund.

Clanwilliam The **Lebanon Citrus Holiday Farm** (*www.lebanon.co.za*) has camping for US$7 per person.

Stellenbosch Try the **Stumble Inn Backpackers** (*www.stumbleinnbackpackers. co.za*). We parked safely outside in the street.

Beaufort West The **Municipal Caravan Park** is just on the southern edge of town. Camping for a car plus two people costs US$10.

Gariep Dam Beside the lake is a superb campsite costing US$10 for a car plus two people, for a site with private kitchen and bathroom.

Bloemfontein North of the city is **Reyneke Park**, a peaceful spot with camping areas. It costs US$7 per person.

Pretoria We stayed at the **North South Backpackers** in Hatfield, where the vehicle just fitted in through the archway. It's well guarded and costs US$13 to camp/ park. Other places are **Kia Oro Lodge Backpackers**, **Backpackers International**, **Pretoria Backpackers** and **Khyalethu Backpackers** for starters, but check that the parking is safe.

Johannesburg The **Africa's Zoo Lodge** (*233A Jan Smuts Av, Parktown North;* *011 880 5108; www.zoolodge.co.za*) has been recommended. **Brown Sugar Hostel** is great but parking is very risky here; bed and breakfast costs US$32 for a double room. For an excellent mechanic, contact William Beets in Jo'burg (m *0833 207244;* e *william_beets@yahoo.com*).

Pietermaritzburg The pleasant out-of-town **Msundzi Caravan Park** has nice camping and is about 5km out on the east side of town.

Top of the Oliviershoek Pass With a wonderful view across the whole range of the Drakensberg Mountains, the **Windmill Resort** was surprisingly inexpensive. It has rondavel bungalows for a little luxury, and a comfortable bar, too. It was temporarily closed for a while for renovations. Across the road, down a steep narrow track, is **Amphitheatre Backpackers**.

Durban It's best to head for the beaches to the north and south, as Durban is not safe for parking overnight, or even in the daytime in many areas. Near the port is **IPA Port Natal Guesthouse** in the Rossburgh area, but it does not have parking.

Eshowe The classic **Hotel George** is great, with a historical atmosphere. Camping is possible in the garden area for US$17 per site, and the hotel serves a great bacon-and-egg breakfast! There are road tolls near Empangeli and two beach campsites before Umlhanga.

Polokwane The **Igloo Inn** has a camping option here. Otherwise try the **Travellers Lodge** (US$45) – nice but pricey. It's off Thabo Mbeki Road south of the central area. From here it's a good road to Tzaneen, but hilly *en route* to Kruger.

Phalaborwa The **Elephant Walk** (US$18) is a small but relaxing camp and backpackers' hostel. Head south off the main road, then right then left.

Kruger Park (*www.krugerpark.co.za*) The roads are good in Kruger, including the dirt tracks; there is a 50km/h limit. Entry costs from US$35, and camping from US$17. From the entry gate east of Phalaborwa it's about 40km to **Letaba Rest Camp**, 40km to a lunch spot at **Satara Rest Camp** and then 145km to **Skukuza Camp**. There are 13 listed rest camps and in season it's best to book in advance. We saw only one lion, but loads of monkeys, elephant, antelope, wildebeest, eland, giraffe, warthog, rhino, buffalo and zebra. A hungry hyena was spotted trying to get through the metal fence surrounding the campsite at evening braai time! In the rainy season the grass is high, giving less chance of seeing elusive creatures. The Crocodile Gate is often closed at times in the rainy season. If you're heading to Swaziland, go for the border south of Komatpoort.

OTHER Crime is really rampant, unfortunately, and ever on the increase in most major towns, so watch out and always carry minimal valuables. Most accommodation and camping places in South Africa offer to place all valuables in a safe. Sadly it is still not advisable for any white person to enter a black township unless with a guide or tour company.

FURTHER INFORMATION
South Africa Highlights Philip Briggs (Bradt Travel Guides)
Southern African Wildlife Mike Unwin (Bradt Travel Guides)
www.southafrica.co.za

SOUTH SUDAN

WARNING! Despite peace agreements, visiting more isolated parts of South Sudan remains a risky venture, with landmines being one hazard apart from general instability. Things do seem to be improving now that both Sudan and South Sudan are holding the peace. Keep an eye on developments in the world's newest country.

CAPITAL Juba

LANGUAGE English (Arabic is widely spoken)

INTERNATIONAL TELEPHONE CODE +211

CURRENCY AND RATE South Sudan pound (SSP); US$1 = SSP2.97

RED TAPE Expect roadblocks and security issues if you're heading outside Juba.

Visas Visitors to the Republic of South Sudan (RoSS) require a visa. Currently these can only be obtained at the embassies in Cairo, Nairobi, Kampala and Addis Ababa. In Kampala the process was taking three days and cost US$100. If you pay

US$25 extra, it is done the same day. Apparently visas can only be obtained in person and it can take two days in Nairobi. Be prepared to queue at the RoSS embassy in Nairobi before it opens and pay in US dollars. The Nairobi embassy is at Bishop's Gate, 6th Floor, 5 Ngong Avenue, Bishop's Road. Some visitors have obtained a visa at the Nimule border for US$50, but check beforehand whether

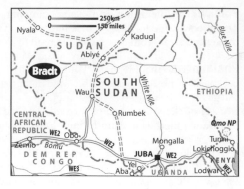

this is possible. Having a Sudan visa in your passport is not a problem at present.

African embassies
www.embassypages.com/southsudan

DRIVING AND ROADS Drive on the right. All the major tarred roads are in good condition, but there are not too many of these. All other roads are pistes and tracks. Roads to Juba are still not entirely safe, although improving. From the north the route is via El Obeid, Dilling, then poor to Keilak, Abiye and on to Wau, Rumbek and Juba. Via Malakal is ill-advised, rough and hard to follow. The road to Uganda via Nimule and Gulu is mostly decent tar and into Kenya work is apparently ongoing via Torit. The road between Yei and Juba is fair.

Fuel costs Diesel: US$2.00; petrol: US$2.00 per litre. Carry as much as you can, as supplies are sure to be erratic as well as expensive.

CLIMATE Don't go during the wet season, April to September, as roads become even grimmer.

HIGHLIGHTS The main highlight of both South and north Sudan is its amazingly welcoming people, such as the Dinka, Shilluk and Nuer. The Dinder National Park and the Nile route to Juba, through the swamps of the Sudd, are a naturalist's haven. South of Juba are some amazingly high boulder outcrops. The Nimule National Park is open at the time of writing. Heading northwest is sure to be a big adventure when it gets more secure.

 WHERE TO STAY

Juba So far most of the options are expensive. The cheapest seems to be the **Christmas Hotel**, where a room with fan costs US$45. Bearable might be the **Palm Hotel** for US$60 a night. The Hai-Thoura area north of the University of Juba has some decent places like the **Alba Hotel** and **Vermont**, also around US$60. Cheaper choices are likely to appear, although some may be payable by the hour or two! Years ago, sleeping in a police compound (not the jail) was the only option, but today that will please no-one, including the police.

Yei In 1980 Yei was a village set in wonderful countryside with very large boulders hosting wildlife. Now the town has had an influx of NGOs and is developing fast. Suggested are the **New Tokyo Hotel**, about US$20, and the **Twins Hotel**, US$25.

Wau When Bob visited in 1976 the only options were the police station and the cemetery! On the Jur River, the **Wau River Lodge** is getting good reviews. It's one of the cheaper options, but still a whopping US$100 a night. Any overlanders who get this far could well bargain for a camping spot in the garden for their novelty value and effort!

Rumbek The **Safaristyle Hotel** has tented rooms as well as classy options aimed at the waves of NGOs. Expect it to be US$100 at least.

Throughout the old country, bush sleeping was the best option, but with mines around this is not generally a good idea yet.

OTHER Photography was a very sensitive matter years ago, but it's not likely to be such an issue these days. As always, beware of photographing military installations, airports, government buildings, post offices and bridges.

For **public transport** travellers heading to Juba from Kampala, there is the Baby Coach bus leaving Kampala at 20.30 and arriving in Juba the next afternoon. The ticket costs UGX70,000. It's about 11 hours to the border. Expect to wait for hours at the border – five hours is a reasonable estimate.

FURTHER INFORMATION
South Sudan Sophie and Max Lovell-Hoare (Bradt Travel Guides)
The official portal of the Government of the Republic of South Sudan is www. goss.org.

SUDAN

WARNING! The route across Darfur is probably still too risky, but there has been a marked reduction in armed incidents. Eventually things may improve, hopefully during the lifetime of this guide. Thankfully the routes from Egypt to Khartoum and south into Ethiopia are safe.

CAPITAL Khartoum

LANGUAGE Arabic

INTERNATIONAL TELEPHONE CODE +249

CURRENCY AND RATE Sudanese pound (SDG); US$1 = SDG5.99. You cannot change any 'old-fashioned' travellers' cheques or use cards in Sudan, but US dollars cash are no problem.

RED TAPE Sudan is wonderful to travel through, but famous for its bureaucracy. Obtaining the relevant permits is a time-consuming, frustrating task. Stay within the restrictions of any permits needed, generally all in Arabic, as these may be checked on the road. Those arriving in Wadi Halfa from Aswan by ferry should study the following:

Before arrival at the port, passports must be taken to the Sudan office on board the ferry behind the kitchen area. We docked at around 10.00 with more form-filling and were off the ferry by noon. A free bus ferries everyone to the customs area, which takes ages. After formalities there are taxi pick-ups into town (cost S£5).

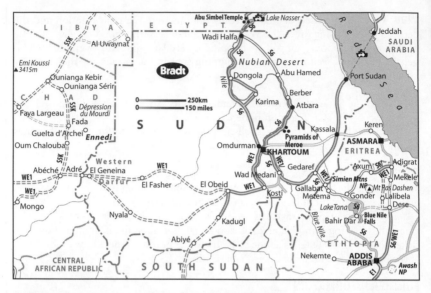

Walking takes 45 minutes and can be rather hot. How long you have to wait in Wadi Halfa for your vehicle on the separate barge is anyone's guess, so be prepared with some luxuries from your vehicle – like bedding, some food goodies and a mosquito net at least. See Wadi Halfa accommodation below.

Registration for all foreign passengers must be done in Wadi Halfa as follows (see map). The procedure is confusing, with so many offices to visit. See the map opposite for a basic plan.

First get copies of the form, visa and passport pages (photo required). Put all this into a folder (green) from office (A). Go to office (B) to pick up a form. Go to (C) and pay S£100+. Go to (A) for sticker. Go back to (B) for signature. Go to (A) for tax: S£3+ each. Finally go to relax after all this commotion.

And let's not forget finding the bank, where you must exchange cash in order to pay the US$20 or so for this purpose.

After this, you may need an 'Alien's Movement Permit', which states the towns and the route you intend to take. Any deviation may cause you trouble, so decide on your route before you apply. These documents were formerly required for all travel within Sudan. Things seem to change constantly, so check at the border and in Khartoum before going too far away. Road and photo permits were required on our last visit, but not before reaching Khartoum. We required them the last time between Khartoum and the Ethiopian border, whereas the first time we did not!

The famous George at the Hotel Acropole will know the latest requirements. The Aliens' office is on Abu Sin Road one block south of the British Council, opposite the Hotel Danolus. There is no fee, but copies are needed of the form, passport, visa plus a photo and registration stamp.

Previously, wherever you stayed overnight you were supposed to check in with the local police. This was exceedingly tedious, especially as the offices were often closed. It is better to camp in the bush, stopping only briefly in the towns for supplies or sightseeing. In case the procedure has been simplified, it would be a good idea to check with Mr Midhat Mahir at Mashansharti For Travel and Tourism (\+249 9 12253484; e midhat@tour-sudan.com, midhat.sudan@gmail.com or w_halfa@yahoo.com; www.tour-sudan.com).

Visas Visas are required for all and the process is lengthy in Europe, particularly in London, as your application will first need to be approved by Khartoum. It could take months. Visas were easy to obtain in Cairo and Addis Ababa. They are not issued at the border.

African embassies
http://embassy.goabroad.com/embassies-in/sudan
www.embassypages.com/sudan

DRIVING AND ROADS Drive on the right. The major tarred roads leading from Khartoum to El Obeid, Gedaref, Port Sudan and Atbara are in good condition. Roads between Wadi Halfa and Khartoum, via Dongola, Karima and Meroë, are now tarmac, as is the road from Gedaref to Gallabat on the Ethiopian border. Tarmac now continues to Gondar. All other roads into the hinterland are desert pistes and tracks. The route to the south is via El Obeid, Dilling, Keilak (poor sections), Abiye and eventually on to Wau, Rumbek and Juba, but the recent border clashes make this a future option. Going via Malakal is ill-advised, rough and hard to follow.

Fuel costs Diesel: US$0.53; petrol: US$0.77 per litre. The further north or west you go, the more expensive fuel becomes.

CLIMATE The summer months in Sudan are extremely hot and dry, reaching 45°C+. The best time to visit is during the winter months from December to mid-March, when temperatures still reach 40°C but evenings are cool and pleasant.

HIGHLIGHTS The main highlight of Sudan is its amazingly welcoming and diverse people, including Dinka, Shilluk and Nuer. Khartoum, the confluence of the Blue and the White Niles, has Kitchener's old steamboat, teashops, an impressive central mosque, and the Mahdi's Tomb in Omdurman. It offers fine dining at one of the restaurants along the waterfront. Further north is the Nubian Desert and the ancient pyramids of Meroë, reputed to be the oldest in the world.

Along the Red Sea near Port Sudan and Suakin are some reportedly excellent diving areas, with fishing excursions possible. On the way to Port Sudan is the town of Kassala, located in spectacular rocky countryside. It could be visited on the way to Eritrea if things ever improve in the region. To the west are the volcanic mountains of Jebel Marra near El Fasher, once a great adventure to reach.

WHERE TO STAY Throughout Sudan bush sleeping is the best option, but keep a good distance from settlements.

Wadi Halfa The infamous **Hotel El Nile** is atmospheric, but the sand floors are crawling with bugs – room US$6. Better is **Hotel Defintood** with concrete floors and a few fans, US$6 each. Showers are lousy everywhere. Food shops are well stocked these days, with yoghurt, tins and water sold in town. The café in the 'square' is Egyptian-run, with OK meals at S£15–20. It's near the hotels. Internet is at

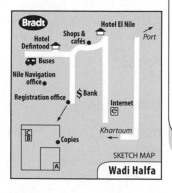

the other end, on the eastern side of town. The Nile Navigation office is also on the southeast side – well hidden and probably moveable. See the map on page 307. A super new sealed road heads south via Dongola to Khartoum (direct, it is approximately 895km). New roads abound from Dongola eastwards.

En route to Omdurman Desert camping is surprisingly difficult, as there is soft sand everywhere. At Km184 before Khartoum on the right side (SW) is a track into the bush area near an abandoned village. Shady acacias give cover, with only the odd passing local. Arriving in Omdurman is confusing – follow the widest roads to find the bridges. It's better to use the 'yellow' Nile bridge to cross the White Nile if you're heading for the campsite in Khartoum. If you've crossed the Blue Nile bridge, you're too far north.

Khartoum The best and most convenient camping is at the **Blue Nile Sailing Club**, on the southern bank of the Blue Nile near the church. It's along the Blue Nile, passing two new bridges and on the left before the railway bridge. An added bonus is the imposing presence of Kitchener's steamboat, marooned here since 1898 (like you if your papers aren't in order). It costs about US$15 for a vehicle and two people. The other place is on the road south to Wad Medani, some 10km out. It's not easy to find and has limited shade. A hotel in town to consider is the Hotel Falcon (US$45+). Staying at the Acropole would be grand; it's expensive (US$90–150) but worth a visit. It seems to have been run by George the Greek since Kitchener's time.

Atbara The **Nile Hotel** was once recommended.

Meroë Wild camping is permitted in the area. There was also a tastefully designed, Italian-run luxury tented camp and restaurant complex. It was not cheap.

Dongola We did not stay here but took the bypass, where there are a couple of fuel stations, and continued on towards Omdurman. The best place is **Olla Hotel**. Others are the **Haifa Hotel** and the **Lord Hotel**, but the desert might be preferable.

Gedaref The only decent spot is the **Hotel El Motwakil**, which claims to have guarded parking; it is not cheap now at US$70. You can bush camp south of town on the grassy plains, but be careful of bush fires, which are common in the dry season. The road to Gedaref is good but bumpy. Last time we camped 107km south of Gedaref in the bush area along a track to the right.

Kassala One hotel is the **Hipton**, with good views of town and the impressive granite Taka Mountain domes.

Port Sudan You may be able to park/camp in the grounds of the **Baasher Palace Hotel**.

El Obeid Parking was possible at the **El Madina Hotel**.

OTHER It is anticipated that the road between Aswan and Wadi Halfa will be derestricted for tourists. High tolls are expected to be imposed that are comparable to, or more than, the total ferry costs – but a week and a lot of nervous energy could be saved. For more up-to-date information call Mr Midhat Mahir at Mashansharti

for Travel and Tourism (📞 *+249 9 12253484;* e *midhat@tour-sudan.com, midhat.
sudan@gmail.com or w_halfa@yahoo.com; www.tour-sudan.com*).

Apparently there is a daily ferry from Port Sudan (Suakin) to Jeddah. Cost
quoted at around US$150 per car and US$500 for a car and two people. Of course,
the snag is that you need a Saudi visa for the northbound trip.

Photography is a sensitive issue and photographic permits are sometimes
suggested, but no-one seems to know if the rule is still enforced. Just be careful and
don't take photos of anything with even the slightest military connection, including
airports, government buildings, post offices, bridges, policemen and even fuel
stations.

FURTHER INFORMATION
Sudan Sophie and Max Lovell-Hoare (Bradt Travel Guides)

SWAZILAND

CAPITAL Mbabane

LANGUAGE English and Swati

INTERNATIONAL TELEPHONE CODE +268

CURRENCY AND RATE Lilangeni (SZL) (plural emalangeni); US$1 = SZL11.32.
South African rand are universally accepted.

RED TAPE None of any significance. Swaziland is within the South African customs
zone. Note that foreign-registered vehicles on a carnet now get only three months
in the South African Union area, which includes South Africa, Botswana, Namibia,
Swaziland and Lesotho.

Visas Most nationalities do not need a visa. Others should check to see if they are
available at the border.

African embassies
http://embassy.goabroad.com/embassies-in/swaziland
www.embassypages.com/swaziland

DRIVING AND ROADS Drive on the left. The main roads are good and secondary
roads are mostly fine.

Fuel costs Diesel: US$1.36; petrol: US$1.34
per litre.

CLIMATE Swaziland has a climate generally
moderated by altitude. The drier but cool season
is from May to August. The main rains are from
November to April.

HIGHLIGHTS On the way from Mozambique
are the well-manicured sugar plantations and
Hlane Royal Park. An encouraging roadsign

reads: '*Motorists, beware of elephants. Cyclists and pedestrians, beware of lions!*' Not far from Mbabane is the beautiful green Ezulwini Valley, ancestral home of the royal family. The Mlilwane Wildlife Sanctuary near Lobamba is a delightful stop. Do go for morning or afternoon tea at Reilly's Rock and enjoy the sumptuous colonial house, slumping in the supersoft armchairs while the overnight guests are out. Other reserves or parks include Malolotja Nature Reserve and Mkhaya Game Reserve for black rhinos.

WHERE TO STAY The country is small, so almost any central location will give access to most places of interest.

Mbabane The **Cathmar cottages** are north of town near Pine Valley.

Manzini Try **Swaziland Backpackers**, or **Myxo's Place**, which offers village visits. To the south of the main road near Mahlanya Market is Sundowners Backpackers, also offering camping.

Ezulwini The picturesque **Lidwala Backpackers** has parking and camping. This is a great option. **Legends Backpackers** is another popular place.

Mlilwane Wildlife Sanctuary There is a lovely campsite in the park with well-kept gardens, bar, restaurant and inquisitive warthogs. Reilly's old house in the park is a superb colonial relic, moderately expensive but good for morning biscuits and tea. Entry costs US$4 each, and camping US$12 for a car plus two people. **Sondzela Backpackers** is another place.

Hlane National Park This is a super spot to camp, with in-house rhinos, hippos and warthogs. Entry (daily conservation fee) is ZAR40 per person (must be paid in rand or local currency) and camping US$8 each. There are no electric lights after dark.

Near Big Bend To the south of Hlane and near Nilliwane there was a poorly signed place to camp on the left.

OTHER With increasing crime in neighbouring South Africa, it's refreshing to visit Swaziland for its peace and tranquillity (except perhaps Mbabane and Manzini at night). Some game parks can only be paid for in rand or local currency, not other cash, even dollars.

FURTHER INFORMATION
Swaziland Mike Unwin (Bradt Travel Guides)

TANZANIA

CAPITAL Dodoma

LANGUAGE English and Swahili

INTERNATIONAL TELEPHONE CODE +255

CURRENCY AND RATE Tanzanian shilling (TZS); US$1 = TZS1,636

RED TAPE Watch out for radar and hefty speeding fines. Yes, this happens even in Africa, although there are no cameras as yet! Road tax is around US$25. Coming in from Burundi, there were no moneychangers until Kasulu. Customs is up the bank on a tall, wonky ladder on the left. Immigration is to the right up the muddy bank.

Visas Visas are required for most, but things change, so do check. A visitor's pass for up to three months may be issued at the border, costing US$50, depending on nationality. A transit visa for US$40 may be available.

African embassies
http://embassy.goabroad.com/embassies-in/tanzania
www.embassypages.com/tanzania

DRIVING AND ROADS Drive on the left. The main roads are mostly in good condition. Arusha to Dar es Salaam and on to Mbeya is fine. The road from Arusha to Ngorongoro is being tarred. The road south from Arusha to Dodoma is said to be atrocious. There are rumours that some of the route from Dar es Salaam via Kilwa to Mozambique may be tarred, except for 40km each side of the border, but we don't have any hard facts, so beware of planning that route with only hearsay.

Fuel costs Diesel: US$1.32; petrol: US$1.38 per litre.

CLIMATE It's hot and humid along the coast (particularly December to March). The rains are from March/April to May and in November. Inland the rains are from January to April. On the central plateau it is warm and drier. The highlands are a little cooler, even cold at times.

HIGHLIGHTS In the north, Arusha is the gateway to the fabulous Serengeti National Park and Ngorongoro Crater. Climbing Mount Kilimanjaro, Africa's highest mountain, is good for those with the inclination and fitness. Bagamoyo, north of Dar es Salaam, is a historic sight with pleasant beaches close by (until the rumoured international shipping port is built). Zanzibar has Stone Town, beautiful winding roads and stunning beaches. In the south are the Ruaha National Park and Selous Game Reserve. Much of the central highland area is very green after the rains and quite wild. South of Dar es Salaam is the former Arab/Omani trading port of Kilwa Kisiwani. Adventurers can try the remote and wild western route described in *Chapter 2*.

WHERE TO STAY
Dar es Salaam In the city you could try the **Safari Inn**, but parking will be a problem. Power cuts are common in Dar. Head 20km north along the Bagamoyo road to Kanduchi Beach, hopefully to still find the **Silversands Hotel and Campsite**. There's more choice going south, such as **Sunrise Beach Campsite** (S 06° 51.033, E 39° 21.540). Others were **Kipepeo Camp** and **Kim Beach Campsite**, but names may have changed! **Bahari Lodge and Campsite** is running down, but the setting is gorgeous. The **Mikadi Beach Campsite** (*www.mikadibeach.com*) has a sheltered cooking area, electric point and light on site with two small braai pits and running salt-water tap! Camping is US$6 with possible upgrades to *bandas* for US$12 each with netting. Mikadi Beach is a high-risk malarial area.

Bagamoyo The **Travellers' Lodge** is one suitable place and another is **Badeco Beach Hotel**, which has camping. Another is **Bora Beach Resort**. Go soon, as it's rumoured that a big international shipping port will be built here.

Zanzibar Various ferries and local pirogues leave daily and hourly from the main wharf in Dar es Salaam. Yellow fever vaccination certificates are obligatory before a ticket is issued. Make sure you find a safe place to park your vehicle before you head over to the island. It's worth the effort, as Zanzibar is really beautiful. There is plenty of accommodation, ranging from hotels to pensions. **Mtoni Marine** has been mentioned for a splurge at US$72 for a double room.

Arusha Stay at the **Masai Camp** (S 03° 23.116, E 36° 43.188) about 2.5km outside town on the old Moshi road. If it's full of overland trucks, don't expect a quiet night in the bush. The cost is US$5–6 each. The **Meserani Snake Park** (*www.meseranisnakepark.com*) has camping and a bar west of town on Dodoma Road. Camping costs US$5–6, which includes entrance to the Snake Park. BJ's workshop here can help with getting cars fixed; they also know where to go to get parts! Another place is **Arusha Vision Camping**. The park has a selection of camping places.

Mombo The **Tembo Lodge and Campsite** is the place to stay here. It's in the grounds of an old saw mill on the right-hand side at the foot of the escarpment. Look out for a white signpost and turn-off on the right about 20km after Mombo. Follow the track over the railway and head up through the village, keeping right. It costs around US$5 each, with good hiking nearby. The **Zebra Camp** is a further 26km (47km from Mombo); camping is US$5. Mosquitoes can be a little bit of a problem. **Pangani Camp** has hot showers and squat toilets. It's next door to Zebra Camp and costs US$5 per person.

Lake Manyara There are a number of camping options outside the park. Choose from **Panorama Campsite**, **National Park Bandas Campsite**, **Migunga Campsite**, **Kiboko Bush Camp**, **Jambo Campsite**, **Wild Fig Camp** and, for a cheaper place, **Lakeview Camp** or **Camp Vision Lodge**. Inside the park are the **Bagayo A & B sites**.

Karatu Further along from Lake Manyara is the small town of Karatu. The **Safari Inn Camping** has a nice open garden and good facilities including restaurant/bar. Cost is US$9 for two. **Karatu Bushman Camp**, **Ngorongoro Camp** and **Kudu Campsite** are other choices.

Mto Wu Mbu The **Twiga Campsite** (\ +255 713 334 297; e *twigacampsite@yahoo.com*) is recommended and has a great pool. There is a restaurant with buffet dinner (US$10) and an internet café adjacent to the bar. Camping costs US$10 per person.

The Serengeti and Ngorongoro Crater As in Kenya, taking your own vehicle into the national parks is quite expensive but offers so much freedom. In some circumstances, though, it might be easier to organise something with a tour company from Karatu or Arusha. Taking a tour might cost in the order of US$85–140 per person per day, depending on the number of people. It should include all park fees, accommodation and meals.

Ngorongoro Crater The crater is a magical place in fine weather but can be cold at night. The **Simba Camps** have been used for years. Facilities are OK but costs are high, from US$30 per person (public), and US$50 per person for special camps. The views are great. Beware of animals at night. Park entry is US$50 per person for 24 hours, plus a vehicle fee of US$150 and an extra 'crater service fee' of US$200.

Serengeti Covering 15,000 square miles, the Serengeti is vast. From Ngorongoro Crater the track passes Olduvai Gorge, famous for its early human remains, and heads to **Seronera**, the central area with most accommodation. Entry is US$50 for 24 hours plus a vehicle charge of US$40; trucks US$100. The lodges are very expensive but camping in designated areas is possible for US$20 per person per day. Further north is **Lobo**, with camping. The wildebeest migrations are amazing in this northern zone. Across the border in Kenya is the Masai Mara. West from Seronera is a track to Mwanza and Lake Victoria. It used to get horribly sticky and muddy in the rainy season. If you make it this way, look for the **Serengeti Stop Over**, with camping near Lake Victoria; it costs US$10 each. It's not unusual to see game around this place, without having to pay any entry fees for that night. If you're coming from Lake Victoria, **Tumbili Campsite** in Seronera is simple with good amenities. With no fence around the campsite, be cautious at night as wild animals do wander about! It's US$30 per person to camp, plus park entrance fees.

Lake Natron There are a couple of camping areas. **Riverside Campsite** and **Waterfall Campsite** both charge US$10 per person. **Wasso Camp** is near Loliondo.

Moshi Suggestions are the **Keys Hotel Campsite** (S 03° 20.308, E 37° 20.813) and **Honey Badger Restcamp**.

Kilimanjaro A good base for climbing Kilimanjaro is the well-known **Marangu Hotel** in Moshi. It is 10km south of the main national park gate and near the start of the most popular route up the mountain. The safe and attractive campsite, with hot showers, has a pool. Climbs can be organised here. A more expensive option is **Coffee Tree Camping**, which also organises climbs. Other choices are **Gilman's Camping Site**, **Njari Camp** and **Amin's Cottages** outside the park. The **Baranco Camp**, **Crater Camp**, **Karanga Camp** and **Lava Tower Camp** are inside the park.

A six-day trek will probably cost well over US$1,200 per person, and depending on what is provided, the sky is the limit. Check online for the many options. Beware of the altitude: do not climb higher if you are suffering from prolonged headaches, nausea and loss of appetite – the effects of pulmonary and cerebral oedema can be fatal.

Musoma The **Tembo Beach Camp/Musoma Camping** is on a nice grassy/sandy area with a great view of Lake Victoria. Contact Raymond (☏ *+255 713 264 287/262 2887*; e *tembobeach@yahoo.com*). It costs US$10 per person.

Tanga Try the **Kiboko Guesthouse** and **Campsite**. **Peponi Beach Resort** had camping to the south. Hotels include **Beach Crab Hotel**, **Panori Hotel** and **Regal Naivera** but camping is not certain at these, so check.

Pangani South of Tanga, look for the **Argovia Tented Camp and Campsite** with a great location. Another option is the **Ushongo Beach Resort**.

Same The **Elephant Motel** south of town allows camping in its large grounds, and has showers. Camping costs US$5 per person.

Korogwe The **White Parrot Motel** (e *motelwhiteparrot@yahoo.com*) has a small campsite with nice grass. Camping is US$10; rooms cost from US$30.

Segera The **Segera Motel** has no real facilities but camping is allowed behind the motel/restaurant. Camping is US$4–5.

Morogoro The **New Acropole Hotel** has camping out in the yard, or you could take a room. The bar is lively at night, with lots of expatriates. It is Canadian-run and very friendly. Some way out of town is the **Kilamatembo Campsite** (S06° 48.255, E 37° 42.988).

Baobab Valley The **Baobab Valley Camp** has a great bar overlooking the Ruaha River. Remember that crocodiles inhabit the river, so swimming is not advised! Camping is US$6 per person. Another choice is **Crocodile Camp** (S 07° 29.100, E 36° 34.080) (*www.crocodilecamp.de*). Run by Jennifer and Frank, it has a restaurant and bar, and upgrades to bungalows are available. Camping costs US$4 per person.

Selous Game Reserve Overlanders can rest up at the **Ndovu Campsite**, a new set-up. Two other rather rustic places with few facilities are **Lake Tagalala** and **Beho Beho Camp**. Inside the park is **Rufiji River Camp** (S 07° 44.664, E 38° 11.641).

Mikumi National Park Try **Melela Nzuri Campsite** (S 06° 56.649, E 37° 16.020) just off the main road on the east side of the park. Three other national park campsites are found here near the main gate, but at US$20 per person they are expensive for the limited facilities they offer. The **TanSwiss Campsite** (*www.tanswiss.com*) costs US$7 per person.

Iringa The **Kisolanza Farm** (S 08° 08.800, E 35° 24.718) (*www.kisolanza.com*) is a wonderful stop 40km south of Iringa. The farmhouse has been restored and has a spacious campsite under the trees. If you want more luxury for a change, stay in one of the beautiful new bungalows. Local farm produce and delicious steak can be bought in the farm shop to cook yourself. There is a cosy bar, but no restaurant. Camping costs US$5–6 per person. Closer to Iringa is the **Riverside Camp**, appropriately beside a river.

Mbeya Staying at the missionary **Karibuni Centre** out of town is a possibility.

Tukuyu The **Landmark Hotel** (*www.rungwetea.com*) has a small garden area around the side for camping – ask reception to let you know about toilets/showers. In Kibis village, the very basic **Bongo Campsite** is 800m from the main road. Camping is US$8.

Matema Beach You can stay on the shores of Lake Nyasa here at the **Matema Beach View Lutheran Centre**, where camping has been offered before. Rooms from US$10–US$20.

Kilwa Masoko If you have come from Mozambique, you could end up here. The budget option is the **New Mjaka Guesthouse**. **Kilwa Masoko Seaview Resort** (S 08° 55.647, E 39° 31.304) and **Paradise Beach Rest Camp** (S 08° 53.876, E 39° 31.074) are other choices. The Omani ruins of Kilwa Kisiwani are some of the best in east Africa.

Mtwara South along the coast is this small town, where **Beach Villas** are at the beautiful Shangani Beach. Also look for **Mikandani campsite** (S 10° 16.947, E 40° 07.144).

Kasulu The friendly **God Bless Hotel** is on the left with parking space – US$10 for a room. Fill up with fuel and water here, as there's nothing much from here south. There is a bank in Kasulu.

Mpanda The **Super City Hotel** on the south side is OK with parking.

Sumbawanga The **Moravian Conference Centre** is paradise, with hot-water showers. Pass two fuel stations on the right, then go uphill to the left and look for Nyere Road, the third or fourth road up. Bed and breakfast costs US$17 for two. There are tarmac roads in town at least!

Tunduma The **Hotel Silver Stone** near the border has outside yard parking left up a small track. It has good rooms for US$12, but they are noisy if the disco is in action.
　　Bush camping is difficult *en route*. The border is hellishly chaotic, with no space for the vehicles to move.

OTHER Most nationalities do need visas, but the majority can be obtained on arrival at the border. The fees vary a lot, from US$10 to US$50 for an entry permit/visa. We still advise prior checking.

FURTHER INFORMATION
Tanzania Safari Guide Philip Briggs and Chris McIntyre (Bradt Travel Guides)
Northern Tanzania – Serengeti, Kilimanjaro and Zanzibar Philip Briggs and Chris McIntyre (Bradt Travel Guides)
Zanzibar Chris and Susie McIntyre (Bradt Travel Guides)
www.tanzania-web.com
www.worldtravelshop.biz/overland/tanzania-campsites-gps

TOGO

CAPITAL Lomé

LANGUAGE French

INTERNATIONAL TELEPHONE CODE +228

CURRENCY AND RATE West African franc (CFA); US$1 = CFA478

RED TAPE Our most recent experience is that touts and officials try to charge you for having the carnet stamped at the southern border of Togo. Crossing the Burkina border in the north in either direction is easy, with no obstructive officials. The military can be officious at times.

Visas Visas are required for all foreigners. They are available at Togo embassies or maybe at French consulates where Togo has no other representation. The main borders issue a seven-day pass; cost US$20+. A yellow fever certificate is required.

African embassies
http://embassy.goabroad.com/embassies-in/togo
www.embassypages.com/togo
www.embassyworld.com

DRIVING AND ROADS Drive on the right. The main roads are in generally good condition. Traffic in Lomé is horrendous, with very few signposts.

Fuel costs Diesel: US$1.46; petrol: US$1.47 per litre.

CLIMATE The rainy season is April to July, with shorter rains in October and November. The temperature is pleasant in the dry season, but hotter inland.

HIGHLIGHTS Lomé has a fetish market. Along the coast from Lomé is Lake Togo, with watersports, and Togoville with voodoo culture. For hiking there are the beautiful hills of Kpalimé. Visit the fortified, tiered, conical compounds (Tata houses) of the Tamberma people and the hilly scenery of the Kandé area. From Kandé it's about 16km to Nadoba, the main village. Niamtougou, which has a good market, is another base for visiting these unusual constructions.

 WHERE TO STAY

Lomé Near Robinson Plage is **Le Ramatou**, where camping is possible. About 12km east of Lomé town, camping and rooms can be found at **Chez Alice** on the beachfront. Camping costs US$5–6 per person.

Lake Togo This shallow lake, 30km (18 miles) east of Lomé, is popular for watersports. On the lake's northern shore lies Togoville, the centre of Togo's voodoo culture. There is rumoured to be a new camping option at an auberge in the vicinity of Agbodrafo.

Kpalimé Try **Chez Fanny,** 2km from town, for 'vehicle camping'. Kpalimé is a great base for hiking enthusiasts.

Sokode The **Campement Tchaoudjo** has rooms from around US$8.

Kandé This makes a good base for visiting the amazing Tamberma Tata houses. There is the basic but friendly **Auberge Oxygène**, which has a large bar with cold drinks. Rooms are cheap (US$12) and there is space to camp. It is possible to 'sleep' on the floor of one of the Tamberma houses if you're 'young at heart'.

Dapaong There are two branches of the **Hôtel Tolérance** here; amazingly there is one on either side of town, on the main road, miles apart. Each has good parking and nice rooms, costing US$20–25.

Atakpamé The **Hôtel Sahelian** is a good-value place to relax with air conditioning. If you're heading south, it's on the left side just before town. Everything works and it has secure parking and camping. Rooms with air conditioning cost from US$25.

FURTHER INFORMATION
West Africa (Rough Guides)

TUNISIA

WARNING! Things are still rumbling on after the Arab Spring began here, but in general there are no obvious threats.

CAPITAL Tunis

LANGUAGE Arabic

INTERNATIONAL TELEPHONE CODE +216

CURRENCY AND RATE Tunisian dinar (TND); US$1 = TND1.63

RED TAPE None of any significance. Visitors with vehicles will probably have the fact stamped into their passports.

Visas Nationals of most western European countries, USA, Canada and Japan, do not need a visa. Nationals of Australia, New Zealand and South Africa may need a visa. Visas are not issued at the border and should be applied for at any Tunisian embassy or consulate beforehand. Israeli nationals are not allowed into the country. Visitor's entry permits are issued at the border.

African embassies
www.embassypages.com/tunisia
http://tn.embassyinformation.com

DRIVING AND ROADS Drive on the right. The roads are generally in good condition. There are a limited number of tracks and pistes in the south near the borders of Algeria and Libya; some are restricted. Watch your speed if a minor road joins the major road you're on; the area around the junction may have a lower speed limit and sometimes there are police checks.

Fuel costs Diesel: US$1.02; petrol: US$1.16 per litre.

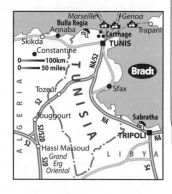

CLIMATE Tunisia has a Mediterranean climate in the north with cool, sometimes rainy, winters. In the south it is hotter, with a dry desert climate inland.

HIGHLIGHTS Tunisia has a number of ancient Roman sites, including those of Carthage (near Tunis), Dougga and Bulla Regia. El Djem has a gem of an amphitheatre. Beaches are found south of Hammamet and on the island of Djerba. In the south are the oasis towns of Douz, where you will find organised camel trips to 'nomadic' camps, plus Tozeur and Nefta, with picturesque palmeries. The vast Chott el Jerid is a shimmering salt lake. In contrast, the lunar landscape of Matmata near Gabès conceals a once-busy community living underground, in caves chiselled out of the rock – you can visit their dwellings.

 WHERE TO STAY There are a few campsites throughout Tunisia.

Tunis The **Hôtel Amilcar**, north of town and close to Sidi Bou Said, is on the beach with fine views. It has safe parking and camping might be allowed. It is also possible, and was safe, to sleep in your car at the ferry port in La Goulette.

Nabeul It was possible to camp at the **Hôtel Les Jardins** close to the beach.

Hammamet There is a nice no-name camping place with olive trees and a small hotel; take the southern motorway exit to Hammamet, and it's at the first crossroads next to a fuel station. Otherwise look for **Camping Les Jasmins**.

Gabès The slightly run-down **Gabès Youth Hostel** has camping in its large grounds. It's hard to find, though. When driving north to south, turn left off the main road at a roundabout with fuel station (near the new bypass ring road), then fork left almost immediately down a narrow road through a dry riverbed on the northwest of town, passing some markets. Turn left at the end and it's on your left.

Tozeur There is a shady pleasant camping place south of town in the palmerie: **Camping Beau Rivages**.

Nefta We used the **Hotel Marhaba**, which at the time allowed camping in the grounds. If it's not open, try the **Dar Zagouni**, which has had good reviews.

Degache Famed for its dates, there is a pleasant campsite in the palmeries.

OTHER Tunisia is easygoing by Muslim standards, particularly in areas frequented by tourists, but outside these areas life is still conservative and revolves around the mosque, *hammam* (local baths) and cafés. Act and dress appropriately.

FURTHER INFORMATION
www.tunisiaonline.com

UGANDA

MILD WARNING! Uganda is generally a very safe destination, with one exception. Northeast Uganda was dominated by the LRA (Lord's Resistance Army) and some areas may still be unsafe.

CAPITAL Kampala

LANGUAGE English

INTERNATIONAL TELEPHONE CODE +256

CURRENCY AND RATE Ugandan shilling (UGX); US$1 = UGX2,511. Money can be changed in Kampala. There are some ATMs, but they only accept Visa credit cards. Cash dollars (US) and cash advances can be obtained at banks.

RED TAPE There are road taxes that add up to about US$30 at the borders. Expect some roadblocks close to the DRC border, and in the north with remnant elements of the LRA rebellion.

Visas Visas are not required for nationals of Denmark, Finland, France, Germany, Israel, Japan, Sweden and most Commonwealth countries – India, New Zealand and Nigeria are exceptions. Visas cost US$50. They can be obtained at the border and are valid for 30 days. Students/ISS cardholders can get a discount.

African embassies
http://embassy.goabroad.com/embassies-in/uganda

DRIVING AND ROADS Drive on the left. The main roads are in generally good condition. Upcountry the condition of some dirt roads can be badly affected by wet weather. Parts of Kampala have big traffic snarl-ups – avoid the main market area. The road to Masaka is mostly good and on to Mbarara it's improving, but you could find some messy bits with pot-holes. To Kabale the road is mostly fine, with some holes. To Lake Bunyonyi the way is very steep and bad in wet weather. The border road to Rwanda has some pot-holes but is fair.

Fuel costs Diesel: US$1.24; petrol: US$1.36 per litre.

CLIMATE Despite Uganda's location on the Equator, its high altitude makes for a mostly pleasant climate. The rainy seasons are March to June and October to December.

HIGHLIGHTS An undoubted highlight of Uganda is tracking gorillas in the rainforests, but it's not a cheap activity. Visit Murchison and Sipi Falls, Queen Elizabeth National Park, go trekking in the Ruwenzori Mountains and relax for a few days on Ssese Island. There's also white-water rafting on the Nile, while staying in Jinja. Lake Bunyonyi (near Kabale) is a very tranquil and relaxing place to spend a couple of days.

WHERE TO STAY
Kampala The **Kampala Backpackers' Hostel and Campsite** (US$3–4 per person) is west of the centre uphill near the Cathedral, with a nice shady garden, bar and food. **Backpackers' Hostel and Campsite** (*6121 Kalema Rd, Lunguja; www.backpackers.co.ug*), just off Naktete Road and west of town, has a relaxed atmosphere. Camping costs US$3–4 per person. **Red Chilli Hideaway** (*www.redchillihideaway.com*) has a garden area out of town to the southeast with camping space, US$5 per person. About 4km east of town, be sure to look for the camping

option at **Andrew's Lakeside Farm**, a charming retreat from town. There is a Bosch agent near the Red Chilli, near Old Port Bell Road.

Entebbe The **Camp Entebbe** charges US$10 each. **Frank's Tourist Hostel and Campsite** charges US$4–5 per person for a nice lawn.

Tororo Try **Hotel Rock Classic**, with rooms for US$15 and camping for US$10.

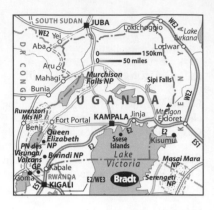

Jinja Apart from Speke (after he left Burton), most people stop over in Jinja for the white-water rafting. In or close to town you can stay at either **Explorers Backpackers** or the **Timton Hotel** for camping. Not far out (9km) is Bujagali Falls. Here you can stay at **Explorers' Campsite** (US$8–10) or **Speke Camp**. The dirt road is OK from town. Also good is **Jinja Backpackers**, just below the Source of the Nile (*Bridge Close, off Bridge St, right on the banks of the Victoria Nile;* m *078 459 1252/077 473 0659; www. jinjabackpackers.com*); camping US$5 per person, dorms US$10. Three companies offer rafting: Adrift (*www.adrift.ug*), Equator Rafting (*www.equatorrafts.com*) and Nile River Explorers (*www.raftafrica.com*). There is also a campsite at Mabira Forest.

Mount Elgon/Sipi Falls To get to Sipi Falls you'll need to climb a steep and treacherous road up into the mountains. Sipi Falls and the surrounding area are beautiful, with green, hilly outcrops and villages dotted around the countryside. You can stay at the **Crow's Nest Campsite**, which is eco-friendly and has a superb view of Sipi Falls. Camping costs US$5 per person. Nearby are **Moses' Campsite** and **Twilight Sipi Campsite**. For rooms check **Lacama Lodge**.

Masaka Look for **Masaka Backpackers** with camping for US$5 per person.

Ssese Islands You'll have to leave your vehicle behind, but camping on Buggala Island is available. There is a 50-minute ferry from Kabassese. A new ferry operates from the Nakiwogo port near Entebbe. Campers can stay at **Hornbill Campsite**, and there are various choices if you want a room.

Lake Mburo National Park This has variously priced tented camps and basic camping.

Mbarara The **Blue Sky Motel** is before town and **Westlands** in town has parking for just US$17 a room.

Kisoro The **Rugigana Campsite** is popular with overland trucks.

Lake Bunyonyi The **Bunyonyi Overland Camp** has excellent camping spots right on the lakeside. This popular overlanders' spot is well maintained, with a pleasant bar and hot showers. Other choices vary from luxury to basic. Try one of the following:

Bushara Island Camp, Nature's Prime Island, Kalebas Campsite, Crater Bay Cottage and Byoona Amagara Island Retreat. None will break the budget.

Fort Portal This is the base for exploring the Ruwenzori peaks. In town the **Ruwenzori Travellers' Inn** is highly recommended. Otherwise it's best to head towards the Kibale Forest National Park, south of Fort Portal, and look out for the **Safari Hotel** on your right at Nkingo village. Camping costs US$5. For the Ruwenzori National Park, stay in Kasese or at **Ruboni Campsite**, a community-run place, for US$5 per person. Kibale Forest National Park also has **Chimpanzee Valley Resort**.

Bwindi The campsites are near the Buhoma Gate of the national park. **Buhoma Community Rest Camp** costs US$4 and **Bwindi Gorilla's Nest Rest Camp** is US$6. Also just outside the park is **Lake Kitandara Bwindi Camp**, another cheap choice.

Mgahinga There is a **Community Campsite** just near the national park entrance gate, with a spectacular setting. Check out the other option, **Mount Mgahinga Rest Camp** nearby – it's only US$180 per person for a double room! For Nkuringo stay at the **Nkuringo Gorilla Camp** for US$5 per tent.

Murchison Falls National Park The **Red Chilli** has a place with camping (US$6); others are **Rabonga Camp, Top of Murchison Falls, Sambiya Lodge and Nile Safari Camp**. The falls are particularly spectacular.

Queen Elizabeth National Park There is abundant wildlife here. You will need to be self-sufficient and carry all your supplies with you. During the rainy season the roads can be treacherous. Camping with basic facilities costs US$6 per person. There is also self-catering, where facilities include a basic hut and a staffed kitchen. A number of private luxury campsites have opened across the area: **Mweya Safari Lodge** is posh, and you could also try **Bush Lodge**. The entry charge is US$20 per person and US$20 per vehicle.

OTHER There are three options for gorilla tracking – Bwindi National Park, Mgahinga National Park and now Nkuringo, part of Bwindi. Most opt for Bwindi, as they have three groups of gorillas that have been habituated, while Mgahinga has only one. It can get cold up in the mountains, so come prepared. Entry fees are from US$30 per night. Gorilla-tracking permits are now US$500. Contact the UWA (Uganda Wildlife Association) office (*Kiira Rd, Kampala;* \ *0414 355000; www.safari-uganda.com/uganda/bwindi*) for up-to-date prices and entry fees.

FURTHER INFORMATION
Uganda Philip Briggs with Andrew Roberts (Bradt Travel Guides)
www.myuganda.co.ug
www.visituganda.com

WESTERN SAHARA

CAPITAL Laayoune

LANGUAGE Arabic

INTERNATIONAL TELEPHONE CODE +212

CURRENCY AND RATE Dirham (MAD); US$1 = MAD8.18

RED TAPE Officials are often extremely helpful. It is advisable to have many copies of the *Personal details* document in *Appendix 2*, plus lots of copies of your passport and driving licence, as these are required at the prolific roadblocks in Western Sahara and in Morocco. Heading north, vehicles may be sent through a scanner and subjected to a sniffer dog session.

Visas Most visitors to Western Sahara/Morocco do not require visas and can remain in Morocco for 90 days. Some nationalities do need visas, so it's still best to check.

African embassies Currently the same as those listed for Morocco.

DRIVING AND ROADS Drive on the right. Roads are generally in good condition on all major routes, apart from more remote desert tracks. Some areas are off-limits to foreigners.

Fuel costs Diesel: US$0.60; petrol: US$0.70 per litre.

CLIMATE Western Sahara has a continental climate, with extremes in the interior and desert in the south. The south is generally hotter and inland nights can be cold in winter. Mist often hangs around along the coast, where cold currents hit hot shores. There can be exceedingly strong, dusty winds at times.

HIGHLIGHTS The nominal capital, Laayoune, has some older mosques and buildings, but is fundamentally a fairly modern town. The beach is not far away at Laayoune Plage. The Atlantic coast is a bleak and often windswept region, but has a stark beauty of its own. Dakhla is the main point of interest on the south coast. Visiting Smara is now possible and some have taken the desert piste to/from Assa, east of Tan Tan. New sealed roads are being added to the network. The Aouinet Asguer rock paintings are well worth the effort to reach.

 WHERE TO STAY There are now several recognised campsites. Desert camping is also an option, but don't end up stopping by accident in any military zone that is not clearly defined.

Tan Tan Along the coast there are a couple of small, narrow but spectacular inlets where parking is allowed. They cost US$3. Otherwise look for **Ksar Tafnidilt**, Tan Tan (N 28° 32.757, W 10° 59.580) (*off the P41 from Tan Tan to Guelmim; http:// tafnidilt.net*). It's like a mini-Alhambra, with breathtaking views over the Oued Draa. The camping area has a place to eat, wash up and barbecue, hot showers and toilets with beautiful tiles, all for US$10. An olive grove below, orange trees above and palm trees all around give shade. The restaurant serves fine Moroccan wine from Meknes.

El Ouata/Tan Tan Plage At the road junction is a restaurant/fuel station, **Les Deux Chameaux**. Rooms are available and there is camping in the yard behind.

Sidi Afkhenir There is camping within the courtyard at **Le Courbine d'Argent**. Twenty-two kilometres south of the town on the north side of the road is the amazing blue lagoon, **La Lagune de Nella**, where camping is allowed for a small fee.

Laayoune There's nothing much in town except hotels, although campervans can park near the airport.

Dawra North of Laayoune is **Le Camp Bedouin**, a beautiful site on the edge of a salt lake amidst wild scrubby dunes (N 27° 27.701, W 13° 03.125) (☎ *0661 090604; www.camp-bedouin-maroc. com*); prices from US$9. Ask for Luc and Hafida.

Boujdour Down by the beach is **Camping Sahara Line**, Plage de Boujdour, a mostly good option, with hot showers and laundry facilities when the power is working. A high wall shelters the site from the pervasive wind. Wi-Fi is erratic and it can be busy with campervans. Also, 20km south of town is a police check-post, from where there is a tarmac road down to an isolated beach. Camping is allowed here on the beach. There are some great kebabs off the Avenue de Corniche (to the right near the top if you are heading away from the sea).

Dakhla Dakhla is set at the end of an amazingly beautiful sandy peninsula. A few kilometres from the turn-off is a place to camp on the south side – look for all the white campervans! There is also a walled campsite, **Camping Moussafir**, about 6km before the centre of town, with incredible sea views and small beach (N 23° 45.831, W 15° 54.416). It has fairly clean toilets and showers with a sparse supply of saline water for US$7–8.

Motel Barbas This small, friendly settlement offers travellers shelter 80km from the border. Rooms, restaurant and free parking are found here. Rooms from US$12 to US$15.

Wild camping The following suggestions are supplied by Simon, Kate and Max, who explored the northeast corner of the country.

Off the N1 There is a good spot off the N1 and north of Centre Bir Gandouz at N 22° 04.275, W 16° 36.105. All with camel bones and white sand dunes in the distance.

Near Portorico Near Portorico (a Moroccan marine post) and the rural commune of Imlili, north of Cintra at N 23° 29.944, W 15° 56.625.

Halfway between Dakhla and Boujdour You can camp at N 24° 36.988, W 14° 54.481, where there are lots of rocks hollowed out by the wind.

Off the N5 to Bir Mogrein Just before the junction with the N14 to Smara at N 26° 41.675, W 13° 01.832. It's surrounded by acacias, cacti, flints and hills covered with green lichen and inhabited by large rabbits.

Smara (58km west) off the N14 At N 26° 32.532, W 12° 09.698. 'The Moroccan police are very friendly yet quite officious at the checkpoint into Smara. They took away our passports even though we had fiche. They wanted to know whether we were staying the night, what hotel we were staying at, and so on. Everyone prefers to speak Spanish rather than French. There are lots of shops, hotels, market stalls and even a youth hostel here. There are lots of cafés along the beautiful tree-lined and arcaded main street.'

Hawza and Km90 (297) This spot is on Chris Scott's Sahara overland M13 Assa–Smara itinerary at N 27° 05.120, W 11° 15.382.

Past Hawza Just before Km190 (197) on the M13 from Smara to Assa at N 27° 31.411, W 10° 36.455. Aeroplane noise all night.

In between Km219 (168) and Km242 (145) on the M13 from Smara to Assa at N 27° 51.107, W 10° 39.463. Camping in a startling white landscape.

Aouinet Torkoz 9km north of Km74 (174) on Chris Scott's M12 itinerary from Tan Tan to Assa, but in reverse (Assa–Tan Tan), at N 28° 17.718, W 10° 03.356. There are some pre-Islamic monuments.

Near Km148 (100) On the M12 from Assa to Tan Tan at N 28° 12.073, W 10° 41.990.

Aguejgal 10km from Aguejgal and off the road running parallel to the Tafnidilt–Fort Bou Jerif (Plage Blanche) piste at N 28° 56.993, W 10° 32.147. See also http://www.voyage4x4.com/Maroc/tafnidilt.html.

Aouinet Asguer rock paintings These can be found at N 27° 51.110, W 10° 39.440. At Km211 (160) you need to take a track to the left at N 27° 41.500, W 10° 27.500. Ancient paintings of giraffes, elephants, lions and hunters with bows and arrows can be observed.

Assa There is a large Moroccan military presence in Assa, as there is in all the towns in Western Sahara. There are well-stocked shops here that sell everything you need.

OTHER Western Sahara was previously known as Spanish Sahara. In 1975 the Spanish colonists left. Morocco and Mauritania then raised claims to the territory, because of phosphates in the area. The native Saharawi people have been in conflict since that time through their Polisario movement.

Morocco virtually annexed the northern two-thirds of Western Sahara in 1976, and the rest of the territory in 1979, following Mauritania's withdrawal. A guerrilla war, with the Polisario Front contesting Rabat's sovereignty, ended in a 1991 ceasefire; a referendum on final status has been repeatedly postponed. In May 2003 the area was granted limited autonomy under Moroccan sovereignty. Over the next few years, some democratic reforms and institutions should be established, followed by a referendum of the Saharawi peoples. The problem is defining who is eligible to vote, and this is the daunting task that the UN has so far been unable to complete. No permanent solution has been found as yet.

Chris Scott's **Sahara overland itinerary M12–Tan Tan–Assa** is a useful summary of a route in the region. Simon and Kate drove from Assa towards Tan Tan, but left the itinerary at Km49 (199) at Aouinet Torkoz and travelled along a piste parallel to the south and along the Oued Draa. It was here that they found many pre-Islamic monuments. They rejoined the M12 at Km145 (103).

FURTHER INFORMATION
Morocco (Rough Guides)

ZAMBIA

CAPITAL Lusaka

LANGUAGE English

INTERNATIONAL TELEPHONE CODE +260

CURRENCY AND RATE Zambian kwacha (ZMW); US$1 = ZMW5.71. Note that the Zambian kwacha was rebased on 1 January 2013, at a rate of 1,000 old kwacha (ZMK) to 1 new kwacha (ZMW). Old currency is no longer legal tender. There are moneychangers and ATMs but not all that many, so stock up with kwachas when possible.

RED TAPE There is not much red tape in general, but the northern border at Nakonde is quite a hassle, with carbon tax, road tax, and even a 'tax' for placing tacky bits of red/white plastic tape to act as rear/front reflectors. Finally there is a ZMW20 road tax after the border. Moneychangers here give poor rates, but there is no choice as the next banking facility is the Barclays ATM in Nakonde. There are quite a lot of police check-posts along the roads.

Visas All visitors except citizens of some Commonwealth countries need a visa. Check whether visas are being given at borders, as has been the case recently.

African embassies
http://embassy.goabroad.com/embassies-in/zambia
www.embassypages.com/zambia

DRIVING AND ROADS Drive on the left. Many roads are being rebuilt, but there are speed traps and police officers everywhere (the fine for overtaking on a white line is US$80 – a legitimate fine!). There aren't many fuel stations, so keep your tank filled up. It's a good road from Tanzania to Kabwe. From Kabwe to Lusaka and east to Malawi, the roads were quite badly pot-holed.

Fuel costs Diesel: US$1.89; petrol: US$2.06 per litre. Expensive!

CLIMATE It is sunny but cool from May to September and hot from October to November. The rains are normally from November to April. Most parks and other resorts shut down during this time, as the majority of roads are impassable.

HIGHLIGHTS Victoria Falls is the most imposing sight. You can try white-water rafting and bungee jumping if you need more adrenalin highs than you get from just driving on Zambian roads. Try taking an easy canoe ride down the Zambezi if you actually want to enjoy the surroundings. A trip to one of the flagship national parks

– South Luangwa, the Lower Zambezi and the Kafue – with their varied and prolific wildlife, is highly recommended, as is the historic Shiwa N'gandu. In the north close to Lake Tanganyika are the Kalambo Falls.

🏠 WHERE TO STAY

Lusaka Lusaka now has several large shopping centres and ATMs throughout the city. Supermarkets and restaurants abound. In town there is camping for US$10 at **Lusaka Backpackers** (formerly Chachacha Backpackers) (*www.lusakabackpackers.com*). **Eureka Camping Park** is 10km south of the city on Kafue Road (S 15° 30.206, E 28° 15.901). It has a bar and restaurant as well as a large grassy camping area with lots of shelters for cooking. Chalets are available and camping costs US$6–7 per person. **Pioneer Campsite** (*www.pioneercampzambia.com*) is signposted 5km south of the Great East Road, 18km east of the city centre, 3km east of the airport turn-off. Camping costs US$5 each. Both campsites are close to public transport into Lusaka.

***En route* to Mpika** Along the scenic road 60km south of the Nakonde border is **Camping Kings Highway** to the left (east side). Some 20km west of Shiwa N'gandu you can camp at **Kapishya Hot Springs**, and there's camping south of Mpika, too, at **Mutinondo**. Closer to Kabwe is the **Forest Inn**.

Mpika The **Hotel Mazongo** before town on the right has loads of garden area. Camping costs US$11 and rooms are US$17 for a double.

Kabwe The **Hotel Garden** on the left when leaving town has camping space and rooms at US$17. **Tuskers Hotel** has a great garden, but it's not a cheap option. To avoid the city rush, consider **Fringilla Lodge**, south of Kabwe and 51km north of Lusaka, also with camping.

Kafue/Harare junction South of Lusaka, at Kafue town, the road splits: southwest to Livingstone; southeast to Chirundu and Harare. The **Riverside Mission** is 3km along a dirt road left off the Harare road, near the junction. It's a lovely place with no fixed charge; donations accepted. Freshly grown fruit and veggies are sold here. Volunteers are welcomed. South on the road to Livingstone is the paradise of **Moorings Campsite**, 2km left off the main road, 50km south of Mazabuka and 11km north of Monze.

Livingstone/Victoria Falls There are plenty of backpacker places in Livingstone that also offer camping. Their names are liable to change periodically, even if the premises don't. **Fawlty Towers** is fine, with parking/camping at the rear; US$10. Closer to the falls is **Livingstone Safari Lodge and Camp** near the misty spray-cloud view. **The Grotto** has a large grassy area, pool, bar, hot showers with plenty of water and power, but normally only accepts overland truck groups. Camping costs US$8. The **Zambezi Waterfront** campsite is huge and based right on the water with a lovely view over the Zambezi River. There is a bar and pool on site plus rooms. It gets rowdy when a big truck turns up. Entrance to the falls was US$20 per person with parking at US$5.

Upstream from Victoria Falls is **Bovu Island** (✆ *323 708; www.junglejunction. info/bovu.htm*). It is popular, so it may be worth checking beforehand.

Kazungula/Shesheke At Shesheke is **Brenda's Best Baobab**, which comes highly recommended, with camping from US$6.

Lake Kariba Look out for **Eagle's Rest**, but beware of crocodiles!

Kafue National Park Riverside camping options are plentiful but not cheap. Central is **Mayukuyuku Bush Camp**; to the east, consider **McBrides'**, **Leopard Lodge** or **Kafue River Camp**; to the south, **KaingU Campsite**, **Puku Pan Safari Lodge**, **Hippo Bay** and **Nanzhila Plains**. **Kasabushi Camp**, accessed off the spinal road inside the southern section of the park, has braai facilities and individual camping areas. **Museksese Fly Camp**, open May to December, has been getting some great feedback. **Mawimbi Bush Camp** has luxury en suite tents, and offers canoeing, bush walks, game drives and fishing.

Chipata *En route* to South Luangwa from Lusaka are **Bridge Camp** and, at Petauke, is **Zulu Kraal Campsite**. The popular **Mama Rula's B&B and campsite** (*www.mamarulas.com*) in Chipata has a small bar, large camping area and lots of showers (hot if you ask for the fire to be lit). Internet is sporadic. Camping costs US$7; rooms start at US$25 each.

South and North Luangwa National Park Park entry is US$25 per person, with a foreign-registered vehicle costing an extra US$30. In general the wildlife is prolific, but the season may dictate the abundance of animals you find. There are reasonable camping opportunities just outside the South Park, at US$5–7 per person. In the North Park is **Natangwe Community Campsite**, US$10.

The **Croc Valley Camp** (*www.crocvalley.com*) is a part of the old crocodile farm. Off the main road about 2km from South Luangwa Park entrance on the right, it is a very friendly campsite. A new bar and restaurant with pool and hot showers are being built. There is a large grassy area to camp on and another camping area for overland trucks, from US$10 per person. With a fantastic setting right on the river's edge, you have the chance to see elephants, hippos and zebra wandering through the campsite. Game drives are US$40 for the first drive and US$35 for the second, plus a park entry fee of US$25 (or US$20 for residents).

Lower Zambezi National Park There is a **community campsite** near Chongwe, and camping at several of the lodges along the river west of the national park. Park entry fees are similar to those for the Luangwa.

Kasanka National Park Area There are two cheap places: **Nkwali Pontoon Campsite** and **Fibre (Fibwe) Campsite**. The Kasanka Trust runs the **Shoebill Island Camp** in the Bangweulu Wetlands area. At Lake Waka Waka is a tranquil place to bush camp if you take all the necessary supplies.

OTHER Zambia is developing very fast, but unfortunately crime is now on the increase, particularly in Lusaka. Take a taxi at night. Be careful around Victoria Falls after dark and watch out for petty theft. The country is getting very expensive, but most things do now work. Activities around Livingstone include scenic flights, elephant-back riding, bungee jumps, jet boat rides and sunset/booze cruises.

FURTHER INFORMATION
Zambia Chris McIntyre (Bradt Travel Guides)
www.zambia.co.zm

ZIMBABWE

At the time of writing, things are much better then they were, but keep an eye on the situation.

CAPITAL Harare

LANGUAGE English, Shona and Sindebele

INTERNATIONAL TELEPHONE CODE +263

CURRENCY AND RATE Zimbabwe adopted the US dollar in 2009 in order to curb rampant inflation. See www.newzimbabwe.com for up-to-date news on whether or not the country will again have its own currency. Old Zimbabwe dollar (and million dollar!) notes can be found as souvenirs, but they have no monetary value.

RED TAPE There are some roadblocks and police checks. There is an entry tax.

Visas Visas are required for most nationalities. They vary in cost; some are free, others are US$40–50. Yellow fever vaccination certificates are obligatory. A visitor's entry pass can be issued at the border.

African embassies
http://embassy.goabroad.cm/embassies-in/zimbabwe
www.embassypages.com/zimbabwe

DRIVING AND ROADS Drive on the left. Roads were in relatively good condition, but there are some poorer sections. It's a good road to Kazungula with no traffic, but watch out for wildlife.

Fuel costs Diesel: US$1.50; petrol: US$1.70 per litre.

CLIMATE Because of its generally higher altitude, the country has a temperate climate. The rainy season is December to March and cool season May to September.

HIGHLIGHTS In the east are the highlands and Chimanimani National Park. Perhaps the best-known site is the Great Zimbabwe ruin near Masivingo. In the northwest is the Lake Kariba district, with its lake of dead trees. The

unmissable Victoria Falls offer a variety of activities, from white-water rafting to helicopter rides over the falls. Other national parks are Hwange, Mana Pools, Matobo and Matusadona.

🏠 WHERE TO STAY

Harare Most overlanders used to head for **Backpackers and Overland Lodge** on Twentydales Road. Camping cost US$5–6. **Small World Backpackers** in Avondale is another place for cheap living. You might also try the **Hillside Lodge** or **York Lodge** in Newlands. Don't walk around at night. The **Coronation Caravan Park** is 6km from town (S 17° 50. 980, E 31° 68.100).

Bulawayo In Burnside near Mabukuwene Nature Reserve is **Burkes Paradise**, where overland trucks abound. There are dorms, rooms, kitchen, pool and lots of grassy areas, with prices from US$7 to US$15.

Mutare Look for the **Municipal Caravan and Camping Park** on Harare Road. Don't walk around at night.

Chimanimani National Park The **Mutekeswane Base Camp** is the place to stay. You can leave your vehicle at the park entrance and take all necessary goods with you while trekking the area for a few days. You'll need to be self-sufficient; camping is possible in the various caves and lodges dotted around the area. Park entry fees were US$10 per day. See www.zimparks.org for the latest park fees.

Victoria Falls With an atmospheric bar, shaded camping and good facilities, **Shoestrings Backpackers' Lodge** (*www.shoestringsvicfalls.com*) is a great place to stay; it costs US$5 per person. Ask for Tim Cherry. **Victoria Falls Backpackers** is another place. Also at Victoria Falls is the **Restcamp and Lodges**, a vast area for campers and overland trucks. Camping costs around US$5–6 per person. Take care if walking around after dark. There are ATMs in town. There is an entrance charge of US$30 to visit the Victoria Falls Park.

Great Zimbabwe National Park Park entry fees are US$15 per person. Camping costs US$10 per person for a site outside the park; camping is no longer allowed in the park. Watch out for the vervet monkeys; they'll steal anything.

OTHER So far tourists have not been directly affected by the politics, but seek the latest advice.

Zimbabwe has a significant **tsetse-fly** problem, particularly along Lake Kariba. You will see blue-and-silver screens dotted along the side of roads, which attract the flies. Tsetse flies can give a very vicious bite, so beware. You may also come across tsetse-fly control stations, where two people with a butterfly net in either hand search every part of your vehicle for the elusive fly. This is a genuine search; you are very unlikely to be asked for any 'donation', but the experience may keep you amused for days. Don't wear blue; it's the flies' favourite colour!

FURTHER INFORMATION

Zimbabwe Paul Murray (Bradt Travel Guides)

THE END

A hazy sunshine greeted us as we parked by the seaside. A couple of tour buses pulled up to share the view. But at this point we were more troubled by our lack of communication with the shipping agents. The internet had crashed at the café down the road. How and when were we going to get our beloved Land Rover home? It's a pity that we took in the significance of the view from the car park too hurriedly; it should have been a moment to savour. Table Mountain was clearly in the picture: the symbolic end of our trip, which had taken us from London to Cape Town. Well, we had made it, but nobody else knew that. American tourists poured from the coach; if it was Wednesday, it must be Cape Town.

10

Guide to Countries on the Return Route via Asia

This chapter contains a brief section on the main countries that you might visit on a return trip through Asia, as detailed in *Chapter 2*.

Only brief details are given here. For comprehensive information pick up the relevant travel guides, such as the Bradt guides!

INDIA

CAPITAL Delhi

LANGUAGE Hindi, English and many others

INTERNATIONAL TELEPHONE CODE +91

CURRENCY AND RATE Indian rupee (INR); US$1 = INR62

RED TAPE A carnet is required plus insurance, obtained in the nearest border/entry town. The carnet is valued at 500% of the vehicle's value, so don't have an expensive model. Normally Nepal can be added to the policy – see www.newindia.co.in.

Visas Most nationalities require visas in advance. Fees have increased to around US$130 for most nationalities, plus a service fee and online prearrangement. A one-month visa may be available at the border, but it's best to get it beforehand. Tourist visas are normally valid for six months.

DRIVING AND ROADS Officially all should drive on the left, but most stick to the middle! Main roads are in quite good condition. Side roads are poor, but driving standards are shocking everywhere. Don't be surprised to find traffic heading along motorways on the wrong carriageway; although this is becoming less common, it's better to assume the most unlikely scenario. Buffalo carts and bicycles may park in the fast lane and be invisible at night.

Fuel costs Diesel: US$0.99; petrol: US$1.25 per litre. See www.mypetrolprice.com.

CLIMATE The winter, from November to early March, is the best time, before the heat of spring and the rains of the summer monsoon. October is still hot but OK.

HIGHLIGHTS There are far too many highlights to list. Between Mumbai and Kathmandu are Ellora, Ajanta, Mandu, Sanchi near Bhopal, Agra, Khajuraho, Varanasi and jolly old grotty Gorakhpur! Elsewhere Rajasthan is fabulous for

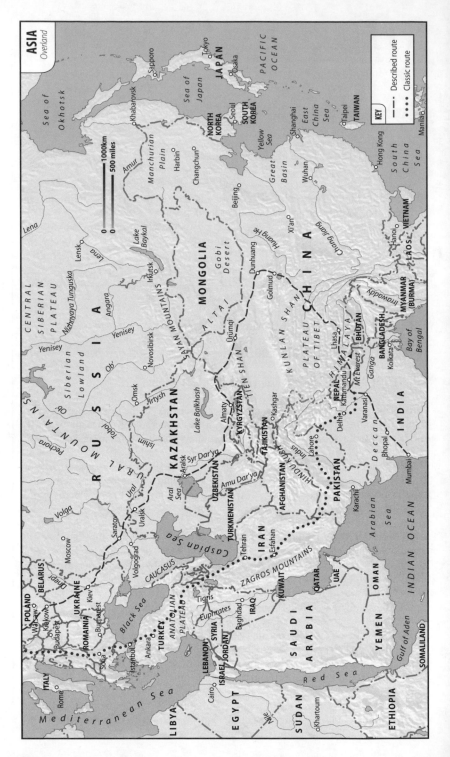

ASIA
Overland

KEY
- - - Described route
···· Classic route

PACIFIC OCEAN

Sea of Okhotsk

JAPAN
Tokyo
Osaka
Sapporo

Khabarovsk

Sea of Japan

NORTH KOREA
SOUTH KOREA
Seoul

TAIWAN
Taipei

Manila

East China Sea

Shanghai

Yellow Sea

Hong Kong

South China Sea

Manchurian Plain
Harbin
Changchun

Beijing

Wuhan

Great Basin

Xi'an

CHINA

Chang Jiang

Huang He

Dunhuang

Gobi Desert

MONGOLIA

Golmud

KUNLAN SHAN

PLATEAU OF TIBET

Lhasa

Mt Everest

HIMALAYA

NEPAL
Kathmandu

BHUTAN

BANGLADESH
Kolkata

Bay of Bengal

MYANMAR (BURMA)
Irrawaddy

LAOS
VIETNAM
Hanoi

ALTAI

Ürümqi

TIEN SHAN

Kashgar

KYRGYZSTAN

TAJIKISTAN

HINDU KUSH

Delhi

Varanasi

Ganga

INDIA

Deccan

Bhopal

Mumbai

Arabian Sea

INDIAN OCEAN

Karachi

PAKISTAN
Lahore

Indus

AFGHANISTAN

TURKMENISTAN

UZBEKISTAN

Amu Dar'ya

Syr Dar'ya

Aral Sea

KAZAKHSTAN

Lake Balkhash

Almaty

SAYAN MOUNTAINS

Lake Baykal

Irkutsk

Lensk

Lena

Angara

Yenisey

Nizhnaya Tunguska

CENTRAL SIBERIAN PLATEAU

Siberian Lowland

Ob'

Novosibirsk

Omsk

Ishim

Irtysh

Tobol

R U S S I A

U R A L M O U N T A I N S

Pechora

Ob'

Yenisey

Lena

1000km
500 miles
0
0

Atyrau

Ural'sk

Ural

IRAN
Tehran
Esfahan

ZAGROS MOUNTAINS

Caspian Sea

Volga

Saratov

Volgograd

Moscow

Dnipr

BELARUS

UKRAINE
Kiev

POLAND
Warsaw
Kraków

Lviv

ROMANIA
Bucharest

Budapest

ITALY
Rome

Black Sea

Sofia

Istanbul

Ankara

TURKEY

ANATOLIAN PLATEAU

CAUCASUS

Tigris

Euphrates

IRAQ
Baghdad

SYRIA
LEBANON

ISRAEL
JORDAN

KUWAIT

QATAR

UAE

OMAN

SAUDI ARABIA

YEMEN

Gulf of Aden

SOMALILAND

Red Sea

SUDAN
Khartoum

EGYPT
Cairo

Nile

LIBYA

ETHIOPIA

Mediterranean Sea

pageantry and colourful palaces. In the north in Punjab is Amritsar and its superb Golden Temple; Kashmir when safe and Ladakh are all possibilities closer to the old classic route. To the east is Calcutta (Kolkata), Darjeeling, Sikkim and remote Assam. Going south, it's beaches, temples, ashrams and the Kerala backwaters; all best explored in winter.

🏠 WHERE TO STAY
There are far too many options to list, but here are a few old favourites. Wild camping is not an easy option in India with so many people around, but a few designated hotel backyards are available in most places. If in doubt, head to one of the State Government (ie: Rajastan Tourism complexes/hotels/bungalows) first, as they usually have parking and gardens.

Mumbai
Accommodation is not cheap here. This is the most likely port of arrival in India; the port itself is called Nawa Durga and it's just across the bay. We stayed at the **Hotel Carlton**, which is not at all grand. It's behind the famous **Taj Hotel** and very near India Gate, from where you will catch the ferry over to the docks when your container has arrived. Camping is not an option.

Delhi
Try the **YMCA**, which has parking and is central near Connaught Place (now called Rajiv Chowk). It's on Jai Singh Road near the Sikh temple.

Amritsar
It's easy to camp here at the famous overlanders' hideaway of **Mrs Bhandari's Guest House** in the cantonment area northwest of town. It's also a super place to park a vehicle for some months if necessary to return to your home country or elsewhere for a while.

Jaipur
An old Maharajah's palace, **Hotel Bissau** will allow campers if it's not busy.

Agra
The most popular place for overlanders to stay/camp was **Hotel Laurie's**, an old colonial place supposedly used by royalty once – it may be closed by now, so ask at guesthouses near the Taj south side.

Dhulia
Once only squalid dives were on offer, but near the east side ring road are a couple of super new quiet hotels, including the **Hotel Manas**, with loads of garden area for parking.

Sanchi
For a quiet retreat, try the **Hotel Sambodhi** on the right, south of the Buddhist monuments.

Khajuraho
There's good parking in the grounds of the **MPTDC Hotel Jhankar** just 200m south of the Raja Café.

Varanasi
The **Surya Hotel** is everyone's favourite. There's good parking/camping, nice rooms and superb north Indian food. The location is away from the bustle in the cantonment area close to a couple of five-star hotel swimming pools. Nearby is Mr Shafiq Junior's excellent workshop, with hoisting gear suspended from a large shady Banyan tree – it's an overlanding institution.

Gorakhpur
You can just squeeze a Land Rover into the secure parking of the **Hotel Amber** opposite the station. Otherwise you'll have to head west to **Hotel Bobina**.

NEPAL

CAPITAL Kathmandu

LANGUAGE Nepali, English and many local languages

INTERNATIONAL TELEPHONE CODE +977

CURRENCY AND RATE Nepalese rupee (NPR); US$1 = NPR99

RED TAPE A carnet is required plus insurance, obtained in the nearest border/entry town. Indian insurance normally covers Nepal, but you must ask for it.

Visas Most nationalities require visas. Visas can be obtained at borders. One month costs US$40 or US$100 for three-month multiple entry.

DRIVING AND ROADS Drive on the left. Main roads are in quite good condition. Side roads are poor. There are a lot of dirt mountain roads that vie to be the most dangerous road in the world, but they'll wreck your suspension. Driving standards are better than India – they couldn't be worse!

Fuel costs Diesel: US$1.03; petrol: US$1.30 per litre.

CLIMATE Autumn and winter (October to April) are the best times, before the heat of late spring and the travel delays of the summer monsoon rains.

HIGHLIGHTS The Kathmandu Valley has enough World Heritage Sites to delay you for days, as well as all the pie shops and restaurants. For superb mountain vistas without having to trek, head to Pokhara. *En route* from India is the Chitwan National Park as well as Bardia Park to the west. Find a place to park (a hotel yard) and take time off to trek into the Himalayan peaks: Everest, Annapurna, Manaslu, Langtang and Ganesh for starters.

WHERE TO STAY

Kathmandu Our favourite is the **Kathmandu Guest House** (double rooms from US$2 to US$180), but parking for long periods is not possible. Elsewhere there is the yard of the 1905 restaurant behind the Tri Devi Marg temples and one where the Greenline bus parks, but neither are very secure in the daytime. Otherwise it's a bit tricky. You might be able to park at Park Village near Budhanikantha if you stay a while – that's not a hardship in any case. In the 1970s everyone parked at Withes Hotel in Teku, when Teku was a field. It's still there, but the parking space is less and now its name is **Hotel Valley View**, although the view of the valley has long gone.

Pokhara The easiest option is to head to the **Comfort Inn** for good parking; it's down a small lane opposite the Fishtail Lodge area – ask for directions or look online. There are dozens of hotels on Lakeside, some with gardens and yards, so try your luck.

Chitwan There are dozens of places, some with gardens. The **Maruni** complex has space, but is a little far away from the action.

Kodari Below the Chinese border a couple of street hotels are fine and so is parking, since it's the end of the road in Nepal.

CHINA

CAPITAL Beijing

LANGUAGE Mandarin, Cantonese, Tibetan, Uighur and others

INTERNATIONAL TELEPHONE CODE +86

CURRENCY AND RATE Chinese yuan renminbi (CNY); US$1 = CNY6.07. The Bank of China is near the top of Zhangmu (which is on a steep hillside), on the left.

RED TAPE The Chinese excel at red tape, so expect months of application processing. All foreign vehicles must take a Chinese guide with them, which is actually a wise idea, since language and bureaucracy would be a big headache otherwise. A temporary Chinese driving licence, vehicle plates and vehicle roadworthiness test (conducted in Shigatse or Yining) and insurance are other requirements. All this is included in the cost, except for hotels and food. Most Chinese travel agents cannot arrange for visitors to drive their own vehicles in China. We used a company called Navo from Chengdu (*www.navo-tour.com*).

Visas Visas are required for most nationalities in advance unless arriving from Nepal, where special arrangements are in force. Your Chinese visa will normally be cancelled by the Chinese embassy in Kathmandu, so don't bother to get it in advance; wait until you get permission from the Chinese to enter from Nepal, through the agent arranging your visit.

DRIVING AND ROADS Drive on the right. There is a newly sealed road between Kathmandu and Lhasa and beyond to Golmud. Some patchy sections are being improved in Qinghai, Gansu and Xinjiang. Ürümqi to Kashgar is a new, modern highway. Between Kashgar and Lhasa via the border highway the road is being sealed and could be done by 2014.

Fuel costs Diesel: US$1.72; petrol: US$1.72 per litre.

CLIMATE Spring and autumn are best for Tibet and across China. Coming from Europe, the late summers in Tibet are also a good time for warmer days but with some misty views on the mountains. Unfortunately the Indian monsoon wreaks havoc on the road into Tibet through Nepal for those heading westwards between early June and until mid-September. Winter is to be avoided completely.

HIGHLIGHTS Stunning parts of the route include crossing the Himalayas and Kunlun Mountains, Everest views, Xegar (Shegar) Dzong, Xigatse (Shigatse), Gyangtse, Lhasa and the lonely Tibetan Plateau. Further north are the Buddhist caves at Dunhunag and the old parts of Turfan. Driving in China is a highlight in itself for its novelty value; however, it could wear a bit thin after three weeks.

WHERE TO STAY
Zhangmu On the left side, **Hotel He Jia** costs US$17.

Nyalam For good parking, with a slope so you can push your vehicle to start it if it's freezing, go to **Hotel Nyalam** (US$17). A heater is available plus electric power, but the loos are grungy.

Xegar (Shegar) Dzong With a toilet at the end of the corridor, **Hotel Ding Ri** (US$17) is rough and ready, but OK. No good food around.

Xigatse (Shigatse) The **Hotel Shandong** is a high-rise monstrosity but has good rooms and great views of the fort and Tashi Lhunpo monastery; double room US$80 (US$20 'special price'). Eat along the road 1–2km south in a student area. Tashi Lhunpo entry costs US$10 per person. If you're lucky, the monks will be at prayer. The old fort has been fully restored and Xigatse is now a substantial town. The vehicle insurance company was north and east of the hotel. The police are south and east of the hotel, while the MOT is on the road in from Lhatse. Your guide will have to take you to all these places.

Nagartze On the shores of Lake Yamdrok, **Hotel Yangua** (US$25) is good, warm and comfortable.

Lhasa Close to the Barkhor and next to the Banak Shol, a double room in the **Dong Cuo Youth Hostel** costs US$20, plus US$2 for parking. You can eat across the road in various noodle places. The **Banak Shol**, one of the first backpacker hotels to open in Lhasa back in the mid 1980s, is now more expensive but has a good restaurant. **Hotel Snowlands** is another old favourite, offering DVD burning and internet. **Hotel Kirey** is decent. The old Barkhor area has been remodelled. To visit Ganden monastery, have a rest from driving and take a taxi. Entry is US$8. It is one hour east of Lhasa and up an extremely big hill to the south – 59km, plus 12km up continuous zigzags.

Nagqu The **Hotel Xin Shu Dai** (US$22) is adequate. It's along the third road on the right, then 100m on the left. We cooked our own food in a snowstorm to avoid dodgy-looking local fare.

Tuo Tuo Beyan A one-street settlement in the middle of nowhere on the high plateau at 4,500m. We were taken to the new **Guesthouse Xin Hwang** (US$20) near the fuel stop on the right side, off the main road. It's then 50m on the right. Good choice with a warmish glasshouse corridor, TV and heating. An icy loo was down the corridor.

Golmud Quite a large town now but still a drab, dreary place. Security checks are normally expected here when staying overnight. Since they were not open at the weekend, we did not waste time! You might be able to stay in the **Hai Ma Hotel** here – although it is not strictly for foreigners' use (US$15 double). Parking is easy and it's very convenient for the roads in and out, being a short way after a right turn at the big roundabout that leads to the city centre. Take-away meals are available nearby.

Aksai The **Hotel Aksai** is a great place (US$30). Good parking in a vast area. Aksai is an impressive modern town with traditional-style new mosques and civic buildings. **Mingboa Guest House** is an alternative (US$17).

Dunhuang Stay at Crescent Moon, 5km south of town on the Qili road. **Dunhuang Zephyr Youth Hostel** complex is a real overlander-style place near the dunes and camel farm (US$40 for a good double room). It has Mongolian-style rooms and camping is possible. Also here is Charley Johng's **Dune Guest House**. The entry to the dunes of Crescent Moon is a whopping US$20 each with camels at US$14. This is not like Algeria, where the dunes are free!

Hami You could stay at the motel by the junction to town, to avoid the traffic. Otherwise head to the cosy **Hotel My Home** (double US$24). It's on the right on a road south of the railway station. There are about four hotels around here, up to US$50.

Turfan The **No Name Hotel** is near the bus station and is OK for US$17. Your guide should be able to find it. Eat in the cafeteria north and west on the opposite side. The ancient city is now hidden behind the new modern streets. The famed mosque minaret is still the big attraction to the east. Three ancient Silk Road historic sights are within a day-trip distance: Gaochang, Bezeklik Caves and Jiaohe, as well as the Flaming Mountains (Huoyan Shan).

Ürümqi There is a small town tax on entry. Try the good **Youth Hostel** (CNY100 for a double room) on the right side (heading north), north of the town rock outcrops. It's about 300m north of the Carrefour superstore!

Jing He There is the nice **Hotel Jing He** for 'Aliens' priced around US$17–US$25. It is the only hotel for foreigners and has good parking.

Khorgos The **Xian Tao Shortcut Hotel** costs US$20 or US$17 for a roadside room, but isn't particularly friendly. There are some welding shops to the south in scruffy local yards. After a three-day delay due to 'all things Chinese', we needed ten signatures, including five from Ürümqi, to exit the country. Two French Landy overlanders took a week to enter here, partly due to the May Day holiday and then paperwork.

KAZAKHSTAN

CAPITAL Almaty

LANGUAGE Kazakh, Russian and some English spoken

INTERNATIONAL TELEPHONE CODE +7

CURRENCY AND RATE Kazakh tenge (KZT); US$1 = KZT185. Note there is no exchange at the Khorgos border, but there was an ATM on the left just after the exit gate. Exchange is possible in Zharkent.

RED TAPE The border was easy going and it only took two hours for the process. Vehicle papers, which must not be lost, are issued at the border. Normally you have to register your passport with the OVIR, since they will not give this extra stamp at the Khorgos border thus far. In Almaty the OVIR office was at the intersection of streets Naurybai and Kabanbai. There is no fee, but expect a brawl to get in. Insurance is not apparently mandatory, but you would be wise to find some. We obtained cover from Nomad for a mere £3 – their office was south of the bus depot in Almaty. If you're coming from Europe, try asking around for insurance – maybe at Campbell Irvine in London.

Visas Required for most nationalities, they must be obtained in advance. It appears they cannot be extended, so plan very carefully and then wait for the Chinese to change it all around!

DRIVING AND ROADS Drive on the right. The main roads are being upgraded but there were some long bad sections – it's a large country to transit. Our route was between Almaty, Taraz, Shymkent, Aral (Aralsk), Aktope, Oral (Uralsk) and into Russia.

Fuel costs Diesel: US$0.66; petrol: US$0.52 per litre.

CLIMATE Spring and autumn are the best time to visit to avoid the hot summers and bitter winters.

HIGHLIGHTS The incredible Charyn Gorge, a smaller version of the Grand Canyon, is east of the capital, in wild country. Almaty is famed for its fabulous, colourful cathedral and easy going flavour, while Taraz is the opposite, notable for its grim Soviet hangover. Shymkent has some history to uncover and Turkestan has some atmospheric central Asian blue mosques. Heading northwest is the depressing, dried-up Aral Sea, the camels of the desert and the Russian style of the city of Oral/Uralsk.

 WHERE TO STAY

Zharkent The **Hotel Zharkent** (US$40) has a family connection with Canada and is the green building in a complex with a bank and ATM shop. It's on the left, after passing a police station on the right.

Almaty The **Motel/Hotel Dostar** is 3km before town on the left side. It's on the top floor of a big complex with shops but no food. Take bus 100 from the bus stop across the road to the Sahyat bus depot in the city. Near the depot is a Land Rover dealer, as well as the Green Supermarket – great supplies here – just behind the main street; ask someone to show you where. Raiymbek road is the way out to Taraz.

Taraz The Hotel Taraz is unfriendly and will not accept foreigners. Drive out on the Shymkent road for 2km and look for the **Motel Green** on the left, a great place with parking and restaurant, plus room service. Double room US$22.

Turkestan The **Hotel Yassi** (US$27 for a room) near the big mausoleum has good parking. **Hotel Eden** (US$33) is good, with the best food – chicken Kiev for US$5.50. To reach the Eden, turn left out of the Yassi Hotel, then right and then left. It's on the right – some guide maps are wrong.

Khosaly This quiet town is off the main road; turn right, then 200–300m on the left side is the two-storey **Guest House Gosterlitz Almaty**, beyond a square. Rooms cost US$35–US$60. There is safe parking in the courtyard behind it.

Aral Although it's a Soviet-style dump, **Hotel Aral** (US$27) has good parking in the yard across the road. Once in town, follow the bigger road over the railway, then go to the right side and take the second left to a café and internet on the main road. It's down a street right towards the old port area.

Aktope It might be possible to camp (signed but unclear) on entry before the ring road. Try the **Hotel Aktope** (US$42) with parking behind some way back. The traffic is bad and chaotic. Follow the ring road, then drive into the centre; turn to the right for the hotel. To leave town, head south and follow signs for Oral.

Oral/Uralsk The **Hotel Sahayat** is a great place (US$35–US$70). Satellite TV at last! Parking behind is fine. The town is an extremely confusing place and it's hard to find the real centre. The main area is on the west side, almost hidden with so many ring roads. Oral is a very interesting town with fine churches, historic buildings and a pleasant atmosphere.

RUSSIA

CAPITAL Moscow

LANGUAGE Russian

INTERNATIONAL TELEPHONE CODE +7

CURRENCY AND RATE Russian rouble (RUB); US$1 = RUB35.27

RED TAPE Surprisingly little hassle by officials, but vehicle documents need to be obtained. Passport registration was not in fact required. Insurance is the main hassle if you're heading from Kazakhstan – hopefully they will send you to the blue office cabin down the road. In our case, we were sent to follow a taxi into a small village on the left about 8km further on, to a man in a small private house! Insurance was US$50 for two weeks. There was no place to change cash into roubles here. If you're coming from Europe, try to find insurance beforehand – try Down Under Insurance (*www.duinsure.com*) in London. Checking into hotels, especially in the countryside, can take ages and they are not cheap.

Visas Visas are required for most nationalities in advance. Allow some time for the process. Transit visas (ten days) are enough and easier to get for a short visit, but fixing the dates in advance is a gamble.

DRIVING AND ROADS Drive on the right. Motorways and main roads are surprisingly poor. Pot-holes abound but they don't seem to deter Russian truckers and motorists from keeping up a high average speed. Beware!

Fuel costs Diesel: US$1.13; petrol: US$0.82 per litre.

CLIMATE The autumn and spring are the best times before the heat of summer and bitter cold of the winter.

HIGHLIGHTS On our route, Saratov has some quaint old buildings and onion-domed churches. The typical grim, run-down Soviet-era architecture of Voronezh and Belgorod is of historic interest. Otherwise the steppe is flat and somewhat endless.

WHERE TO STAY
Saratov Try the **Hotel Slovakia**; it has some unrefurbished rooms (which were perfectly fine) for US$60 and better rooms at US$150. The ATM here works; you'll

need it! From the northern ring road, head into town and go left at a fuel station roundabout. Continue downhill, passing an onion-dome church. Then head left to the waterfront area. The hotel suggested we needed to register our passports, but they couldn't do it at the weekend. They implied we had seven days' grace, but in the event we didn't do it as we left the country within that period. The **Shoreline Hotel** is close by and cheaper, but they had registration issues. Parking was OK on the street square.

Borisoglebsk The no-name **pink-coloured motel** here was off the main highway on the right near factories, and then on the left side. It was very expensive for a simple double room (US$60), but had parking in a gated yard. Check-in took an hour over paperwork and there was no food. We cooked and ate dinner long before finishing the check-in.

Belgorod There is a modern, swish brightly coloured motel 15km before town on the right that is excellent. Beware, though, that the meat meals are priced by weight, so your US$26 dish suddenly becomes US$36 plus!

OTHER Exiting Russia into Ukraine south of Belgorod is slow but not particularly stressing. Customs is straightforward (in room 7). Insurance should be available and you might try to get it to cover Poland, since we could not get any on entry to Poland. Our UK insurance could not be reissued and we had to find insurance by email and phone from Krakow for the transit across Europe.

UKRAINE

CAPITAL Kiev

LANGUAGE Russian/Ukrainian

INTERNATIONAL TELEPHONE CODE +38

CURRENCY AND RATE Ukraine hryvnia (UAH); US$1 = UAH8.85

RED TAPE Perhaps surprisingly, you shouldn't have to contend with too much red tape. Papers for the vehicle are easily sorted but don't lose them.

DRIVING AND ROADS Most main roads are decent, in places a little rough with a few pot-holes, but they are being improved.

Fuel costs Diesel: US$0.93; petrol: US$1.03 per litre.

HIGHLIGHTS There are a lot for such a little-known country. Kiev has a plethora of churches and monasteries, like the Lavra complex. Don't miss Kamyanets and Kotyn castles, the old Jewish town of Medzhybizh and the old city of Lviv. Further off the route are Odessa and the Crimean attractions.

 WHERE TO STAY

***En route* to Kiev** there is a motel on the right side, trucker-style, 10km west of the capital. A double room costs US$20, plus US$1.50 parking.

Kiev The popular **Hotel and Camping Prolisok** (US$25 for two to camp, including vehicle) is in a beautiful forest on the left along the Lviv road, 1km west of a major junction. Bus 37 goes to the metro lines, then into the centre on the red line (seven–eight stations).

Chirvona Zirka The **Motel Dam** (US$25) is on the left, 10km past Medzhybizh.

Kamyanets The new town has the **Gala Hotel** (US$45).

Lviv The BP Motel (US$20) is good and easy to find on the south-side ring road.

POLAND

CAPITAL Warsaw

CURRENCY Polish złoty (PLN); US$1 = PLN3.03

DRIVING AND ROADS EU money has radically improved motorways, although the road from Ukraine to Krakow will take a while to be done, so some narrow sections through towns and villages can still be expected.

 WHERE TO STAY

Krakow West of the Zakopane road and south of the centre, **Camping Borek** (camping for two including vehicle US$20) is close to the ring road, near a supermarket and BP garage. Tram 8 goes into town. Also try **Camping Korona**, a long way south of the motorway.

Wroclaw Camp at the **Olympic Park** on the east side; cross an old suspension bridge and then follow the signs. Take trams 9, 12 and 17 to get to the city centre.

OTHER You can proceed at your own pace across Europe. When you reach **Calais**, sleep at the docks and get a morning ferry for the final run of the trip.
Readjust to normal life – another journey!

10

Appendix 1

LANGUAGE

FRENCH AND ARABIC TRANSLATIONS You may well speak conversational French, but perhaps the technical terms for vehicle parts will not spring easily to mind. We have listed (in alphabetical order) all relevant vehicle parts in French. As for Arabic, *Salaam aleikum* with a smile can get you a long way, but not knowing the translation of vehicle parts or tools may stump you. The Arabic translation is phonetic, ie: as spoken rather than spelt.

French

accelerator jet	*gicleur de pompe*
alternator	*alternateur*
anti-roll bar	*barre de stabilisateur*
armature	*induit de démarreur*
axle casing	*corps de pont*
ball bearings	*roulement à billes*
ball joint	*rotule*
battery	*batterie*
bearing	*coussinet*
body	*carrosserie*
bolt	*boulon*
brake hose	*flexible de frein*
brake lining	*garniture de frein*
brake master cylinder	*maître-cylindre de frein*
brake shoe	*mâchoires de frein*
brush	*balai*
bumper	*pare chocs*
camshaft	*arbre à cames*
carburettor	*carburateur*
chassis	*chassis*
clutch	*embrayage*
clutch master cylinder	*pompe d'embrayage*
clutch plate	*disque d'embrayage*
clutch slave cylinder	*recepteur d'embrayage*
coil	*bobine d'allumage*
condenser	*condensateur*
conrod	*bielle*
contact points	*jeu de contacts, rupteur*
cotter pins	*bagues d'appui*
crankshaft	*vilebrequin*
crescent spanner	*clé plate*
crown wheel and pinion	*couple conique*
CV joint	*joint homocinétique*
cylinder block	*bloc-cylindres*
cylinder head	*culasse*
diesel	*gazole*
differential	*différentiel*
dipstick	*jauge d'huile*
disc brakes	*freins à disque*
distance recorder	*compteur kilométrique*
distributor	*allumeur*
engine mounting	*tampon*
exhaust valve	*soupape d'échappement*
fan	*ventilateur*
fan belt	*corroie de ventilateur*
float	*flotteur*
float chamber	*cuve à niveau constant*
flywheel	*volant*
fracture in tyre	*déchirure*
fuel gauge	*indicateur de niveau, jauge*
fuel line	*canalisation*
fuel pump	*pompe à essence (gazole)*
fuel tank	*réservoir*
fuse	*fusible*

A1

gasket	*joint*	reverse gear	*marche arrière*
gearbox	*boîte de vitesses*	ring spanner	*clé à oeillet*
(see also third gear and reverse gear)		rocker	*culbuteur*
generator	*dynamo*	rockershaft	*axe de culbuteur*
gudgeon pin	*axe de piston*	rotor arm	*rotor de distributeur*
hammer	*marteau*	rubber bush	*coussinet en*
handbrake cable	*cable de frein à main*		*caoutchouc*
handbrake lever	*levier de frein à main*	screwdriver	*tournevis*
heater plug	*bougie de*	set of pads	*jeu de mâchoires*
	préchauffage	shock absorber	*amortisseur*
hose	*durite*	slow idle jet	*gicleur de ralenti*
ignition switch	*contacteur d'allumage*	socket	*douille*
inlet valve	*soupape d'admission*	socket spanner	*clé à tube*
jack	*cric*	solenoid	*solenoid, bendix*
leaf spring	*lame de ressort*	spanner	*clé*
leakage	*fuite*	spare wheel	*roue de secours*
limited slip	*différentiel*	spark plug	*bougie*
differentials	*autobloquant*	speedo cable	*flexible de tachymètre*
lock nut	*contre écrou*	speedometer	*compteur, tachymètre*
locking washer	*arrêtoir*	spring	*ressort de suspension*
main jet	*gicleur d'alimentation*	starter motor	*démarreur*
manifold	*collecteur*	steering column	*colonne de direction*
needle valve	*pointeau*	steering wheel	*volant de direction*
nut	*écrou*	thermostat	*thermostat*
oil cooler	*radiateur d'huile*	third gear	*pignon de la troisième*
oil filter	*filtre à huile*		*vitesse*
oil seal	*bague d'étanchéité*		(1st *première*,
patch	*rustine*		2nd *deuxième*,
petrol	*essence*		4th *quatrième*,
petrol cap	*bouchon de réservoir*		5th *cinquième*)
piston	*piston*	throttle valve	*papillon*
piston ring	*segment*	tie road	*barre de connexion*
pitman arm	*levier de direction*	torque spanner	*clé dynamométrique*
pliers	*pince*	tube	*chambre à air*
pressure plates	*plateau de pression*	tyre	*pneu*
prop shaft	*arbre de transmission*	tyre lever	*démonte pneu*
pulley	*poulie*	universal joint	*cardan de roue*
puncture	*crevaison*	valve	*soupape*
push rod	*tige de culbuteur*	valve cover	*couvercle de culasse*
(motor/engine)		valve guide	*guide de soupape*
push rod	*tige de poussoir*	valve spring	*ressort de soupape*
(transmission)		water pump	*pompe à eau*
push rod tube	*couvercle de tige*	wheel	*roue*
radiator	*radiateur*	wheel hub	*moyeu de roue*
rear axle	*pont arrière*	wheel rim	*jante*
regulator	*régulateur*	windscreen	*pare-brise*
release bearing	*butée d'embrayage*		

Arabic When reading the imitated pronunciation, stress the part of the word that is underlined. Pronounce each word as if it were an English word and you should be understood sufficiently well.

General

accident	haadethah	north	shemaal
accommodation	maskan	office	maktab
border	hodood	passport	jawaaz safar
bread	khobz	policeman	shortee
camel	jamal	police station	noqtat ash- shortah
campsite	moAskar	post office	maktab bareed
coffee	qahwah	reply to greeting	al laikoum salaam
doctor	tabeebh	riverbed	oued
drinking water	maa' lesh-shorb	road	shaarea
east	sharq	road or piste	tric
exchange rate	seAr at-taHweel	sick	mareed
flat stony plain	hammada	small rock standing	gara
Go away!	Emshee!	in the plain	
greeting	Salaam al Laikoum	small shops	souks
How long will it	Qad aysh waqt	south	janoob
take?	tastaghreq be-	Stop!	Geff!
	taakhoz?	tea	atai
How much?	Kem?	thank you	shukran
journey	rehlah	tip	baksheesh
map	khareetah	valley between dunes	gassi
married	motazawaj	water	mey
morning	sabaah	west	gharb
mountain	jebel	Where can I park?	Wayn awqef as-
night	layl		sayaarah?
no (response)	laa	yes	noam

Vehicle

accelerator	dawaasat al-banzeen	inner tube	anboob daakhelee
anti-freeze	modaad let-tajmeed	long (as in	taweel
battery	bataareeyah	How long?)	
brake	faraamel	mechanic	meekaaneekee
breakdown	ta Atal	motorbike	daraajah
camshaft	amood al-kaamuh		bokhaareeyah
car	sayaarah	oil	zayt
carburettor	karboraateere	park (the vehicle)	hadeeqah
clutch	debreiyaaj	piston	makbas
diesel	deezel	puncture	haqb
distributor	destrebyooter	radiator	raadiyateer
drive	yasooq	screwdriver	mafakk
to drive	yasooq	seatbelt	hezaam al-maqad
engine	moHarrek	spanner	meftaah sawaameel
exhaust	shakmaan	spares	qetaa ghiyaar
fan belt	sayr al-marwahah	spark plug	belajaat
funnel	qomA	speedometer	adaad as-sorah
garage (for fuel)	mahattat banzeen	spring	soostah
garage (for repairs)	garaaj meekaaneekee	steering wheel	ajalat al-qiyaadah
gears	geer	to tow	yashab
handbrake	araamel	transmission	naql al-harakah
ignition	jehaaz al-eshAal	tyre	etaar or taayer
indicator	mo'asher	wheel	ajalah

Appendix 2

PERSONAL DETAILS

Wherever you go in Africa, it's worthwhile having some copies of the following information sheet, in order to speed up some of the bureaucracy. Use A4 paper, then use this and copies of your passport and driving licence for presentation as required. Of course, the information can be written out at each police post, but the officials don't mind the copied material, so why waste time? Alternatively, make a photocopy of your passport photo page and copy the relevant information below on to the same page before photocopying it again many times.

Surname ....

Name ....

Date of birth ....

Place of birth ....

Nationality ....

Passport number ....

Date of issue ....

Date of expiry ....

Place of issue ....

Profession ....

Permanent address ....

Father's name ....

Mother's name ....

Purpose of visit ....

Vehicle make and plate numbers ....

Driving licence number ....

Appendix 3

CHECKLIST

Below is a suggested checklist so that you can see at a glance whether you have everything you might want.

Item	Have or not	Details	Cost
FINANCES			
Travellers' cheques			
US dollars			
British pounds			
Euros			
Other denominations			
Credit cards			
ROUTE PLANNING			
Where, ie: planned route			
For how long			
Suggested itinerary			
Guidebooks and maps			
Africa guidebooks			
North Africa			
West Africa			
Central Africa			
East Africa			
South Africa			
Africa maps			
Michelin 741 – North and West			
Michelin 745 – North East			
Michelin 746 – Central and South Africa			
Michelin 743 – Algeria and Tunisia			
Michelin 742 – Morocco			
Michelin 747 – Ivory Coast			
BUREAUCRACY			
Visas			
For which countries			
Cost estimate			
Can get beforehand			
Other			

Item	Have or not	Details	Cost
Paperwork			
Passport			
Validity			
Number of unused pages			
Vaccination certificates			
Cholera			
Diphtheria			
Hepatitis A and B			
Meningitis			
Polio			
Rabies (optional)			
Tetanus			
Tuberculosis			
Typhoid			
Yellow fever			
NB: Certificate signed by GP/clinic			
Other			
Bond or insurance			
Carnet de passage (carnet) organised for every country mentioned that you will visit			
International certificate for motor vehicles, ie: carte grise (grey card)			
Insurance			
Medical insurance			
Vehicle insurance (optional)			
International driving licence			
References			
in English			
in French			
Passport photos			

Item	Have or not	Details	Cost
VEHICLE SELECTION			
4x4/2WD			
Type			
Registration number			
Chassis number			
Engine number			
Other			
Motorbike			
Type			
Registration number			
Chassis number			
Engine number			
Other			
Bicycle			
Type			
Other			

Item	Have or not	Details	Cost
4X4/2WD			
Preparation			
Sleeping requirements			
Tent			
Rooftop tent			
Inside the vehicle			
Mattresses			
Pillows			
Sleeping bags			
Covers for pillows, etc			
Roof rack			
Security			
Padlocks and hasps			
Windows			
Curtains			
Safety box			
Alarm system (optional)			
Bull bar			
Baffle/bash plate			
Suspension			
Heavy-duty suspension fitted			
Spare battery and split-charge system			
Oil cooler			
Raised air intake			
Tyres			
Spare tyres			
Inner tubes			
Valves			
Foot or electrical tyre pump			
Tyre-repair kit			
Pressure gauge			
Fuel and water tanks			
Capacity			
Fuel			
Water			
Storage boxes			
Seat covers			
Steering-wheel cover			
Stereo			
Type and make			
Serial number			
Canopy			

Item	Have or not	Details	Cost
EQUIPMENT			
Recovery gear			
Electronic or manual winches			
Type and make			
Guarantees			
High-lift jack			
Hydraulic jack			

Item	Have or not	Details	Cost
Blocks of wood to jack on			
Sand ladders			
Towing points			
Towing straps			
Shackles			
Compass and/or Global Positioning System (GPS)			
Type and make			
Mounting and storage system			
Serial number			
Guarantee			
Shovel or sand spades			
Axe or machete			
Warning triangles (2)			
Jerrycans			
Carrying capacity for:			
Fuel			
Water			
Oil			
Fire extinguisher			
Water			
Water purification (eg: Chloromyn T, Puritabs)			
Water filter			
Type			
Capacity of filter before replacement			
Guarantee			
Table and chairs			
Mosquito net/s			
Refrigerator			
Type and make			
Runs on 12V DC or 240V AC or gas or all three			
Serial number			
Guarantee			

Lighting

Item	Have or not	Details	Cost
Car lights			
Fluorescent strip light			
Map light			
Torch and batteries			

Cooking equipment

Item	Have or not	Details	Cost
Petrol stoves			
Kerosene stoves			
Container for kerosene			
Meths burners			
Container for methylated spirits			
Gas stoves			
Gas bottle fitted			
Cooking utensils			
Saucepan			

Item	Have or not	Details	Cost
Deep straight-edged frying pan			
Cooking pot or cast-iron pot			
Kettle			
Pressure cooker or wok (optional)			
Decent sharp knife			
Wooden spoon			
Strainer (optional)			
Tin-opener			
Bottle-opener			
Chopping board			
Plates and bowls (plastic or enamel)			
Mugs (plastic)			
Assortment of cutlery			
Matches and/or firelighters			
Fire grill (optional)			

Cleaning up

Item	Have or not	Details	Cost
Plastic bowl			
Washing-up liquid			
Washing-up cloth			
Scourer			
Drying-up cloth			

Spares and tools

Item	Have or not	Details	Cost
Workshop manual			
3 x oil filters			
4 x fuel filters			
2–3 x air filters			
Engine oil (enough for two changes)			
5 litres of gearbox and differential oil			
Grease			
1–2 litres brake and clutch fluid oil			
1–2 litres coolant (you can use water)			
Heater plugs/spark plugs			
One spare diesel injector			
Set of engine gaskets			
Set of all oil seals			
Set of wheel bearings			
Set of engine mounts			
Set of radiator hoses			
Accelerator cable			
2 x fanbelts			
Set of brake pads			
Brake master cylinder rubbers			
Clutch master and slave cylinder rubbers (as above)			
Wheel cylinder kit – rubbers (or kit for disc brakes)			
Water pump			
Lift pump			
Suspension rubbers and bushes			
Condenser			

Item	Have or not	Details	Cost
Distributor cap			
Contact breaker points			
Spare fuel cap			
Spare radiator cap			
U-bolts centre bolts for leaf springs			
Main leaf springs (coil springs rarely break with careful driving)			
Track rod ends			
Clutch plate			
Wheel nuts			
Water temperature sensor unit			
Sump/gearbox drain plugs			
Propshaft UJ			
Brake hose			
Alternator (complete or at least the brushes)			
Fuses			
Light bulbs			
Other optional parts			
Starter (for remoter areas)			
Fan (for remote areas)			
Injector pipes			
Injector pump (for remote areas)			
Injector pump solenoid if applicable			
Useful items			
Funnel (make sure it fits the filler of your fuel tank)			
Jubilee clips			
Cable ties			
Electrical tapes			
Electrical wires			
Masking tape/duct tape			
Assortment of wire			
Assortment of nuts, bolts and washers			
Plastic fuel line and connectors			
Contact adhesive			
Prately putty/flexible 'bathroom' sealant			
2m fuel hoses (long enough to be used as a siphon)			
Rapid araldite/plastic metal glue			
Plastic padding/instant fibreglass			
Instant gasket paste			
Exhaust repair putty			
Gasket paper			
Can of WD40 or Q20			
Radiator sealant			
Towing eye/cable			
Assorted small sheet metal, short drain piping, square tubing, etc			

Item	Have or not	Details	Cost
Assorted bits of rubber, inner tube, old stockings			
Old rags – lots and lots			

Tools

Item	Have or not	Details	Cost
Good set of spanners (imperial or metric as required)			
Good set of sockets with power bar and ratchet			
Extra large sockets (check sizes needed)			
Assortment of screwdrivers			
Adjustable spanner			
Mole wrench (large and small)			
Pipe wrench			
Grease gun			
Metal and rubber hammers			
Torque wrench			
Pliers (various)			
Circclip removers			
Multi-size puller			
Jump leads			
Set of feeler gauges			
Hacksaw and spare blades			
Multi-meter electrical tester			
Flat metal file			
Small round file			
Coarse flat file			
Hand drill and kit (9V cordless drills can be connected directly to your battery)			
Tyre levers			
Tyre valve tool			
Set of Allen keys			
Centre punch/assorted punches and metal drifts			
Wet and dry sandpaper			
Length of pipe (to extend your power bar for those stubborn nuts)			
Arc welding rods – a few			
G clamp/small vice to attach to bumper			
Magnetic retrieving tool			

MOTORBIKE
Spares and tools

Item	Have or not	Details	Cost
Repair manual			
1 x spare rear tyre			
1 x front and rear heavy-duty inner tubes			
1 x good-quality puncture repair kit with lots of patches			
1 x small mountain-bike pump			
A few spare spokes			
Connecting links for chain			

Appendix 3   CHECKLIST

A3

Item	Have or not	Details	Cost
1 x clutch lever			
1 x brake lever			
1 x clutch cable			
1 x throttle cable(s)			
1 x air filter			
3 x oil filters			
1 x fuel filter			
2 x spark plugs			
Fuel hose and jubilee clips			
Bulbs and fuses			
Electrical wire and connectors			
Assorted nuts, bolts and washers			
Main gaskets			
Duct tape			
Assorted cable ties (lots)			
Spare bungee rope/straps			
Instant gasket			
Silicon sealant			
Epoxy glue			
Liquid steel			
Loctite (for nut threads)			
Small tub of grease			
About 1 litre engine oil (for top up and oiling air filter)			
Standard small toolkit (combination spanners, ³/₈in drive ratchet + relevant sockets, screwdrivers)			
Leatherman's or Swiss Army knife			
Feeler gauges			
File			
Spark plug spanner			
Tyre levers			

Personal equipment

Item	Have or not	Details	Cost
Jacket with built-in shoulder and elbow pads			
Spine protector with a waist band			
Full-length motorcross-style boots (optional)			
Helmet and goggles			
Gloves			

BICYCLE
Spares and tools

Item	Have or not	Details	Cost
Panniers – Overlander by Carradice			
2 x spare tyres			
10 x inner tubes			
Puncture repair kit			
Cables			
Brakepads			
Grease and oil			

Item	Have or not	Details	Cost
Bearings			
Wires and straps			
Pliers			
Set of Allen keys			
Cable cutter			
Spoke tensioner			
Set of spanners			
Screwdriver			
Bottom bracket tensioner			
Front bearing spanner			
Spokes			
Box of nuts and bolts, etc			
Chain link extractor			
Toothbrush			

Personal equipment

Item	Have or not	Details	Cost
Helmet			
Gloves			
Sunglasses			
2 x whistles (as a warning and signal)			
Compass			

CAMPING: MOTORBIKE/BICYCLE

Item	Have or not	Details	Cost
Tent			
Sleeping mat			
Sleeping bag			
Nylon string			
Towel			
Torch			
Thermarest mattress			

Cooking

Item	Have or not	Details	Cost
Stove, eg: MSR high-quality petrol stove or Coleman's multi-fuel cooker			
2 x spoons			
2 x plastic bowls			
2 x plastic cups			
Saucepan			
Penknife			

Water

Item	Have or not	Details	Cost
2 x Travelwell military water purifiers			
2 x 10-litre water bags			
Water bottle			
Filter			

Food

Item	Have or not	Details	Cost
Salt and pepper			
Herbs and spices			
Tea and coffee			
Sugar			
Powdered milk			
Muesli/cereals/oats			
Jam/marmalade			

Item	Have or not	Details	Cost
Rice and pasta			
Tubes of tomato purée			
Stock cubes			
Marmite/Vegemite			
Tinned meat			
Tinned vegetables and fruit			
Packets of instant foods, ie: ready-made pasta, etc			
Oil			
Vinegar			
Flour or cornflour			
Dried beans			
Mustard			
Kendal Mint Cake			
Dried mushrooms or other			
Dried fruit and nuts			
Biscuits and crackers			
Boiled sweets			
Packets of dried food (specific for cyclists and bikers)			
Instant mashed potato			
Small packets Parmesan cheese			

MEDICAL KIT

Seek medical advice before use of any medicaments and read the instructions.

Analgesics (painkillers)

Aspirin for sore throat and mild pain			
Paracetamol for mild pain and temperature			
Ibuprofen for joint inflammation and pain			
Paracetamol/codeine for moderate pain			

General

Stemetil for severe nausea, vomiting and vertigo			
Loperamide for acute diarrhoea			
Oral-rehydration sachets for dehydration			
Senokot tabs for constipation			
Lozenges for sore throats			
Indigestion tabs for excessive acid and indigestion			
Antihistamines for allergies			
Pseudoephedrine (Sudafed) for nasal and sinus congestion			
Clove oil for toothache			

Antibiotics

Amoxycillin for chest, ear, cellulitis and urinary tract infection (general antibiotic)			

Item	Have or not	Details	Cost
Ciprofloxacin for gut and urinary tract infections			
Tinidazole for amoebic dysentery and giardia			
Flucloxacillin for skin infections			
Erythromycin for skin and chest infections (if allergic to penicillin)			
Mebendazole for thread-, round- and hookworm infections			
Malaria (prevention and treatment)			
Anti-malarial tablets			
Treatment for malaria			
Bilharzia			
Biltracide			
Eye, ear and nose			
Chloramphenicol for eye infections			
Normal saline sachets for eye wash			
Eye bath as an eye-wash unit			
Ear drops			
Nose drops			
Powder and creams for the skin			
Hydrocortisone for skin allergies and insect bites			
Lactocalamine for sunburn, itching and rashes			
Daktarin cream for fungal infections			
Cicatrin powder for wound infections (antibiotic)			
Magnesium sulphate for treatment of boils			
Comprehensive first-aid kit			
Granuflex dressing for tropical ulcers			
Gauze swabs for cleaning wounds			
Melolin of varying sizes for non-sticky wound dressing			
Micropore or zinc-oxide tape used as surgical tape			
Assortment of plasters			
Crêpe bandage for muscular injuries			
Steristrips for wound closures			
Wound dressing for heavily bleeding wounds			
Triangular bandage for securing broken limbs			
Safety pins			
Steripods (disposable antiseptic sachets)			
Water gel or Jelonet dressing for burns			
Scissors			
Tweezers			
Disposable gloves			

Item	Have or not	Details	Cost
Lancets (sterile needles which can be used for popping blisters)			
Betadine as antiseptic solution			

Sterile surgical equipment (optional)

Item	Have or not	Details	Cost
Sterile surgical gloves			
Scalpel (disposable)			
Mersilk suture of varying sizes			
Suturing forceps			
Stitch cutter			
Dental needles			
Syringes of varying sizes			
Variety of needles			
Pink and green Venflon for intravenous administration			
Sterile gauze to cleanse area of sterilisation			
Medical set for intravenous administration			

Other items for the medical kit

Item	Have or not	Details	Cost
Thermometer			
Permethrin mosi-net treatment			
Repellent coils to burn at night			
Insect repellent			
Anti-itch cream			
Flu medication			
Medication for personal ailments			
Condoms, pill or other			
Tampons			

PERSONAL KIT
Clothes

Item	Have or not	Details	Cost
Jeans			
T-shirts			
Light cotton trousers			
Skirt			
Tunic dress			
Smarter trousers			
Long-sleeved shirts			
Short-sleeved shirts			
Swimming costumes			
Wraparound skirts (also used as towels)			
Light scarf or shawl			
Sweatshirts			
Thick jerseys			
Woolly hats			
Hiking boots			
Sandals			
Raincoats			
Socks and underwear			

Item	Have or not	Details	Cost
Toiletries			
Soap			
Shampoo			
Flannel			
Toothbrush and toothpaste			
Towels (or sarongs)			
Portable washing machine			
Bucket with lid			
Washing liquid/powder			
Nylon or other string			
Clothes pegs			
Miscellaneous			
Pens and pencils			
Writing paper			
Diary or other writing material			
Address book			
Games/playing cards			
Books and magazines			
Music on either tapes or CD			
Short wave radio			
Pocket calculator			
Swiss Army knife or Leatherman's			
Hammock			
Binoculars and various books on fauna, flora and wildlife			
Driver's logbook			
Gifts			
Photographic equipment			
Dust-proof storage system			
Camera			
Polaroid camera			
Lens/es			
Cleaning gear			
Film			
Other			
Serial number(s)			

A3

Appendix 4

VISA REQUIREMENTS AT A GLANCE

Prices quoted by UK embassies for single entry. Details shown for tourists, not African nationals, although South African overlanders need to check. Many visas are cheaper procured in Africa, but some must be obtained in advance. See also Travcour (*www.travcour. com*).

AFRICA

Country	Visa requirements	Approx cost
Algeria	Required for all except nationals of other Arabic countries	£85
Angola	Required for all; use within 60 days of issue.	£40
Benin	Required for all countries.	£60–70
Botswana	Cheaper 48-hour visa normally available at border. Not required for nationals of USA, UK, Europe and most Commonwealth countries	
Burkina Faso	Required for all	£30
Burundi	Required for all nationals	£50
Cameroon	Required for all	£62
CAR	Required for all when safe; €50 (in Paris)	€50
Chad	Required for most	£100
Congo	Required for most	£60
DRC	Required for all	£60
Djibouti	Required for all (try Paris or in Addis Ababa)	€70
Egypt	Required for most but available	£15
Equatorial Guinea	Required for all except USA maybe	£100
Eritrea	Required for all; try the embassy direct	£40
Ethiopia	Required for all in advance	£14
Gabon	Required for all	£60
Gambia	Not required by European nations, but USA do	
Ghana	Required for all	£56.25
Guinea	Required for all	£65
Guinea Bissau	Required for all, obtain *en route*	US$50
Ivory Coast	Required for most, in person in Paris	€110
Kenya	Required for all (single–multiple)	£30
Lesotho	Not required for most nationals	
Liberia	Required for all	£60
Libya	Visa situation fluid	£50

Country	Visa requirements	Approx cost
Malawi	Not required for most nationals	
Mali	Required for all	£50
Mauritania	Required for all, get in Morocco	£55
Morocco	Not required for most nationals except South African	
Mozambique	Required for all	£40
Namibia	Not required for most nationals	
Niger	Required for all	£120
Nigeria	Required for all	£94.50
Rwanda	Not required for some (UK, Germany, USA)	£35
Senegal	Required for most. Rules have recently changed. You have to attend the embassy in person and cannot use a visa agency!	
Sierra Leone	Required for all	£50
Somalia	Required for all	unknown
Somaliland	Required for all (in London)	£30
South Africa	Not required for most nationals	
South Sudan	Required for all	£35
Sudan	Required for all (best to obtain this in Cairo)	£55
Swaziland	Not required for most	
Tanzania	Required for all	£40
Togo	Required for all (in Paris)	£35
Tunisia	Not required for most nationals	
Uganda	Required for all	£25
Zambia	Required for all	£35
Zimbabwe	Now required for most nationals at border	varies

MIDDLE EAST

Country	Visa requirements	Approx cost
Iraq	Required by all when safe	unknown
Jordan	Required by all	£44
Lebanon	Required by most	£25
Syria	Required by all when safe	£32
Turkey	Obtained at borders, or now e-visa online	£12

ASIA

Country	Visa requirements	Approx cost
China	Special Tibet entry must be obtained in Kathmandu	US$100
India	Required by all, obtain in advance	$150
Kazakhstan	Required by all; obtain in advance	US$55
Nepal	Obtained at borders or embassies	£25–75
Russia	Required by all; Kathmandu embassy	US$90

Appendix 5

FURTHER INFORMATION
BOOKS
History and politics

Butcher, Tim *Blood River* Vintage, 2008. A travelogue following the Congo River in the footsteps of the early reporter, Henry Morton Stanley.

Goldsworthy, David *Tom Mboya: The Man Kenya Wanted To Forget* Heinemann, 1982. Fascinating book on the former Kenyan trade union leader and politician who was murdered in 1969. Provides an insight to Kenya's history in the 1950s and 1960s.

Mandela, Nelson *Long Walk to Freedom* Little Brown, 1995. The autobiography of Nelson Mandela and the story of the ANC – a great insight into the apartheid era.

Marable, Manning *African and Caribbean Politics* Verso, 1987. A good overview of African history and politics, with particular reference to Ghana.

Matar, N I *Islam for Beginners* Writers and Readers, 1992. A brief introduction to the basic precepts of Islam.

Milne, June *Kwame Nkrumah* Panaf Books, 2000. An introduction to the man who led Ghana to freedom in 1956 and also led the Pan-African liberation movement.

Moorehead, Alan *The Blue Nile* Hamish Hamilton, 1972. The story of the exploration and history of the Blue Nile River.

Moorehead, Alan *The White Nile* Penguin, 1972. It covers the story of the exploration and history of the White Nile River.

Nkrumah, Kwame *Sékou Touré* Panaf Books, 1978. The story of Guinea's unique road to independence and of its charismatic first leader.

Odinga, Oginga *Not Yet Uhuru* Heinemann, 1967. The autobiography of the man who was Kenya's vice-president under Jomo Kenyatta and who later became a leading opposition force in exile.

Pakenham, Thomas *The Scramble for Africa* Abacus, 1992. A well-indexed account of Africa's development – and its colourful cast of characters – from 1876 to 1912.

Reader, John *Africa: A Biography of the Continent* Penguin, 1998. The complete reference book: Africa from its origins until the end of the 20th century.

Sankara, Thomas *Thomas Sankara Speaks* Pathfinder, 1988. Some key speeches by the inspiring and popular former president of Burkina Faso.

Bradt guides (*www.bradtguides.com*)
Africa

Algeria Jonathan Oakes

Angola Mike Stead and Sean Rorison

Benin Stuart Butler (available as an e-book only)

Botswana: Okavango, Chobe, Northern Kalahari Chris McIntyre

Burkina Faso Katrina Manson and James Knight
Cameroon Ben West
Congo: Democratic Republic and Republic Sean Rorison
East African Wildlife Philip Briggs
Eritrea Edward Denison
Ethiopia Philip Briggs
Ethiopia Highlights Philip Briggs
Ghana Philip Briggs
Kenya Highlights Philip Briggs
Malawi Philip Briggs
Mali Ross Velton
Mozambique Philip Briggs
Namibia Chris McIntyre
Nigeria Lizzie Williams
North Africa: The Roman Coast Ethel Davies
Northern Tanzania Philip Briggs and Chris McIntyre
Rwanda Philip Briggs
Sierra Leone Katrina Manson and James Knight
Somaliland Philip Briggs
South Africa Highlights Philip Briggs
South Sudan Sophie and Max Lovell-Hoare
Southern African Wildlife Mike Unwin
Sudan Sophie Ibbotson and Max Lovell-Hoare
Tanzania Safari Guide Philip Briggs and Chris McIntyre
Uganda Philip Briggs with Andrew Roberts
Zambia Chris McIntyre
Zanzibar Chris and Susan McIntyre
Zimbabwe Paul Murray

Middle East and Asia
Eastern Turkey Diana Darke
Iran Patricia Baker and Hilary Smith
Jordan Carole French
Kazakhstan Paul Brummell
Kyrgyzstan Laurence Mitchell
Lebanon Paul Doyle
Syria Diana Darke
Tajikistan Sophie Ibbotson and Max Lovell-Hoare
Tibet Michael Buckley

Other guidebooks
de Villiers, Marq and Hirtle, Sheila *Into Africa* Weidenfeld & Nicolson in Great Britain, Jonathan Ball Publishers in South Africa, 1997
Oliver, Roland *The African Experience* Pimlico, 1991
Philips *Essential World Atlas,* in association with the Royal Geographical Society and the Institute of British Geographers
Running Press *The Quotable Traveler,* 1994
Scott, Chris *Adventure Motorcycling Handbook* Trailblazer, 6th edition 2012, reprinted with amendments 2013
Scott, Chris *Desert Biking: A Guide to Independent Motorcycling in the Sahara* The Travellers' Bookshop, 1995 – for those planning a desert trip by motorbike

Scott, Chris *Morocco Overland,* Trailblazer, 2nd edition 2013
Scott, Chris *Sahara Overland* Trailblazer, 2nd edition 2004 reprinted with amendments 2007
St Pierre White, Andrew *The Complete Guide to a Four Wheel Drive in Southern Africa* National Book Printers, 1998/1999
Werner, David et al *Where There Is No Doctor: Village Health Care Handbook for Africa* Macmillan Education, 1994

Language

Berlitz *Arabic for Travellers*
Berlitz *Swahili Phrase Book and Dictionary*
Eyewitness Travel Guides *Arabic Phrasebook*
Lonely Planet *Swahili Phrasebook*

Wildlife Enthusiasts may need information tailored to a specific country or area; in this case see recommendations in the appropriate travel guides.

Briggs, Philip *East African Wildlife* Bradt Travel Guides
Kingdon, Jonathan *The Kingdon Field Guide to African Mammals* Academic Press, 1997. Recommended by Philip Briggs, author of many Bradt Africa guides, as 'the most detailed, thorough and up-to-date of several field guides covering the mammals of the region'.
Perlo, Bervan *Illustrated Checklist to the Birds of Eastern Africa* (Collins, 1995) and *Illustrated Checklist to the Birds of Southern Africa* (Collins, 1999) between them cover bird species recorded in countries including Eritrea, Ethiopia, Kenya, Uganda, Rwanda, Tanzania, Zambia, Malawi and South Africa.
Unwin, Mike *Southern African Wildlife* Bradt Travel Guides

Other useful reading

Davies, Miranda and Longrigg, Laura (eds) *Half the Earth: Women's Experience of Travel Worldwide* Thorsons, 1986. An excellent collection of encounters by women travellers, based on their experiences around the world.
Hibbert, Christopher *Africa Explored* Penguin, 1982
Pryce, Lois *Red Tape & White Knuckles* Century, 2008. The story of Lois Pryce's solo motorbike trip from London to Cape Town.
Simon, Ted *Jupiter's Travels* Penguin, 1980. The classic story of a round-the-world journey by motorbike, including the trip from Tunis to Cape Town from 1974 to 1978. Dated but the spirit of the book makes it unmissable.

Easy reads

Blixen, Karen *Out of Africa* Putnam & Co Ltd, 1937 (1st edition)
Foden, Giles *The Last King of Scotland* Faber & Faber, 1999 and *Ladysmith* Faber & Faber, 2000. *The Last King of Scotland* revolves around Idi Amin through the eyes of his personal physician, and has been made into a film. *Ladysmith* is about the British occupation of this small town in southern Africa.
Galman, Kuki *I Dreamed of Africa* Penguin, 2007. This author has written several novels regarding her time with her family in Kenya.
Godwin, Peter *Mukiwa* Picador, 2007. This book depicts Rhodesia in 1964 as seen through a young boy's eyes, continuing on through the freedom years to the dawn of Zimbabwe.
Mail and Guardian Bedside Book, 1999. A selection of superb journalism from Africa's best.

SOURCING AFRICAN LITERATURE AND MAPS All of the above-mentioned books can be ordered through Amazon on www.amazon.co.uk or www.amazon.com. All Bradt guides are available via www.bradtguides.com. Old, out-of-print books (in bookshops worldwide) can sometimes be tracked down via www.usedbooksearch.co.uk.

UK
Africa Book Centre Ltd www.africabookcentre. com
Blackwells e london@blackwell.co.uk; www. blackwells.co.uk. Many shops countrywide.
Daunt Books www.dauntbooks.co.uk
Map World Direct Ltd Alton; e service@map-guides.com; www.map-guides.com
Stanfords 12–14 Long Acre, London WC2E 9LP; ☏020 7836 1321; www.stanfords.co.uk. Excellent selection of maps & books.

USA
Book Passage San Francisco; www. bookpassage.com
The Savvy Traveller www.thesavvytraveller.com
Wide World Books and Maps Seattle; www. wideworldtravels.com

South Africa
Exclusive Books Johannesburg plus 29 other stores; www.exclusivebooks.co.za

MAGAZINES

Trailbike and Enduro Magazine (TBM) is a UK-based monthly publication with up-to-date information on the latest trailbikes. For information and subscriptions, phone ☏080 8840 4760.

WEBSITES
Expedition planning
www.africanet.com Africanet (general information on Africa including history and politics)
www.africa-overland.net, **www.overlandclub.com** Independent Africa Overland Club (a general overview on travelling overland in Africa)
www.bradtguides.com Bradt Travel Guides
www.expeditionworld.com Authors' website
www.horizonsunlimited.com A very useful source of information for overlanders
www.sahara-overland.com Sahara Travel Information (specific to Saharan countries, with travellers' tales and much more)
www.wtgonline.com Columbus World Travel Guide

Off-road
www.4x4mag.co.uk Internet magazine – particularly good classified section on used vehicles
www.4x4offroad.co.uk Of general interest regarding off-road issues
www.4xforum.co.za Offering information on all aspects of four-wheel driving in Africa
www.muddymotor.com For some fun before leaving, perhaps

Biking
www.adventure-motorcycling.com
www.berndtesch.de
www.horizonsunlimited.com
www.ibike.org/ibike

For luggage and accessories
www.davidlambeth.co.uk
www.acerbis.com
www.adventure-spec.com
www.coreuk.co.uk
www.kriega.com
www.longroad.co.uk

www.metalmule.com
www.touratech.de
www.wunderlich.de
www.xr-only.com

Other

www.africa.com
www.africaguide.com An excellent source of general information on individual African countries
www.africanconnections.com
www.africanet.com
www.africaonline.com
www.allafrica.com News from all over the continent
www.ananzi.co.za
www.arab.net
www.ase.net A useful source of information on accommodation
www.autotrader.co.za
www.backpackafrica.com
www.escapeartist.com
www.finance.yahoo.com/currency
www.freightquote.com
www.geography.about.com
www.i-cias.com
www.infoplease.com
www.interknowledge.com
www.loisontheloose.com
www.odci.gov CIA website including details of every African country
www.places.co.za For countries in southern Africa and, strangely, the Maldives
www.safarinow.com
www.sas.upenn.edu/African_Studies An excellent site from the University of Pennsylvania
www.tracks4africa.co.za
www.travelinafrica.co.za Includes visa information in some detail
www.travel.state.gov/travel
www.wncountries.com World news for every country
www.worldtravelguide.net
www.yellowpages.co.za

INDEX OF ADVERTISERS

Index